Situational Analysis

For Anselm and Allan, without whom . . .

Situational Analysis

Grounded Theory
After the Postmodern Turn

Adele E. Clarke
University of California, San Francisco

SAGE Publications
Thousand Oaks ■ London ■ New Delhi

For information:

Sage Publications, Inc.
2455 Teller Road
Thousand Oaks, California 91320
E-mail: order@sagepub.com

Sage Publications Ltd.
1 Oliver's Yard
55 City Road
London EC1Y 1SP
United Kingdom

Sage Publications India Pvt. Ltd.
B-42, Panchsheel Enclave
Post Box 4109
New Delhi 110 017 India

Printed in the United States of America

Library of Congress Cataloging-in-Publication Data

Clarke, Adele.
Situational analysis: Grounded theory after the postmodern turn / Adele E. Clarke.
   p. cm.
Includes bibliographical references and index.
ISBN 978-0-7619-3055-6 (cloth)—ISBN 978-0-7619-3056-3 (pbk.)
   1. Social sciences—Research—Methodology. 2. Grounded theory.
I. Title.
H62.C498 2005
001.4'33—dc22

                       2004022902

This book is printed on acid-free paper.

08   09   10   9 8 7 6 5 4 3 2

Acquisitions Editor:	Lisa Cuevas Shaw
Editorial Assistants:	Margo Beth Crouppen and Karen Gia Wong
Production Editor:	Melanie Birdsall
Copy Editor:	Barbara Coster
Typesetter:	C&M Digitals (P) Ltd.
Proofreader:	Cheryl Rivard
Indexer:	Kathy Paparchontis
Cover Designer:	Janet Foulger

Brief Contents

Contents

Chapter 5

Chapter 6

Chapter 7

Epilogue

Acknowledgments

The roots of this book go deep. As a student in the scientistic 1960s, my exposure to qualitative research was minimal. But at Barnard College, Renee Fox had us read Laura Bohannan's *Return to Laughter* on doing ethnography, and I was inspired. At NYU in sociology, we were trained only in statistics and survey methods, although Eliot Freidson brought Howie Becker in to give a talk and we read their qualitative work and that of Goffman, Garfinkle, and others. When I worked in survey research, I noticed that some of the most interesting data were left in the file cabinets—answers to "open-ended" questions—because no one knew what to do with them. I had done the interviews and was haunted.

A decade later, I sought a doctoral program in sociology that would allow me to specialize in qualitative research, medical sociology, and women's health. A most generous colleague at Sonoma State University, Kathy Charmaz, directed me to the University of California, San Francisco, her alma mater. In 1980 at UCSF, I finally "came home" (Clarke & Star 1998). We pursued our own hands-on "do-it-yourself" research projects from design to final presentations with superb faculty: Ginnie Olesen and Lenny Schatzman taught field research while Anselm Strauss followed with qualitative analysis organized as a small working group. We were welcome to sit in on his ongoing analysis group as long as we desired. We desired! And

AUTHOR'S NOTE: Earlier versions of Chapter 1 were presented at meetings of the Stone Symposium of the Society for the Study of Symbolic Interactionism, Nottingham, England (July 1996), the American Sociological Association (August 1997), the Pacific Sociological Association (April 1998), the Conference in Honor of Anselm Strauss at the University of Magdeburg, Germany (June 1999—see www.ucsf .edu/anselmstrauss/), and the conference "Intersections: Society, Technology, and Geographic Thought" at the University of Kentucky (1999). Segments of Chapters 1 and 3 appeared in Clarke (2003).

we simultaneously read Anselm's draft chapters for *Qualitative Analysis for Social Scientists* (1987) that presented our group sessions. My cohort also traveled to Marin, California, for analysis sessions offered by Barney Glaser, who was no longer at UCSF.

As a doctoral student, I began working in science and technology studies, joining this rich intellectual world at a key moment. Those engagements are inscribed throughout this book, and special thanks are due to Leigh Star, Joan Fujimura, Nelly Oudshoorn, Donna Haraway, Bruno Latour, and Geof Bowker. At UCSF I studied the history of medicine and the life sciences with Gert Brieger and Dan Todes, who were exceptionally supportive. I have since undertaken collaborative projects with historians, including Jane Maienschein, Gregg Mitman, Warwick Anderson, Guenter Risse, Jack Lesch, Garland Allan, and the late Merriley Borell and Gerry Geison. All helped me think through using grounded theory and situational analysis with historical materials.

In the late 1980s, I had the privilege of a 2-year National Institute of Mental Health (NIMH) postdoc led by Dick Scott at Stanford University, sharpening my understanding of symbolic interactionism and social worlds through deep engagement with organizations theory (Clarke 1991). Very special thanks to Dick and to my adviser Carol Connell for extraordinary professional and intellectual generosity, and to Marc Ventresca and Brian Powers for collegial support ever since.

To my considerable surprise, I was then hired into the faculty position vacated by Anselm Strauss at UCSF when he was required to retire at age 70. I began coteaching the nearly yearlong sequence of courses in qualitative research and analysis with very methodologically sophisticated colleagues from nursing—Jeanne DeJoseph, who specializes in feminist narrative interpretation, and Kit Chesla, who specializes in interpretive phenomenology. Our doctoral students and many auditors come from sociology, nursing, occasionally anthropology, but also from a host of other disciplines (from rhetoric to urban studies, psychology, medicine), and from near and far, Taiwan and Thailand to Poland to Botswana. We are routinely pushed to translate across languages and cultures—including the cultures of nursing, sociology, and so on that we "discover" in the classroom by tripping over our own blind spots. I inherited Ginnie Olesen's superb syllabi and have, with cofaculty, continued to elaborate these (e.g., Clarke & Chesla 2001). Special thanks are due to my wonderful cofaculty and students who asked great questions and did great projects. My confidence in developing situational analysis and writing this book really comes from sustained and serious engagements with them over the years.

In 1995, I participated in a Residential Research Group at the University of California Systemwide Humanities Research Institute at UC Irvine on "Feminist Epistemologies and Methodologies." Convened by Val Hartouni, the group included Patti Lather, Katie King, Leslie Rabine, Jane Newman, Joan Tronto, Nancy Hartsock, and several graduate students. We focused on research methods and feminist scholarship, informing my earliest work on this book. My special thanks to them and Patricia O'Brien, then director, Deborah Massey Sanchez, then assistant director, and the wonderful staff. Being at HRI was truly intellectual nirvana.

Most of all, I thank those who have supported and read this work. Janet Shim and Debora Bone, both UCSF alumna, magnanimously consented to my using their work as major exemplars and helped me to do so thoughtfully and incisively. The book has greatly benefited from comments from Isabelle Baszanger, Howie Becker, Pat Benner, Geof Bowker, Antony Bryant, Monica Casper, Brian Castellani, Kathy Charmaz, Kit Chesla, Patricia Clough, Jeanne DeJoseph, Norman Denzin, Jennifer Fishman, Jenny Fosket, Carrie Friese, Peter Hall, Francis Harvey, Katie King, Nick King, Krzysztof Konecki, Patti Lather, Karen Locke, Laura Mamo, Lisa Jean Moore, Ginnie Olesen, Janet Shim, Sara Shostak, Leigh Star, Stefan Timmermans, and anonymous reviewers. Carrie Friese also served as a grounding research assistant. Lisa Mix of Archives and Special Collections at the UCSF Library was exceptionally helpful.

I thank Anselm Strauss yet again not only for being a superb teacher but also a superb colleague (Clarke & Star 1998). Through working with him, I have been most fortunate in "finding a creative present in the context of a revered past" (Dunning 2003:10). Anselm and Fran Strauss were "Franselm" on my autodialer, our friends, and Fran continues to inspire us. As always, I thank last but most of all for incredibly loving and sustained support my friends Pam Mendelsohn, Jenny Ross, Dan Doyle, and my partner through truly stunning changes in our lives over 30-plus years, Allan Regenstreif, without whom . . .

projects drawing on interview, ethnographic, historical, visual, and/or other discursive materials, including multisite research. Situational analysis allows researchers to draw together studies of discourse and agency, action and structure, image, text and context, history and the present moment—to analyze complex situations of inquiry broadly conceived. Thus it can support researchers from heterogeneous backgrounds pursuing a wide array of projects.

Situational analysis has a radically different conceptual infrastructure or guiding metaphor from the action-centered "basic social process" concept that undergirds traditional grounded theory. In situational analysis, that is replaced with Strauss's situation-centered "social worlds/arenas/negotiations" framework.[3] Building upon and extending Strauss's work, situational analysis offers three main cartographic approaches:

1. **Situational maps** that lay out the major human, nonhuman, discursive, and other elements in the research situation of inquiry and provoke analysis of relations among them;

2. **Social worlds/arenas maps** that lay out the collective actors, key nonhuman elements, and the arena(s) of commitment and discourse within which they are engaged in ongoing negotiations—meso-level interpretations of the situation; and

3. **Positional maps** that lay out the major positions taken, and *not* taken, in the data vis-à-vis particular axes of difference, concern, and controversy around issues in the situation of inquiry.

All three kinds of maps are intended as analytic exercises, fresh ways into social science data that are especially well suited to contemporary studies from solely interview-based to multisited research projects. They are intended as supplemental approaches to traditional grounded theory analyses that center on the framing of action—basic social processes. Instead, these maps center on elucidating the key elements, materialities, discourses, structures, and conditions that characterize the situation of inquiry. Through mapping the data, the analyst constructs the situation of inquiry empirically. The *situation per se becomes the ultimate unit of analysis,* and understanding its elements and their relations is the primary goal. Thus situational analysis can deeply situate research projects individually, collectively, organizationally, institutionally, temporally, geographically, materially, discursively, culturally, symbolically, visually, and historically.

Situational analysis supplements traditional or basic grounded theory with alternative approaches to *both* data gathering and analysis/interpretation.

In addition to producing and analyzing interview and ethnographic data, situational analysis promotes the analysis of extant narrative, visual, and historical discourse materials. It enhances our capacities to do incisive studies of differences of perspective, of highly complex situations of action and positionality, of the heterogeneous discourses in which we are all constantly awash, and of the situated knowledges of life itself thereby produced. What I am ultimately grappling toward are approaches that can simultaneously address voice and discourse, texts and the consequential materialities and symbolisms of the nonhuman, the dynamics of historical change, and, last but far from least, power in both its more solid and fluid forms. The outcomes of situational mappings should be "thick analyses" (Fosket 2002:40), paralleling Geertz's (1973) "thick descriptions." Thick analyses take explicitly into account the full array of elements in the situation and explicate their interrelations.

With deep roots in pragmatist philosophy and symbolic interactionist sociology, the grounded theory method can be viewed as a theory/methods package.[4] While scholars utilizing grounded theory have ranged from positivist to social constructivist, recent work is shifting toward more constructivist assumptions/epistemologies (Baszanger & Dodier 2004; Charmaz 1995a, 2000). Situational analysis is part of these shifts. I seek with Charmaz (2000:510) to "reclaim these tools from their positivist underpinnings to form a revised, more open-ended practice of grounded theory that stresses its emergent, constructivist elements" and to "use grounded theory methods as flexible, heuristic strategies." Charmaz emphasizes that a focus on meaning making furthers interpretive, constructivist, and, I would add, relativist/ perspectival understandings. My goal is to further enable, sustain, and enhance such shifts.

In the remainder of this chapter, I first briefly frame what I mean by "the postmodern turn" (discussed more extensively in Chapter 1). I then offer the grounds for a new method based around the postmodern turn. Next is a sketch of the main parameters of basic grounded theory as it has been done over the past 30-plus years, followed by an outline of doing the new situational maps and analysis. Last, I provide an overview of the book.

The Postmodern Turn

> Postmodernism is "the as yet unnamable which begins to proclaim itself."
>
> —Derrida (quoted in Lather 1991:160)

This book is part of a long-term project of regenerating and expanding grounded theory after the postmodern turn that has been taking place over the past several decades. I frame this expansion by situating grounded theory methods within current transdisciplinary conversations on doing qualitative research after the postmodern turn, traversing and hopefully erasing some of the boundaries amongst social sciences, humanities, and professional practices of inquiry.

The postmodern turn has occurred across the academy in the social sciences, humanities, and professional schools (e.g., nursing, education, business, social work) and throughout other sites of knowledge production such as the media, and sites of creativity in the arts, film, architecture, and so on. Postmodernism consists of many things and interpretations, today essentially ubiquitous if also contested (e.g., Best & Kellner 1991; Lather 2001a). If modernism emphasized universality, generalization, simplification, permanence, stability, wholeness, rationality, regularity, homogeneity, and sufficiency, then postmodernism has shifted emphases to partialities, positionalities, complications, tenuousness, instabilities, irregularities, contradictions, heterogeneities, situatedness, and fragmentation—complexities. Postmodernism itself is not a unified system of beliefs or assumptions but rather an ongoing array of possibilities, "a series of fragments in continuous flux . . . abandoning overarching paradigms and theoretical and methodological metasystems" (Fontana 2002:162). Postmodern scholarship seeks to address "almost unthinkably complex, interrelated and interactive global" situations while simultaneously acknowledging the "ungraspable of this world" (Usher 1997:30). It involves us in "the ontological politics of staying true to complexity" (Landstrom 2000:475), however partially and contradictorily.

One fundamental issue taken up throughout postmodernist literatures and projects and particularly pertinent to research concerns the nature of knowledge. "'Postmodernism' is the continuation of modernism except that confidence in the extension of reason has been abandoned" (Latour 1999:308). As part of the theoretical turn of the mid/late 20th century, postmodernism thus offers a way of describing the broadening and now relentless challenges to the Western Enlightenment, humanism, and positivist sciences as the assumed pinnacles of human achievement globally. Instead, postmodern perspectives view *all* knowledges (including the natural and social sciences and humanities, "lay" knowledges of all sorts, and knowledges from all sites globally) as socially and culturally produced (e.g., Berger & Luckman 1966; McCarthy 1996). Key interlocutory questions of the postmodern turn thus feature those of the sociology of knowledge concerning the relations of knowledges to the sites of their production and consumption practices—aspects of "ecologies of knowledge" (Rosenberg 1979; Star 1995).

Since the postmodern turn, then, all knowledges are understood by major segments of scholarly worlds and beyond as *situated* knowledges (e.g., Haraway, 1991b)—produced and consumed by particular groups of people, historically and geographically locatable. Claims of universality are considered naive at best and much more commonly as hegemonic strategies seeking to silence/erase other perspectives (Gramsci 1971). Genealogies of knowledges, their discourses and practices—histories of the present—are routinely undertaken (e.g., Foucault 1972, 1973, 1980). In fact, taking on social analysis of "the hard cases" of knowledge production is what studies of science, technology, and medicine (my own research area) do.

Others in other studies have also been busy with parallel yet distinctive projects in the sociology of knowledge, often focusing on the involvement of particular racial, gendered, and related social formations in projects of knowledge production (e.g., Omi & Winant 1994; Poovey 1998). Over the past several decades, many explicit ruptures of "difference" have been asserted through postcolonial, feminist, diasporic, ethnic, queer, multicultural, and "other" theories and studies. Each of these innovative approaches to examining knowledge production has challenged the kinds of knowledges and discourses circulating about differently situated people, things, and issues, often produced by and circulating especially among those situated in positions of greater power, legitimacy, and/or authority. These projects ask: Who is authorized and not authorized to make what kinds of knowledges about whom/what, and under what conditions? Together they have initiated a disruptive and truly stunning appreciation of the complexities and heterogeneities of our individual and collective situations, discourses, and the complexities and heterogeneities of our knowledge production—our interpretations of those situations.[5]

But postmodernisms have not been unopposed, and there are several strands of pertinent critique. The main critique is, of course, the positivist denial of the sociology of knowledge, of the socially constructed nature of all categories, and of the theory of linguistic indeterminacy that undergirds postmodern theory (e.g., Ashman & Barringer 2001; Gross & Levitt 1994). There are softer versions of such realisms as well that are more common among qualitative researchers and remain problematic. Another strand of critique objects to slick, quick, and trendy pomo framings and statements that lack depth and attention to history and context. A third critical edge concerns the "collapse of optimism of the modernist project" (Jenkins 1997:5), and belief in human progress. To some critics, an ultimate nihilism must (logically to them) flow from the abandonment of realism, the acceptance of the partiality of all knowledge, and the moves to integrate constructionism. While I have some sympathy with the latter two critiques, I can only make sense of the world with the tools of the sociology of knowledge and constructionism, and I seek here to add to those tools. Further, as Latour (1999:23) points out, nihilism is not required:

> In opening the black box of scientific facts, we knew we would be opening Pandora's box. There was no way to avoid it. . . . Now that it has been opened, with plagues and curses, sins and ills whirling around, there is only one thing to do, and that is to go even deeper, all the way down into the almost empty box, in order to retrieve what, according to the venerable legend, has been left at the bottom—yes, hope. It is much too deep for me on my own; are you willing to help me reach it? May I give you a hand?

This is not to say that very dark readings indeed of the human condition today are "wrong." It is to say that when, with Foucault (1991:84), we ask, "What is to be done?" we need to address that darkness and proceed in the face of it.

To sustain the challenging endeavors of "opening Pandora's box[es]," our research processes and assumptions need enhanced capacities to grasp and interpret the complexities and heterogeneities of social life empirically (e.g., Haraway 1999; Lather 2001a, n.d.). We need methods for research and analysis to support our yearnings (hooks 1990), our desires to know (savoir), and our will to know (Burchell, Gordon, & Miller 1991; Foucault 1972, 1973), both for the knowledge itself and for the potential such knowledges may offer for making life on the planet better. We need methods that can support research on social suffering and anguish that also allow the hope that dwells at the bottom of Pandora's box to emerge, nourish, and be nourished. But that hope cannot be naive. In Richardson's (2000:928; emphasis added) terms:

> The core of postmodernism is the *doubt* that any method or theory, discourse or genre, tradition or novelty, has a universal claim as the "right" or the privileged form of authoritative knowledge. Postmodernism *suspects* all truth claims of masking and serving particular interests in local, cultural and political struggles. But it does not automatically reject conventional methods of knowing and telling as false or archaic. *Rather it opens those standard methods to inquiry and introduces new methods, which are also, then, subject to critique.*

Thus not only are more scientist quantitative approaches challenged through postmodernism and the sociology of knowledge, but so too are interpretive qualitative approaches to knowledge production. Clough's (1992) provocative

Some years ago, Katovich and Reese (1993:400-405) interestingly argued that Strauss's negotiated order and related work recuperatively pulled *the social* around the postmodern turn through its methodological (grounded theoretical) recognition of the partial, tenuous, shifting, and unstable nature of the empirical world and its constructedness. I strongly agree and would argue that Strauss also particularly furthered this "postmodernization of the social" through his conceptualizations of social worlds and arenas as modes of understanding the deeply situated yet always also fluid organizational elements of negotiations and discourses.[7] He foreshadowed what later came to be known as postmodern assumptions: the instability of situations; the characteristic changing, porous boundaries of both social worlds and arenas; social worlds seen as mutually constitutive/coproduced in the negotiations taking place in arenas; negotiations as central social processes hailing that "things can always be otherwise"; and so on. Negotiations also signal micropolitics of power and the powers of discourses—decentering the subject and power in its more fluid and discursive forms (e.g., Foucault 1979, 1980)—as well as "the usual" meso/macro structural elements.

Through integrating the social worlds/arenas/negotiations/discourse framework with grounded theory as a new conceptual infrastructure, I hope to sustain and extend these methodological contributions of grounded theory. Thus situational analysis is especially useful for understanding and elaborating what has been meant by "the social" in social life. This is valuable precisely because the social has too often been analytically elusive and ungrounded in research.

There are several key methodological issues here. First, methods are needed that can address and elucidate the complexities of situations as the grounds of social life. That is, methods are needed that intentionally aim at capturing complexities rather than aiming at simplifications; that elucidate processes of change in situations as well as they elucidate patterns and stabilities; that detangle agents and positions sufficiently to make contradictions, ambivalences, and irrelevances clear. Second, methods are needed that can allow and encourage the analyst to elucidate heretofore illegitimate and/or marginalized perspectives and subjugated knowledges of social life— to lucidly communicate what it means to be dwelling heterogeneously all over this planet in the new millennium in complicated and unstable situations (e.g., Ferguson, Gever, Minh-Ha, & West 1990). Here, some threads of symbolic interactionism have been moving toward postmodern cultural studies in ways that I seek to extend through this project (Becker & McCall 1990; Denzin 1992, 1997, 2000). Cultural symbologies have always been of concern in symbolic interactionisms, if not routinely featured.

Third, methods are needed that go beyond "the knowing subject" as centered knower and decision maker to also address and analyze salient discourses within the situation of inquiry. We are all, like it or not, constantly awash in seas of discourses that are constitutive of life itself. Situational analysis therefore integrates aspects of Foucault's poststructural approaches, enrolling him in pushing grounded theory around the postmodern turn. Specifically, situational analysis follows "Foucault's footsteps" (Prior 1997) into sites of his serious theorizing—historical, narrative/textual, and visual discourses. The decentering of "the knowing subject" common in poststructuralism needs to be integrated more deeply into empirical research. Grounded theory aided and abetted by situational analysis can facilitate such moves.

Having begun down this path, it quickly becomes obvious that if the subject is decentered, "the object is also and always decentered" (Dugdale 1999:16). This means that fresh methodological attention needs to be paid to objects in situations. This includes cultural objects, technologies, media— all the nonhuman, animate and inanimate things that also constitute the situations in which we live (e.g., Foucault 1972; Latour 1987; McCarthy 1984). Some are products of human action (and we can study the production processes); others are construed as "natural" (and we can study how they have been constructed as such). In the postmodern moment, studying action is far from enough.

Further, I would argue that we need at least a century's worth of attempting to take differences seriously empirically through a variety of innovative methodologies. Individual and collective difference(s) in our situatedness and practices need to be capable of being taken into account in social life and in social policies of all kinds from education to welfare reform to health coverage and caregiving to social security in old age. If we lack both an adequate vocabulary and research methods to specify at least genres of difference, we will continue to be paralyzed in terms of constructing ways of sharing the planet that work effectively toward greater social justice and more democratic participation.

Such visionary Deweyian aspects of pragmatism are alive and well after the postmodern turn for good reason—because they are sorely needed (e.g., Denzin & Lincoln 2005; Nicholson 1999; Rorty 1982). But they also need to be recast in ways that allow the *explicit acknowledgment and incorporation of the complexities of situatedness, variation, and difference(s)* rather than promoting their erasure through various assimilations or hopes for transcendence through shared education or shared beliefs. At the same time, we cannot assume (it would be naive and/or more than arrogant to do so) that our research will lead directly or indirectly to the changes we may envision and desire. Herein lies the skeptical and dubious postmodern "rub," the challenge with which we must come to terms.

Basic Grounded Theory

Social phenomena are complex. Thus they require complex grounded theory.

—Strauss (1987:1)

This is not a book for beginners in grounded theory or qualitative inquiry. It assumes some familiarity with basic or traditional grounded theory methods, and the greater the familiarity, the easier the read. This section is for those unfamiliar. A modest framing is offered by Atkinson, Coffey, and Delamont (2003:150): "[G]rounded theory is not a description of a kind of theory. Rather it represents a general way of generating theory (or, even more generically, a way of having ideas on the basis of empirical research)." Very briefly, grounded theory is an empirical approach to the study of social life through qualitative research and analysis. In this method, the analyst initially codes the data (open coding)—word by word, segment by segment— and gives temporary labels (codes) to particular phenomena. The analyst determines whether codes generated through one data source also appear elsewhere, and elaborates their properties. Related codes that have endured are then densified into more enduring and analytically ambitious "categories," and these are ultimately integrated into a theoretical analysis of the substantive area. Thus a "grounded theory" of a particular phenomenon of concern is composed of the analytic codes and categories generated inductively in the analysis and explicitly integrated to form a theory of the substantive area that is the focus of the research project—an empirically based "substantive theory." In traditional grounded theory, over time, after multiple substantive theories of a particular area of interest have been generated through an array of empirical research projects, so the argument went, more "formal theory" could be developed (see esp. Strauss 1995).

Unique to this approach has been, first, its requiring that analysis begin as soon as there are data. Coding begins immediately, and theorizing based on that coding does as well, however provisionally (Glaser 1978). Second, "sampling" is driven not necessarily (or not only) by attempts to be "representative" of some social body or population or its heterogeneities but especially and explicitly by *theoretical* concerns that have emerged in the provisional analysis to date. Such "theoretical sampling" focuses on finding *new data sources* (persons or things—and not theories) that can best explicitly address specific theoretically interesting facets of the emergent analysis. Theoretical sampling has been integral to grounded theory from the outset, remains a fundamental strength of this analytic approach, and is crucial for situational analysis.[8] In fact, "The true legacy of Glaser and Strauss is a collective awareness of the heuristic value of developmental research designs [through theoretical sampling] and exploratory data analytic strategies, not a 'system' for conducting and analyzing research" (Atkinson, Coffey, & Delamont 2003:162-163).

Since its inception in the late 1960s (Glaser 1978; Glaser & Strauss 1967; Strauss 1987), the focus of most research using grounded theory has relied on fieldwork to generate interview and/or ethnographic data through which to analyze human action (e.g., Glaser 1993; Strauss & Corbin 1997). Conventional grounded theory has focused on generating the "basic social process" occurring in the data concerning the phenomenon of concern—the basic form of human action. Studies have been done, for example, on *living with* chronic illness (Charmaz 1991; Orona 1990), *crafting* scientific work (Fujimura 1992), *disciplining* the scientific study of reproduction (Clarke 1998), *classifying* and its consequences (Bowker & Star 1999; Star 1989), *organizing* the specialty of pain medicine (Baszanger 1998a), *making* hospitals appear accountable for their practices (Wiener 2000b), *making* CPR the main emergency response to sudden death (Timmermans 1999), and *creating* a new social actor—the unborn patient—via fetal surgery (Casper 1998a, 1998b).

In a traditional grounded theory study, the key or basic social process is typically articulated in gerund form connoting ongoing action, and at an abstract level. Around this basic process, the analyst then constellates the particular and distinctive conditions, strategies, actions, and practices engaged in by human and nonhuman actors involved with/in the process and their consequences. For example, subprocesses of disciplining the scientific study of reproduction include *formalizing* a scientific discipline, *establishing* stable access to research materials, *gleaning* fiscal support for research, *producing* contraceptives and other technoscientific products, and *handling* the social controversies the science provokes (e.g., regarding use of contraceptives).

Many superb projects have been done using basic grounded theory, and this action-centered approach will continue to be fundamentally important analytically. What I propose is to supplement basic grounded theory with a situation-centered approach that in addition to studying action also explicitly includes the analysis of the full situation, including discourses—narrative, visual, and historical. Such work can enrich research by addressing and engaging the important complexities of postmodern theoretical and methodological concerns. In many ways, as I argue more elaborately in Chapter 1, grounded theory was always already around the postmodern turn while in other ways it was not particularly so, and/or not clearly so. Situational maps and analyses make it so.

Situational Maps and Analysis

[A]ll aspects of human being and knowing are situated.

—McCarthy (1996:107; emphasis in original)

My goal is to revise and regenerate the grounded theory method toward new approaches to grounded theorizing that take postmodern turns in social theory and qualitative research more fully into account. I seek to do so by

- Disarticulating grounded theory from its remaining positivist roots in 1950s and 1960s social science and enhancing its always already present but heretofore often muted postmodern capacities;
- Supplementing the traditional grounded theory root metaphor of social process/ action with an ecological root metaphor of social worlds/arenas/negotiations/ discourses as an alternative conceptual infrastructure that provokes situational analysis at the meso-level, new social organizational/institutional/discursive/ practice sitings;
- Supplementing the traditional grounded theory analysis of a basic or key social process (action) with alternatives centered on cartographic situational analysis—maps of key elements; maps of social worlds, arenas and their discourses in meso-level negotiations; and maps of issues and axes focused around difference(s) of positionality—the dense complexities of the situation of inquiry broadly construed;
- Generating sensitizing concepts and theoretical integration toward provocative yet provisional analytics and grounded theor*izing* as an ongoing process rather than the development of substantive and formal theories as the ultimate goals; and
- Framing systematic and flexible means of research design that facilitate multisite research, including discursive textual, visual, and archival historical materials and documents, as well as ethnographic (interview and observational) transcripts and field notes to more fully take into account the complexities of postmodern life.

Because epistemology and ontology are joined at the hip, methods need to be understood as "theory/methods packages" (e.g., Star 1989). I therefore make the theoretical groundings of grounded theory in early-20th-century Chicago School sociology, in pragmatist philosophy, and in post-World War II symbolic interactionism explicit. I do so precisely because over the past 20 or so years, grounded theorists have been widening their theoretical gazes and moving around the postmodern turn, shifting to more fully developed constructionist framings, which I seek to further (e.g., Charmaz 1995b, 2000). This book therefore not only offers situational analysis as a new approach to constructionist/postmodern grounded theorizing but also elaborates some key theoretical shifts that undergird it.

Situational analysis arose in and through my own work since I entered the University of California, San Francisco as a graduate student in sociology in 1980, especially through my teaching of grounded theory and other qualitative research methods at UCSF since 1989. It also emerged from my reading and teaching feminist theory, interactionist theory, Foucault, cultural studies and science, technology, and medicine studies. As a student, I learned grounded theory from Anselm Strauss long before he began on the *Basics of Qualitative Research* books, so the method I learned was much less codified and closer to that discussed in his *Qualitative Analysis for Social Scientists* (1987). Strauss was also then deeply engaged in elaborating his social worlds/arenas/discourse/negotiations framework, and I was thus raised in what Miller (1997:2) calls the "institutional studies tradition" in qualitative research.[9] Some aspects of the *Basics* books (Strauss & Corbin 1990, 1998) work very well for me, while others do not, and I engage those here. The basic coding procedures of grounded theory as they appear in the earlier works remain invaluable,[10] and are used in developing situational analysis as well as in analyzing basic social processes.

While an emphasis on variation and/or difference(s) was clearly not part of either Strauss's or Glaser's agendas (see Glaser 1992, 2002; Strauss 1993:210-212), nor those of other current elaborators of grounded theory (see note 2), it is central to mine. In fact, the long-established grounded theory strategy of theoretical sampling can be explicitly directed toward seeking the broadest range of variation within salient data sources. That is, thoughtful theoretical sampling strategies can be used to pursue particular aspects of situatedness, difference(s), and variations. Heterogeneous positions and relations can be explicitly sought out, pursued, analyzed, and discussed. This is in direct and vivid contrast with their explicit erasure through various data homogenization and simplification strategies common in traditional positivist social science, but also too frequent in qualitative pursuits. To be able to do such purposive theoretical sampling involves elaborated attention to research design previously underdeveloped in the grounded theory tradition (aside from theoretical sampling), discussed at length in Chapter 2 and elsewhere.

A key feature of the postmodern turn has been an enhanced theoretical grasp of the analytic importance of the nonhuman in our complex situatedness, and I emphasize this here (also discussed in Chapter 2). Distinctively, grounded theory analysis does not center on properties of persons or "variables" as is common in most social science. Therefore it has never been limited to the study of humans, but it can in principle easily accommodate nonhuman objects (technologies, animals, discourses, historical documents, visual representations, etc.). Such material entities in our situations of concern deserve more explicit and intentional inclusion in our research and analyses. Just as "nature" and "society" are not separate but "make each other up"—are coconstitutive—so too do humans and nonhuman objects (e.g., Haraway 1989, 2003; Latour 1987; McCarthy 1984; Mead 1934/1962). The semiotics of materiality matter and materiality is relational (Law 1999:4). Any method that ignores the materialities of human existence is inadequate, especially today as humans and various technosciences are together transforming the planet from the inside out (e.g., Clarke, Shim, Mamo, Fosket, & Fishman 2003).

It was, in fact, the very openness of grounded theory in its Straussian incarnations to allow analysis of a wide range of nonhuman objects that initially attracted me. This openness allowed me while a student to begin doing grounded theory studies of discourses—historical materials and later visual cultures—and ultimately prompted this attempt to regenerate grounded theory methodology within a postmodern framework. It also provoked me to draw explicitly and deeply on the work of Michel Foucault in pushing grounded theory around the postmodern turn (discussed in Chapter 2).

Although Glaser and Strauss did not initially emphasize context/situatedness, Strauss (e.g., 1987:77-81) later did so. With Corbin, he also engaged situatedness through their conditional matrices (e.g., Strauss & Corbin 1990:163, 1998:184). These are analytic devices intended to push grounded theorists to consider seriously the various contexts of their research focus and to portray how contextual elements "condition" the action that is the central analytic focus. But, while pointing in some "right directions," I find the conditional matrix approach inadequate to the task (see also P. M. Hall 1997). I offer instead the considerably more elaborated modes of situational analysis. Here, *the situation of inquiry itself broadly conceived is the key unit of analysis.*[11]

The situation of inquiry is empirically constructed through the making of three kinds of maps and following through with analytic work and memos of various kinds. The first maps are the **situational maps** that lay out the major human, nonhuman, discursive, historical, symbolic, cultural, political, and other elements in the research situation of concern and provoke analysis of relations among them. These maps are intended to capture and discuss the messy complexities of the situation in their dense relations and permutations. They intentionally work *against* the usual simplifications so characteristic of scientific work (Star 1983, 1986) in particularly postmodern ways.

Second, the **social worlds/arenas maps** lay out all of the *collective* actors, key nonhuman elements, and the arena(s) of commitment within which they are engaged in ongoing discourse and negotiations. Such maps offer meso-level interpretations of the situation, explicitly taking up its social organizational, institutional, and discursive dimensions. They are distinctively postmodern in their assumptions: We cannot assume directionalities of influence; boundaries are open and porous; negotiations are fluid; discourses are multiple and potentially contradictory. Negotiations of many kinds from coercion to bargaining are the "basic social processes" that construct and constantly destabilize the social worlds/arenas maps (Strauss, 1993). Things could always be otherwise—not only individually but also collectively/organizationally/institutionally/discursively—and these maps portray such postmodern possibilities.

Third, **positional maps** lay out the major positions taken, and *not* taken, in the data vis-à-vis particular axes of variation and difference, focus, and controversy found in the situation of concern. Perhaps most significantly, positional maps are not articulated with persons or groups but rather seek to represent the full range of *discursive* positions on particular issues—fully allowing multiple positions and even contradictions within both individuals and collectivities to be articulated. Complexities are themselves heterogeneous, and we need improved means of representing them.

All three kinds of maps are keyed to taking the nonhuman—including discourses—in the situation of inquiry seriously. In doing initial situational maps, the analyst is asked to specify the nonhuman elements in the situation, thus making pertinent materialities and discourses visible from the outset. The flip side of the second kind of map, the social worlds/arenas map, is a discourse/arenas map. Social worlds are "universes of discourse" routinely producing discourses about elements of concern in the situation. Such discourses can be mapped and analyzed. Last, positional maps seek to open up the discourses per se by analyzing positions taken on key analytic axes. Discourses can thereby be disarticulated from their sites of production, decentering them and allowing further analytic bite.

Bowker and Star (1999:10) discuss "infrastructural inversion" wherein the infrastructure of something is (unusually) revealed and even featured. An example of this would be the Pompidou Center in Paris, where all the pipes, stanchions, conduits, and other building innards are instead "outards"— exposed and attached to the exterior walls rather than hidden *in between* the interior and exterior walls. Situational maps and analyses do a kind of "social inversion" in making the usually invisible and inchoate social features of a situation more visible: all the key elements in the situation and their interrelations; the social worlds and arenas in which the phenomena of interest are embedded; the discursive positions taken and not taken by actors (human and nonhuman) on key issues; and the discourses themselves as constitutive of the situation. This is the postmodernization of a grounded theory grounded in symbolic interactionism and Foucaultian analytics.

Situational maps and analyses are postmodern approaches in a wide variety of ways elaborated above and throughout this book. Let me end this introductory moment by emphasizing that an "analysis" of any kind is no more than one or a few "readings" of a situation—understandings, interpretations. An analysis or reading thus does not claim adequacy or validity in the modern methodological usages of those terms. Rather, an analysis is what it is understood to be, in all its partialities. Obviously, I believe the analytic strategies I have developed and laid out here are worthy of attention and useful in terms of doing the kinds of work in research worlds that I think need doing. But other approaches are always already available and may also be provocative and interesting, perhaps in combination with situational analyses.

My project, then, is to regenerate grounded theory in ways that can support researchers from the social sciences, humanities, professions, and beyond in a wide array of projects drawing on historical, visual, textual, ethnographic, and interview materials. Here the researcher becomes not only analyst and bricoleur but also a cartographer of sorts. Because the codes and categories of a particular analysis can be both generated and applied across the full range of possible data sources, the new mapping approaches are especially useful for what is being called multisite research. They are equally useful with small or large interview-based research projects as well as ethnographic field projects and analysis of extant discourses of many kinds. Everything is situated, and situational analysis maps and elucidates this facet of postmodern understanding.

Overview of the Book

There is always a question of how and where to enter any book. In fact, some readers may want to peruse Chapter 3 first, before reading Chapters 1 and 2, to get a deeper grasp on where I am going with situational analysis.

Chapter 1 focuses on why grounded theory needs to be updated and aptly takes up "pushing and being pulled by grounded theory/symbolic interactionism around the postmodern turn." It first lays out how grounded theory is "always already" around the postmodern turn through its symbolic interactionist roots, including the Meadian notion of perspective, its materialist social constructionism, its relational ecological frameworks, and its postmodern capacities to handle the complexities of situatedness, variation and difference(s), positionality and relationality. Yet grounded theory also needs to be pushed around that turn, actively pulled away from its positivist roots in 1950s and 1960s sociology. These problematic recalcitrancies include a lack of reflexivity about research processes and products, oversimplifications, interpretations of "negative" cases, and searching for grounded purity. I then begin to push grounded theory around the postmodern turn by regrounding grounded theory in the broader symbolic interactionist concept of the situation of action, assuming the situatedness of all knowledges and their producers. Knowledges always bear the inscriptions of their production processes. I also emphasize elucidation of variations/difference(s)/heterogeneities of position, and assert the sufficiency of sensitizing concepts and analytics for a fresh approach to grounded theor*izing* rather than the development of high modernist formal theory.

Chapter 2, "From Chicago Ecologies to Situational Analysis," frames the new approach of situational analysis historically and theoretically. It traces Chicago School tradition/symbolic interactionist mapping strategies from the relational ecological maps of the early ethnographies (1920s-1940s) to Strauss's social worlds/arenas maps and my own (1980s-present). It is important to grasp the ecological roots of this conceptual infrastructure as the guiding metaphor for doing situational analysis. Next, three "new roots" for theoretically grounding situational analysis are laid out. First, the major push of grounded theory around the postmodern turn through situational analysis is, through Foucault, the turn to discourse. I briefly situate Foucault among the interactionists by placing him in conversation with Strauss about three sites of their conceptual articulation: discourse/discipline and social worlds/arenas; the field of practice(s) and negotiated/processual ordering; and the gaze and perspective.

Second, a featured aspect of situational analysis is taking the nonhuman elements in that research situation explicitly and seriously into account. Understanding how such materialities matter and how they are *constitutive* of the situation of action are next discussed at length. Third, I turn to an extended critique of Strauss and Corbin's conditional matrices of action, their major effort to ground grounded theory in the situation being researched, and offer my alternative framing of this problem—making the situation the unit of analysis. This is the third new root. Situational analysis also requires some innovative strategies for project design and data gathering, topics generally unaddressed in traditional grounded theory, and I discuss these. The need for enhanced reflexivity and new forms of researcher accountability as fundamental to grounded theorizing after the postmodern turn are also taken up.

Chapter 3 on "Doing Situational Maps and Analysis" is very much an introductory "how-to" explication of each of the three modes: situational maps, social worlds and arenas maps, and positional maps. It offers a thorough description of each, followed by extended examples from two different research projects that are carried through the chapter. One example is a small interview study, while the other is a multisited project. My examples throughout the book are taken largely from studies of health and medical scientific domains where I dwell as a scholar. Obviously, many other kinds of exemplars are possible. Readers, especially faculty considering teaching with this book, might well want to locate substantively appropriate (and hence much more familiar) studies to assign in article form along with this book. These works can then be mapped in class as locally relevant working exemplars in action.

Chapter 4 is predicated on the increasing complexities of genres of data that can be pertinent to particular research projects. As we dwell, in postmodern times, in the society of the spectacle, analyzing individual and collective human and nonhuman actors and actants will not suffice. Chapter 4 therefore pivots situational analysis into the domains of discourse. It lays out why the turn to discourse is crucial and maps the major genres and foci of discourse analysis to date. It then provides short and long examples of multisite research that include discourse analysis as parts of larger projects as well as projects unto themselves. Last, it frames how to do situational analysis of extant discourses, including issues of research design, how analysis of extant discourse is different, and possibilities for integrative and/or comparative mapping of different genres of data.

Chapter 5 is the first of three "how to analyze discourse" chapters and focuses on working with extant narrative discourses. Issues of choosing a discourse, locating, situating, documenting, and tracking materials are addressed. The chapter then turns to actually doing each of the three kinds of situational maps using discursive data with an exemplar from my own work. It ends with a section on doing project-specific maps based on narrative materials.

Because so few grounded theorists have studied visual discourse, Chapter 6 offers a theoretical and conceptual overview of this domain. I then lay out the distinctive methods for doing situational analysis of visual materials. These include the complexities of deciding upon and gathering the materials, doing initial locating, big picture, and specification memos, and then doing the three kinds of situational maps. The exemplar is from my ongoing work on anatomies with Lisa Jean Moore.

Chapter 7 takes up mapping historical discourse—using historical materials to either historicize a research project focused on a contemporary situation or to pursue a "full-on" history project. Again using my own work as an exemplar (of the latter version), doing the three kinds of situational maps is explicated. Doing the same maps for different historical moments and their comparative provocations is the focus. A project map is also offered.

Last, "Epilogue: FAQs and Conversations," takes up questions and comments about situational analysis raised to me by students and colleagues to date. I respond to theoretical/philosophical questions, technical methods questions, miscellaneous questions, and critiques of situational analysis. I end with unanswered questions. As McCarthy (1996:111) has argued, "Situated knowledges are, by their nature, unfinished. But that is the character of all things human and alive."

Notes

1. See, e.g., Rosaldo (1989), Marcus and Fischer (1986), Denzin and Lincoln (1994, 2000), Atkinson, Coffey, Delamont, Lofland, and Lofland (2001), and Lather (1993, 2001a, 2001b). Bryant (2002) also uses the phrase "regrounding grounded theory."

2. See Glaser and Strauss (1967), Glaser (1978, 1992, 2002), Glaser and Holton (2004), Strauss (1987, 1991b, 1991d, 1993, 1995), and Strauss and Corbin (1990, 1994, 1997, 1998, 2005). It has been further elucidated especially by Charmaz (1983, 1995a, 1995b, 2000, 2001, 2002a, 2002b, 2003a, 2003b, 2005, in press), Charmaz and Mitchell (2001), Clarke (1991), Clarke and Montini (1993), Dey (1999, 2004), Locke (2001), and others: Annells (1996), Bartlett and Payne (1997), Baszanger and Dodier (2004), Corbin (1997, 1998), Ezzy (2002), Flick (1998), Konecki (2000), Melia (1996, 1997), Schreiber and Stern (2001), Soulliere, Britt, and Maines (2001), Starrin, Dahlgren, Larsson, and Styrborn (1997), van den Hoonaard (1997), and Wuest (1995).

3. Strauss's work on social worlds/arenas/negotiations was undertaken over many years at the same time as he developed grounded theory. See Strauss, Schatzman, Bucher, Ehrlich, and Sabshin (1964), Baszanger (1998b), and Strauss (1978, 1979, 1982a, 1982b, 1984, 1988, 1991a, 1991b, 1993). For Clarke's work in this area, see Clarke (1990a, 1990b, 1991, 1998). For Clarke's earliest articulation of the analytic importance of the situation, see Clarke and Fujimura (1992/1996).

4. On theory/methods packages, see Star (1989), Star and Griesemer (1989), and Fujimura (1992). Symbolic interactionism provides the ontological grounding. See Charmaz (2000) for an excellent discussion of the range of epistemologies associated with grounded theory, past and present. I discuss the Glaser/Strauss debate and Glaser and Holton's (2004) refutation of interactionist roots in Chapter 1.

5. Each of these is a huge literature in itself. For entrée to postcolonial studies, see Gandhi (1998); on feminist studies, see Olesen (1994, 2000); on diasporic studies, see Appadurai (1996); on race/ethnic/multicultural studies, see Twine and Warren (2000) and Ladson-Billings (2000); and on queer studies, see Plummer (1995) and Gamson (2000). See also Denzin and Lincoln (2005).

6. The phrase "always already" is used from Derrida (1978). It infers that the roots of present phenomena can always already be discerned in the past. We often enter always already ongoing flows later constructed as histories.

7. See note 3 for full citations to Strauss's work in these areas.

8. See, on theoretical sampling, Glaser and Strauss (1967:45-77), Glaser (1978:36-54), Strauss (1987:38-39), and Strauss and Corbin (1998:201-215).

9. By and large, I do not see Strauss as having theoretically elaborated upon his social psychology after 1959, although he routinely applied it in his research. See www.ucsf.edu/anselmstrauss/ for topic bibliographies that demonstrate this point.

10. On classic grounded theory coding, see especially Glaser and Strauss (1967:21-43), Glaser (1978:55-82), Strauss (1987:22-109), and Strauss and Corbin (1998:55-181). For more recent formulations, see Charmaz (2000, 2001, 2002b, 2002c, 2003b, in press). On diagramming, see especially Strauss (1987:130-230) and Strauss and Corbin (1990:195-224, 1998:217-242).

11. There is an extended discussion of the concept of situation in Chapter 1 and a critique of the conditional matrices in Chapter 2.

1

Pushing and Being Pulled
Around the Postmodern Turn

[M]ethodology embraces the entire scientific quest and not merely some selected portion or aspect of that quest.

—Blumer (1969:24)

S ymbolic interactionism is the theoretical tradition in sociology that nourished one of the two founders of the grounded theory method, Anselm Strauss. Symbolic interactionism sits simultaneously in some exceptionally comfortable and other highly awkward positions vis-à-vis postmodernism. In some ways, symbolic interactionist theory has always already been situated around the postmodern turn, especially but not only through its incorporation and elaboration of George Herbert Mead's concept of perspective. That is, much of symbolic interactionism has thereby always been distinctly perspectival in ways fully compatible with producing through research what are today understood as situated knowledges (Haraway 1991b, 1997). This especially involves the commitment to representing those we study on their own terms/through their own perspectives. Yet in other ways, symbolic interactionism can be seen to hark back to positivist empiricisms deeply reliant upon assumptions of an ultimately shared reality (e.g., Charmaz 1995a, 2000; Denzin 1996a, 1996b, 1996c; Maines 1996).

The grounded theory method, when itself explicitly situated with/in symbolic interactionism (which it has not always been), is similarly situated vis-à-vis postmodern insights—both always already there and also needing a push around the turn. This chapter centers on both being pulled by and pushing grounded theory/symbolic interactionism further around the postmodern turn, explicating how and why grounded theory needs to be renovated, and elucidating what that demands methodologically.

In important recent contributions, Charmaz (1995a, 2000), Locke (2001), and others have recently laid out the range of stances *within* grounded theory work from positivist to social constructivist, arguing that more recent work is shifting toward more constructivist assumptions/epistemologies. For example, while Charmaz (2000:510) and Locke (2001:12-13) both see positivisms in Strauss and Corbin's *Basics* books (1990, 1998), they both find as well that Strauss and Corbin's position moves toward postpositivism because they focus on giving voice to those they study. Charmaz (2000:510) sees the grounds for constructivist grounded theory as lying in its "tools for understanding empirical worlds" that can be used in "more open-ended practice[s]" as "flexible, heuristic strategies rather than as formulaic procedures" (see also Atkinson, Coffey, & Delamont 2003:148-152).

My goal is to further enable, sustain, and enhance such shifts through situational analysis. Methods are needed that are simultaneously epistemologically/ontologically based in the soil that nurtured pragmatism, symbolic interactionism, and grounded theory, and that also address demands for empirical understanding of the heterogeneous worlds emerging from this "fractured, multi-centered discursive system" of new world orderings. With Lather (n.d.:preface), I am seeking "a fertile space and ethical practice in asking how research based knowledge remains possible after so much questioning of the very ground of science . . . gesturing toward the science possible after the critique of science."

In this chapter, I first frame grounded theory as a theory/methods package rooted in symbolic interactionism. I next elucidate the ways in which grounded theory may be viewed as always already around the postmodern turn since its inception, pulling us along. I then describe its positivist recalcitrancies. Last, I introduce the main strategies I am advocating for pushing grounded theory more fully around the postmodern turn by providing alternative grounds for grounded theorizing.

Grounded Theory/Symbolic Interactionism as a Theory/Methods Package

> *Scientific theories begin with situations. . . . Theories are responses to the contingencies of these situations—courses of*

action articulated with yet more courses of action. The theories that scientists form about nature are the actions that both meet specific contingencies and frame future solutions.

—Star (1989:15-16)

Foundational to my project is the assumption that grounded theory methodology is itself grounded epistemologically and ontologically in symbolic interactionist theory. Historically, Glaser and Strauss (1967), Glaser (1978), and Schatzman and Strauss (1973) argued that grounded theory as a methodological approach could be effectively used by people from a variety of theoretical as well as disciplinary perspectives. That is, they initially took a "mix and match" approach. Their challenge—which they ably met—was to articulate a new qualitative methodology in the belly of the haute positivist quantitative sociological beast of the 1960s. They sought to do so through a systematic approach to analyzing qualitative research data.[1] Their emphases in the early works cited were on taking a *naturalistic* approach to research, having initially *modest* (read substantively focused) theoretical goals, and being *systematic* in what we might today call the interrogation of qualitative research data in order to work against what they and others then saw as the "distorting subjectivities" of the researcher in the concrete processes of interpretive analysis.

Strauss and Glaser sought to make qualitative sense within an increasingly quantitative and scientistically oriented discipline of sociology increasingly reliant upon mechanistic methods. They sought to do so by providing what was then most obviously missing from the disciplinary toolbox—a reasonable inductive approach to collecting and analyzing qualitative data that seriously attempted to be faithful to the understandings, interpretations, intentions, and perspectives of the people studied on their own terms as expressed through their actions as well as their words. The groundedness of good traditional grounded theorizing is not only in the data per se but, I would argue, most deeply in the seriousness of the analyst's commitment to representing *all* understandings, all knowledge(s) and action(s) of those studied—as well as their own—as *perspectival*. Strauss's later work noted this vividly, leading off with the need to "bring out the amazing complexity of what lies in, behind, and beyond, those data" (e.g., Strauss 1987:110, 1993, 1995). In terms of promoting inductive conceptual work, grounded theory has been exceptionally influential in the domains of qualitative research almost since its inception (e.g., Atkinson, Coffey, & Delamont 2003:148-152; Bryman & Burgess 1994:220).

Another fundamental desire of Strauss and Glaser was for a method that could travel across some of the usual divides of the academy without violating core disciplinary and/or social science/humanities concerns. In this too they succeeded, perhaps beyond their wildest dreams. Grounded theory has become one of the major approaches in qualitative research not only in sociology (e.g., Strauss & Corbin 1997) and nursing (e.g., Benoliel 1996; Schreiber & Stern 2001), where it was originally taught, but also in organization and management studies (e.g., Locke 2001; Turner 1983), education (e.g., Bogdan & Bicklen 2003; Creswell 2002; Merriam 2002), cultural studies (e.g., Gelder & Thornton 1997), computer and information science (e.g., Bryant 2002; Star 1992; Star & Strauss 1998), social work (e.g., Riessman 1994), science, technology, and medicine studies (e.g., Clarke & Star 2003), and queer studies (e.g., Ekins 1997; Gamson 2000; Plummer 1995). A Current Contents database search on "grounded theory" found 1,353 citations, 435 of which were after 2002 (done May 25, 2004).

Glaser and Strauss seem, at least initially, not to have been particularly concerned about other users shearing off key aspects of the epistemological apparatus of the method.[2] In contrast, I would argue that such shearing off of epistemological and ontological roots (intentionally or not) is the usual means of making a method transportable, capable of traveling to new sites of application. For example, in social research more broadly, qualitative research has recently gained a certain recognition of its strengths and hence a certain panache. This has led to many "quickie courses" for quantitatively trained investigators to help them "expand their research repertoires" to meet the new interests of (often U.S. federal) funding sources for projects that combine quantitative and qualitative approaches. Many if not most such projects put epistemology and ontology aside—sometimes with awareness but more often without—and thus never seriously engage with qualitative methodologies, but merely give the appearance of doing so (e.g., Patton 2000). Superficial appearances of compliance often suffice for such organizational purposes (Wiener 2000a).

In considerable contrast, I begin from the assumption that grounded theory/symbolic interactionism constitutes a theory/methods package.[3] Star (1989) framed such packages as including a set of epistemological and ontological assumptions along with concrete practices through which a set of practitioners go about their work, including relating to/with one another and the various nonhuman entities involved in the situation. This concept of theory/methods package focuses on the integral—and ultimately nonfungible—aspects of ontology, epistemology, and practice as these are coconstitutive. Specifically, I am arguing that grounded theory is a methodology inherently predicated upon a symbolic interactionist theoretical and philosophical ontology. Grounded theory is thus one method among many of "performing" (Butler 1993; Goffman 1963a, 1974) or "doing" (Fenstermaker & West 2002) interactionism.

"Method, then, is not the servant of theory: method actually grounds theory" (Jenks 1995:12).

There are, of course, many symbolic interactionisms and many related interpretive empirical approaches all situated and grounded somehow in contrast to most scientistic positivisms. With Carey (2002:200), "Wanting a tradition within which to work, I invented my own take on symbolic interactionism." The interactionisms I see as grounding grounded theory and situational analysis conceptually resonate most strongly with the work of Mead (perspective); Park (the "big picture" and ecological framings); Blumer (sensitizing concepts and group position); Becker (commitment, social worlds, the importance of the visual); Strauss (action theory, social worlds/arenas/negotiations/discourses, the importance of history); Denzin, Charmaz, Richardson, Fontana, Ellis, Bochner, Clough, and Star (postmodern turnings); and Hall, Maines, Strauss, Wiener, and myself (meso-level, institutionally/ecologically informed symbolic interactionist efforts), among others.[4] This conceptual toolbox is not necessarily disciplinary but has dwelled especially in linkages between sociology and cultural studies (e.g., Becker & McCall 1990; Carey 2002; Denzin 1992). Obviously I cannot detail all this interactionist work here. Instead, I next use it to illustrate how grounded theory/interactionism was/is always already around the postmodern turn.

Grounded Theory/Symbolic Interactionism as Always Already Around the Postmodern Turn

> We inhabit a cultural moment that has been dubbed the postmodern. A cultural studies and interpretive interactionism informed by poststructuralism, Marxism, feminism, and the standpoint epistemologies aims to make sense of this historical moment called the postmodern. . . . The postmodern is our project.
>
> —Denzin (1996c:349)

Through grounding grounded theory and situational analysis in symbolic interactionism as a theory/methods package, they are positioned as always already around the postmodern turn in many ways. As Manning (1995:248; emphasis added) has noted: "Postmodernism also shares many intellectual roots with symbolic interactionism, and the postmodern challenge is consistent with the mandate of the leading school of American pragmatism. . . . Symbolic interactionism has a long tradition of detailed description of symbolic aspects of life. It elevates to centrality the spontaneous interpretive self and the role of the *situated and negotiated order* and has shown a passionate resistance to formalization and systematization. A final parallel exists. Like symbolic interactionism, postmodernism is not a theory but a perspective."

There are a number of "always already" postmodern properties of a grounded theory grounded in interactionism.[5] These include the following:

**Being Pulled Around the Postmodern Turn
Through Grounded Theory/Symbolic Interactionism by**

1. The Meadian notion of perspective through which both partiality and situatedness are assumed;

2. Its materialist social constructionism;

3. Its foregrounding of deconstructive analytic interpretation via open coding and the legitimacy of multiple simultaneous readings/interpretations;

4. The orientation toward action, processual analyses, and negotiations as anticipating instabilities;

5. Range of variation as an always significant but underdeveloped and underemphasized featuring of difference(s); and

6. The long-standing ecological and social worlds/arenas bent of both interactionism and grounded theory as presaging relational forms of analysis such as situational analysis and positional maps.

Perspectives, Partialities, and Situatedness

First is the Meadian notion of perspective, perhaps our strongest foundational element and most powerful tool:

> This perspective of the organism is then there in nature. What in the perspective does not preserve the enduring character of here and there, is in motion. . . . [T]his [is a] conception of *nature as an organization of perspectives*, which are there in nature. . . . *This principle is that the individual enters into the perspectives of others, insofar as he is able to take their attitudes, or occupy their points of view.* (Mead [1932] in Strauss et al. 1964:343-346; emphasis added)

Mead's brilliance here lies not only in his articulation of the concept of perspective as social but also in his assertion that nature too is socially constructed. For Mead, there is no ultimate "biology" as the undergirding arbiter of "nature," but only other social (read human-made) perspectives, of which biology qua discipline is one. That is, inherent if not wholly explicit in Mead is the conceptual infrastructure of social constructionism that theoretically undergirds postmodern theory. At its simplest, constructionism assumes that the only realities possible are those that we construct, which we must do through shared language, and that we agree to agree about, however unstable those meanings and agreements may be in linguistic and related practices. Mead's concept of perspective underwrote the early Chicago sociology tenet known as the Thomas's theorem: *Situations defined as real are real in their consequences.* Or, perspective dominates interpretation. This theorem served Chicago School sociology well until constructionism in its own name emerged circa 1966 with the publication of Berger and Luckmann's *The Social Construction of Reality: A Treatise in the Sociology of Knowledge.* While there are likely thousands of forms of constructionist theory circulating today, the key point here is that its American seeds lay in Mead and have been manifest in the sociological work that constitutes symbolic interactionism ever since (e.g., Reynolds & Herman-Kinney 2003).

A Materialist Constructionism

Second, I count among our epistemological blessings that interactionist constructionism is a *materialist* social constructionism. To some, this is an oxymoron, but for me and for grounded theory, it is foundational. Many people (mis)interpret social constructionism as concerned only with the ephemeral or ideological or symbolic. But the material world is itself constructed—given meaning(s)—by us, by those whom we study, and is what we study (our own constructions of our research problems, including nonhuman material aspects). It is present and to be accounted for in our interpretations and analyses. This materialism, this importance of things, this sociality of things was also argued by Mead (1934/1962), as McCarthy (1984) has most elegantly demonstrated. More recently, Law (1999:4) has argued that symbolic interactionism is predicated on what he calls a "relational materiality." We routinely make meaning about, within, through, and as embodied parts of the material world—human, nonhuman, and hybrid. The social is relentlessly material, not "merely" epiphenomenal. As elsewhere, those meanings (Meadean attitudes, points of view, and perspectives) are not to be assumed but to be empirically examined. (I discuss the importance of taking the nonhuman into account in Chapter 2.)

Deconstructive Analysis

The third way in which grounded theory/symbolic interactionism can be viewed as always already around the postmodern turn is its foregrounding of a deconstructive mode of analysis via open coding. Open coding connotes just that—data are open to multiple simultaneous readings/codes. Many different phenomena and many different properties can be named, tracked, and traced through reams of all different kinds of data. There is no one right reading. All readings are temporary, partial, provisional, and perspectival—themselves situated historically and geographically. There are no essences—we are postessentialist.

As analysts, we can ourselves attempt to read the data from different perspectives and for different purposes. In fact, Strauss developed a concrete practice approach to producing multiple readings—working groups for data analysis that take up individual members' project data. Multiple readings are routinely and explicitly sought and produced through group effort. This is also the usual pedagogical tradition for teaching/learning grounded theory—to bring multiple perspectives together so that you can *more easily* produce multiple readings, multiple possible codes. In this way of working, the analyst is constantly banging into and bouncing off the interpretations of others. This also ultimately legitimates and enhances the capacity of analysts themselves to come up with multiple possible readings on their own and to abandon ideas about "right" and "wrong" readings. Strauss so much believed in this process that he incorporated transcripts of group analysis sessions into one of his major methods books (Strauss 1987). Later in the research process, of course, the analyst will need to negotiate among the multiple readings produced to decide on those to be preserved and pursued through further theoretical sampling and final analytic products. But this does *not* mean reduction to a singular interpretation or representation (or a single basic social process).

Yet the idea of deconstruction is even stronger here. Recently, grounded theory and other *analytic* approaches have been criticized for "fracturing" data, for "violating" the integrity of participants' narratives, for "pulling apart" stories, and so on (e.g., Mattingly & Garro 2000; Riessman 1993). To me, this is not a weakness or problem but instead the key to grounded theory's *analytic,* rather than (re)representational, strength. Analysis and (re)representation are two deeply different qualitative research approaches, both valuable and both of which I support.[6] These different qualitative approaches can themselves be viewed as standpoints (Miller 1997) or perspectives that privilege different facets of social life.

In grounded theory, the capacity for critical analysis is furthered through open coding such that actions, situated perspectives, symbolism(s), and the heterogeneity of discursive positions and their relations can be discerned and creatively grasped. Here the goal is not preserving and re-representing a "truth" or series of "truths" as expressed (usually) by narratives or quotes from one or a series of individuals. Instead, the goal is critically analyzing to produce "a truth" or possible "truths"—distinctive analytic understandings, interpretations, and representations of a particular social phenomenon. Such critical analysis can also be used to trace genealogies of extant "systems of thought" (e.g., Foucault 1978, 1979). Re-representation usually centers on individuals (occasionally on collectivities). Analysis centers on social phenomena.

Processes and Contingencies

The fourth way in which grounded theory/symbolic interactionism is always already around the postmodern turn lies in the orientation of traditional grounded theory toward action, processual analyses, and negotiations (at least in Strauss's formulations). This approach facilitates representation of the instabilities and contingencies of postmodern concern. The now almost century-long, more general tradition within symbolic interactionism of refutation of dualisms has allowed instabilities and other kinds of teeterings captured so well by analytic gerunds to become robust. In a good grounded theory analysis, it is *routinely* possible to see "how things could have been otherwise" (Hughes 1971). In fact, there is an elaborate conceptual vocabulary of ruptures, turning points, trajectories, careers, and so on elucidating fateful moments (see Glaser 1978; Strauss 1993), and epiphanies (Denzin 1992). Each of these concepts points to "how things could have been otherwise." There are also interesting linkages to be made between this mode of analysis and Foucauldian genealogies that similarly seek to construct "histories of the present" by tracing sites and moments of discursive change (e.g., Dean 1994). I discuss some of these linkages in Chapter 2.

Difference(s)

The fifth way in which grounded theory is always already around the postmodern turn concerns difference as range of variation. Variation has always been attended to in grounded theory, a postmodern inflection. Strauss (1993:49) returned to this point in his capstone book and emphasized it as follows: Social science activity "is directed at understanding the entire range of human actions, of which there are so many that the dictionary can scarcely refer to them all. That is, an interactionist theory of action should address action generally and be applicable to specific types of action, so that in effect the theory can also help us understand the incredibly variegated panorama of human living." I seek here to emphasize this "incredibly variegated panorama of human living" through situational mapping and analyzing differences of all kinds. Building on extant potentials within traditional grounded theory, making differences more visible and making silences speak (also often about difference) are two of the explicit goals of situational analysis.

Ecologies

Sixth and last, the long-standing ecological bent of symbolic interactionism also is alive and well in grounded theory, a form of analyzing relationality that is highly compatible with postmodern concerns with difference. Deep within this sociological ecology, born in the emerging metropolis of Chicago, lie concepts and metaphors of territory, geographic space, maps, relations among entities in a shared terrain, and so on. "The main point . . . was to make an inventory of a space by studying the different communities and activities of which it is composed, that is, which encounter and confront each other in that space" (Baszanger & Dodier 1997:16, 2004).

In Strauss, the Chicago ecological bent was translated through urban geography and imagery into his analyses of social worlds and arenas and later undergirded the conditional matrix. Strauss's handling of social worlds also echoes Blumer's (1958) conceptualization of race as meaningfully constructed through relative *collective positionality*. As usual, in his capstone book, Strauss (1993) emphasized the fluidities and processual facets of social world relations that are also simultaneously structural elements. Borrowing from Carey (2002:202), Strauss's was "a sociology of structuration before Anthony Giddens invented the word."

The particular power of the social worlds/arenas/discourses framework is that because social worlds are "universes of discourse," the framework explicitly goes beyond "the usual suspects"—the usual highly bounded sociological framings of organizations, institutions, and even social movements. These are displaced by a more open, fluidly bounded, discourse-based framing of collective action (Clarke 1991). This displacement of supposedly clearly bounded collective actors by problematically bounded discursive arrangements opens up the broader situation for analysis.

While the ecological bent of grounded theory itself has been comparatively underdeveloped, I feature it in situational analysis. That is, I use social worlds/arenas/discourses and the more general framings of ecology and cartography as the root metaphors for situational analysis. Strauss himself did not "see" his own social worlds framework as building toward this but was certainly agog at and intrigued by the idea of situational analysis as based on it the one time I discussed it with him, sadly just the week before he died.

While these aspects of grounded theory/symbolic interactionism demonstrate how it has always already been around the postmodern turn conceptually and potentially in practice, other features and practices hark back to more positivist empiricisms.

Grounded Theory as Recalcitrant Against the Postmodern Turn

It is as if postmodernism were a choice, or an option.

—Denzin (1996c:347)

Next I turn to what I see as recalcitrancies within grounded theory that need to be explicitly addressed in order to push grounded theory more fully around the postmodern turn. The notion of recalcitrancies is, of course, relative to one's goals. My goals, emerging in part from feminisms, antiracisms, and related commitments to equity, are to create approaches to empirical research that take difference(s), power, contingency, and multiplicity very seriously. I seek approaches that not only do not erase/paper over differences but also seek to address silences in data, silences of resistance, protection, cooptation, and collusion (e.g., Patton 2000). Like Strauss, I see social structures as highly consequential and push analytically on this front as well, drawing upon poststructuralist decenterings and reframings of these analytic concerns to do so.

The recalcitrancies of traditional grounded theory that concern me generally tend to preserve in grounded theory analyses tastes and flavors of 1950s and 1960s styles of American positivism and scientism. Positivist tendencies were clearly present in the original works done by Glaser and Strauss (Atkinson & Coffey 2003; Bryant 2002; Charmaz 2000; Locke 2001). Manning and Cullum-Swan (1994) assert that this was utterly common in the 1960s, when Goffmanian and ethnomethodological approaches were considered radical. While many scholars working in the grounded theory tradition have long since embraced constructionism and truth with a small "t," a certain (sometimes) naive realism or "bottom line-ism" also lurks. This can be manifest in the following "recalcitrancies" of which grounded theorists may or may not be aware in their empirical practices.

Recalcitrancies of Traditional Grounded Theory

1. A lack of reflexivity about research processes and products, including a naive notion of giving "voice" to the unheard from "their own" perspective, including the pretense that the researcher can and should be invisible;

2. Oversimplifications such as emphases on commonalities and strains toward coherence;

3. Oversimplifications such as singular rather than multiple social processes as characteristic of a particular phenomenon or situation;

4. Interpretations of data variation as "negative cases"; and

5. The search for "purity" in grounded theory.

A Lack of Reflexivity

In most grounded theory work, there has been inadequate reflexivity about research processes and products per se and their relations to various nexes of power and authority, especially vis-à-vis the production of official and unofficial knowledges. As Denzin (1996c:352) has argued, "Self-reflection in ethnographic practice is no longer an option," and a significant aspect of the postmodern turn in qualitative/interpretive research has been an intensive focus on the presence and consequences of the researcher in the research—as an actor, designer, interpreter, writer, coconstructor of data, ultimate arbiter of the accounts proffered, and as accountable for those accounts, and so on (e.g., Kleinman & Copp 1993; Olesen 1994, 2000). No longer is Francis Bacon's phrase "About ourselves we remain silent" deemed acceptable (Ree 2001:53). Key questions to be addressed include the following: Whose knowledge about what counts to whom and under what conditions? Who is the researcher? How is who they are consequential? Who/what is researched? With what consequences? For whom? Who paid for it and why? Who/what is placed at risk by this research? How? Who/what is advantaged by this research? How?

In grounded theory, there has historically been a problematic pretense that the researcher can be and/or should be invisible. This is the continued and multiply faceted denial that *we are, through the very act of research itself, directly in the situation we are studying.* This is specifically manifest in Glaser's (1992:50; emphasis in original) belief in researchers as tabula rasa (blank slates), able to virginally enter new research sites: "The analyst should just *not know* as he [*sic*] approaches the data." In contrast, I assert that we cannot help but come to almost any research project already "knowing" in some ways, already inflected, already affected, already "infected."

Further, researchers' own experiences of and interests in their particular areas of research are often quite extensive and important to put on the table in the research per se (e.g., Bartlett & Payne 1997; Frank 1995). Strauss generally assumed that people had personal interests in their research topics and encouraged students to draw upon and reflect upon that knowledge (Strauss 1987:10-13, 160-162; Strauss & Corbin 1998:43-48). He himself wrote on living with chronic illness for the entire two-plus decades during which he lived with a severe heart condition. The questions are: How can we be present and hold ourselves accountable in our research? Without discrediting our research through "personal bias"? And without displacing it with what Daly (1997:361) calls an "intellectual narcissism" that goes over the reflexive edge to produce a study that becomes too much of "us" and too little of "them"?

Another related reflexivity issue concerns the uses of our prior experiences and knowledge in our research. Responding to Glaserian critiques of grounded theory after Strauss's death, Corbin (1998:122) asserted: "We certainly had no intention of conveying the idea that we use 'experience' as data. Rather, experience is an analytic device used to stimulate reflection about the data at hand." One's own experiences offer but one among many perspectives on the issue, here neither falsely denied nor weighted in privileging ways. This multiplicity of perspectives on a research topic is, of course, aided and abetted by Straussian group analysis of data, often rupturing the analyst's framings as well.

Further, in terms of prior knowledge, many researchers have extensive coursework and literature reviews of an area under their belts before beginning the empirical research project.[7] Such reviews are commonly required as part of dissertation and grant proposals. I see prior knowledge of the substantive field as valuable rather than hindering. We do not need to invest precious research time and energies to reinvent wheels. And none of this prior knowledge can be or should be erased from researchers' conscious awareness. There is actually "something ludicrous about pretending to be a 'theoretical virgin'" (Robert Loescher, quoted in Elkins 2003:31).

Moreover, after a half to full century of social science research in some topic areas, little that is new is coming forward except through paradigm shifts, such as the postmodern turn. Using "received theory" *instead* of doing one's own analysis is always a danger, especially for students, but grounded theory has always worked against such tendencies. Regardless, scholars need to situate their own work vis-à-vis the substantive field.

Certainly social scientists have "been around the block" with these issues over the past two decades—or even century. But these issues are worth returning to again and again and are fundamental to postmodern interrogations of research methods. I am reminded here of a wonderful piece of art: In dripping black paint along the top of a very large white canvas was written "1. Language is not transparent."[8] Neither are we. Instead of hiding behind method, I am proposing with many others that as researchers, we become more visible and accountable for, in, and through our research.

Weber (1946) long ago raised these issues of personal involvement and values in research. He asserted that we are usually personally involved and revealed in the act of research problem selection but should seek objectivity in the research process itself. More recently, at the height of the deeply politicized Vietnam War era in the United States, Becker (1967/1970) discussed how people construct "hierarchies of credibility" that implicate researchers on the basis of what/who we choose to study. We are clearly slotted by others into distinctive positions based on our choice of research topic. Anyone who has chosen to study a "hot" or controversial topic can attest to this, including, for example, sex (Moore 1997), genetics (Rapp 1999b), reproductive science (e.g., Clarke 1990a, 1998), and fetal surgery (Casper 1997, 1998a). Becker's article title, "Whose Side Are You On?" tells us that we can and will be positioned by others, like it or not (see also Atkinson & Coffey 2003:ch. 3).

Significantly, such positionalities and hierarchies are constructed not only by academics and others inside the research community and academia more broadly but also and increasingly by those being researched and certainly by other audiences of the work. Scholars in science studies, where studying controversy has a long history as being a useful research strategy for seeing "science in action," have found themselves positioned as tacitly if not explicitly supporting the "underdog" by studying the controversy.[9] That is, researchers are typically seen as *advocates* of underdog positions precisely because the intervention of social science research as a representational event itself gives greater visibility and voice to underdog positions. This occurs *regardless* of researchers' efforts to be "unbiased." As philosopher Ian Hacking (1983) asserts, representation *is* intervention. This point is also partly what Donna Haraway (Haraway 1991b) means when she asserts that there are no innocent positions. And it is what Pnina Abir-Am (1985) means when saying we cannot help but be hagiographic of what we choose to study at least in the sense that *any* advertising is "good" advertising (see also Clarke & Montini 1993).

This, then, is the first of several sites where greater reflexivity on the part of grounded theory researchers is needed. How and why have we come to study X topic? With what goals in mind? For whom? Cui bono? Is it possible to "do no harm"? Given that we *are* intervening, are we clear about our goals and means? Nancy Naples (2003; Naples & Sachs 2000; Naples & Clarke 1995) and others (e.g., Lewin & Leap 1996) have recently pursued the issues of personal involvement in research, "outing" themselves as *fully* participant observers in the social worlds they have studied and/or having themselves personally experienced the social problem(s) they pursue. They have reflexively addressed their *simultaneous* situatedness as participants *and* as researchers. There are no easy "answers," only processes of seeking more ethical reflexivity.

Another problematic of reflexivity manifest in some grounded theory accounts concerns (sometimes naively framed) notions of giving unmediated "voice" to the unheard—from "their own" perspective(s). Recent scholarship in qualitative inquiry has instead asserted, rightly I believe, that *all* reports are deeply mediated by the researcher.[10] Moreover, without taking difference(s) fully into account, I suspect representations of participants' "own perspectives" are rather narrowed at best. A key question here becomes, To what extent are *different* perspectives "given voice" by the researchers—even perspectives repugnant to the researcher? Who/what is omitted or silenced by the researchers themselves? Wittingly or not? What is sanitized and dressed up? Why and how? How are participants' *contradictory* responses addressed and handled? Patti Lather's work addresses these questions assiduously (see also Kitzinger 2004). My own experiences in studies of science and technology empirically rendered "voice" problematic in another way: Scientists' voices usually have much more power than mine, and I have sometimes inadvertently lost my own voice as the researcher in representing theirs "too" assiduously for my own good/goals. Reflexivities are needed that enhance our capacity to address all kinds of differences, certainly including those of power and authority.

Oversimplifications

The second major area of recalcitrance of grounded theory is oversimplification in research reports such as strains toward coherence and commonalities. These can often be construed as intentionally deleting distinctiveness and heterogeneities in favor of creating a monolithic "Other." I am reminded here of an account by a former student, Linda Hogle (1999), who studied transplant medicine in Germany. One day, during observations in the room with a fresh cadaver, she watched the physician in charge of explantation working at the preparation bench deal with a just-removed liver. He was carving and shaping it like a sculpture before placing it in the preservative container in which it would be delivered to the recipient. We ourselves do such carving and sculpting as well in constructing our data, our memos, and our research reports, and we also usually do *not* talk or write about it.

Instead, I propose that we complicate our stories, represent not only difference(s) but even contradictions and incoherencies in the data, note other possible readings, and at least note some of our anxieties and omissions. That is, we need to find ways of discussing that which we have in the past scraped or trimmed off or somehow left behind in our research process while still telling coherent analytic stories. We need to address head-on the inconsistencies, irregularities, and downright messiness of the empirical world—not scrub it clean and dress it up for the special occasion of a presentation or a publication. This does not at all mean presenting raw data—but rather doing even more analysis and extended reflection that can take rawness into fuller and more explicit account.

A Singular Basic Social Process

Several other recalcitrancies are found in grounded theory that I shall merely mention now but return to in detail later. One consists in subtle or blatant pressures toward analyzing for a singular "basic social process" rather than allowing for the possibility of multiple social processes as characteristic of a particular phenomenon. That is, the canonical grounded theory texts all encourage the analyst to select one main process and to describe other processes as "subprocesses," seemingly regardless of how complicated the situation may be. Again, this may well effect erasure of difference(s). Instead, I would analytically allow the possibility of multiple major processes and that some processes may even be paradoxical or contradictory.

"Negative" Cases

Another recalcitrance involves interpretations of data variation as "negative" cases (e.g., Glaser 1978; Glaser & Strauss 1967; Strauss 1987). "Outlier" data are thus characterized within the dated framework of "normalcy" versus "deviance," which has its American origins in Parsonian functionalism and was both challenged and reframed through labeling theory by interactionists in the 1960s and 1970s (e.g., Becker 1963; Pfohl 1985; Rubington & Weinberg 1968). The questions are: Why is a particular data point "negative"? Another "positive"? Negative to whom? For whom? Who gets to do the labeling? Who does not? Of whom or what? And ultimately, why is social life being structured as binary through grounded theory research? *It need not be and it should not be.* In my era as a student in his classes after circa 1980, Strauss taught this as "range of variation" that should be taken into analytic account. But if this was a shift in his thinking, it did not make it into his writing that I have found.

The Search for "Purity"

The last recalcitrance is the search for "purity" and "objectivity" by more positivist grounded theorists who tend to believe methodological (and perhaps other) purity is not only possible but desirable. Over the past decade or so, Glaser and others have devoted much energy to policing boundaries, trying to keep things and people apart, and promulgating methodological "antimiscegenation laws" intended to prevent change and innovation in grounded theory. Glaser himself has made a wealth of fresh assertions regarding what counts as "real" grounded theory, many in direct response to Strauss and Corbin's collaborative works.[11] While careful readers of this book will recognize my deep appreciation for many facets of classic grounded theory, I also find myself in deep disagreement with many of Glaser's fundamental(ist) points. I address several of them here and others passim.

To begin, I see Strauss as more and perhaps increasingly constructionist in how he used and understood grounded theory in both his teaching and independent writing (e.g., Strauss 1987). I see the epigraph on the dedication page of Strauss and Corbin's *Basics* (1990, 1998) as a commentary on the importance of change to keeping grounded theory vital—and I believe it was addressed to Glaser: "If the artist does not perfect new vision in his process of doing, he acts mechanically and repeats some old model fixed like a blueprint in his mind"—John Dewey, *Art as Experience,* 1934, p. 50. Strauss and Corbin (1994:283) also noted that "no inventor has permanent possession of the invention—certainly not even of its name—and furthermore we would not wish to do so."

Moreover, for Glaser (with Holton 2004:sec. 2:7), grounded theory "is not underlined by symbolic interaction, nor constructed data. GT uses 'all as data,' of which these are just one kind of data." I read this as constituting two distinct points. First, Glaser disavows symbolic interactionism as grounding (his version of) grounded theory. I agree with this as his version is deeply positivist, most significantly eschews Mead, and even includes "core variable" language. In sharp contrast, Strauss clearly *was* deeply rooted in interactionism and commented on this as a difference between them (esp. Corbin 1998:125-126). Second, Glaser demonstrates here (and passim in his recent work) that he does not understand social constructionism as an epistemological/ontological position. He thinks *some* data are "constructed" while *other* data are "pure." Constructionism asserts that *all* meanings are constructed by people as they "do" life, and there is, therefore, no space outside/beyond constructions (e.g., Berger & Luckman 1966; Blumer 1958; see also earlier discussion of Mead).

Related to this are several issues about researchers' reflexivity. The first concerns the role of the researcher. When Strauss and Corbin's (1990) *Basics* was published, Glaser (1992) accused Strauss of abandoning their original version of grounded theory and "forcing data" through the procedures outlined in *Basics* rather than "letting the data speak for themselves." Locke (1996:240-241) attributes their methodological disagreements to fundamental differences in perspective on the role/presence of the researcher in the research process:

> Strauss locates agency for [grounded] theory development in human researchers, whereas Glaser confers agency on neutral methods and data. . . . Thus Strauss and Corbin's (1990) rewriting expresses a very active, even provocative, role in which researchers essentially interrogate the data they

gather to arrive at conceptual categories. . . . Glaser [assumes] a one-way mirror through which the natural world might be revealed. . . . Clearly, in this tradition, the natural world is "out there." This portrayal of researchers presented in Glaser's 1992 publication is consistent with the images scientists in the positivist tradition present of themselves. . . . [In contrast, Strauss and Corbin] view researchers as interpreters of the data they study who can build good complex theories by actively "opening up" the data to discovery.[12]

Strauss himself also noted a lack of reflexivity on Glaser's part (Corbin 1998). My own position here is very much allied with Strauss and Corbin in terms of "opening up" data, and I seek to go even further in abandoning positivist goals for postmodernist ones. (See also the discussion of research design in Chapter 2.)

Another point of serious concern is that Glaser (with Holton 2004:sec. 4) asserts that grounded theory pertains only to social psychology. I certainly see it as conceptually much broader—not only fully sociological but also as pertaining to meso/organizational/institutional concerns, as did Strauss (e.g., 1987, 1993) and also relevant far beyond sociology. Furthermore, according to Glaser (with Holton 2004:sec. 2:8), "Context must emerge as a relevant category or as a theoretical code like all other categories in a GT. It cannot be assumed as relevant in advance." I profoundly disagree. In fact, I have predicated situational analysis on the analytic necessity of addressing "context." Strauss's own prolonged disagreement with Glaser on this very point is demonstrated through the conditional matrices (see Chapter 2).

Also serious is Glaser's (with Holton 2004:sec. 2:9) position that "the goal of GT is conceptual theory abstract of time, place and people." Or, grounded theory should be ahistorical, acultural, and transcendent. Others of us (e.g., Haraway 1991b) argue, au contraire, that there is no meaningful "voice from nowhere" (1997) that will guide us to some heavenly methodological redemption from messes, ambiguities, contingencies, materialities, multiplicities, embodiments, and even contradictions. There is no "god's-eye view" position from which to write up research. *Knowledges and knowledge productions are situated and noninnocent.*

Taking all this into account is part of the paradigm-rupturing transition from modern to postmodern that Haraway (1991b:186) brilliantly calls "a kind of epistemological electro-shock therapy." Pushing grounded theory/ symbolic interactionism around the postmodern turn, then, *does* require abandoning naive hopes of theoretical transcendence, complete (macro or other) theoretical explanations, universal cures, transhistorical solutions, and the possibility of interventions without unintended side effects. But there are other alternatives, certainly for modestly improving qualitative research methods.

Pushing Grounded Theory
Around the Postmodern Turn

> *Methods are mere instruments designed to identify and analyze the*
> *obdurate character of the empirical world, and as such their value*
> *exists only in their suitability in enabling this task to be done.*

—Blumer (1969:27)

Next I focus on the six strategies I advocate to push grounded theory/symbolic interactionism even further around the postmodern turn than it always already is. This involves both pushing against the force of the recalcitrancies elucidated above and elaborating upon its always already postmodern strengths. One of the core criteria of a good grounded theory is that it is modifiable—responsive to new data. I want to do a subversive reading of this criterion toward modifying the theory of grounded theory per se. I want to shift and augment the undergirding assumptions of grounded theory from positivist to postmodern, from Western scientific universalizing master narratives "explaining variation" to creating representations that basically assume differences and multiplicities and seek to explicitly map and represent them. I am interested in the following:

Pushing Grounded Theory Around the Postmodern Turn by

1. Assuming and acknowledging the embodiment and situatedness of all knowledge producers, and assuming the simultaneous "truths" of multiple knowledges;

2. Using the *situation* of the research phenomenon as the site of analytic grounding;

3. Shifting from assumptions and representational strategies of simplifying normativities and homogeneity to complexities, differences, and heterogeneities;

4. Asserting the analytic sufficiency of sensitizing concepts and theoretically integrated analytics rather than the pursuit of formal theory;

5. Doing situational analyses throughout the research process, including making situational maps, social worlds/arenas maps, and positional maps; and

6. Turning to discourses—narrative, visual, and historical—to expand the domains of social life included in grounded theory research.

Acknowledging Embodiment and Situatedness

The first move toward pushing grounded theory around the postmodern turn is not only assuming but explicitly acknowledging the embodiment and situatedness of knowledge producers—both us (the researchers) and them (who and what we are studying). Historically, grounded theory had a foot (and sometimes more than one) in the positivist domain that, since the scientific revolution, has assumed that "nature" determines what is known about the "natural." In brief, across the 16th century, a set of changes took place in the West called "the scientific revolution" (itself now also under reinterrogation), and the reframing of knowledge production it engendered was centered around a new human character who Shapin and Schafer (1985) described as "the modest witness." This new modest witness is not the medieval conquering hero embodying a masculinity constructed through participation in Christian Crusades in the "Orient" (Said 1978), the knight in shining armor who epitomized the white, male-gendered ideal human being of the previous historical epoch. Rather, the new Renaissance hero is a freshly gendered white male form—the modest scientist. In this shift from religious to Western scientific modes of knowledge production as the legitimate "way of knowing" the world, the modestly witnessing scientist claims to provide an account that offers a "mirror" of nature (Rorty 1979). This modest man comes from what Sharon Traweek (2000) has called "the culture of no culture," a space of *self*-invisibility, that crucial hegemonic space claimed and dominated by modern Western science. His elite class status was rendered invisible, until recently, by the invisibility of the technicians and other servants who historically performed the physical and craft labor of his science.[13] The modest witness can thus be free of the burdens of corporeality (e.g., Hayles 1999). He "doesn't have a body; therefore, he alone sees everything in the great communicator's empire of the Global Network" (Haraway 1991b:183).

Personally apparently unintrusive, stable, and therefore unbiased, Haraway (1997:24) notes that the modest witness claims he adds "nothing from his mere opinions, nothing from his biasing embodiment. And so he is endowed with the remarkable power to establish the facts" in a pattern of human activity that we have come to name "objectivity."[14] This new expert knowledge—positivist science—is "the founding gesture of what we call modernity. It is the founding gesture of the [*claimed*] separation of the technical and the political" (Haraway 1997:24; see also Foucault and Latour), and the technical from the religious/spiritual.

I want new directions in grounded theory to both address and push these issues further. I am arguing more broadly that the scientistic framework of the modest witness was not only constitutive of gender, race and class, empire and colony. That framework was also constitutive of new domains of legitimate and illegitimate knowledges, narrowings of epistemology/ontology that to this day delegitimate many knowledges. Modest witnesses instituted much more elaborate calculi of what kinds of knowledges can "count" and what kinds cannot, especially "officially."[15] The race, gender, class, and geographic locations of "modest witnesses" were claimed to be rendered silent and invisible by their pretense of disembodiment and their explicit denial of the salience of the embodiment of the knower. But they were not.

In sharp contrast, recent scholarship on qualitative methods and related work instead asserts that knowers *are* embodied, regardless of denial strategies.[16] That embodiment is inscribed on the knowledge produced in the very act of its claiming objectivity. Embodiment, so long refused, is thus today ever more salient and must increasingly and reflexively be taken into greater account. New knowledge studies also seek to specify what has gone and goes unstudied—what Evelynn Hammonds (1994) calls "black (w)holes"—sites of particular tensions of omission (e.g., Poovey 1998). What goes unstudied may not be seen or perceived, or may be refused—and is worthy of note regardless (Star 1991b). In fact, we need to become *immodest witnesses*— acknowledgedly embodied knowers—and produce new and even blatant framings of what can and should be known. Representing the heterogeneity of perspectives remains a quite radical act, especially in the United States where the default assumption is that of the binary, hegemonically reinforcing a repressive and distorting two-party political system and a two-sided adversarial legal system—as if there "really" are only two perspectives that "matter." Fascism has many faces, and insisting upon binaries is one.

Grounding in the Situation

My second strategy for pushing grounded theory around the postmodern turn is making the broader *situation* of the phenomenon under research the analytic ground.[17] "The situation is both an object confronted and an ongoing process subsequent to that confrontation. . . . Situations have a career-like quality and are linked in various ways . . . to other situations" (Morrione 1985:161-162). The term "situation" signals for me four particular scholarly contributions of which I am intellectually inordinately fond. First is William Thomas's and Dorothy Swayne Thomas's (1923/1978, 1928/1970) conception of "the definition of the situation." In short, they argued three-quarters of a century ago that *situations defined as real are real in their consequences.* Or, perspective dominates the interpretation upon which action is based. To me, this is relentlessly relational and ecological. It echoes Mead's (1927/1964:315) assertion that *situations are organizations of perspectives that stratify nature*—that make genres of distinctions that carry meaning and are consequential. It is also relentlessly relativist: These stratifications "are the only forms of nature that are there."

My second inspiration regarding the concept of situation is C. Wright Mills's classic and deeply pragmatist paper from 1940 (1940/1970:472; emphasis added) on "Situated Actions and Vocabularies of Motive," where I draw on his elucidation of situated action:

> The postulate underlying modern study of language is the simple one that we must approach linguistic behavior, not by referring it to private states in individuals, but by *observing its social function of coordinating diverse action*. . . . [L]anguage is taken by other persons as an indicator of future actions. . . . [M]otives are the terms with which *interpretation* of conduct by social actors proceeds. . . . First, we must demarcate the general conditions under which such motive imputation and avowal seem to occur. . . . The importance of this initial task for research is clear. Most researches on the verbal level merely ask abstract questions of individuals, but *if we can tentatively delimit the situations* in which certain motives may be verbalized, *we can use that delimitation in the construction of situational questions.*

Situational questions are a focus of data gathering for situational analyses.[18] Here we embrace the limitations of analyzing a particular situation rather than attempt to overcome them through the generation of formal theory. Partial perspectives suffice.

My third key resource on the concept of situation is Donna Haraway's (1991b:188; emphasis in original) classic feminist theory paper on "Situated Knowledges" in which she states:

> I would like to insist on the embodied nature of all vision, and so reclaim the sensory system that has been used to signify a leap out of the marked body and into a conquering gaze from nowhere. . . . I would like a doctrine of embodied objectivity that accommodates paradoxical and critical feminist science projects: feminist objectivity means quite simply *situated knowledges*. . . . In this way we might become answerable for what we learn how to see.

It was through feminisms, including hard-won appreciations that the term needed to be pluralized, that many of us came to understand that knowers are embodied and knowledges are situated, as discussed above (e.g., King 1994; Lather 2000). Accountability—becoming "answerable for what we learn how to see"—is of signal import (see also Chapter 2). Hence we need to know what the situations are—especially but not only of knowledge production. Situations become the fundamental units of analysis.

Another significance of the concept situation for interactionists lies in its gestalt—how a situation is always greater than the sum of its parts because it includes their relationality in a particular temporal and spatial moment. Peter Hall (1997:400; emphasis added) wrote: "Anselm Strauss (1993) has contributed more than any other interactionist to the conceptualization of social organization and our understanding of *relations among situations.*" Writing on relations between U.S. Steel and the United Steelworkers union, Blumer noted: "The point is that very frequently the power relationship between them was the result of the situation rather than the situation being the result of their respective power positions as they entered it. *This important feature is characteristically ignored in the usual analysis in terms of power*" (Blumer, quoted in Hall 1997:405; emphasis added). Blumer is arguing for a gestalt understanding of situations as generating "a life of their own." This is a very poststructuralist reading, granting a kind of agency to the situation per se similar to the agency discourses have/are in Foucaultian terms, an important facet toward understanding situational analysis.

A final pleasure in focusing on the situation of inquiry itself is that the situation is being taken up in social theory today in new ways. For example, I see Massumi (2002:211) as building on this gestalt of situations, arguing that the "excess"—that which makes the situation greater than the sum of its parts—"*belongs to their joint situation. More precisely, it enters their situation.*" Massumi (2002:209-210; emphasis in original) also recently said, "[T]here are other ways of approaching the situation than bare-braining it. For one thing, you could try to *think* it. . . . In other words, what is at stake is no longer factuality and its profitability but rather *relation* and its *genitivity.* The question is: what new thoughts does this nexus of productively experienced relation make it possible to think?"

Differences and Complexities

My third strategy for pushing grounded theory around the postmodern turn therefore concerns the assumption and representational strategies of focusing on normativity/homogeneity versus differences/complexities/heterogeneities. The capacity of grounded theory techniques to fracture data and permit multiple analyses is its key contribution to the capacity to represent difference(s), complexities, multiplicities. But to empower this capacity of grounded theorizing, to feature it, involves an array of efforts. Most foundationally, it involves analyzing *against* the assumptions of the normal curve that are implicit throughout the social sciences. The normal curve is the implanted default drive of Western science, black-boxed inside the hardwares of knowledge production and inside the softwares of social science training.

Many/most of us fall back into it automatically in our thinking. It is today, I would argue, a *cultural* assumption of the Western educated mind/person and deeply embedded in a wide array of discourses. It is one of the ways in which a distinctively functionalist positivism and scientism have become culturally and transnationally taken for granted—that is, naturalized (Foucault 1965, 1975)—and rendered invisible as part of the intellectual colonization processes that Gramsci (1971) described as hegemonic.

Normal Curve

imagine a drawing of the normal curve here
[it won't be hard]

The normal curve is a measure of central tendency. The foundational assumption is that frequencies of X phenomenon will distribute themselves in a patterned way, with most of the variation falling at two "opposite" "ends" of a binary continuum. The "nonvariation"—"normal"—or majority will fall in the "middle." Again, this is frequency based and also commonly appears as a bar graph. Representationally, it is as if the blanket of inquiry has been thrown over the data points and pushed them down and forward into a single dimension at the bottom of the page/figure, carefully containing them within their "natural" classificatory slots. The normal curve is clearly a high modern concept that embodies Enlightenment thinking and thereby produces knowledge that fits its ordered and orderly preconceptions.

The normal curve lies at the metaphoric heart of the concept of a "Basic Social Process."[19] The historic centering of a grounded theory of a given phenomenon on a single social process has been based on profoundly universalizing and essentializing assumptions of the homogeneity of individuals and/or experiences embedded in the concept of the normal curve. The key intervening questions here are: Basic for whom? Basic for what? What/whose perspectives have been ignored or given short shrift? And why only one process?

The normal curve operates both graphically and metaphorically: While the fringes or margins are literally contiguous with the center, we are led to assume they are not constitutive of the "normal." Certainly Canguilhem (1978), Foucault (1965, 1975), and many symbolic interactionists struggling with functionalists in the 1960s and 1970s (e.g., Becker 1963, 1967/1970; Blumer 1969) and others have argued otherwise. It is the boundaries/margins that *produce* the center, the peripheries/colonies that constitute the core/metropole (Bhabha 1994; Gieryn 1999; Said 1978; Star & Griesemer

1989). Moreover, in narrowly focusing on what is construed as "the normal," the broader situation in which the phenomenon has been historically and otherwise located recedes to the point of invisibility. But methodologically, I do not think these arguments have been "heard" or been adequately consequential in research.

My alternative grounding for grounded theory as it keeps traveling around the postmodern turn draws deeply on social worlds and arenas approaches and metaphors. I seek to replace metaphors of normal curves and normativity with relational metaphors of ecology and cartography. See Figure 1.1, Mapping Positionality. My argument is that we need to conceptually replace modernist unidimensional normal curves with postmodern multidimensional mappings in order to represent lived situations and the variety of positionalities and human and nonhuman activities and discourses within them. Otherwise we merely continue performing recursive classifications that ignore the empirical world.

This alternative relational modality of representation does not concern itself particularly with frequency but instead with positions and their distribution across some kinds of situational or topographical maps that do the work of helping us to "see" the range of positions. This alternative seeks not to frame a "basic social process" or even processes but to draw maps. The goal is to understand, make known, and represent the heterogeneity of positions taken in the situation under study and/or within given (historical and/or visual and/or narrative) discourses in that situation.

Such maps draw deeply on postmodern concerns with the concrete representation of difference. They thereby disarticulate grounded theory from traditional positivist concerns and rearticulate the approach within a postmodern frame. This is especially vivid in terms of elaborating the traditional strength of grounded theory in getting at the range of variation, always present but never featured in the analytic foreground. In postmodern grounded theorizing, it is front and center.

I use the term "differences" often in this book, and it means multiple things simultaneously. My usage has its origins in feminist theory, which from the outset took up issues of sex/gender difference but very quickly expanded to include differences among women—*within* the "category" "women"—on the basis of race, ethnicity, class, sexuality, physical ability, and so on. Very quickly again, it became vividly clear that while there might be certain differences on the basis of any of these and other related identity politics categories, extending far beyond feminism to postcolonial sites and beyond, there are also extensive and serious within-category differences and many other kinds of differences as well. That is, the categories of "received theory" do not suffice for taking differences into account.

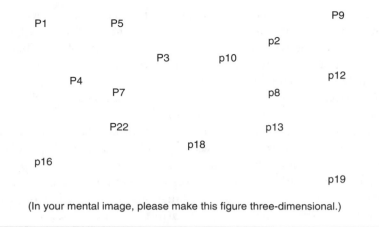

(In your mental image, please make this figure three-dimensional.)

Figure 1.1   Mapping Positionality

Historicizing how "difference" has been taken up in the human sciences, Stepan (1986:275-276) argues that before World War II, difference was usually linked to hierarchical discourses that legitimated various inequalities. In contrast, after World War II, similarities were emphasized and linked to equality. In more recent discourse, equality has been explicitly asserted as appropriate regardless of difference. Furthermore, difference and rights have also been linked around arguments that differences need to be taken into account to protect rights.

The concept of difference also takes up marginalities—and the study of those at the margins has a long and deep history within interactionism (e.g., Ferguson, Gever, Minh-ha, & West 1990; Hughes 1971; Simmel 1903/1964, 1908/1993; Wirth 1928). Today, this is more broadly inflected, and with Tsing (1993:36), I seek "encounter[s that] encourage me to begin from the marginal—not to head back to an imagined center, but to extend my account to other marginalities." All these differences also need to be mapped, acknowledged, and their implications understood. In addition, poststructuralist theory, including the work of Derrida, attended to difference and its ramifications. In short, the concept of "differences" has exploded during my lifetime as a scholar, and it is very much to offer a means of addressing this that I developed situational analysis.[20]

The main goal of situational analysis vis-à-vis differences is to enhance their *empirical* study. That is, we cannot assume what any kinds of differences mean to those in a given situation and need more and better methods to explore those meanings and their consequences in concrete social practices, including the production and consumption of discourses as practices (Schwalbe et al. 2000).

Harris (2001:456) captures the principle well focusing on inequality; the word "difference" can also be inserted:

> [T]he strength of interactionism derives from its attention to the meanings that putatively equal or unequal situations have for those whose behavior one attempts to understand. These diverse meanings tend to be obscured when sociologists [or other scholars] define inequality, identify its manifestations, measure the extent of its existence, explore its causes and document its effects, and advocate ways of diminishing it. In contrast, the primary task for interactionists should be researching the meanings inequality has *for people*.

Differences need to be de-reified through empirical research. This is, of course, not to say that feminist theory, race theory, research, and so on are useless. It is to say that specificities of meanings *within* particular situations are important to grasp while also grasping and using theory and other research to enhance our understanding. We need to grasp variation within data categories, range of variation within data, complexities, contradictions, multiplicities, and ambivalence(s) manifest individually, collectively, and discursively. Situational maps are each and all designed to do precisely this work.

But all is not differences either. In one of the most interesting recent interventions in race theory that has implications for many other domains, "sameness" and the work that sameness can do within particular situations has been raised (Essed & Goldberg 2002). That is, there can be preferences for doing something with or being with people who are "like me" rather than "different from me" that work against differences in discriminatory ways without focusing explicitly on any particular differences per se. That is, while seeking sameness may be the intent, rather than seeking to exclude, discriminatory exclusion may nonetheless be a consequence. Differences and samenesses are reified in all kinds of social practices, including discourses, and those practices and discourses need to be understood.

A key means of entrée where differences tend to be more than usually vivid is to research situations featuring conflict and controversy. In such situations the workings of power are often clearer. Peter Hall (1997:401) has argued that "while Strauss is cognizant of power and domination, he has not made them central or even conceptualized them." Dingwall and Strong (1985; Dingwall 1999) similarly critiqued Strauss's inattention to "the nonnegotiable in social life." Situational analysis seeks to rectify this in a number of ways. Analyses of power are facilitated in conflictful and controversial situations because issues that may be tacit, unspoken, or even hidden suddenly become explicit and stated—if not shouted. Interactionism has a conceptual vocabulary of such Meadean moments of rupture: turning points, trajectories, fateful moments, epiphanies, and so on (Reynolds & Herman-Kinney 2003:47). Each points to "how things could have been otherwise" (Hughes 1971), usually in ways related to power in the situation, and allows a more Foucaultian genealogical approach to be taken that opens past and present to analysis. This strategy of studying controversy has a long history and has ably demonstrated its utility in science, technology, and medicine studies (e.g., Collins 1981; Garrety 1997, 1998; Nelkin 1995; Scott, Richards, & Martin 1990). There one analytically seeks the actors with sufficient power to effect "closure" of the controversy, but other approaches are certainly viable.

Sensitizing Concepts, Analytics, and Theorizing

My fourth strategy for pulling grounded theory around the postmodern turn is asserting the analytic sufficiency of sensitizing concepts, analytics, and theor*izing* for solid grounded theory research. This replaces the pursuit of substantive or formal theory advocated in traditional grounded theory (including by Strauss 1995). There, in principle and over time, multiple studies would be done in a particular substantive area; a series of substantive theories would be generated through integrating concepts; and ultimately these would be drawn into a formal theory. Glaser and Strauss themselves did this in their research on dying.[21] The idea of generating formal theory through grounded theory was a high modernist project, itself situated in an elaborate set of assumptions about the making of sociology as a science parallel to the natural sciences.

In contrast, I agree with Denzin (1992:23; emphasis added) that "[s]ociety, like interaction, is an emergent phenomenon, a framework for the construction of diverse forms of social action. *It makes no sense to write a grand theory of something that is always changing.*" Thus, a key aspect of the alternative approach developed here is focused on grounded theor*izing* through the development of *sensitizing concepts* and integrated analytics. Blumer (1969:147-148; emphasis added) said:

> [T]he concepts of our discipline are fundamentally sensitizing instruments. Hence, I call them "sensitizing concepts" and put them in contrast with definitive concepts. . . . A *definitive concept* refers precisely to what is *common* to a class of objects, and by the aid of a clear definition in terms of attributes or fixed bench marks. . . . A *sensitizing concept* lacks such specification. . . . Instead, it gives the user a general sense of reference and guidance in approaching empirical instances. Whereas definitive concepts provide prescriptions of what to see, *sensitizing concepts merely suggest directions along which to look.*

Significantly, this does *not* mean "analysis lite," a characteristic of too many grounded theory projects according to an array of critics.[22] As Locke (1996:244) noted, the grounded theory label is used too often as a "rhetoric of justification as opposed to a rhetoric of explication." It does mean "interpretive sufficiency" (Charmaz 2005, in press). It does mean more explicitly situated analytic claims making and the avoidance of overgeneralization and overabstraction (e.g., van den Hoonarrd 1997). In Daly's (1997:360, 353) words, the challenge for presenting a theoretical text, then, is to present theory "not as objective truth but as a located and limited story. . . . [T]o keep theory in play but to redefine theory in a way that keeps the theorist in play—all within the bounds of science."

More modest and partial but serious, useful, and hopefully provocative grounded analyses, sensitizing concepts, analytics, and theorizing are adequate. Analytics are unlike theory in that they do not presuppose a transcendent origin or cause of phenomena. "We aren't, nor do we have to put ourselves, under the sign of a unitary necessity" (Burchell, Gordon, & Miller 1991:78). Furthermore, rather than focusing on commonalities, we can pursue directions and angles of vision that reveal difference(s) and complexities, heterogeneous positionings, including but not limited to differences in power in situations. The goal is not prediction but what Fosket (2002:40) called "thick analysis." The possibility of analytic extension of theorizing into other parallel or related situations certainly remains, but here it is accomplished through the use of comparisons rather than theoretical formalization and claims of transcendence.

Doing Situational Analysis

My fifth strategy for bringing grounded theory around the postmodern turn is making empirical analytic maps of situations and doing *situational analyses* of several kinds—the focus of most of this book. Situational analyses seek to analyze a particular situation of interest through the specification, re-representation, and subsequent examination of the most salient elements in that situation and their relations. Some of these elements have traditionally been discussed as "context." For example, Hall and McGinty (2002:303; emphasis added) have ably argued that some

interactionists have in varying ways elaborated how context matters but have been extremely leery of conventional assumptions about social structure. . . . [Instead they have] actively engaged in clarifying the nature of social organization (a term chosen in lieu of social structure). . . . Words like society, the state, bureaucracy, and group mask contradiction, complexity, ambiguity and incompleteness. *The nature and degree of social organization must be an empirical question.* In addition, interactionists have disputed views of social organization as external and constraining, as standing above and apart from social actors. They have argued for its embeddedness and active conditional influence and its continual . . . [re]constitution by those actors. The resulting interactionist view of social organization is one that is complex, processual, dynamic, variably coupled, and open.

I strongly agree but take this one step further: The important so-called contextual elements are actually *inside the situation itself.* They are *constitutive* of it, including structural and power elements, and we can map and analyze them as such.

Why situational *maps?* Why not narratives? There are a number of reasons. Let me start with some advantageous properties of maps elucidated by David Turnbull (2000) and elaborated by me. Because maps are visual representations, they helpfully rupture (some/most of) our normal ways of working and may provoke us to see things afresh (e.g., Latour 1986, 1988b; Suchman 1987). Maps also work more easily as discursive devices for making assemblages and connections—relational analyses. Maps are excellent "devices to materialize questions." Maps are tools of control, appropriation, and ideological expression. Mapping is a fundamental cognitive process—we can "just do it." Mapping opens up knowledge spaces. Maps are great boundary objects—devices for handling multiplicity, heterogeneity, and messiness in ways that can travel. Maps work well as spatial and temporal narratives. Maps allow unmapping and remapping. In addition, maps are very much part of the Chicago tradition as devices for analyzing relationality (see Chapter 2). Most important here, one can move around on/in maps much more quickly and easily than in narrative text, excellent for analytic work. Last, at least since the postcolonial era began, maps have been widely understood as very political—and shifting—devices. Hopefully, this will provoke enhanced reflexivity. The limitations of maps remain, of course, what can be "seen" by a particular analyst in a particular time and place. No method overcomes the situatedness of its users. A method can, however, attempt to use situatedness to improve the quality of the research.

Turning to Discourse(s)

The sixth and last strategy for pushing grounded theory/symbolic interactionism further around the postmodern turn consists in turning through Foucault toward discourse, including situational analyses of narrative, visual, and historical discourses in grounded theory research to expand the domains of social life addressed. I am pushed here by C. Wright Mills "with his insistence that social theory must connect biography to history, connect the stories we tell ourselves about ourselves, which are impositions of a narrative line on the phantasmagoria of experience, with the stories the narrative machinery of society tells not only about us but about the society itself" (Carey 2002:201). We need more and better understandings of the various "narrative machineries" and the discourses they produce. Four chapters of this book (Chapters 4-7) facilitate making this turn, aided and abetted by Foucault.

Chapter 2 elucidates more specifically how I take up these six means of pushing grounded theory around the postmodern turn through situational analysis.

Reflections and Anticipations

> All *components of the desire [for "better" science] are paradoxical and dangerous, and their combination is both contradictory and necessary.*
>
> —Haraway (1991b:187; emphasis in original)

Let me summarize this chapter with a chart while also appreciating the irony of offering one in the postmodern (Lather 1991:159). See Figure 1.2, From Traditional/Positivist to Postmodern/Constructivist Orientations to Grounded Theory. The chart does not and is not intended to represent grounded theory as usually done. Far from it. I seek to highlight some of the more problematic in practice tendencies that have gotten played out in traditional grounded theory because of the lingering aura/promises of positivism and how this is manifest. Similarly, I seek to highlight some of the goals of constructivist grounded theory work—perhaps ideally more than in practice as yet. The chart maps the directions in which I am pushing grounded theory to get it more fully around the postmodern turn.

There are three main take-home messages from this chapter. First, a grounded theorizing approach can valuably be used to construct situational analyses as well as to frame basic social processes. Second, a core goal of such analyses is to improve the representation of difference(s) and complexities of all kinds—especially situated in practice differences rather than in abstracted differences. And third, perhaps the radical reflexive act we perform as mapmakers is to reveal ourselves in and through analyzing what "we" do as well as what "they" do.

TRADITIONAL/POSITIVIST GROUNDED THEORY	POSTMODERN/CONSTRUCTIVIST GROUNDED THEORIZING
***All of the following should be assumed to hold only part and never all of the time/in all cases.	***All of the following should be assumed to be followed by "if and as found in the data."
Positivist/realist	Constructivist/relativist
Dualism of subject and object	Continuities of subjects and objects
Discovering/finding	Constructing/making
Correspondence theory of truth	Constructionist theory of knowledge production
Naive objectivity	Noninnocent subjectivity/reflexivity
(Over)homogenization; (over)generalization	Multiple positions; heterogeneous representations
A priori rejection of contradiction as possible	Representation of contradiction(s) as analyzed/interpreted
Simplification desired	Complexity represented
Seeks to be conclusive	Tentative, opening, jarring, troubling
Authority of author/"expert" voice dominant	Multiple voices, perspectives, intensities, reflexivities
(False/overdrawn) clarity	Ambiguity of representation
"Normal"/average plus "negative cases"	Difference, range of variation, outliers, positionality
Tacitly progressive; linear	Doubtful; reads against the grain
Assumption of normativity	Assumption of positionality
Metaphors of normal curve	Metaphors of cartography
Goal: To delineate a basic social process (BSP) and formal theory	Goal: To construct processes, sensitizing concepts, situational analytics, and theorize

Figure 1.2   From Traditional/Positivist to Postmodern/Constructivist Orientations to Grounded Theory

Studying action is not enough. We need analytic maps to plot positions taken and their relative locations and power. We need improved methods for grasping the constructions of terrain—altitudes, topographies, scales, textures, and so on. We need methods that can simultaneously address actors in action and reflection and discursive constructions of human and nonhuman actors and positions and their implications. We need cartographies of discursive positions. This is not to say that splendid studies have not been produced through analyzing basic social processes. They have been and will be. Nor do I seek to end or replace processual approaches and action analyses using grounded theory. I do seek to address situational analyses to multiple audiences who will find these approaches useful in addressing the empirical world in postmodern times.

Notes

1. See also Atkinson and Coffey (2003:148-152). Glaser (1978, 2002) and Glaser with Holton (2004) argue that grounded theory could also be used with quantitative research.

2. Strauss was, in person, often quite critical of studies that claimed to be using grounded theory but which he found lacking in this regard. He knew one cannot control what others do with one's work, but was still, like Glaser (2002; Glaser & Holton 2004), quite disappointed and exasperated when users "didn't get it." Significant aspects of his exasperation concerned the conceptual and epistemic/ontological absence of symbolic interactionism in many such works. His intense analytic pursuit of the work of other symbolic interactionists at the end of his life (e.g., Mead, Blumer, Hughes, Davis) attests to the continuing importance of interactionism to him (see Strauss 1991a, 1996a, 1996b, 1996c). I would argue that those absences in published grounded theory research drove him, in part, to the intense writing he did on research methods during the final years of his life (Strauss 1987, 1993, 1995; Strauss & Corbin 1990, 1997, 1998).

3. Leigh Star, Joan Fujimura, and I have elaborated this notion in symbolic interactionist science studies focused on actual practices—known earlier/elsewhere in symbolic interactionism as the sociology of work (see Clarke 1987/1995, 1998, 2003; Clarke & Fujimura 1992/1996; Fujimura 1992, 1996; Star 1989, 1991a, 1991b, 1995, 1999). Star (1989) demonstrates the materiality and consequentiality of such theory/methods packages (in brain research). Fujimura (1996) pushed on the modes through which theory/methods packages can travel—by being widely accepted (part of a "bandwagon"), often because they perform increasingly well in situations at hand (e.g., creating "doable problems" for research scientists to address), as they are further standardized. Bowker and Star (1999) elucidate how, through classification and standardization processes, computer and information science are aiding and abetting such travel.

4. See, e.g., Mead (1927/1964, 1934/1962), Park (1925, 1952), Blumer (1958, 1969), Becker (1967/1970, 1982), and Strauss (1991b, 1993). On meso-level symbolic interactionism, see, e.g., P. M. Hall (1987, 1997), Hall and McGinty (2002), Maines (1988), Strauss (1991b), Wiener (2000a, 2000b), Clarke (1991), and Clarke and Montini (1993). See also Fine (1993).

5. See Maines (1996:334) for a more elaborated list. See also Maines (2001) and Denzin (1992, 1996c).

6. By re-representation, I mean attempting to successfully represent in another medium—such as oral interview into scholarly writing. I applaud, celebrate, and routinely teach the clearly postmodern re-representational interventions produced by Denzin (1989, 1991), Ellis (1995), Ellis and Flaherty (1992), Ellis and Bochner (1996), Bochner and Ellis (2001), Richardson (1992, 2000), Clough (1992), Ronai (1995, 1997), Lather and Smithies (1997), and others. I also celebrate more phenomenological work (e.g., Benner 1994; Benner, Tanner, & Chesla 1996; Chesla 1995), narrative analysis (Bell 2000; Messias & DeJoseph n.d.; Riessman 1993, 2002). These are excellent and wholly worthwhile projects, but not mine.

7. Glaser (1978) especially advised against this. However, Glaser has also chosen not to pursue research funding or publish in conventional academic venues since he left the University of California, San Francisco, in the late 1970s.

8. This "conceptual art" was done by Mel Bochner in 1970.

9. A quite sophisticated debate took place in science studies on this topic. See Scott et al. (1990) and the special issue of *Social Studies of Science* edited by Ashmore and Richards (1996).

10. See, e.g., Clifford and Marcus (1986), Visweswaran (1994), Denzin and Lincoln (1994, 2000), Lather (1993, 1995, 1999, 2001a, 2001b), Lather and Smithies (1997), Fine (1994), Fine, Mun Wong, Powell, and Weis (1996), and Fine, Weis, Weseen, and Mun Wong (2000).

11. See Glaser (1978, 1992; Glaser with Holton 2004) and Baker, Wuest, and Stern (1992) on "method slurring," Wilson and Hutchinson (1996) on research mistakes, and Stern (1994) on preserving the earliest (Glaser & Strauss 1967), most positivist and narrowest version of grounded theory. For extended comparisons of Glaserian and Straussian perspectives, see commentary by Bryant (2002, 2003), Charmaz (1995a, 2000), Corbin (1998), Dey (1999, 2004), Locke (1996), and Melia (1996). See also Annells (1996), Atkinson, Coffey, and Delamont (2003), Bartlett (2001), Bartlett and Payne (1997), Rennie (1998), and Strubing (1998). On Glaserian perspectives, see the Grounded Theory Institute's Web site at www.groundedtheory.com.

12. Glaser is clearly *not* animating data as the "nonhuman actant" in some version of semiotic actor-network theory (see Chapter 2). Locke (1996:241) notes that, au contraire, Glaser is using a rhetorical device named by Charles Bazerman (Bazerman & Paradis 1991) as "the active seeking of passive restraints"—attempting to use methods that will constrain the influence of the researcher. I find that Glaser goes beyond this to further claim that using such methods erases all traces of the researcher, and agree with Locke (2001), Bryant (2002, 2003), and many others

that this is a conceptual and practical impossibility. See also Melia (1997), Corbin (1998), Charmaz and Mitchell (2001), and Atkinson, Coffey, and Delamont (2003:esp. 148-152).

13. On technicians and related workers in science, see, e.g., Clarke (1987/1995), Shapin (1989), and Clarke and Fujimura (1992/1996); in medicine, see Strauss et al. (1964).

14. On the historical construction of objectivity in the sciences and beyond, see Daston (1992/1999), Daston and Gallison (1992), Porter (1995), Potter (2001), and Harding (1991, 1998).

15. On contemporary attempts to further narrow and standardize what legitimate research can be, see the two special issues of *Qualitative Inquiry* (Vol. 10, Nos. 1 and 2) on "Dangerous Discourses I and II." While these focus especially on U.S. federal support of education research, the implications of both the politics and the processes of standardization of research methods are much broader. See also Bowker and Star (1999).

16. See, e.g., Fine (1994), Kleinman and Copp (1993), Johnson (1975), Fine et al. (2000), Haraway (1997), Lather (1999, 2001a, 2001b), Visweswaran (1994), and Denzin and Lincoln (2000).

17. The term "situation" has been used in related ways by others. Reynolds and Herman-Kinney (2003:47) trace early uses in Pierce and Dewey. Goffman (1964) titled a paper "The Neglected Situation," meaning the *immediate situation of interaction* as "an environment of mutual monitoring possibilities." Goffman's (1974) *Frame Analysis* also takes up the definition of the situation in this immediate interpersonal sense. Gubrium and Holstein (1997:163) call Goffman's approach "situational analysis," referring to largely face-to-face situated interaction as "sites of interpretive practice." My use of the term is much broader and includes pertinent institutional and other meso/macro social formations, though possibilities of mutual monitoring are very much a part of it (see also McHugh 1968; Morrione 1985; Snow 2001). Because "the process involving the definition of the situation is a significant act of power," Altheide's (2002b:173) "main interest concerns the role of the mass media and popular culture in shaping such definitions." This fits well with the inclusion of discourse analysis in postmodern grounded theorizing. Last, a group of French artists and social/political theorists, including Guy Debord, called themselves the "Situationists." Their work contributed extensively to the students' and workers' revolt of May 1968. Many but not all of their ideas are compatible with what I am writing about here. See, e.g., Brooker (1999:204-205) and Dark Star (2001).

18. C. Wright Mills (Mills & Mills 2000) apparently wrote to David Riessman in 1952 that he was not content with this publication, and had reworked it as a chapter of *Character and Social Structure,* coauthored with Hans Gerth (Gerth & Mills 1964). The reworkings do not appear to be pertinent to the present argument.

19. See, for example, Glaser's (1978:109-110) "BSPs Compared to Units" [of analysis—people, institutions, etc.]. While I agree with some of his points, others are classically modernist and universalizing, articulated from and through a positivist

perspective. For example, his #5 asserts that "freedom from perspective" is not only possible but desirable. To me, Glaser confounds level of abstraction with generalizability and universality.

20. See Derrida (1978), Hekman (1999), Dugdale (1999), Epstein (2004), Essed and Goldberg (2002), Fenstermaker and West (2002), Friedman (1998), Gilman (1985), S. Hall (1990, 1996, 1997), and Hammonds (1997a). On complexity, see Landstrom (2000) and Law (1999). A recent book edited by Lincoln and Denzin (2003) on *Turning Points in Qualitative Research* actually begins with a section on "the revolution of representation" that centers on representations of difference.

21. See Glaser and Strauss (1964, 1965, 1968), Strauss (1970), and Strauss and Glaser (1970). See also Timmermans (1994) and Mamo (1999), who both theorize these issues further.

22. On "liteness" and the absence of theory, see, e.g., Bryman and Burgess (1994), Dey (1999, 2004), Bryant (2002), Locke (2001), Glaser (1992), and Atkinson et al. (2003). There are certainly exceptions (e.g., Kearney 1998). There also appear to be some slippages viz. the meanings of "sensitizing concepts" among Glaser, Strauss, Blumer (see van den Hoonaard 1997:5-6).

2

From Chicago Ecologies
to Situational Analysis

Moving across levels of the particular and abstract, trying to avoid a transcendent purchase on the object of study, we set ourselves up for necessary failure in order to learn how to find our way into postfoundational possibilities.

—Lather (1999:137)

This chapter provides the historical theoretical background and conceptual foundations for the new methodological approaches to grounded theory called situational analysis. At the same time that the canonic grounded theory approach centered on analyses featuring basic social processes, others of us—including Strauss—also used that approach to do what we have called social worlds/arenas/discourse analysis.[1] The new approaches of situational analysis are rooted in this work. Here the root metaphor for grounded theorizing shifts from social process/action to social ecology/situation—grounding the analysis deeply and explicitly in the broader situation of inquiry of the research project.

In simplified form, situational or relational ecology is closest to policy arena analyses. We assume multiple collective actors (social worlds) in all kinds of negotiations and conflicts in a broad substantive arena focused on matters about which all the involved social worlds and actors care enough to be committed to act and to produce discourses about arena concerns. In this broader situation, there are also individuals, an array of nonhuman and hybrid actors (discussed below), discourses on related topics (narrative, visual, historical), and so on. The social worlds/arenas/discourses framework relies strongly upon Mead's key concepts of perspective and commitment—all actors have their own perspectives and commitments vis-à-vis the situation/arena articulated through discourse.

Arenas are discursive sites in often complicated ways. Particular social worlds are constructed in others' discourses as well as producing their own. But arenas usually endure for some time, and long-standing ones will typically be characterized by multiple, complex, and layered discourses that interpolate and combine old(er) and new(er) elements in ongoing, contingent, and inflected practices. Furthermore, because perspectives and commitments differ, arenas are usually sites of contestation and controversy, especially good for analyzing both heterogeneous perspectives/positions on key elements, and to see power in action (a lesson from technoscience studies; see Chapter 1, note 10).

Arenas are also especially amenable conceptual frames through which to work at a more meso/organizational level, analyzing *collective* actors (social worlds), their work and discourses in those arenas. For example, Peter Hall (1997:397) noted: "A view of social organization is offered that emphasizes relations among situations, linkages between consequences and conditions, and networks of collective activity across space and time." It is through such frames that symbolic interactionist studies can address more global elements, increasingly important today. But like the basic social process/action frameworks fundamental to traditional grounded theory, social worlds/arenas/discourses analyses also cannot do everything we want to do analytically; hence my expansion of them into the several forms of situational analysis offered in this book.

I begin by very briefly laying out the historical roots of situational analysis within Chicago School symbolic interactionism as it shifted from what could be called the early social ecologies to the more contemporary framing of social worlds/arenas/discourses. This is followed by discussion of three "new roots" that reground grounded theory through situational analysis, innovations that become parts of the constructionist conceptual infrastructure. The first new root sets Foucault among the interactionists. I place him in conversation with Strauss about discourse/discipline and social worlds/arenas; the field of practice(s)/conditions of possibility and negotiated ordering/situations; the gaze and perspective.

The second new root concerns taking the nonhuman explicitly into account, including not only material "things" but also discourses (including visual and historical materials) and other virtual realities. Nonhuman elements are important actors in situations of action and hence in situational analyses. Next I discuss the expansion from social worlds/arenas to the broader framework of situational analysis through a critical analysis of Strauss and Corbin's conditional matrices. Finally, one more area of innovation within grounded theorizing is proposed—a more grounded and situated accountability accomplished through design-stage and subsequent data selection and gathering strategies.

Root Metaphors: From Chicago School Social Ecologies to Social Worlds/Arenas/Discourses

> *Symbolic interactionism is grounded on a number of basic ideas, or "root images," . . . [which] refer to and depict the nature of the following matters: human groups or societies, social interaction, objects, the human being as an actor, human action, and the interconnectedness of lines of action. Taken together, these root images represent the way in which symbolic interactionism views human society and conduct. They constitute the framework of study and analysis.*
>
> —Blumer (1969:6)

The Chicago School ecological and social worlds/arenas/discourses approaches become the root images or metaphors for the supplemental mapping strategies of situational analysis—the conceptual/philosophical infrastructure for this innovative approach to qualitative analysis. Blumer (1969:24-25; emphasis added) discussed such root metaphors as follows:

> *The Possession and Use of a Prior Picture or Scheme of the Empirical World Under Study* . . . [T]his is an *unavoidable* prerequisite for any study of the empirical world. One can *see* the empirical world only through some scheme or image of it. The entire act of scientific study is oriented and shaped by the underlying picture of the empirical world that is used. This picture sets the selection and formulation of problems, the determination of what are data, the means to be used in getting data, the kinds of relations sought between data, and the forms in which propositions are cast.

In many ways, the root metaphor or conceptual infrastructure of an analytic approach may be somewhat tacit. For example, I see many traditional grounded theory studies as tacitly rooted in a metaphor of human action as an arrow or arrows moving forward through time, where the key actions are to be specified during the research and the path of the arrow(s) may well thus become understood as convoluted. This is what Blumer calls a "prior scheme" or metaphor of basic social process analysis used by many qualitative researchers.

However, Strauss was also deeply interested in how social structures operate as "conditions" under/through/over/in/around/within which social processes occur. These are ultimately *constitutive* of social processes—integral and nonfungible features. And, perhaps most importantly, Strauss was interested in specifying these methodologically in fresh ways that sought to push the conventional boundaries of social science research and capture the interactive nature of structure/process, practice/negotiation—conditional elements in situations. In early work with Glaser they stated (Glaser & Strauss 1967:239-242): "One of the central issues in sociological theory is the relationship of structure to process. . . . Sociological theory ordinarily does not join structure and process so tightly as our notion of 'structural process' does. . . . A major implication of our book is that structure and process are related more complexly (and more interestingly) than is commonly conceived." Thus from the outset, grounded theory was aimed at "deconstructing" and complicating this age-old, tired if not exhausted, binary.

In his later work, Strauss pursued two avenues through which he sought to incorporate and integrate analyses of structural process in new ways. The first was conceptual—his pursuit, along with other symbolic interactionists (Shibutani, Becker), of the social worlds/arenas/discourses framework.[2] Second is the methodological framework of the conditional matrix. Both are discussed at length below. I argue, however, that these were ultimately neither integrated with each other nor with grounded theory methodology in coherent ways. Such integration is precisely what I seek to accomplish through situational analysis.

Roots in Chicago Ecologies

The cartographic alternatives of situational analysis that supplement the classic grounded theory approach of studying social processes have deep roots in Chicago School social ecologies. These early Chicago ecologies developed over time into symbolic interactionist studies of social worlds and arenas where multiple worlds come together (Clarke 1991). Early Chicago School studies focused on communities of different types (e.g., ethnic communities, elite neighborhoods, impoverished slums), distinctive locales (e.g., taxi dance halls, the stockyards), and signal events of varying temporal durations (e.g., a strike).[3] The sociological task was "to make *the group* the focal center and to build up from its discoveries *in concrete situations,* a knowledge of the whole" (Eubank in Meltzer et al. 1975:42; emphasis added). But as Baszanger and Dodier (1997:16) have asserted:

> Compared with the anthropological tradition, the originality of the first works
> in the Chicago tradition was that they did not necessarily integrate the data

collected around a collective whole in terms of a common culture, but in terms of territory or geographic space. The problem with which these sociologists were concerned was based on human ecology: interactions of human groups with the natural environment and interactions of human groups in a given geographic milieu. . . . The main point here was to make an inventory of a space by studying the different communities and activities of which it is composed, that is, which encounter and confront each other in that space.

These "inventories of space" often took the form of maps. Traditional Chicago School studies were undergirded by an aerial field model—a "map" of some kind done from "above" such as a city map (e.g., Blumer 1958; Hughes 1971:esp. 267, 270; Park 1952). Mapmaking was very much a part of the Chicago School sociological tradition in this era. Most significant for my purposes, the communities, organizations, kinds of sites, and collectivities represented on such maps were to be explicitly viewed *in relation to the sitings or situations of one another, and within their larger contexts*. Relationality was a featured concern. "The power of the ecological model underlying the traditional Chicago approach lies in the ability to focus now on the niche and now on the ecosystem which defined it" (Dingwall 1999:217). See Figures 2.1-2.4.

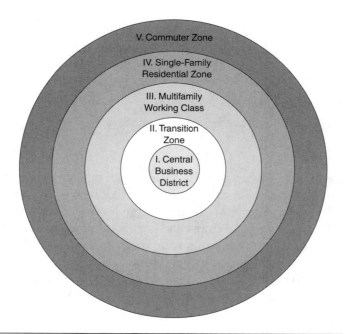

Figure 2.1   Park/Burgess Model of Natural Urban Areas

SOURCE: Pfohl 1985:148. Reproduced by permission of The McGraw-Hill Companies.

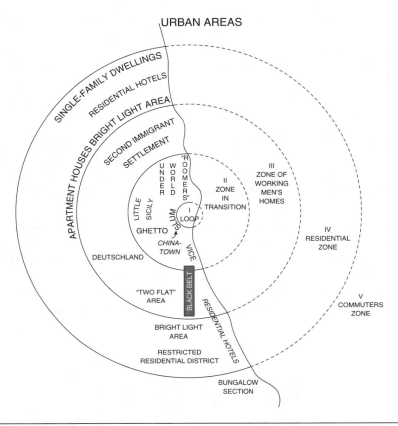

Figure 2.2   Anatomy of the City

SOURCE: Zorbaugh 1929:230. Reproduced by permission of The University of Chicago Press.

These maps frame Chicago School aerial field models historically. They demonstrate how the ecological root metaphor has been expressed over time in this tradition and allow us to examine the productive tension between what Park (1952) called "the big picture" and more local particularities of interest in the maps. Today, after the postmodern turn, problems with the level(s) of abstraction of the Park/Burgess model (Figure 2.1), especially in terms of its attempts at universality, have been widely elaborated (e.g., Atkinson et al. 2001; Burawoy 2000). But also in the time of Burgess and Park, the model was intended as such—as a general model that would "work" well enough to be useful transgeographically and not as a site-specific map.

In fact, early Chicago School work is also full of highly detailed site-specific maps focused on the geographical distribution of objects of research

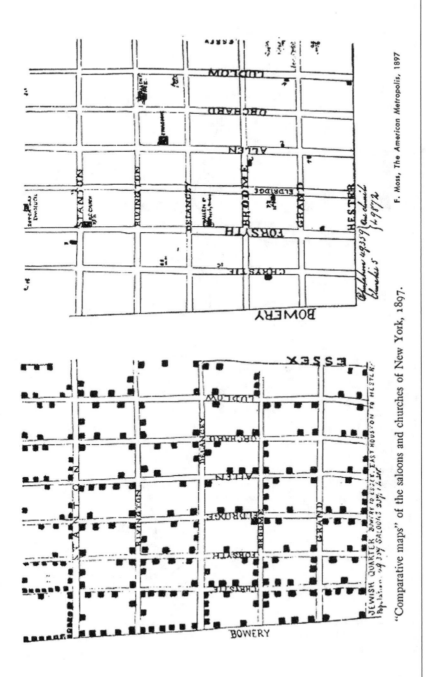

"Comparative maps" of the saloons and churches of New York, 1897.

F. Moss, *The American Metropolis*, 1897

Figure 2.3   Comparative Maps, New York City

SOURCE: Strauss 1976:175. Reproduced by permission of Transaction Publishers.

43

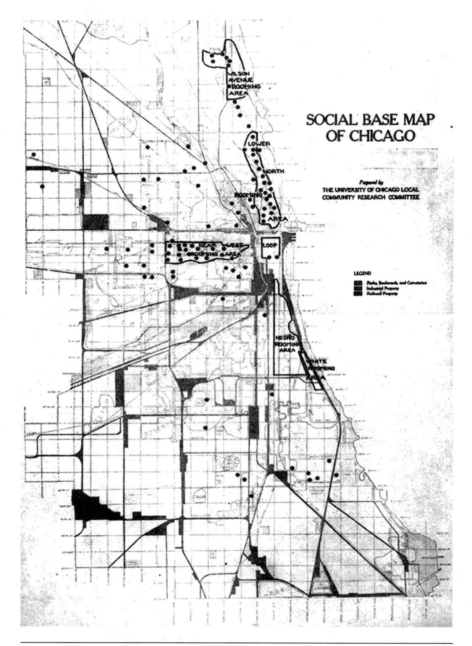

Figure 2.4   Social Base Map of Chicago

SOURCE: Cressey 1932:227. Reproduced by permission of The University of Chicago Press.

such as churches, taverns, taxi dance halls, and ethnic neighborhoods (see Figures 2.2, 2.3, and 2.4). From 1923 to 1930, the University of Chicago's Local Community Research Committee received external (Rockefeller) support that funded a wave of graduate student and faculty research and seriously fostered empirical ethnographic social science.[4] Interest in ethnic neighborhoods and urban ethnography has remained strong in urban studies and has also been resurrected in recent cultural studies (e.g., Gelder & Thornton 1997) and popular culture (e.g., Conniff 1991:57).

Specific topics were also pursued in neighborhood studies, illustrated in Figure 2.3. Here we have "comparative maps" of the locations of saloons and churches in the Lower East Side neighborhood of New York City in 1897. These were mapped as local institutional sites of collective commitments and activities—the kinds of community sites important to geographically based ethnographic studies. These particular maps were included by Strauss (1976) in his book on urban imagery, demonstrating his long-standing ecological interest.

In the 1950s and 1960s, researchers in this tradition continued the study of "social wholes" in new ways, shifting to studies of work, occupations, and professions, moving from local to national and international groups.[5] Geographic boundaries were dropped as necessarily salient, replaced by *shared discourses* as boundary making and marking. Perhaps most significantly, they increasingly attended to the relationships of those groups to other "social wholes," *the interactions of collective actors and discourses.* In today's methodological vernacular, many such studies would be termed "multisited" (e.g., Marcus 1995, 1998), including Freidson's (1970, 1975) on the profession of medicine and Bucher's (1962) on a reform-oriented segment of pathology as a social movement inside a profession.

Concepts in Social Worlds/Arenas/Discourses Theory

Several sociologists then initiated explicit social worlds theory development—the high modern version of studies of "social wholes" (see Clarke 1991). Social worlds (e.g., a recreation group, an occupation, a theoretical tradition) generate shared perspectives that then form the basis for collective action (Shibutani 1955, 1962, 1986), while individual and collective identities are constituted through commitments to and participation in social worlds and arenas (Becker 1960, 1967; Strauss 1959). Commitment was understood as both part of identity construction and as predisposition to act. Strauss (Strauss et al. 1964; Strauss 1978) and Becker (1974, 1982) then more ambitiously defined social worlds as groups with shared commitments to certain activities sharing resources of many kinds to achieve their goals, and building shared ideologies about how to go about their business. Social worlds are *universes of discourse* (Mead 1938/1972:518) and principal affiliative mechanisms through which people organize social life. Insofar as it meaningfully exists, society as a whole, then, can be conceptualized as consisting of layered mosaics of social worlds and arenas.

Strauss argued (1978:122) that each social world has at least one primary activity, particular sites, a technology (inherited or innovative means of carrying out the social world's activities), and, once under way, more formal organizations typically evolve to further one aspect or another of the world's activities. Hughes (1971) offered the more informal notion of a *going concern* in which certain assumptions about what activities are important and what will be done can be taken for granted.[6] People typically participate in a number of social worlds/going concerns simultaneously, and such participation usually remains highly fluid. *Entrepreneurs,* deeply committed and active individuals (Becker 1963), cluster around the core of the world and mobilize those around them (Hughes 1971:54). Shibutani (1986:109) viewed social worlds as identity- and meaning-making segments in mass society, drawing on distinctive aspects of mass culture, with individuals capable of participation in only a limited number of such worlds.

There can also be *implicated actors* in a social world and/or arena, actors silenced or only discursively present—constructed by others for their own purposes (Clarke & Montini 1993). This concept provides a means of analyzing the situatedness of less powerful actors and the consequences of others' actions for them and raises issues of discursive constructions of actors and of nonhuman actants. I will therefore discuss it at some length. There are at least two kinds of implicated actors. First are those implicated actors who are physically present but are generally silenced/ignored/invisibled by those in power in the social world or arena. Second are those implicated actors *not* physically present in a given social world but solely discursively constructed; they are conceived, represented, and perhaps targeted by the work of those others; hence they are discursively present. *Neither* category of implicated actors is actively involved in the actual negotiations of self-representation in the social world or arena, nor are their thoughts or opinions or identities explored or sought out by other actors through any openly empirical mode of inquiry (such as asking them questions). They are neither invited by those in greater power to participate nor to represent themselves on their own terms. If physically present, their perceptions are largely ignored and/or silenced. The difference between the two types turns on the issue of their physical presence.

Let me give several examples here. First, those actors present but silenced/invisibled in the situation of inquiry can be exemplified by women scholars and scholars of color in traditional histories of academic disciplines and professions. They were there in those worlds, doing many things, but their presence and contributions have been largely ignored and/or erased, requiring archaeologies to excavate, resuscitate, and resituate them. For another example, let us look at Baszanger's (1998a) study of the specialty of pain medicine. Here patients in pain are *both* physically present in the social worlds of pain medicine *and* are discursively constructed by the physicians and others creating this new medical specialty. That is, patients in pain are reconstituted by the emerging discipline of pain medicine (a social world), which itself has two competing paradigms (two main segments of that world) and two different discursive constructions of patients (one originating in each segment). In one construction, patients are deemed largely capable of controlling their own pain through education in what current research has deemed to be the most effective behavior modification strategies (e.g., biofeedback). In the second construction, the patients are generally deemed needful of powerful medications for pain control.

Baszanger's key point is that in *neither* of these constructions by the physicians from the two different social world segments are the patients reconstituted on their own terms or in their own interests, nor are their heterogeneities and individual variations over time and situation taken into adequate account. Both patients' own voices and differences among them are suppressed in favor of advancing the discursive constructions/professional ideologies of the social world's two segments. Quite radically, Baszanger actually included in-depth empirical interviews with pain clinic patients in her study. Even more radically, she organized it so that she interviewed them in their homes—away from the clinics where they sought treatment. Thereby, in the eyes and minds of these patients, she distanced herself dramatically from the physicians. Through often highly responsive interview data, Baszanger was able to discover and reveal considerable heterogeneity among the patients, to seriously grasp analytically what "their own terms" were, often quite complicated in terms of self-management of their pain within the particular complexities of their own daily lives.

There can, of course, also be *implicated actants*—implicated nonhuman actors in situations of concern.[7] Like humans, implicated actants can be physically *and/or* discursively present in the situation of inquiry. That is, human actors (individually and/or collectively as social worlds) routinely discursively construct nonhuman actants from those human actors' own perspectives. The analytic question here is: Who is discursively constructing what, and how and why are they doing so? For example, a very widely and heterogeneously constructed implicated actant is the male (birth control) Pill. Most people, if they have heard of it at all, will have done so in the question: "Whatever happened to the male Pill?" Nelly Oudshoorn's (2003) new book, *The Male Pill: A Biography of a Technology in the Making,* answers that question. Though technically feasible since the 1970s, the very intensity of the discursive constructions of the male Pill have delayed its going on the market for decades.

The concept of implicated actors and actants can be particularly useful in the explicit analysis of power in social worlds and arenas. Such analyses are both complicated and enhanced by the fact that there are generally *multiple* discursive constructions circulating of both the human and nonhuman actors in any given situation. Analyzing power involves analyzing: Whose constructions of whom/what exist? Which are taken as "the real" constructions or the ones that "matter" in the situation by the various participants? Which are contested? Whose are ignored? By whom? Through understanding the discursive constructions of implicated actors and actants, analysts can grasp a lot about the social worlds and the arena in which they are active and some of the consequences of those actions for the less powerful.

Every complex social world characteristically has *segments,* subdivisions or subworlds, shifting as patterns of commitment alter, reorganize, and realign. Two or more worlds may intersect to form a new world, or one world may segment into two or more worlds (Bucher & Strauss 1961; Bucher 1962, 1988; Clarke n.d.). As these collective actions and structures became clear to Strauss, especially through his work on negotiations (e.g., Strauss 1979, 1982a, 1993), he began diagramming them. See Figure 2.5. Larger *arenas* of concern are constituted of multiple social worlds focused on a given issue and prepared to act in some way (Strauss et al. 1964:377). The empirical questions here are: "Who cares and what do they want to do about it?" In arenas, "various issues are debated, negotiated, fought out, forced and manipulated by representatives" of the participating worlds and subworlds (Strauss 1978:124).

What this means methodologically is that *if one seeks to understand a particular social world, one must understand all the arenas in which that world participates and the other worlds in those arenas and the related discourses, as these are all mutually influential/constitutive of that world.* This is the basic project of social worlds/arenas mapping, one form of situational maps proposed here (see Figure 2.6). Such maps can handle specific organizations and their negotiations without the reductionist and closed-systems feel of traditional approaches to organizations (Clarke 1991; cf. Hall 1997: 401; Scott, Meyer et al. 1994). (For orienting examples of actual social worlds/arenas maps, see Figures 3.12 and 3.13.)

As part of Chicago School interactionism, social worlds/arenas theory is a conflict theory—over differences at least of perspective (e.g., Park 1952; Simmel 1955/1964). There typically exist *intra*-world differences as well

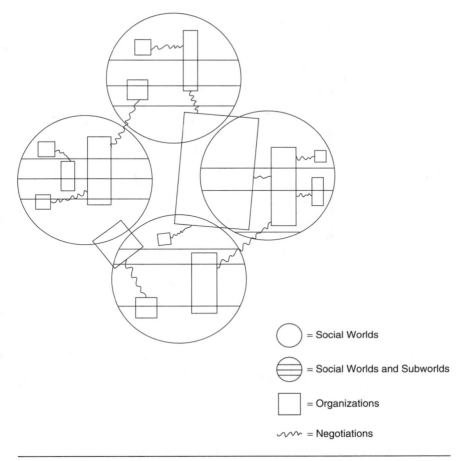

= Social Worlds

= Social Worlds and Subworlds

= Organizations

= Negotiations

Figure 2.5   Strauss's 1982 Map of Social Worlds, Subworlds, Organizations, and Negotiations

SOURCE: Strauss 1982b: Figure 7. Reprinted by permission of Sage Publications.

as the more conventionally expected *inter*-world differences of perspective, commitment, and inscribed attributes (see, e.g., Clarke & Montini 1993). For Strauss (esp. 1978, 1993), *negotiations* of various kinds—persuasion, coercion, bartering, educating, discursively and otherwise repositioning, and so on—are strategies to deal with such conflicts and are routinely engaged.

Key sociological differences emerge when researchers focus on studying the social world's work activities, organization, and discourses rather than studying individuals. Placing work—action—in the analytic foreground

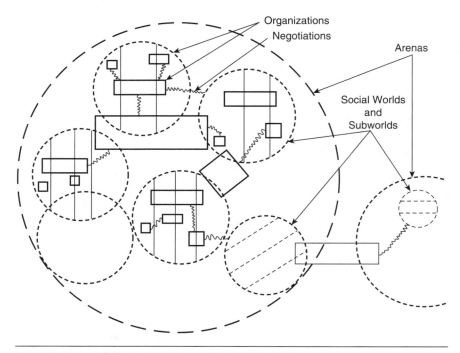

Figure 2.6   Clarke's 1991 Map of Social Worlds/Arenas

SOURCE: Clarke 1991:123. Reprinted with permission from *Social Organization and Social Process,* by David R. Maines (Ed.), Copyright © 1991, Walter deGruyter, Inc. Published by Aldine deGruyter, Hawthorne, NY.

facilitates the analysis of social worlds qua worlds and elucidation of the human and nonhuman elements. In Shibutani's (1955, 1962, 1986:109-116) social world perspective, individuals were commonly the units of analysis and were studied in relation to their social worlds, very much in line with classic symbolic interactionist concerns about the relations between individuals and institutions (e.g., Goffman 1959; Hughes 1971). In contrast, for Strauss (1978), Becker (1982), and others (e.g., Star, Fujimura, Baszanger, Garrety, Casper, and myself), the social worlds and arenas themselves become the units of analysis in studies of collective discourse and action (see note 1).

Star and Griesemer (1989) developed the concept of *boundary objects* for things that exist at junctures where varied social worlds meet in an arena of mutual concern. Boundary objects can be treaties among countries, software programs for users in different settings, even concepts themselves. Here the basic social process is "translating the object" to address the multiple specific needs or demands placed upon it by the different worlds involved. Boundary objects are often very important to many/most of the worlds involved and hence can be sites of intense controversy and competition for the power to define them. For example, in Star and Griesemer's (1989) study of a regional zoology museum founded at the turn of the 20th century, the museum's specimens were boundary objects. There were collections of multiple specimens of each species and subspecies, which, for the zoologists to find them useful, had to be very, very carefully tagged as to date and where collected, and very, very carefully preserved and taxidermied. Aerial temperature, humidity, rainfall, and the precise habitat information on specimens were all important. The mammal and bird specimens were usually killed, gathered, and sent to the museum by amateur collectors and "mercenaries" (paid collectors) of varied backgrounds. Also involved were university administrators, a patron (herself an amateur collector), curators, research scientists, clerical staff, members of scientific clubs, and taxidermists. *All* had particular concerns about the specimens that needed to be addressed and mutually articulated for the museum's collections to "work" well for *all* those involved. Thus the study of boundary objects can be an important pathway into often complicated situations, allowing the analyst to study the different participants through their distinctive relations with and discourses about the specific boundary object in question. This can help frame the broader situation of inquiry as well. Boundary objects can be human or nonhuman.

Based on Bucher's (1962, 1988; Bucher & Stelling 1977; Bucher & Strauss 1961) insights, interactionists have examined fluidity and change *within* social worlds and arenas by extending social movements analysis to include studies of reform movements of various kinds undertaken by segments or subworlds within professions, disciplines, and other work organizations (Strauss et al. 1964, 1985/1997). Such reform movements can cut across whole arenas, such as rationalizing and standardizing hospital quality assurance in the late 20th-century United States (Wiener 2000a, 2000b). Fujimura (1988, 1996), who studied the molecularization of biology, called such larger-scale processes "bandwagons." In many arenas, reform movements have centered around processes of homogenization, standardization, formal classifications—things that would organize and articulate the work of the social worlds in that arena in parallel ways (e.g., Bowker & Star 1999; Clarke & Casper 1996; Timmermans & Berg 2003).

In sum, then, social worlds/arenas theory is distinctive in permitting analyses of a full array of collective human social entities and their actions, discourses, and related nonhuman elements in the situation of concern. The key analytic power of social worlds/arenas theory, so rooted in Chicago social ecologies, is that one can take advantage of the elasticity of the concepts to analyze at multiple levels of complexity. Next we turn to three new roots that help (re)ground grounded theory after the postmodern turn: the work of Michel Foucault, the importance of the nonhuman in research, and the shift from Chicago School ecologies to situational analysis.

New Roots I: Foucault and the Interactionist Project

Interactionism, if it is to thrive and grow, must incorporate elements of poststructural and postmodern theory (e.g., the works of Barthes, Derrida, Foucault, Baudrillard, etc.) into its underlying views of history, culture, and politics.

—Denzin (1992:xvii)

Symbolic interactionist grounded theory is not only always already around the postmodern turn, but also needs to be pushed around that turn through infusion with postmodern/poststructural theory, precisely as Denzin has asserted. For me (and some other interactionists), the primary path around the postmodern turn is *through* Foucault.[8] I next briefly take up several conceptual overlaps that not only reinvigorate some interactionist concepts important to situational analysis but also have the capacity to transform them.

If action is at the heart of Strauss's project, and power at the heart of Foucault's,[9] they meet in related conceptualizations of practices as fundamental processes of action and change and in the ways in which their particular meso-level concepts interrelate.[10] These include (leading with Foucault) discourse/discipline and social worlds/arenas; the field of organizing practices/conditions of possibility and negotiated ordering/situations; the gaze and perspective. My caveat here is that these are *not* equivalences—there are serious differences, including differences of emphasis. But there are also sites of articulation. One can envision Strauss and Foucault standing next to each other, looking, pointing in the same direction, talking together. Working on these concepts at about the same time, both assumed the materiality of the world, both were developing what Blumer (1969) called "sensitizing concepts" of the meso level, and both were concerned with practices—the doingness of life. Here I place some of those concepts in provocative dialogue pertinent to situational analysis, but again they do not mean the "same" things.

Simon (1996:319) asserted that the work of Foucault "might be called a postmodern version of middle range theory." Foucault decentered the "knowing subject" to focus instead on the social as discursive practices and on discourses as elements of practices that are constitutive of subjectivities. After formulating a sociological social psychology (Strauss 1959), Strauss et al. (1964) quickly moved analytically to more meso-level concerns, framing social worlds/arenas and negotiated ordering (discussed at length above). The concepts of *both* Strauss and Foucault are social, institution*al*, and organization*al*—though not necessarily and certainly not only about institutions or organizations. Regimes of practices and negotiated orderings are kindred concepts.

Both Strauss and Foucault were primarily in dialogue with linguistic and political/theoretical structuralisms, hermeneutics, and social psychologies, although they came to those dialogues from different initial engagements. Dreyfus and Rabinow (1983) view Foucault's work as moving *Beyond Structuralism and Hermeneutics*. That is, Foucault (1991:75; emphasis in original) especially sought to refute both the determinisms of French Marxisms of his time and the subject-centeredness of hermeneutic interpretation. He laid out his alternative project in part as follows:

> [A]s in my other earlier work, the target of analysis wasn't "institutions," "theories" or "ideologies," but *practices*—with the aim of grasping the conditions which make these acceptable at a given moment; the hypothesis being that these types of practice are not just governed by institutions, prescribed by ideologies, guided by pragmatic circumstances—whatever role these elements may actually play—but possess up to a point their own specific regularities, logic, strategy, self-evidence and "reason." It is a question of analyzing a "regime of practices"—practices being understood here as places where what is said and what is done, rules imposed and reasons given, the planned and the taken-for-granted meet and intersect.

We can hear Foucault's focus on the ongoing "how"—the ways in which a regime of practices must be sustained through performance of those practices over time. To me, there are strong echoes between Foucault's "regime of practices" and Strauss's "negotiated ordering," which similarly assumes ongoing practices but instead focuses on the management of contingencies in those practices through strategic negotiations.

In contrast to Foucault, Strauss's work can be seen as taking interactionism *beyond astructuralism and social psychology*. Strauss began by arguing against the atomism of American functionalism through creating a relentlessly *social* social psychology based in Mead's assertion that selves are constitutively social (Strauss 1959). Here identity "meant linking individual identities with collective ones" (Strauss 1992:4). Next he took on the critique of interactionism as astructural and, without entering into direct dialogue with Marxisms, engaged structuralist sociological (*not* linguistic) concerns explicitly. Mounted initially in the 1960s, the astructural critique asserted that symbolic interactionism took neither power nor social structures seriously enough and was too devoted to micro-level analytics.[11] While, for Strauss, structure and power are always relentlessly processual (enacted and hence existing in and through actions/concrete practices), they are also relentlessly social, organizational, and structural through the plastic/elastic forms of social worlds, arenas, discourses, and negotiations at the meso level. At any given moment, there is some version of a negotiated or processual ordering—ways of working, sets of operant if continually revised practices, close to what Foucault called a "regime of practices."[12] In the 1990s, Denzin (1992:63) declared: "The problem of the astructural bias in symbolic interactionism is a dead issue." Insofar as it is dead, this is due in significant part to the work of Strauss—the very work I am arguing met Foucault on his own middle-range ground.

Discourse/Discipline and Social Worlds/Arenas/Discourses

Foucault's concepts of discourse and discipline are interrelated. He began (1972) with the concept of "the order of discourse," asserting that ways of framing and representing linguistic conventions of meanings and habits of usage together constitute specific discursive fields or terrains—discourses as modes of ordering the chaos of the world. His concept of "discursive practices" described ways of working that could, when historicized, be understood to produce distinctive "discursive formations" or dominant discourses that bound together injunctions about particular ways of being in the world (Dreyfus & Rabinow 1983:59). For example, the institutions of medicine and the media together produce extensive discourses on health and the responsibilities of citizens to pursue it. Discursive formations are also capable of and routinely contain contradictory discourses, a point significant to my argument about social worlds. It is *through* this containment that some stability is achieved—however temporary, elusive, or conditional.

Dominant discourses are reinforced through extant institutional systems of law, media, medicine, education, and so on. A discourse is effected in disciplining practices that produce subjects/subjectivities through surveillance, examination, and various technologies of the self—ways of producing ourselves as proper disciplinary/disciplined subjects (e.g., Foucault 1973, 1975, 1978, 1988). Rose and Miller (1992:174) capture this well: "Power is not so much a matter of imposing constraints upon citizens as of 'making up' citizens capable of bearing a kind of regulated freedom. Personal autonomy is not the antithesis of political power, but a key term in its exercise, the more so because most individuals are not merely the subjects of power but play a part in its operations."

Strauss was similarly concerned with the invariably *social/organizational* ways in which what he frames as identities (rather than subjectivities) are produced and transformed throughout life through relations in social worlds in which people participate.[13] While Blumer (1958) took up meaning making, boundary making, and group positioning through what are now termed the identity politics of race and racial formations and the movements of "the color line" (e.g., Omi & Winant 1994), Strauss (1978, 1993) was more abstract here. His social worlds theory focuses on worlds as *"universes of discourse."* Traceable back to Mead (1934/1962, 1938/1972:518), the interactionist concept of discourse was used as a general term for what happens in interactions. Shibutani, Strauss, and Becker all used the term as characterizing social worlds, noting that a particular social world "ends" where its distinctive discourses are no longer in use, no longer practiced. But interactionists did not feature this concept and Foucault did.

Also traceable back to Mead, both Blumer and Strauss understood individuals as *constituted through* such collectivities, and collectivities as *constituted through* interaction with other collectivities. Castellani (1999:263) points out that "[a]s both Foucault and Blumer [and Strauss] understood, one can never escape one's social context. Foucault learned this lesson from Nietzsche (Dreyfus & Rabinow 1983), Blumer [and Strauss] learned it from pragmatism (Blumer 1969) [Strauss 1993]."

Placed in conversation with the interactionist concept of social worlds and the Straussian emphasis on arenas and conflict within them, Foucault's concepts of discourse/discipline situate these more explicitly in (historical and other) matrices of power. Key here is that social worlds are *"universes of discourse"* (Strauss 1978). For Foucault, both individuals and collectivities are *constituted* through discourses and disciplining. For Strauss, both individuals and collectivities are *produced* through their participation in social worlds and arenas, including their discourses. While Foucault's language of disciplining and the constitution of subjectivity(ies) is more insistent and decenters "the knowing subject" much more thoroughly, these productions are accomplished through routine practices. Later in his career, when issues of agency concerned him more, Foucault (1988:11; emphasis added) stated:

> I would say that if now I am interested, in fact, in the way in which the subject constitutes himself in an active fashion, by the practices of self, these practices are nevertheless *not* something that the individual invents by himself. They are patterns that he finds in his culture and which are proposed, suggested and imposed on him by his culture, his society *and his social group.*

This, to me, is a key point of articulation with Strauss—and with interactionism more broadly.

Fields of Practice(s)/Conditions of Possibility and Negotiated Ordering(s)/Situations

The concepts of practice, action, conditions, situations, and negotiations are key sites where the linkages between some lines of interactionism and the work of Foucault can be articulated. Practice is at the center of Foucault's work, but differently inflected. Foucault shared with interactionism the idea that action is always interaction, "a set of actions upon other actions (Foucault 1983:220), [b]ut . . . it is not simply an interaction between people. It is the interaction of practice itself. . . . It is the interaction of *strategies,* the interaction of power relations themselves as a diffuse *field of organizing practices*" (Castellani 1999:263, 254-255; emphasis added). In interactionist terms, we would say that the processes are foregrounded. This foregrounding emphasizes the fluidities of power relations, from local/micro capillary flows to more thundering meso/macro tides. Indeed, Foucault's writing gives distinctive meaning to the concept of "power surge."

Foucault's conceptualization of the power/knowledge relationship as "the field of organizing practices" has been very widely taken up (e.g., Schatzki et al. 2001). He emphasizes disciplining as a series of organizing practices that produce the rules through which individuals (I would add collectivities of various types) make themselves up as subjects. Dreyfus and Rabinow (1983:109; emphasis added) said, "Now this field or clearing is understood as the result of long term practices and as the field in which those practices operate. . . . *These are social maneuvers of great consequence for those involved.*" Thus Foucault's field of practices is not alien to Strauss's social worlds/arenas. "[T]he work of Michel Foucault suggests a connection between the collectively representational and the interactional, arguing that interpretive structures are embodied in discourse. . . . [H]is recognition of discourse-as-practice hints at the importance of understanding the more interactional side of language-in-use" (Gubrium & Holstein 1997:117).

A Foucaultian (1975) analysis would attempt to clarify the "conditions of possibility" in a specific field of organizing practices pertaining at a given historical moment. I read this concept as consisting of the constellation of constraints, opportunities, resources, and other elements in "the situation" at hand. That is, the conditions of possibility compose possible developments based in that specific constellated site of practice/situation. Foucault's question is: Where can things go from here?

Strauss's parallel but differently inflected question is: What's the action here? His sociological vision is grounded in related framings of the sociology of action/work/practice, of social worlds/arenas/discourses/negotiations, and the spaces in between. Action is always at the center for Strauss. But the action is generally grounded in the actual work people are doing, individually and collectively.[14] In Strauss, that work is usually organized as a set of practices related to the social world(s) in which they are involved and committed for whatever reasons. Serious conflicts may occur between or among segments of social worlds. Power relations for Strauss (1979, 1982a, 1993) are constituted in the practices of addressing such conflicts that he termed "negotiated ordering." Here, "[t]he various *interactional processes*—negotiation, persuasion, manipulation, education, threat, and actual coercion—will each have different salience" (Strauss 1993:250; emphasis in original). This obviously parallels Foucault's assertion that discourses contain conflict and contradiction.[15]

Part of the work social worlds do is monitoring the discourses and actions of the other social worlds in the arenas in which they participate. That is, *negotiations* based around discourses are at the heart of the work of social worlds and arenas and those who represent them in a particular situation. Foucault's (1975) similar "conditions of possibility" also reject (pre)determined outcomes. Castellani (1999:267; emphasis added) argues that viewing practice as twofold/two-way (I would say *n*-way)

> allows us to make important use of Strauss's (1978) concepts of negotiation and negotiated order. . . . *Strauss's concepts are significant to a theory of discursive interactionism.* . . . [T]hey reveal that practice is a negotiated order, both in terms of the interaction of practice and the interactions of the individuals involved in those practices. . . . Like power relations, interaction-as-negotiation is fundamental to any and all states of interaction, be they domination or any other form of control. *As such, the overall organization that emerges from practice is a negotiated order.*

If Foucault focuses on conditions of possibility, Strauss focuses on negotiations. My argument is that both deserve analysis, and the concept of the situation seeks to capture all of the above—the situation qua conditions of possibility and the action, discourses, and practices in it.

The Gaze and Perspective

> *Just a gaze. An inspecting gaze, a gaze which each individual under its weight will end by interiorizing to the point that he is his own overseer, each individual thus exercising this surveillance over, and against, himself.*
>
> —Foucault (1980:155, "The Eye of Power")

Placed in conversation with the Meadian interactionist concept of perspective (see Chapter 1), it can be argued that Foucault is often looking over the shoulder of power, while interactionists have a long tradition of attempting to see the world from the perspectives of all those in the situation, including the underdog(s)—those with less (but never no) power (e.g., Becker 1967/1970; Goffman 1959). This difference, I argue next, can be turned into a new analytic tool.[16]

Foucault's (1975, 1979) concept of the gaze situates perspective in (historical and other) matrices of power. "*The* gaze" is not "*a* gaze" or *one among many* perspectives. It is the gaze that emanates from a site of power and authority, always already appropriating the right to look and to see, attempting to do so hegemonically, and thereby invisibling/silencing other perspectives/gazes. Foucault (1979) articulated this surveillance mode of disciplining using Jeremy Bentham's panopticon, a circular form of (literal/metaphorical) prison in which the guard tower is in the middle and the prisoners' cell walls facing in that direction are transparent. The guards can always see in, though they themselves are not visible—and may not even be present. Disciplining refers to the ways in which the prisoners come to restrain themselves—regardless of whether anyone is actually watching, which cannot be known.

Foucault's (1988) radical theoretical innovation here is understanding that to effect disciplining, the surveilling gaze of power is always already internalized so that disciplining is what he later called a "technology of the self" rather than imposed from without. Foucault's emphasis on the processes of disciplining also decenter the subject/the self. That panopticon, that position of power, can be patriarchal, disciplinary/institutional, the gaze of medicine, the gaze of the state, the gaze of empire, racializing, otherwise marking, and so on. This conceptual linkage of discourse and power to perspective via the gaze is analytically central to pushing interactionism further around the postmodern turn, and grounded theory with it.

But the interactionist concept of perspective can also be deployed to complicate "the gaze" of Foucault and has the capacity to make such analyses more radical and transgressive of "the powers that be" in the very ways of which Foucault himself was fond. I start here from the insight of Abir-Am (1985) that *all* representations, however critical, are also hagiographic—somehow "worshipful" of that which is represented. They cannot *not* be "in the service of" that which is represented, at minimum in the sense that "any advertising is good advertising." Analyses in the Foucauldian tradition tend to focus largely if not exclusively on the *source* of "the gaze," the surveilling and disciplining work the gaze does in what I call the situation at hand, and its consequences. This is very important analytic work. However, it is centered on power and hence hagiographic of "the powers that be."

Adding to such analytic consideration of the gaze, similar consideration of the perspectives of other entities (individual and/or collective, human and/or nonhuman) in that situation can disrupt the hagiographic moment *without* abandoning analysis of the gaze. Representing the multiplicity of perspectives in the situation, the various prisoners of various kinds of panopticons, "minority" views, "marginal" positions, and/or the "other(s)"/ alterity, also disrupts *representational* hegemony. Representing *is* intervening (Hacking 1983). Epstein (1996:357-358), for example, discusses how a Foucaultian genealogical approach is compatible with his "democratic" approach to claims making, which seeks to recover the full panoply of knowledge claims, not only those that "count" as formal, accredited knowledge. This, of course, has been at the heart of feminist projects (e.g., Hekman 1999; Lather & Smithies 1997). It also links back to the concept of implicated actors.

Complicating the analysis of the gaze in this way can also be seen as engaging Foucault's (Morris & Patton 1979:52) ideas about resistance as "something which in some way escapes the relations of power; something in the social body, in the classes, in the groups, in the individuals themselves which is not at all the more or less docile or reactive raw material, but which is the centrifugal movement, the inverse energy, that which escapes." Considerable interactionist work analyzes such junctures where resistances are manifest—where individuals "meet" institutions, from Goffman's (1959) total institutions such as the asylum to Strauss's (Strauss et al. 1964, 1985/1997) patients in hospitals (see also Covaleski et al. 1998).

In sum, then, the meso level of action/negotiation/discourse/practice produces, under historically specific "conditions of possibility," subjectivities, collectivities, and discourses. "Structure is replaced by the concept of practice" (Castellani 1999:269). I began this conversation by stating, "If action is at the heart of Strauss's project, and power at the heart of Foucault's,[17] they meet in related conceptualizations of practices as fundamental processes of action and change and in the ways in which their particular meso-level concepts interrelate." I conclude by asserting that a worthy project, and part of doing situational analyses, is to learn how to productively tack back and forth among these useful and provocative concepts analytically. I am explicitly *not* arguing here for some dialectical synthesis of Strauss and Foucault. I *am* arguing that using the analytics of both considerably strengthens situational analysis. Castellani (1999:269; emphasis added) points clearly to what can be gained:

Individuals [and groups] are productive, and not just reactionary or passive, forces in the games of truth. Difference therefore increases in importance. Differences, in terms of race, class, gender, psychological composition, personality, geographical location, individual intention and desire, group affiliation, status, irrational and unconscious need, economic ability, educational background, and professional affiliation *all influence how practice is practiced.*

Understanding such differences in their heterogeneous engagements is at the heart of the project of situational analysis.

My renderings of Foucault here are primitive and stunningly partial.[18] My point is that Foucaultian forms of attention to power, to disciplining, to discourses as meso-level social forms that produce subjectivities—individual and collective—and to the ordering of things that produces how we can know those things are invaluable analytic tools. I am attempting to address these concerns through the relational practices of situational analysis. As Foucault said, "What is interesting is always interconnection, not the primacy of this or that" (quoted in Brooker 1999:1).

New Roots II: Taking the Nonhuman Explicitly Into Account

> *Theory is of value in empirical science only to the extent to which it connects fruitfully with the empirical world. Concepts are the means, and the only means of establishing such connection.*
>
> —Blumer (1969:143)

Next I insert a second "new root" for situational analysis that addresses postmodern concerns that have not yet been taken into explicit account in either social worlds/arenas/discourse theory or the grounded theory method qua method—taking the nonhuman in the situation *explicitly* into account. That is, many of us actually using grounded theory have been taking the nonhuman into account in our substantive research for decades (Clarke & Star 2003), but we have done so without the methodological reflexivity that would make these innovations adequately visible or accessible to others seeking to use grounded theory in such postmodern ways. Let me begin by discussing the term "nonhuman."

Nonhuman Actors/Actants/Elements

Over the past several decades, the theoretical importance of things—materialities—has been retheorized in a number of ways through poststructural lenses. Certainly Foucault's (1973) *The Order of Things* raised fresh ways of conceptualizing the ways in which things order the world. That is,

Foucault's displacement of "the knowing subject" as the sole/main focus of analysis opened that space to allow inclusion of a wondrous array of things as well as persons. It was through actor-network theory, developed since circa 1975 especially by Latour, Callon, Law, and Akrich in the transdisciplinary field of science and technology studies and pursued both qualitatively and quantitatively, that I first encountered this move. Actor-network theory initiated a much more explicit and full(er) theoretical and methodological status for the nonhuman, and explicitly uses that term. To study actor-networks, the analytic task (much simplified) is to follow the leaders, describe what they do (including production of and interaction with the nonhuman), how they (both human and nonhuman) interest potential allies through translations of what they have to offer to meet potential allies' needs, and then enroll them as allies in the actor-network through a funneling process. Alternatively, one can follow a nonhuman object on its travels through its network(s), or follow the semiotic network itself as the central focus as it links both human actors and nonhuman actors/actants (heterogeneous elements such as scientific facts, rules, consumers, resources, technical workers, microbes, factories). Actor-networks thus expand through "interessement" and enrollment, and contract through withdrawals. Power in such a network resides especially at sites or nodes of particular power through which other actors *must* proceed, called "obligatory points of passage."[19]

The status of "nonhuman actants," not only present as nodes in the network but which also have agency in this approach, especially distinguishes actor-network theory. In science and technology studies, such conceptions exploded dualistic notions of a technical core and social superstructure. Instead, the social and technical together become a "seamless web," coconstructed and mutually embedded (Latour 1987; Pinch & Bijker 1987). Woolgar (1991) captured this vividly in research on "how computers configure their users," a phrase featuring the agency of the nonhuman. In another example, Latour (1988a) a argued that in the 19th-century actor-network created by Louis Pasteur in France, microbes became actants fully capable of recruiting allies for Pasteur and his institute as a "center of authority." Pasteur and his institute became an "obligatory point of passage" for all persons *and things* interested in and related to bacteriological work, from wine makers and farmers to physicians, cows, grapes, and the microbes themselves. In France, grapes are very serious nonhumans.

To me, the agencies of nonhuman actants may differ from those of humans in ways I will not attempt to specify here. Furthermore, such agency(ies) may be conditional upon their being constructed by humans in specific ways in the specific situation. In Dumit's (1997) terms, agencies are sticky and distributed. Others too are critical of the lack of attention to the consequences of different agencies in some actor-network research.[20] Regardless, this reconceptualization is both deeply provocative and productive. *Adequate analyses of situations being researched must include the nonhuman explicitly and in considerable detail.* "Seeing" the agency of the nonhuman elements present in the situation disrupts the taken-for-granted, creating Meadian moments of conceptual rupture (e.g., Mead 1927/1964, 1934/1962) through which we can see the world afresh. For example, "Magazines exist to sell readers to advertisers" ruptures the taken-for-granted and offers a different perspective. The agency of magazines per se in the distribution of advertising discourses, normally invisible or at least not the lead point, is here rendered explicit and primary.

Things have also had an important place in interactionism (e.g., Park & Burgess 1921/1970). As McCarthy (1984:108-109) has argued:

> Mead speaks of the continuity that is established between the individual and the object world—a continuity which implies that the experience of self is bound up with physical things with which one has social relations. . . . To experience the resistance response of objects is to experience their action in relation to one-self. . . . Objects play a central role in the constitution and maintenance of social identities.

I would push further and assert that objects are central to collective identities as well (see also Cohen 1993).

Blumer (1969:10-11; emphasis added), drawing deeply on Mead, offered a specific framework:

> *Nature of Objects.* The position of symbolic interactionism is that the "worlds" that exist for human beings and for their groups are composed of "objects" and that these *objects are the product of symbolic interaction.* An object is anything that can be indicated, anything that is pointed to or referred to—a cloud, a book, a legislature, a banker, a religious doctrine, a ghost, and so forth. For purposes of convenience one can classify objects into three categories: *(a) physical objects,* such as chairs, trees, or bicycles; *(b) social objects,* such as students, priests, a president, a mother, or a friend; and *(c) abstract objects,* such as moral principles, philosophical doctrines, or ideas such as justice, exploitation, or compassion. . . . *The nature of an object—of any and every object—consists of the meaning that it has for the person [and/or social world] for whom it is an object.*

This explicit constructionist and materialist view of the nonhuman has tacitly informed the research of a number of us in science and technology studies and is a site of articulation of our projects with semiotic actor-network theory (Clarke & Star 2003).[21] My own work here has emphasized how research materials and other "tools of the trade" organized the work of scientists, affecting theory as well as research practices, discussed in the next chapter (Clarke 1987/1995; Clarke & Fujimura 1992/1996; Daston 2000). Star's

(1989) project emphasized the work brain maps did in turn-of-the-century neurophysiology, triangulating apparent stability into the field by importing the knowledge products of other specialties as "truth." The instabilities of these knowledge products were shorn off when they were imported/ traveled.

Including the nonhuman as agentic actors/actants in research takes up the postmodern challenge of posthumanism—the idea that only humans "really" matter or "matter most." "By acknowledging nonhumans as components and determinants of the arrangements that encompass people, this line of research *problematizes the social and challenges traditional renderings of it as relations between people*" (Schatzki et al. 2001:11; emphasis added). A key argument in science and technology studies has been that the nonhuman and the human are coconstitutive—together constitute the world and each other. Similar arguments have also been made in material culture studies: "[M]aterial forms were often of significance precisely because being disregarded as trivial, they were often a key unchallenged mechanism for social reproduction and ideological dominance. . . . [S]ocial worlds were as much constituted by materiality as the other way around" (Miller 1998:3; see also Hodder 2000). Consumption studies—focused on relations between humans and things—is another site where taking the nonhuman seriously has occurred (e.g., Appadurai & Kopytof 1986; DeGrazia with Furlough 1996).

I argue in this book that such processes of coconstruction and coconstitution can be studied through using the situation as the locus of analysis and explicitly including all analytically pertinent nonhuman (including technical) elements along with the human in situational maps. This is one of the key ways in which grounded theory rooted in symbolic interactionism offers a distinctively materialist constructionism. Nonhuman actants structurally condition the interactions within the situation through their specific material properties and requirements and through our engagements with them. Their agency is everywhere. Situational analysis explicitly takes the nonhuman elements in the situation of inquiry into account both materially and discursively.

Hybrids, Cyborgs, Discourses, Whatevers

> *Despite our desperate, eternal attempt to separate, contain, and mend, categories always leak.*
>
> —Trinh Minh-ha (1989:94)

Having set up a binary—human/nonhuman—I must as a postmodern immediately destabilize it. The boundaries between these categories are rather leaky, and furthermore, many entities are conceived as hybrids—various kinds of combinations of human and nonhuman. Some hybrids are closer to the idea of *cyborgs*—originally combinations of humans and information technologies (*cyb*ernetic *org*anism*s*) (Haraway 1991a). In material practice, biomedically enhanced humans are probably the most common form of cyborg—adding everything from eyeglasses to modified organs to titanium rods and screws (e.g., Gray 1995; Hogle 1996). Hybridity signifies a merger with at least some stability over time, while heterogeneity connotes difference(s) of perspective, positionality, and so on (Goldberg 2000).

Interestingly, not everything can be defined as human or nonhuman. For example, Casper (1994, 1998a, 1998b) studied one of the most charged cultural objects/icons today—human fetuses—as the work objects of several different categories of workers, from fetal surgeons to fetal cell researchers to right-to-life movement advocates. Fetal cell researchers (now known as stem cell researchers) harvest cells from conceptuses that they view as not (yet) human. In sharp contrast, for right-to-life advocates, they are human from the moment of conception. Fetal surgeons also use a "baby" rhetoric about fetuses that renders them human well before they could survive outside the womb/mother.

Discourses and other virtual realities can also be viewed as nonhuman elements of situations, dwelling in most if not all situations with more or less analytic import. They must therefore be taken into account in adequate situational analyses and grounded theorizing. Strauss did this routinely. He constantly read and analyzed and used discursive data and took them into account, using novels, art, photography, newspapers, anything that came to hand and seemed relevant and/or provocative vis-à-vis his current project (Clarke & Star 1998). He did this; we, his students, have done this. Under his tutelage, I used grounded theory on historical documents, analyzing published discourses as well as private archival correspondence. As we wrote about the nonhuman routinely, we also studied discourses all the time, and performed multisite research. But we never discussed them as such, much less attended to them methodologically. Nor did Strauss integrate such concerns explicitly or systematically in his methodological writings. They were data, then, not discourses or the nonhuman per se.

The time has come to be explicit. Discourses and other nonhuman objects/actants have lives of their own. They can be gendered, raced, and classed (Appadurai & Kopytoff 1986; DeGrazia & Furlough 1996; Naples 2000); they can have biographies or careers (Daston 2000). Over the past several decades, many approaches have been developed and applied in the inter/transdisciplinary area of discourse analysis and these are mapped in Chapter 4. Situational analyses will contribute here particularly by allowing comparative and/or integrative studies of discourses and actions in terms of (a) what is framed as in the situation, (b) the social worlds and arenas involved in the situation and their discourses, and (c) positions on key issues in those discourses.

New Roots III: From Social Worlds/ Arenas to Situational Maps and Analysis

Conception is not merely a stop-gap to perception, but a fashioner of perception.

—Blumer (1969:155)

Earlier in this chapter I explicated the conceptual shift from Chicago School social ecologies to social worlds/arenas theory. I then discussed two new roots for grounding situational analysis—the work of Michel Foucault and the analytic importance of the nonhuman. Here I explicate the third new root—the expansion from social worlds/arenas/discourses to situational analyses by mapping. In my own methodological development this was triggered by my and others' continuing critiques of Strauss and Corbin's conditional matrices. I next lay out these critiques and how they are addressed by situational analysis.

The Conditional Matrices: Structural Conditions of Action

For interactionists, structures are the enduring, "given" aspects or *conditions* of situations, the aspects we can bet with relative assuredness will remain basically stable, "in place" and predictable for some time. Structures are the consequences of prior actions sustained through past and present practices and experienced as obdurate (e.g., Blumer 1969; Strauss 1993). For example, it is likely that physicians will remain at the top of the hierarchical heap in the operating room if not the hospital well into the 21st century. However, computer-driven technologies of visualization and surgical intervention could, if we analyze the nonhuman in the surgical situation with appropriate care, be argued to be displacing them, or the surgeons could themselves be construed as cyborg entities (at least during surgery), highlighting how the work of surgery is now commonly done by humans and machines acting inextricably together in practice (e.g., Zetka 2003). In another example, it is likely that the state in some form or another will continue to be a significant actor in most major arenas of social concern, though this was not always the case and today multinational companies such as Nike and Reebok sit at negotiating tables with activist NGO groups and universities without state presences (e.g., Gupta & Ferguson 1997). As these examples imply, structural elements are not unchanging; rather, they are just slower to change—more obdurate in Blumer's terms—than other aspects of situations—even if shape-shifting.

Toward the end of his career, Strauss (Corbin & Strauss 1990; Strauss 1987, 1991b, 1993, 1995; Strauss & Corbin 1990, 1998) worked assiduously on framing and articulating ways to do grounded theory research that included *specifying structural conditions*—literally making them visible in the analysis. Strauss's interactionist sociology was rooted most of all in understanding action as situated activity. The conditional matrices are thus situating devices for him—means of enabling researchers to more easily and more fully capture the specific conditions under which the action of concern occurs. His capstone theoretical book (Strauss 1993) was titled *Continual Permutations of Action,* nicely capturing the centrality of action in his work. Earlier, in *Negotiations,* Strauss (1979:98-99) had distinguished between a broader structural context and a narrower and more immediate negotiation context (see also Glaser & Strauss 1964). Strauss and Corbin (1990:100), in *Basics,* then, distinguish among causal, intervening, and contextual conditions. While I would agree that some elements are more important than others, and some are certainly experienced by those in the situation as "closer in" than others, it is precisely such an in-principle dualism that I am struggling against. Instead, I am arguing in favor of focusing empirically on the situation as a whole and on examining distinctions made there from the perspectives of different actors, rather than a priori, categorically, and solely from the perspective of the researcher.

That is, clinging to a postmodern pragmatism (Lindesmith 1981), I do not distinguish between "causal, intervening, and contextual conditions" (Strauss & Corbin 1990:100), nor do I want to trace conditional paths (Strauss & Corbin 1990:168). Rather, I am pushing on that edge of grounded theory in which "The focus . . . seems to be fixed on multiple and conjunctural forms of causation" (Dey 1999:180). I attempt to specify all the key elements in a given situation and understand them as coconstitutive—as in part constituting each other—assuming that origins, meanings, and change lie in relationality. Taking things even further, I am hoping situational analysis will push on contingency—how "Chance and indeterminacy, not causality and correlation, are central to explanation" (Manning 1995:250).

Strauss's and Corbin's (Corbin 1991:37; Strauss & Corbin 1990:163, 1998:184; Strauss 1991b:457) several versions of the conditional and conditional/consequential matrices were intended to provide a systematic path for grounded theorists to follow in order to facilitate specifying the salient structural conditions that obtained for the phenomenon under study (see also Dey 1999:esp. ch. 7). See Figures 2.7-2.10.

These conditional matrices frame a number of concerns that are to be considered by the analyst in terms of salience to the project at hand. They are generally organized into "levels": international (economic, cultural, religious, scientific, and environmental issues); national (political, governmental, cultural, economic, gender, age, ethnicity, race, particular national issues, etc.); and, depending upon where the research is undertaken, community, organizational, institutional, or local group and individual/(inter)actional setting. At the core is action—both strategic and routine. Both macro-to-meso-to-micro and micro-to-meso-to-macro impacts can be significant (Strauss et al. 1985/ 1997:210-272; Strauss & Corbin 1990).

In the conditional matrices, Strauss specifies more fully than in *Negotiations* how to detail the structural conditions of a particular situation within which interactive negotiations occur. Looking at the older versions of the conditional matrix (Figures 2.7 and 2.8), we see action in the center,

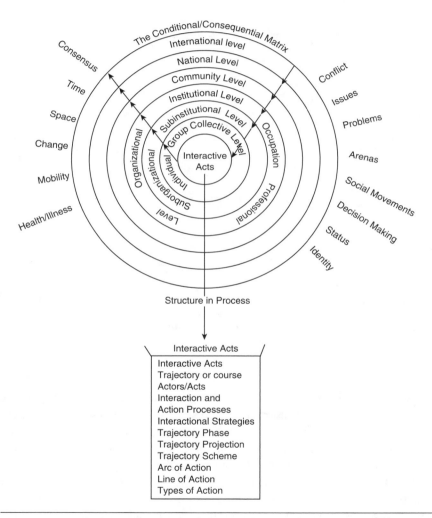

Figure 2.7   Corbin's 1991 Map of Strauss's Structural-Interactionist Theory of Action

SOURCE: Corbin 1991:37. Reprinted with permission from *Social Organization and Social Process*, by David R. Maines (Ed.), Copyright © 1991, Walter deGruyter, Inc. Published by Aldine deGruyter, Hawthorne, NY.

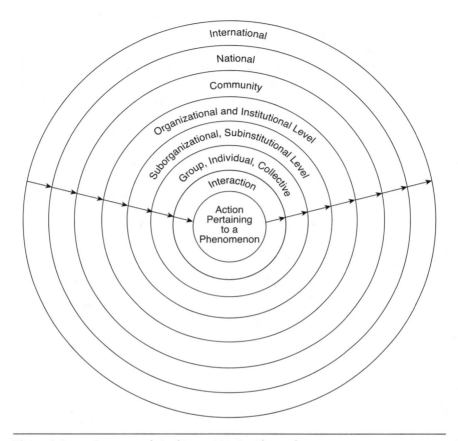

Figure 2.8   Strauss and Corbin's 1990 Conditional Matrix

SOURCE: Strauss & Corbin 1990:163. Reprinted by permission of Sage Publications.

classic Straussian framing, surrounded in widening circles by possible structural/contextual conditions rendered abstractly. The links to the Chicago School ecological maps by Burgess and others (e.g., Figure 2.1) are clear. The Conditional/Consequential Matrix published in the second edition of *Basics* in 1998 (Figure 2.9) is much the same, with the major exception of having "the individual" at the center, building up to smaller groups, and so on, in a reification of micro to macro levels. I doubt Strauss would have made this revision (this was a posthumous publication), as action was *always* at the heart of his analyses rather than persons.

Looking at the two *Basics* matrices (Figures 2.8 and 2.9), we can see that in the first (Strauss & Corbin 1990:163), the concentric circles apparently

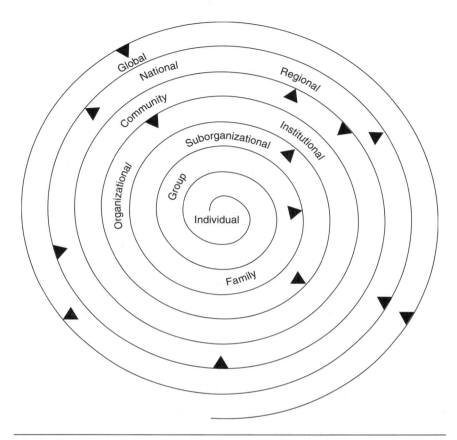

Figure 2.9   Strauss and Corbin's 1998 Conditional/Consequential Matrix

SOURCE: Strauss & Corbin 1998:184. Reprinted by permission of Sage Publications.

NOTES: The conditional/consequential matrix represents constant interplay inter/action (process) with conditions/consequences (structure) and the dynamic evolving of nature of events.
Dark lines = Evolving interaction
Spaces between = Sources of conditions/consequences that make up structure or context
Arrows = Intersection structure with process

represent the more structural conditions *within* which the focus of analysis dwells. The structural conditions are portrayed as *context,* arrayed *around* the central action focus from local to global (from near the center/core to far away places on the periphery). In the second revised version (Strauss & Corbin 1998:184), the conditions spiral around the central focus of analysis (now restricted to the individual), with a similar surrounding local/global

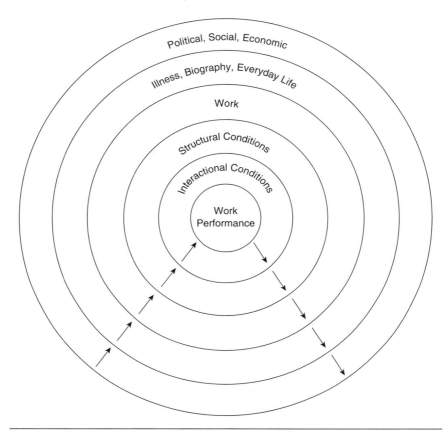

Figure 2.10   Strauss and Corbin's 1991 Project Matrix
SOURCE: Strauss 1991a:457. Reproduced by permission of Transaction Publishers.

display. Here the spiral implies that these conditions may move in more closely or, alternatively, move to the periphery. In both, the micro/macro range of conceptualization is preserved. In the latter version, more movement, fluidity, and a sense of changing conditions are implied. It is important to fairly note that these are *abstract models of matrices,* intended to offer ideas about how analysts might grow actual substantive grounded theoretical matrices for their own projects. Yet, all in all, especially given the primacy of the nation-state, it remains a very modernist vision. Peter Hall's (1997:401) critique on this point, which I share, is that "the imagery of the conditional matrix as a set of concentric circles, while perhaps simply a heuristic device, conveys an erroneous vision of social topography, one that I would rather leave to empirical examination."

Strauss and Corbin advocated constructing a specific conditional matrix for each study (perhaps more than one) and tracing conditional paths for different stories/situations in the data. Figure 2.10 is an example. This is the research-based matrix they generated for their study of "ward work" in American veteran's hospitals—"including its caring features, and broader political, social and economic conditions that might impinge on this work. Moreover, there is a multitude of organizational conditions that have to be taken into account . . . both external to and internal to the wards" (Strauss & Corbin 1990; also in Strauss 1993:457). Strauss and Corbin's project-specific matrix here is *not* organized micro/macro, has work performance—action—at the center, different categories of concern, and so on. The chapter in which this matrix was originally published is titled "Tracing Lines of Conditional Influence: Matrix and Paths," and they do trace some of those paths quite eloquently, with irony and wit—but only in the narrative is there sufficient specificity. There is no fully detailed matrix where you can see what is in the situation of concern with any clarity (but see Wiener 1991: 185-186). There is no map of the situation through which relations among elements can be systematically seen and analyzed.

Strauss and Corbin (1990; also in Strauss 1993:455) also offer a methodological lament: "It is not enough simply to declare or suggest connections between these levels of conditions. Alas, that is of course frequently done. Worse yet, the broader conditions may be described as a kind of contextual background. Their readers are then expected somehow to make the specific connections. . . . But analytically speaking this is done in a haphazard way." Their lament foreshadows my own. To me, the conditional matrices do not do the conceptual analytic work Strauss wanted done in terms of grounded theory method. Strauss was gesturing too abstractly toward the possible salience of the structural elements of situations rather than insisting upon their concrete and detailed empirical specification and clear explication as a requisite part of grounded theory *analysis*. Hence I have attempted to analytically reground the structural conditions of situations through the three mapping strategies of situational analyses detailed in this book.

From Conditional Matrices
to Situational Maps and Analyses

The conditions of the situation are in the situation. There is no such thing as "context." The conditional elements of the situation need to be specified in the analysis of the situation itself as *they are constitutive of it*, not merely surrounding it or framing it or contributing to it. They *are* it. Regardless of whether some might construe them as local or global, internal or external, close-in or far away or whatever, the fundamental question is *"How do these conditions appear—make themselves felt as consequential—inside the empirical situation under examination?"* At least some answers to that question can be found through doing situational analyses.

Ultimately, what structures and conditions any situation is an empirical question—or set of questions. Certainly there are expectable elements of any situation that we would consider in the abstract and seek out in their specificities in the concrete—in the empirical data. These are, I believe, what Strauss and Corbin were pointing toward with "national," "regional," "community," and "professional" analytic signposts. And many of the elements Strauss and Corbin included are also present in my Situational Matrix (see Figure 2.11). This is an interim diagram, standing between the conditional matrices and situational analyses. It also frames situational analysis. In it we can see that the elements formerly arrayed *around* the action are now imaged as *in* the action, as actual *parts of* the situation of action.

Obviously drawing deeply on Strauss's and Strauss and Corbin's conditional matrices as conceptual resources, I see a wide array of structural/conditional elements as potentially constitutive of situations in their ethnographic, discursive, nonhuman, technological, and other specificities. This matrix, like those of Strauss and Corbin, is an abstract version. The diagram as a whole *is* the situation of inquiry. Many kinds or genres of people and things can be in that situation and the labels are intended as generic.

The fundamental assumption is that everything in the situation *both constitutes and affects* most everything else in the situation in some way(s). Everything actually in the situation or understood to be so conditions the possibilities of action, constitutes "the conditions of possibility" (Foucault 1975). People and things, humans and nonhumans, fields of practice, discourses, disciplinary and other regimes/formations, symbols, controversies, organizations and institutions, each and all can be present and mutually consequential. Here the macro/meso/micro distinctions dissolve in the face of presence/absence. For example, Michael (2004:13-14) analyzes the presence in his research situation of things like the university sector (as sponsoring his research) and Burger King (as employing a participant) as "mediation of the macro," allowing us to see the "enactment of large-scale actors within local situations, and the role of the nonhuman in this enactment."

But we need to take this analytic quite a bit further—into the three modes of mapping that are situational analyses. As a part of doing systematic grounded analysis, we need maps of situations, maps that specify what is there empirically in considerable detail from multiple angles of perception. Situational analyses also include adequate representations of the researcher and *their* position(s) on/in the maps developed. Precisely because of these demands upon the analyst(s), before we turn in Chapter 3 to "how to do"

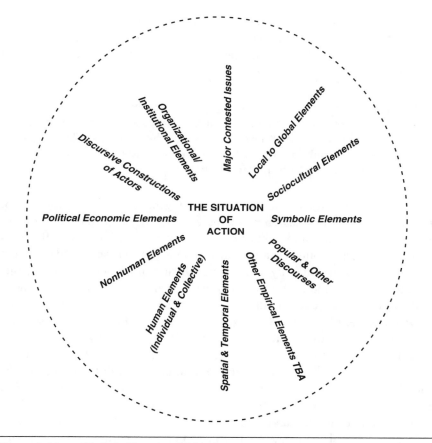

Figure 2.11   Clarke's Situational Matrix

situational analyses, I need to discuss some distinctive data-gathering strategies and reflexivities that facilitate doing them.

Project Design, Data Gathering, and Accountability

> *Working both within and against disciplinary conventions, my sense of task is to explore methodological economies of responsibility and possibility that engage our will to know through concrete efforts to both produce different knowledge and produce knowledge differently.*

> —Lather (2001a:201)

Accountability has new faces. For feminists and some others, accountability for research has gained considerable import since the postmodern turn (e.g., Denzin 1997, 2001c; Fine 1994; Fine et al. 1996, 2000). Haraway (1997:36) is quite explicit:

> The point is to make a difference in the world, to cast our lot with some ways of life and not others. To do that, one must be in the action, be finite and dirty, not transcendent and clean. Knowledge-making technologies, including crafting subject positions and ways of inhabiting such positions, must be made relentlessly visible and open to critical intervention.

For feminists and postmodernists more generally, then, questions of the accountability of research per se increasingly include extended efforts to understand the finer and subtler dynamics of the workings of differences especially but not only vis-à-vis sites of injustice. These include but are far from limited to "identity"/"difference" issues of gender, race, class, age, sexuality, transgender, ethnicity, nationality/ism, colonialism, imperialism, and so on, studied across multiple situations and in their intersectionalities as well (e.g., Arrighi 2001; Collins 1990; Denzin & Lincoln 2005; see also Chapter 1 herein). Such concerns are central to situational analysis.

One challenge to researchers is that many aspects of these dynamics are *not* commonly discussed in conversation, making it difficult to elucidate them during interviews or ethnographic observations. For example, Anna Deavere Smith (1993:xii) states that Americans have difficulty "talking about race and talking about differences. This difficulty goes across race, class and political likes. . . . [There is] . . . a lack of words. . . . [W]e do not have a language that serves us as a group." I am arguing that we are ethically and morally responsible and accountable to seek out data that can speak to such areas of silence and difficulty in the situations we choose to study—subtle as well as blatant racism and/or sexism, ways in which cooptation and collusion take place including our own, silences of active resistance, refusal to engage with the "Other."

For example, a recent study reported in the *New England Journal of Medicine* (Canto et al. 2000; and see Persaud 1999) and taken up in *Time* and the *New York Times* analyzed how a patient's race was often highly consequential for his or her medical treatment—consequential in ways that horrified some of the practitioners studied themselves. They were unaware of the biases embedded in their own assumptions and practices. We as researchers need to assume that we too are unaware of our own partialities of understanding of all the myriad ways in which "differences" operate deleteriously for some people, or the ways they may enhance lives or even not be deemed very important in particular situations. Nor do we ourselves necessarily "know" how we may be shaping our own research in terms of particular issues of difference. These need to be sites of our own learning, opportunities to confront the inadequacies of our own understanding. This is in part what Lather means by "the will to know" in the epigraph—trying to stay open enough to learn possibly difficult things. Qualitative research is especially amenable to the pursuit of differences and their heterogeneous meanings to those actually in the situation of inquiry (e.g., Schwalbe et al. 2000). As we shall see in Chapter 3, the positional maps in situational analysis push the envelope here to open up data to reveal silences and allow pathways into thorny problem areas.

Further, as experienced researchers and scholars—or at least as graduate students aspiring to be such—we often "know" that it is quite likely that such dynamics are present in the situations we are studying even if the data are silent. This raises ethical questions of accountability: Whose data are these anyway? What data have been and should be gathered to fully understand X situation? How can we develop data-gathering strategies that will enable us analytically to better get at silences, at tacit knowledges and practices, at sites of the heretofore inchoate? I noted in Chapter 1 that to me, no researcher is a tabula rasa, and most of us usually have at least a working sense of the field of concern through coursework and literature reviews. Here I am arguing further that these are important to accountability in research. Theoretically informed and knowledgeable research is not nor should it pretend to be innocent, naive, or outside the highly political and even politicized arenas of knowledge production so characteristic of the 21st century. Instead, we attempt to hold ourselves open and accountable through thoughtful reflexive design and data gathering (see also Denzin & Lincoln 2000:367-378).

Here I am directly challenging the ways in which Glaser and Strauss originally talked about "the data," which often had a magical quality predicated on their being separate from the researcher and somehow sacred. The phrase "letting the data speak for themselves" captures this "autonomous" quality they imputed to "the data." In the many courses and analysis groups I sat in with Anselm throughout the 1980s, likely triggered in part by my own and others' feminisms, he routinely asserted that such social aspects as race, class, gender, disability, and so on had to "earn their way into the analysis" by "emerging from the data" rather than be preconceived as salient or significant. I routinely argued with him then. My long-considered response, laid out in this book, is "Yes, but you also need, then, to be sure to *collect* data that can *explicitly address the salience or lack of salience of any of these issues* for the situation at hand." Awaiting "emergence" from the data is not enough. It/we can be all too easily complicitous with the powers that be and the all-too-normalized practices of racism, sexism, homophobia that we too have internalized as participants in our cultures. In the Unites States, at least, there is little space outside of racism, sexism, and so on. We ourselves as researchers construct the data, and we need to take fuller responsibility for that in designing grounded theory studies. Power operates to create silences and gaps, and the sins of omission in sociology and the social sciences more broadly have been profound (e.g., Collins 1990; Denzin 1992; Denzin & Lincoln 2005; Smith 1987).

Atkinson and Coffey (2003) assert that, while not emphasizing design in an a priori conventional sense, traditional grounded theory research actually "bootlegs" design into itself via theoretical sampling across the duration of the project. While also relying on traditional theoretical sampling, I am arguing that we also need to *design* our research from the outset in order to explicitly gather data about theoretically and substantively underdeveloped areas that may lie in our situations of inquiry.[22] One goal here is to enhance our understandings of and capacities to represent power and the dynamics of influence in their capillary as well as venous forms. Including the study of extant narrative, visual, and historical discourses is a valuable design consideration to accomplish this.

My point is that while Strauss and his colleagues were brilliant at analytically finding all kinds of "invisible work" (Star 1991b) and carefully attending to all levels of workers (Strauss et al. 1964, 1985), we need to become stronger at generating the kinds of data in which we can find often "invisibled issues and silences," topics such as the importance of race in medical practices noted above, and implicated actors. Empty spaces and silences have implications. Stereotypes still abound, even if in more subtle incarnations. Dealing with research design and data gathering as active practices, as part of the theory/methods package of grounded theory/symbolic interactionism, is requisite. These have been lacunae in grounded theory (Charmaz, personal communication; Atkinson & Coffey 2003).

At the same time, we need to reject as inadequate the too pat simplifications common in narrow versions of identity politics, the kinds of gratuitous and hence patronizing empathy that can essentialize and/or revictimize (e.g., Lather 1999, 2001b). How can we gather and analyze data without reinscribing narrow identity politics? How can we move toward what Fekete calls a more "mixed economy" of the postmodern that avoids the "too quick re-moralization" that inappropriately crams heterogeneity back into old boxes and slots (Lather 2001b:479)? How can we get beyond knee-jerk stereotypes and silent racisms to the lived complications of the empirical world in all their often difficult heterogeneities? How can we simultaneously study and problematize experience (Scott 1992)? We become invested in various versions/meanings, and calcification and reification are serious risks.

Issues of design also take us into the debates between Straussian and Glaserian versions of grounded theory around the uses of sensitizing concepts and received theory. There has now been about a century's worth of social science research and it has expanded exponentially. The kinds of open-ended projects that worked in academia 40 or 50 years ago no longer "fit" especially but not only because of heightened specialization. Garnering research funds also requires considerable specificity in proposals. Knowledge of the substantive and theoretical literatures is requisite. Specific research questions are requisite (Melia 1996:372).

How, then, can one initially frame and focus the research, drawing on extant literatures and situating the proposed research within those literatures *without* doing premature theoretical closure? My answer to this ongoing conundrum is *through the use of sensitizing concepts* (see also Chapter 1). Blumer (1969:147-148) argued that "[w]hereas definitive concepts provide prescriptions of what to see, sensitizing concepts merely suggest directions along which to look." What I am trying to point at is the difference between using extant concepts as research tools versus gluing received theory onto the proposal and/or the findings without adequate analysis.

For example, Debora Bone's research, which serves as an exemplar in Chapter 3, used the extant concept of "emotion work" (Hochschild 1979) to frame her project and then looked at what counted as such work for hospital nurses and how they handled it in managed care institutions. The extant concept framed "directions along which to look" but not what to see. In contrast, asserting that a proposal about individuals' experiences of a disease is part of the "stress and coping literature" *predefines* that having that disease primarily involves stress and coping. Rather than examining the lived experiences of the illness in their heterogeneity, it co-opts the analysis by directing "what to see" and—more important—"what not to see" (anything *not* stress and copingish). My counterexample is a woman with AIDS who said of her condition, "If it weren't for AIDS, I wouldn't be alive" (Lather & Smithies 1997), referring to her no longer being a serious heroin addict. Living with AIDS as a chronic condition was easier and healthier. The "stress and coping" rubric clearly did *not* fit her experience. Thus some concepts can operate to delineate generic processes or analytic sites (e.g., emotion work, boundary objects, social worlds/arenas, implicated actors), while others perform premature theoretical/analytic closure (e.g., stress and coping, role theory). Our task is to find out how others frame their experiences (e.g., Harris 2001; Schwalbe et al. 2000). Empirically seeking what counts as emotion work in an unstudied area both focuses and opens up possibilities. Deciding that something will count as stress and coping before you even study it closes off one's view of the empirical world.

We need again and again to seek strategies that will destabilize us as researchers and challenge our most cherished positions, to attempt to read against the grain of our own "good intentions." We need to go beyond our "comfort zones" (De Joseph personal communication; Kitzinger 2004) and risk "getting lost" (Lather 2001a, 2001b, n.d.).[23] Ultimately, as Spivak (1994:20, quoting Derrida) asserts, "Perhaps there is no answer to this question [of responsibility/accountability] but the constant attempt 'to let oneself be approached by the resistance which the thinking of responsibility may offer thought.'"

Temporary Closures

> *Always already swept up in language games that constantly undo themselves, we are all a little lost in finding our way into ethnographic practices that open to the irreducible heterogeneity of the other as we face the problems of doing feminist research in this historical time.*
>
> —Lather (2001a:222)

This chapter attempted to historicize the situational analyses proposed in this book as supplemental to grounded theorizing focused on basic social processes. It traced the origins of the root metaphors that undergird situational analysis approaches from early-20th-century Chicago School social ecologies to late-20th-/early-21st-century social worlds/arenas frameworks, as they outgrew their geographic constraints, began to address meso-level organizational and institutional domains of concern, and took up traveling.

I planted three new roots for constructionist grounded theory and situational analysis. First is the work of Foucault, which I see in intense and productive dialogue with Strauss and other interactionists. Second, I argued strongly that situational analyses must take salient nonhuman elements in situations of interest *explicitly* into account. Nonhuman actors/actants/ elements pervade social life, constituting, constraining, and enhancing it, providing opportunities and resources, surveilling and patrolling. Salient nonhumans are everywhere—in all situations—and deserve our serious analytic attention, including discourses and other virtual realities that might well "matter" in the situation at hand.

The third metaphoric new root is the shift and expansion from social worlds/arenas to situational analysis. This was framed and illustrated through a critique of Strauss and Corbin's conditional matrices, assessed as pointing in important directions analytically but not going far enough. Instead, I asserted that the conditions of the action are inside the situation and that we therefore should study the situation itself as the focus of analysis. Situational maps analyses supplement grounded theory by providing means of laying out those conditions in all their density and detail, centering on the interactionist concept of the situation broadly conceived. Last, I raised the thorny issues of accountability in project design and data gathering. Next, we turn to exactly "how to do" situational analyses.

Notes

1. See Strauss et al. (1964), Strauss (1978, 1979, 1982a, 1982b, 1991a, 1991c, 1993), Baszanger (1998a), Bucher (1988), Casper (1998a, 1998b), Clarke (1986, 1990a, 1990b, 1991, 1998, n.d.), Clarke and Montini (1993), Fosket (2002), Fujimura (1988, 1996), Garrety (1997, 1998), Star (1989), Timmermans (1999), and Wiener (1981, 1991, 2000a, 2000b). Becker (1982) and Shibutani (1955, 1962, 1986:109-116) have also written on social worlds, though not using grounded theory methods.

2. While Strauss had a number of more theoretical publications focused on social worlds/arenas, the major published empirical studies were *Psychiatric Ideologies and Institutions* (Strauss et al. 1964), through which, I would argue, he and his colleagues created the framework rather than used it, and Strauss et al. (1985/1997:esp. 287-289). See Strauss (1993:209-244) and note 1. Wiener and Strauss also wrote an (unpublished) social worlds/arenas analysis of the early years of HIV/AIDS in the San Francisco Bay Area, available on the Strauss Web site: www.ucsf.edu/anselmstrauss/.

3. See Kurtz (1984) for an annotated review of the classic Chicago studies. For explications of the problem of organization as it was taken up by Chicago faculty across disciplines, see Redfield (1942) and Mitman, Clarke, and Maienschein (1993).

4. The Laura Spellman Rockfeller Memorial granted $451,000 in basic grants and $180,509 in matching grants for local community research, which largely went to the political science and sociology departments. Many of the most famous Chicago community studies were funded. See Bulmer (1984:129-150 at 140, 257:footnote 59) for a list of those books.

5. Burawoy (2000:10) misreads these moves. He mistakenly calls the symbolic interactionist research of the Becker, Strauss, Goffman, Freidson, Shibutani era "institutional ethnography," when that term was never used by them. In fact, that term has been ably taken up by Dorothy Smith (1987, 1990, 1999) and others working in the

tradition she has established at Toronto and elsewhere (Campbell & Monicom 1995, 1998; Campbell & Gregor 2002; Devault 1996, 1999). Burawoy does not grasp that by studying hospitals, and other such institutions at the meso level, this research moved beyond the local.

6. The boundaries of social worlds may crosscut or be more or less contiguous with those of formal organizations. This element fundamentally distinguishes social worlds theory from most organizations theory. See Strauss (1978, 1982b, 1993) and Clarke (1991, n.d.).

7. Special thanks to Laura Mamo for discussions on this point.

8. See, e.g., Balsamo (1996), Bowker and Star (1999), Clarke (1998), Clarke, Shim, Mamo, Fosket, & Fishman (2003). I am particularly indebted here to a provocative paper by Brian Castellani (1999).

9. Thanks to a term paper by Chris Ganchoff for this point.

10. Today the concept of practices is central across the social sciences (Schatzki, Knorr Cetina, & von Savigny 2001:56).

11. A summary to 1975 is in Meltzer, Petras, and Reynolds (1975:83-123). See also Huber (1973), Benson (1977), Day and Day (1977), Burawoy (2000), and Wacquant (2002). For key interactionist responses, see Denzin (1977, 1992:62-63), Farberman (1975), Dingwall and Strong (1985), Dingwall (1999), Maines (1978, 1988, 1995, 2001:esp. 69-95; Maines & Charlton 1985), P. M. Hall (1987, 1991, 1997), Hall and McGinty (2002), and Prendergast and Knotterus (1993).

12. See especially Strauss (1993), but also Strauss's (1992:4) new introduction to the French translation of *Mirrors and Masks:* "'Identity' treated in this way—and by a sociologist—meant linking individual identities with collective ones. So, it is not surprising to find the book opening with an emphasis on that most quintessential collective process, the use of language." For the English version of this new introduction, see the Strauss Web site: www.ucsf.edu/anselmstrauss/.

13. See esp. Strauss (1959/1997) and the new introduction cited in note 12.

14. In his sociology of work, Strauss (1978, 1979, 1982a, 1984) used the word "work" conceptually to frame what we do to accomplish something. It has nothing necessarily to do with employment, jobs, or careers, though of course it can. For Strauss, work could be visible or invisible (Star 1991b), and he particularly attended to articulation work (Strauss 1988)—work that enabled people to "do things together" (Becker 1986).

15. See Foucault (1972, 1973, 1980), Strauss (1978, 1979, 1982a, 1982b, 1984, 1993), and Clarke and Montini (1993).

16. In comparing Latourian actor-network theory (ANT) with social worlds/ arenas theory, it has been said that the centralized nature of power in ANT is very French, while the pluralism of perspective of social worlds theory is very American (though I have not seen this in writing). A similar argument could be made vis-à-vis Foucault and social worlds/arenas theory. Bowker and Latour (1987) do make a somewhat similar argument in their paper comparing French and Anglo-American science and technology studies. They argued that the rationality/power axis so natural to French technocracy (and explored in Foucault inter alia) is precisely that

which must be proven in Anglo-America, since, in the Anglo-American context, it is "assumed" that there is no relationship between the two to start with. Special thanks to Geof Bowker (personal communication, July 2003).

17. Thanks to a term paper by Chris Ganchoff for this succinct point.

18. See especially Foucault (1980), Dreyfus and Rabinow (1983), Burchell, Gordon, and Miller (1991), Jones and Porter (1994), Rose and Miller (1992), and N. Rose (2001).

19. See, on actor-network theory, Latour (1987, 1988a, 1988b, 1991), Akrich (1992, 1995), and an evaluative edited volume (Law and Hassard 1999).

20. For interactionist critiques of actor-network theory, see Star (1991a, 1995), Fujimura (1991), and Clarke and Montini (1993). Especially on nonhuman agency, see Casper (1994) and Law and Hassard (1999).

21. Keating and Cambrosio (2000) have in fact critiqued symbolic interactionist science and technology studies for not taking the nonhuman seriously enough. Sadly, they ignored a considerable body of interactionist work, including studies of research materials, technologies, etc. (see Clarke & Star 2003), but their critique also provoked fuller and more explicit treatment of the nonhuman here.

22. On classic/traditional theoretical sampling in the grounded theory approach, see Glaser and Strauss (1967:45-78) and Glaser (1978:36-54). For more recent considerations, see Strauss (1987:16-21, 38-39, 274-277; 1995) and Strauss and Corbin (1990, 1994, 1998:201-216).

23. See also, e.g., Kinchelow and McLaren (2000), Essed and Goldberg (2002), Fine (1994), Fine et al. (2000), Stanfield (1994), Olesen (2000), Wolf (1996), Visweswaran (1994), Ladson-Billings (2000), Schwalbe et al. (2000), Twine and Warren (2000), Trepagnier (2001), and Denzin (2001c).

3

Doing Situational
Maps and Analysis

*As I wrestle with what it means to "do" critical, emancipatory
science in a post-foundationalist context, the following questions become key. What is the special status of scientific knowledge? What work do we want inquiry to do? To what extent
does method privilege findings? What is the place of procedures
in the claim to validity?*

—Lather (1994:103)

It is now time to lay out how to do the three kinds of situational analyses proposed in this book. There are several caveats. First, and perhaps
most important, the maps produced using any or all of the strategies laid
out here are not necessarily intended as forming final analytic products.
While they may, of course, do so, the major use for them is "opening up"
the data and interrogating it in fresh ways within a grounded theory framework. As researchers, we constantly confront the problem of "where and
how to enter." Doing situational analyses offers three fresh paths into a full
array of data sources that can lay out in various ways what you have to date.
These approaches should be considered *analytic exercises*—constituting an
ongoing research workout of sorts—well into the research trajectory. Their
most important outcome is provoking the researcher to analyze more deeply.

Second, the approaches can be used with coded data (using conventional grounded theorizing approaches to coding) or even, at least partially, with uncoded but carefully read and somewhat "digested" data. (I will not reexplicate here those aspects of grounded theory, such as coding and diagramming, that I believe can and should be used essentially as laid out in the earlier works.[1]) Thus these new approaches can address the problem I term "analytic paralysis" wherein the researcher has assiduously collected data but does not know where or how to begin analysis. Analytic paralysis is, of course, not supposed to happen in a traditionally pursued grounded theory project wherein analysis, coding, and memo writing begin at the same time as data collection and theoretical sampling then guides further data collection. But it does happen, for a wide array of reasons, especially but not only among neophytes, and usually due to fear of analysis and/or fear of making premature and/or "erroneous" analytic commitments.

Situational maps and analyses can be used as analytic exercises simply to get the researcher moving into and then around in the data. There is nothing more important than making this happen as soon as possible in the research process. But these exercises won't work well at all unless researchers are quite familiar with the data and can move around in them/with them relatively comfortably in their own mind. Coded data—at least preliminarily and partially—are thus much better. Codes, like all other aspects of analysis, are provisional. One tries different codes on data, discards most, and then struggles to select those that fit best—and there can be and probably should be more than one! Furthermore, coding decisions can and sometimes should be delayed. The digesting and reflecting that typically happens *after* an analysis session can be important in such decision making.

Third, precisely *because* the purposes of these approaches is to stimulate your thinking, they should always be undertaken with the possibility for simultaneous memoing, using the precepts of basic grounded theory.[2] A pad and a tape recorder that is sound-sensitive can be used so that you can speak your memos while you continue to lay out the map(s). The goal is multitasking insofar as you are comfortable precisely because these *relational* modes of analysis should provoke new insights into relations among the elements that need memoing promptly. In addition, in the kinds of "wallowing in the data" requisite to doing these maps, the researcher will notice new things already in the data that should receive analytic attention now or later, note areas of inadequate data where further materials should be gathered, note areas of theoretical interest where particular kinds of additional data are requisite (theoretical sampling lives[3]), and so on. Inadequate memoing is the major problem of almost all qualitative research projects—scribbled notes are always better than nothing, and thoughtful memos on the computer are intellectual capital in the bank. And just because they are etched in silicon does not mean you cannot change your mind.

The last caveat is perhaps the most radical. *Researchers should use their own experiences of doing the research as data for making these maps.* There is a saying in the world of qualitative inquiry that the person doing the research is the "research instrument." I am further asserting that that instrument is to be used more fully in doing situational analyses. (See also Chapter 2.) Ethnographic work of multiple kinds is always ongoing in qualitative inquiry. Participant observation is part of the "invisible work" of research— sometimes also invisible to us (Star 1991b; Star & Strauss 1998). Beginning even before a research topic is decided upon, we notice and store information, impressions, and images about topic areas and issues. Not only are there no tabula rasa researchers, but also we usually come with a lot of baggage. Such ideas and preconceptions become intellectual wallpaper of sorts, background tacit assumptions sometimes operating, as it were, behind our backs in the research process. *Part of the process of making situational maps is to try and get such information, assumptions, and so on out on the table and, if appropriate, into the maps.* There it can be addressed in terms of utility, partiality, theoretical sampling, and other criteria. Otherwise we often do not even know such assumptions are there, though they may be doing analytically consequential work in fruitful and/or unfruitful ways.

Furthermore, and also radical, as trained scholars in our varied fields, usually with some theoretical background, we may also suspect that certain things may be going on that have not yet explicitly appeared in our data. In seeking to be ethically accountable researchers, I believe we need to attempt to articulate what we see as the *sites of silence* in our data. What seems present but unarticulated? What thousand-pound gorillas do we think are sitting around in our situations of concern that nobody has bothered to mention yet? Why not? How might we pursue these sites of silence and ask about the gorillas *without* putting words in the mouths of our participants? These are very, very important directions for theoretical sampling.[4]

The three modes of situational analysis offered here should help constitute the overall research analysis per se. The main work that they do is to provide what early Chicago sociologist and journalist Robert E. Park (1952) called "the big picture" or "the big news." Together these maps should answer the questions: Where in the world is this project? Why is it important? What is going on in this situation? Furthermore, the usefulness of these maps consists in part in helping the researcher think *systematically* through both the design of research, especially decisions regarding future data to collect, and the vast amounts of data that one "uploads" into one's brain and other sites during the research process. The researcher may later want to highlight selected parts of the situational analyses in final products of various kinds such as presentations and publications and/or in designing "interventions" in education, social policy, clinical nursing or medicine, and so on. Those are downstream decisions best made long after the analysis has been basically articulated.

There are three main types of **situational maps and analyses:**

1. **Situational maps** as strategies for articulating the elements in the situation and examining relations among them

2. **Social worlds/arenas maps** as cartographies of collective commitments, relations, and sites of action

3. **Positional maps** as simplification strategies for plotting positions articulated and not articulated in discourses

While the format of this chapter explicates them one at a time, they can potentially be used together, some aspects simultaneously, which I discuss in the conclusions. Also, the maps may initially seem quite solid and fixed, but their fluidities and changeability soon become more visible.

The three basic modes of situational analysis are applied in this chapter to ethnographic and interview data. In Chapters 4-7, they are applied to extant narrative, visual, and historical discourses. They may also be used comparatively across different data sources (see Chapter 4). Two other kinds of maps are possible within the framework of grounded theory: traditional grounded theory diagrams and project maps. Traditional diagrams link the analytic codes and categories in an integrated grounded theory analysis (see note 1). I highly recommend doing them. Project maps are, quite simply, maps of particular projects. They can be based on any of the situational maps, draw inspiration from such maps, and/or elaborate or integrate a grounded theory analytic diagram. I discuss and illustrate project maps at the end of this chapter.

Doing Situational Maps

> *What does it mean to recognize the limits of exactitude and certainty, but still have respect for the empirical world and its relation to how we formulate and assess theory?*
>
> —Lather (1994:103)

The locus of analysis here is the situation. The goal is first to descriptively lay out as best one can all the most important human and nonhuman elements in the situation of concern of the research broadly conceived. In the Meadian sense, the questions are: Who and what are in this situation? Who and what matters in this situation? What elements "make a difference" in this situation? Once these maps are drafted, they are used in doing relational analyses, taking each element in turn, thinking about it in relation to the other elements on the map, and specifying the nature of that relationship (described further below).

Abstract Situational Maps

Figure 3.1 offers the Abstract Situational Map: Messy/Working Version. A situational map should include all the analytically pertinent human and nonhuman, material, and symbolic/discursive elements of a particular situation *as framed by those in it and by the analyst.* The human elements (individuals, groups, organizations, institutions, subcultures, and so on) are generally fairly easy to specify. It is likely that, over time, not all will remain of interest, but *all should be specified here.* Nonhuman actors/actants structurally condition interactions within the situation through their specific agencies, properties, and requirements—the demands they place on humans who want to or are forced to deal with them. Their agencies and obduracies must routinely be taken into account by other actors.

Some examples of nonhuman actants that should be taken into account in a situational map may be helpful. Drawing upon my own research (Clarke 1987/1995), in modern Western life sciences, access to all kinds of research supplies is assumed to be available as is a certain level of physical infrastructure to do scientific work. Reliable electricity is a generally assumed, usually "invisible" nonhuman actor in such situations. Yet today, in many parts of the world, steady sources of power are far from common—in parts of the "first world" as well as where we might expect it in the "third world."[5] (I would have said this even if I did not live in California amid rolling blackouts during some of this writing.) Specifying this nonhuman actor might be important downstream. For Western medical scientists, research materials can usually be ordered today by fax or e-mail (e.g., pure-bred rats, cages, food, medical and surgical supplies, lineage forms, chemicals, cell lines, hormones, etc.). Historically, before World War I, no such research supply houses existed, and just getting your research materials into the laboratory was a do-it-yourself project of the first magnitude for scientists themselves, as there also were no technicians. So in a contemporary ethnographic study of a lab or other work site, for example, ease of access to needed supplies and technologies might well be worth analytic consideration. Access certainly deserves a few moments of contemplation. What

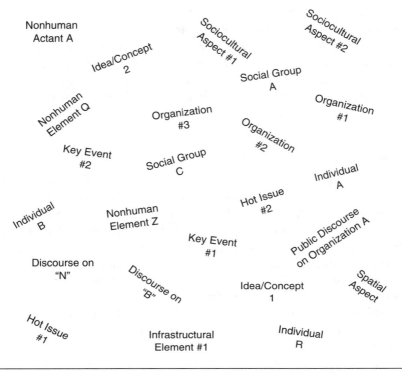

Figure 3.1   Abstract Situational Map: Messy/Working Version

facilitates access? What hinders it? Are these represented on the map? *The key question is: What nonhuman things really "matter" in this situation of inquiry, and to whom or what?* It is the researcher's responsibility to get these into the data—through ethnographic observations, field notes about interviews, and so on, as well as through interview questions. It can be most interesting to see what is taken for granted.

We also need to ask what ideas, concepts, discourses, symbols, sites of debate, and cultural "stuff" may "matter" in this situation. Here I want to highlight the symbolic meanings/discursive constructions of some research materials. To many if not most people, there are tremendous symbolic differences between using rats and mice in research wherein they are sacrificed/killed compared to using cats and dogs, monkeys, and human stem cells. Research using pets historically mobilized major segments of antivivisection movements, unlike the use of rats and mice. The symbologies of monkeys as nonhuman primates "close to us" triggers yet other reactions, and fetal/stem cells evoke in the United States about 150 years of debate about abortion and women's rights. Enough said. The symbolic and discursive meanings of elements in situational maps may be of tremendous significance in the analysis. Again, researchers need to make sure they are present in the data (through careful theoretical sampling if not already present) and on the situational map. If they turn out to be of no particular importance, they will drop away in later stages of the research process.

This first abstract example is very messy—intentionally so. Hence it is very accessible and manipulable by the researcher. Some people will prefer to continue working in this fashion for some time. Make copies, date, and keep all versions.

Figure 3.2 offers the second Abstract Situational Map: Ordered/Working Version. This map is made using the messy one as data. I have framed these categories generalizing both from my own work and from Strauss's (1993: 252) several "general orders" within his negotiated/processual ordering framework: spatial, temporal, technological, work, sentimental, moral, aesthetic, and so on. In terms of laying out the major elements in situations, these categories seem basic to me. Using your own messy map to build this one allows for new and different inductive categories and/or modifications of these.

There is no absolute need to have all of these categories in any given analysis. You may also have other categories. What appears in *your* situational map is based on *your* situation of inquiry—your project. The goal here is *not* to fill in the blanks but to really examine *your* situation of inquiry thoroughly. Some people may not even want to do the ordered working version. That's fine. It isn't necessary.

The situational map will not, of course, have absolutely everything in the situation on it, but it should at least start out erring on the side of inclusivity. Having a big piece of paper with almost everything that you can figure out is important in the research situation written on it in some way can be extraordinarily powerful and empowering of the analyst. It allows you to get a grip on your research, which, in turn, allows analysis to proceed. Simply staring at the situational map, revising it via collapsing and expanding categories/items, adding and deleting, is analytically very provocative.

This is a moment when the art of research is often strong, as one versus another form of representation of something will usually seem "right or wrong" or at least "better or worse." One makes some analytic commitments (however provisional) and moves on. Memoing at the end of a mapping session about that session can be very important as well, noting new insights, signaling shifts of emphasis or direction, detailing further directions

INDIVIDUAL HUMAN ELEMENTS/ACTORS	**NONHUMAN ELEMENTS/ACTANTS**
e.g., key individuals and significant (unorganized) people in the situation	e.g., technologies; material infrastructures; specialized information and/or knowledges; material "things"
COLLECTIVE HUMAN ELEMENTS/ACTORS	**IMPLICATED/SILENT ACTORS/ACTANTS**
e.g., particular groups; specific organizations	As found in the situation
DISCURSIVE CONSTRUCTIONS OF INDIVIDUAL AND/OR COLLECTIVE HUMAN ACTORS	**DISCURSIVE CONSTRUCTION OF NONHUMAN ACTANTS**
As found in the situation	As found in the situation
POLITICAL/ECONOMIC ELEMENTS	**SOCIOCULTURAL/SYMBOLIC ELEMENTS**
e.g., the state; particular industry/ies; local/regional/global orders; political parties; NGOs; politicized issues	e.g., religion; race; sexuality; gender; ethnicity; nationality; logos; icons; other visual and/or aural symbols
TEMPORAL ELEMENTS	**SPATIAL ELEMENTS**
e.g., historical, seasonal, crisis, and/or trajectory aspects	e.g., spaces in the situation, geographical aspects, local, regional, national, global spatial issues
MAJOR ISSUES/DEBATES (USUALLY CONTESTED)	**RELATED DISCOURSES (HISTORICAL, NARRATIVE, AND/OR VISUAL)**
As found in the situation; and see positional map	e.g., normative expectations of actors, actants, and/or other specified elements; moral/ethical elements; mass media and other popular cultural discourses; situation-specific discourses
OTHER KINDS OF ELEMENTS	
As found in the situation	

Figure 3.2   Abstract Situational Map: Ordered/Working Version

for theoretical sampling. (I am assuming that researchers reading this book use some version of a running research journal or audit trail, some means of chronicling changes of direction, rationales, analytic turning points, etc.)

Despite their appearance of fixity, these maps are not static, in the way that we think, say, of street maps as representing fixed entities in more or less constant relationship with one another and unlikely to change very much. (Of course, this is also an incorrect assumption about street maps.) In sharp contrast, there can be considerable fluidity through negotiations, repositionings, and so on in the relations portrayed in these maps, including the addition and deletion of actors and actants and so on over time. Finally, while represented here two-dimensionally, multidimensional maps are also possible. Be sure to date each version of your situational maps and make a couple of photocopies so that you can tinker with them later and still file at least one clean copy of the earlier versions.

Introducing the Two Exemplars

While I use my own research projects as exemplars in the narrative, visual, and historical discourse analysis chapters (5-7), none worked well here. Yet for these exemplars, I needed quite different projects that I also knew deeply. The two exemplars used here are therefore based on the research of former UCSF students on whose dissertation committees I served as a member. (I did not think it would be fair to ask those for whom I had chaired.) Significantly, the situational maps and analyses of their work presented here were done by me in consultation with them. I have tried to be thorough, but these exemplars are only partially represented. Readers are encouraged to consult the published works for fuller treatments (and for citations to the appropriate substantive literatures not duplicated here). These exemplars were selected in part because there are extant publications that allow such consultation. There are also other grounded theory projects that can be easily used for mapping exercises.[6]

The first exemplar here is Debora Bone's (2002) study of "Dilemmas of Emotion Work in Nursing Under Market-Driven Health Care."[7] Over 30 years ago, sociologist Arlie Hochschild (1979) conceptualized "emotion work" as the management of feelings according to socially mediated display and feeling rules that indicate what can or should be felt and expressed, by whom, and under what circumstances, especially in contexts of employment. Part of feminist and other revelations of "invisible work" and often "invisible workers," this sensitizing concept provoked the first scholarly recognition of such activities as "work" and as "part of the job." Hochschild's project focused on airline stewardesses (as they were then known) and their emotional management of passengers, safety, delays, rough weather, other crew, themselves, and one another.

Bone used Hochschild's sensitizing concept, from the now classic paper routinely taught in our doctoral program, to frame her study of hospital-based nursing, reframing certain aspects of the caring nurses do as emotion work and then studying it. Therapeutically oriented emotion work is one of the kinds of work performed by hospital-based nurses as they manage their own, their patients', and others' expressions of their feelings in often very high-tech, very tightly calibrated diagnosis and treatment situations, including a wide array of personnel (from orderlies to specialists) and emotions (e.g., anxiety, fear, pain and suffering, containment, exhaustion, confusion, joy, horror).

Recent structural changes implemented throughout the United States and many other health systems under the increasingly rationalizing and system-atizing logics of managed care have paradoxically both diminished and accentuated the importance of nurses' emotion work, especially but not only in hospitals. In some ways, Bone's study is close to a "salvage ethnography" (Marcus & Fischer 1986)—a project that attempts to capture a particular phenomenon before it disappears from social life as we know it. Bone sought to portray nursing work, especially emotion work, in the transition to man-aged care, as she sought to preserve knowledge of that broader caregiving culture of nursing before it completely disappears—transmogrified into new social forms. She sought to capture the discourse of those for whom that *was* hospital nursing. She herself had spent 20 years as a labor and delivery nurse mostly in a small California town.

For her dissertation research, Bone pursued multiple sites. She did a dis-course analysis of nursing textbooks around the issues of caregiving; she analyzed the literature on hospital nursing care vis-à-vis the shift to managed care; and she did very focused interviews with 18 practicing hospital nurses who she carefully recruited because they were particularly well known among their nursing colleagues for their expertise at "emotional skills" and "caring" (e.g., Benner, Tanner, & Chesla 1996). My situational maps and analyses are based on my reading of her dissertation and publications and my own 30-plus years as a medical sociologist.

Emotion work in nursing is often part of the "invisible work" done in the interstices between clinical and documenting tasks. Bone sought to answer the question: What happens to interpersonal labor in nursing when the time allotted to accomplish it is dramatically reduced, yet demands on nurses by hospital management for improved patient satisfaction and quality "cus-tomer relations" have increased? "I wanted to learn from the 'experts' what they did, how they spoke about it, and how it fit in with the overall demands of their work. I presented myself as both nurse and sociologist, inviting col-laboration and dialogue in this quest to give language to under-acknowl-edged and often unspoken aspects of nursing work" (Bone 2002:141). She was concerned with how nurses handled conflicting demands made upon them—it is not only their emotion work that is "getting squeezed" (one of her "in vivo" codes)—and how they understood and felt about the conse-quences for themselves, for nursing work, and for nursing as a profession.

The second exemplar is Janet Shim's research on two different sets of people concerned with cardiovascular disease (CVD) in the United States today.[8] First are epidemiologists and related researchers who study the racial, sex/gender, social class, ethnic, geographic, and other distributions of CVDs in populations. Second are people of color who have themselves been diagnosed as having CVDs and conditions. Shim's explicitly comparative approach centers on the *meanings* of race, class, and sex vis-à-vis CVDs constructed by the epidemiologists, on the one hand, and by the people of color diagnosed with CVDs, on the other.

In the United States, race, class/SES (socioeconomic status), and sex/gender are key variables in all the social sciences and have been central historically. In fact, all of these elements of individual and collective identity have been becoming increasingly socially and culturally important in the United States, and consequential for the organization of health research, especially health disparities/population health research (e.g., Epstein 2004). This provoked Janet Shim's research on what they *mean* to differently situated people involved in cardiovascular health (see also Schwalbe et al. 2000; Harris 2001). She has both bachelor's and master's degrees in public policy with emphases in health and, hence, long-standing knowledge of epidemiology as a discipline and its practices.

Over roughly the latter half of the 20th century, studies of CVDs have played a central role in the development of the discipline of epidemiology. CVD studies were significant in terms of the kinds of research designs and data accorded scientific legitimacy, the elaboration of more sophisticated methods, and debates over the etiological roles of genetic, other biological, lifestyle, environmental, and social factors in disease distribution. While much if not most medical research on CVDs was conducted on white males prior to circa 1990, racial, socioeconomic, and sex categorization have all consistently been attended to in the U.S. epidemiologic research endeavor. (This is not the case in all first world countries; France, for example, does not collect data on race.) In the United States, population variations are identified and mined for clues to the etiology of disease. Recently, persistent disparities in CVD incidence and outcomes along racial, socioeconomic, and sex lines have raised public concerns and prompted research explicitly aimed at uncovering the causes of such inequalities. In light of such concerns and research, the *meanings* of race, class, and sex/gender must be understood as socially constructed, invoking and mobilizing particular conceptions of bodily and social "differences." Therefore Shim sought to grasp the array of such constructions and who holds which conceptions.

Shim's questions for the people of color diagnosed and living with CVDs centered around how they interpret their experiences as being of a specific race, class, and sex/gender in terms of their CVDs. She also examined their perceptions and engagements with current biomedical "dogma" regarding what constitutes their risk factors and what they "should do" to ameliorate their conditions. These interviews thus examined people's experiences with clinical providers, the advice and recommendations offered to them, and also discursive claims circulating in various media about CVD risks and causes. Shim also attended to their awareness, comprehension, acceptance, strategic invocation, and sometimes rejection of the dominant constructions of "difference" circulating within the "expert" social worlds in the CVD arena.

These two exemplars were chosen in part because they are quite different from each other. Bone's in-depth interview materials are focused more narrowly on the topic of emotion work, centering on interpersonal interaction work situated in contemporary American small-town hospitals under managed care. Shim did both in-depth interviews (with both epidemiologists and people of color diagnosed with CVDs) and ethnographic observations at professional conferences, meetings, health education forums, and related venues. Her approach is explicitly comparative, and at a more meso level of analysis.

Using Bone's and Shim's work, I next offer two examples each of situational maps, of social worlds/arenas maps, and of positional maps. After reading through the chapter, you might want to go back and read continuously through each exemplar one at a time to see a relatively complete situational analysis of one study. The exemplars are labeled to facilitate such moving about in the text.

Situational Maps: The Exemplars

Situational Map Exemplar I: Bone's Project

The fundamental question to be answered in constructing the situational map is: Who and what are in the broader situation? Certainly we know in this study that nurses and patients were there in the hospital settings, but they were far from alone. Who else was involved? What material things were involved and required for providing nursing care? How were various medical technological devices involved? What discursive constructions of patients, nurses, managed care, and other phenomena were circulating? What cultural symbologies and discourses were evoked by the caregiving situations? What social institutions were involved? Were emotion work and caregiving issues controversial or not? If so, to whom? And what were other controversial issues? (This anticipates the later need for issues and axes to develop positional maps.) I will not list in this narrative all the elements on the maps. Please look at Figure 3.3 carefully now.

I tend to work on my own maps in a very informal, often downright messy and seemingly disorganized way. I have reproduced here, therefore, such a map as Figure 3.3, my situational map of Bone's project (considerably

Figure 3.3   Messy Situational Map: Nurses' Work Under Managed Care

neatened by having typed labels). It was, in fact, my own making of maps such as these, both for my own work and to better grasp students' projects while teaching qualitative research methods over the past decade or so, that led me to develop—quite inductively—the concept of situational maps. A messy map such as this is a perfectly reasonable way of working analytically, especially at the early stages of a project. In fact, for many of us, too much order provokes premature closure, a particular hazard with grounded theory. Instead, keeping such a map going over time, returning to it occasionally, adding, deleting, rearranging, can be analytically useful. It is far too easy to become analytically caught up in a few stories and lose sight of the big picture, which needs to be brought back into view regularly in various ways. It is also far too easy to lose sight of other elements that might be important that may have dropped off later maps. Old maps can be truly invaluable.

Figure 3.4 is the Ordered Situational Map: Nurses' Work Under Managed Care. I find it useful to have both messy and orderly versions available to work with simultaneously. I analyze relationally (discussed below) with the messy version. Yet when I want to be sure I have not overlooked or forgotten some relation, the neatness of Figure 3.4 is helpful as I can check through at a glance and not get dizzy. Again, these maps are for thinking with—on *your* own terms.

The situational maps of Bone's project are almost classic demonstrations of the density and significance of structural and material conditions even in a situation where the researcher is deeply focused on small-scale intimate human interaction. And *all* the human interaction is constituted in and through the properties and conditions of this broader situation. What is important here is to specify those elements, and Bone has done so in her published work. For example, note the extensive number and complex relations among structural elements from company mergers and health maintenance organizations[9] to corporate hospital chains, work redesign strategies, management consultants, home health aides, and so on. My maps of her project are full of business terminology—signaling vividly the changes in the health care environment from a situation of the hospital as still a site of at least charitably guided caregiving to the health care domain as just another place of business and site of consumption. Nurses, patients, physicians, and other workers are all still present, but awash in managerial and related calculative schemes and discourses of various kinds.

Yet the nonhuman elements in Bone's situation of concern are not limited to things like "work redesign strategies" and "restructuring plans," no matter how ubiquitous these may be. There are also three sets of things that are ever present for hospital nurses:

- Old, current, and new/emergent medical technologies
- Old, current, and new/emergent pharmaceutical drugs and devices
- Old, current, and new/emergent information technologies and protocols

Each of these is complex, often specialized in terms of particular diseases, takes time to learn, constitutes a serious area of job responsibility, and is often changing and sometimes rapidly. Interestingly, the new information technologies are often used at least in part to track what the nurses themselves are doing while on the job. Whether and how emotion work can/should be tracked or not is an important consideration (e.g., Bowker & Star 1999).

INDIVIDUAL HUMAN ELEMENTS/ACTORS

Nurses (RNs) and nursing aides (LVNs)
Patients and patients' families and friends
Physicians
Hospital managers/administrators/
    consultants
Home health aides

*COLLECTIVE HUMAN
ELEMENTS/ACTORS*

Nurses', physicians', and others'
    professional organizations
Hospitals, chains, and hospital associations
HMOs, state and private insurers
Pharmaceutical and medical supply
    companies

*DISCURSIVE CONSTRUCTIONS OF
INDIVIDUAL AND/OR COLLECTIVE
HUMAN ACTORS*

Nurses as caring/angels of mercy/"good
    mothers" imagery
Patients as needy, demanding
"Everybody's so different"/patient uniqueness
Physicians as unavailable
Administrators as manipulative
Management consultants as heartless

POLITICAL/ECONOMIC ELEMENTS

Rising costs of hospitalization
Expansion of outpatient services
Limits/caps on insurance coverage

TEMPORAL ELEMENTS

Caring as invisible nursing work that takes time
Nursing time per patient and overtime issues
Invisible aspects of caregiving

*MAJOR ISSUES/DEBATES
(USUALLY CONTESTED)*

Nurse/patient ratios as formulas of time
    per patient
Caring as proper nursing work
Caregiving—(invisible) emotion/caring work
Caregiving—technical/clinical work
Work redesign/restructuring plans

NONHUMAN ELEMENTS ACTANTS

Information technologies
Medical technologies
Pharmaceutical drugs and treatments
Work redesign/restructuring plans
Cost containment and patient/customer
    satisfaction goals

*IMPLICATED/SILENT
ACTORS/ACTANTS*

Patients
Patients' families and friends

*DISCURSIVE CONSTRUCTIONS
OF NONHUMAN ACTANTS*

Managed care as antipatient, antinursing
Medical technologies as lifesaving and/or
    dehumanizing

*SOCIOCULTURAL/SYMBOLIC
ELEMENTS*

Caring as important, skilled
    professional work
Variations of expectations of caregiving
    and receiving among patients and nurses

SPATIAL ELEMENTS

Distribution of patients on ward/floor
Invisible aspects of caregiving
Hospital design issues

*RELATED DISCOURSES (HISTORICAL,
NARRATIVE, AND/OR VISUAL)*

Crisis of American health care

OTHER KEY ELEMENTS

Emotion work
Emotions of patients, nurses, families, others

Figure 3.4   Ordered Situational Map: Nurses' Work Under Managed Care

Bone (2002:147) insightfully asks, "Is it possible that the 'invisibility' of some aspects of emotion work actually protects it from commodification?"

One particular discourse seems especially important to this project on emotion work—the extant historical and contemporary discursive cultural constructions of nursing that circulate widely. Nurses have long been discursively constructed as "angels of mercy," good mothers incarnate, caregivers extraordinaire, key sources of help and solace. The magazine of the UCSF School of Nursing is titled *The Science of Caring*, which captures a high modern version of that discourse. Furthermore, it is not only patients and their families and friends who engage this discourse but nurses themselves, nursing educators, and others in the hospital from physicians to managers. How it operates and the work the discourse itself does are both interesting topics. All of the nonhuman elements, as well as many human elements in the situation, contribute to what Bone calls "the intensification of work" under managed care.

In sum, emotions and emotion work almost stick out like sore thumbs as "different" from the main business of what is going on in my maps of Bone's situation of concern. These situational maps thus make it easy to see how and why some nurses see emotion work as getting short shrift and/or being displaced in current hospital care.

Situational Map Exemplar II: Shim's Project

Looking at the messy situational map of Shim's project (see Figure 3.5), first note that many institutional/collective actors are in this situation. Professional expertise is central to Shim's project, and federal research funding fuels the whole arena. Recently the U.S. National Institutes of Health (NIH) implemented revised "inclusion rules" whereby federally funded research using human subjects must include women and people of color or satisfactorily explain why they cannot be included. The long tradition of white males as the "standard medical research subjects" whose outcomes could supposedly be generalized to all others has begun to collapse (Epstein 2004). At the NIH in 1990, both an Office of Research on Minority Health and an Office of Research on Women's Health were founded. They both remain politically controversial and highly vulnerable. All of these developments, deeply charged with "identity politics," have emerged in response to various social movements active over the past 50-plus years: civil rights/ antiracism, women's health, AIDS, queer (lesbian, gay, bi- and transsexual), and others. Today in the United States, ongoing movement organizations with complex agendas actively monitor federally funded research vis-à-vis these inclusion rules and other identity-based criteria.

Figure 3.5   Messy Situational Map: Race, Class, Sex/Gender, and
Cardiovascular Epidemiology

For the epidemiologists, the most important nonhuman elements in this situational map are likely the computers and software programs that perform highly complex statistical manipulations on data from giant population samples, and the International Classification of Diseases of the World Health Organization, the major means of globally systematizing distributional statistics.

Figure 3.6 is the Ordered Situational Map: Race, Class, Sex/Gender, and Cardiovascular Epidemiology. Note that *some elements appear multiple times*—under different headings—as their salience can be quite differently inflected and *all* sites of their appearance deserve consideration.

For example, "individualism" appears under Discursive Constructions of Nonhuman Actants, Political/Economic Elements, Sociocultural Symbolic Elements, National Historical Frame, and Major Issues/Debates. This signals that individualism needs to be understood in multiple ways in this project. Individualism here is the notion that phenomena related to disease and illness—ranging from causes, progression, manifestations and symptoms, outcomes, treatment, and amelioration—can be appropriately and adequately understood at the level of the individual. Thus it is assumed by most epidemiologists that epidemiologic research into the etiology of CVDs can be conducted with the individual as the basic unit of analysis, potential factors and determinants can validly be conceptualized and measured at the individual level, and treatment and prevention efforts can be predicated on individual change and aimed at individual actors. It is this form of individualism that social epidemiology as a professional segment challenges.

In Shim's analysis here, individualism first needs to be explicated as an idea/concept salient in the conduct of mainstream epidemiology and as a focal point for commentaries and critiques about epidemiologists' practices. Then its historical importance vis-à-vis causal theories in health generally and cardiovascular risk specifically need to be laid out. Third, individualism constitutes a central and distinctively American public discourse, structuring the ways Americans are encouraged to think about many things, including bodies and multiple health-related phenomena and the origin, location, and amelioration of illnesses. For Shim, analytic considerations might therefore include the following: How do people diagnosed with CVDs engage or not with individualistic rhetorics about disease causes, risks, and cures? How do epidemiologists so engage or not? How do they discuss—give language to— these issues in their work and their lives?

Questions for Shim's situational maps include the following: Who and what things matter in the broad situation of attending to racial, class, and sex/gender differences in CVDs? Who and what things are involved in producing knowledge about such differences? What discourses, ideas, scientific criteria, and concepts shape how epidemiologic experts and laypeople think about, conceive, and define the nature of racial, socioeconomic/class, and sex/gender differences? What economic, regulatory, political, and cultural conditions affect how research into such differences gets conducted? What professional and social values are taken for granted and by whom, and what if any cultural ideologies underwrite these? What are the consequences of varying kinds of conceptions of "difference" for how researchers conduct epidemiologic studies of differences and for how people "manage" their CVDs? These questions both helped produce the map and were produced by it.

INDIVIDUAL HUMAN ELEMENTS/ACTORS

Participants in Shim's research:
1. People of color with CVDs
2. Key social epidemiologists: Krieger, Cassel, Syme, Susser, Berkman, Kawachi, Diez-Roux

COLLECTIVE HUMAN ELEMENTS/ACTORS

U.S. Congress; U.S. FDA; U.S. NIH and its Offices of Minority and Women's Health Research; ICD of the WHO; epidemiology as discipline: mainstream and social segments; professional organizations: APHA, ACE, NMA, ABC, AMA, ACC, AHA, SER; patient care institutions: local hospitals, ERs, HMOs, clinics, private physicians' offices; big pharma; big biomedicine; civil rights, women's health, and HIV/AIDS movements

DISCURSIVE CONSTRUCTIONS INDIVIDUAL AND/OR COLLECTIVE HUMAN ACTORS

Racial and ethnic stereotypes; sex/gender stereotypes; class/SES stereotypes; stereotypes of patient care; individualism

POLITICAL/ECONOMIC ELEMENTS

U.S. health care politics; Medicare and Medicaid policies; health insurance politics; concepts of citizenship; concepts of individualism

TEMPORAL ELEMENTS: U.S. NATIONAL HISTORICAL FRAME

Histories of race, sex, and class and (bio)medicine; Tuskegee research abuses; histories of routine exclusion of women and minorities from health research; histories of scapegoating and individualism

MAJOR ISSUES/DEBATES (USUALLY CONTESTED)

Focus on meanings and consequences of race/ethnicity, class/SES, and sex/gender vis-à-vis CVDs and CVD epidemiology; individualism

NONHUMAN ELEMENTS/ACTANTS

Computers (hardware, software, and databases for epidemiology); reports: prior clinical trials/studies, e.g., Framingham community studies; CVD procedures, drugs, devices and tests; data collection instruments; key epidemiological concepts (see below)

IMPLICATED/SILENT ACTORS/ACTANTS

People of color with CVDs

KEY EVENTS IN SITUATION

NIH Office of Research on Women's Helath (1990)
NIH Office of Minority Health and Research (1990)

DISCURSIVE CONSTRUCTIONS OF NONHUMAN ACTANTS

Concepts of race/ethnicity; class/ socioeconomic status; sex/gender; sameness/difference(s); statistical significance; correlation; correlation is not causation; multifactoral causation; measureability; standardization; environment; curing; individualism

SOCIOCULTURAL/SYMBOLIC ELEMENTS

Symbolisms of health and illness, esp. of CVDs; curing; individualism

SPATIAL ELEMENTS

Local and regional variations, esp. re race/ethnicity and health care

RELATED DISCOURSES (HISTORICAL, NARRATIVE, AND/OR VISUAL)

Public service health education; media coverage of health; marvels of modern medicine; identity politics discourses; "minority" discourses; women as reproductive bodies; victim blaming discourses; illness and duty to be healthy discourses; individualism discourses

---

Figure 3.6   Ordered Situational Map: Race, Class, Sex/Gender, and Cardiovascular Epidemiology

Doing Relational Analyses With Situational Maps

Once a situational map is done, the next step is to start asking questions based on it and memoing your answers. *Relations* among the various elements are key. You might not think to ask about certain relations within the situation, but if you do what I think of as quick and dirty *relational analyses based on the situational map,* they can be very revealing.

The procedure here is to first make a bunch of photocopies of your best version to date of the situational map. Then you take each element in turn and think about it in relation to each other element on the map. Literally center on one element and draw lines between it and the others and *specify the nature of the relationship by describing the nature of that line.* One does this systematically, one at a time, from every element on the map to every other. Use as many maps as seems useful to diagram yourself through this analytic exercise. This to me is the major work one does with the situational map once it is constructed. I often do some of this out loud to make myself articulate relations more clearly. You could use a sound-sensitive tape recorder with this as well. Sometimes it is tedious or silly—but at other times it can trigger breakthrough thinking, and this is, after all, the main analytic goal. This is one of those sites where being highly systematic in considering data can flip over into the exciting and creative moments of intellectual work. Or not.

Relational analyses can be done very informally and can be personalized to suit your ways of working. I often work with a highlighter and draw these relations on the copies in different colors. The maps can diagram particularly interesting relations by circling (and boxing, triangling, etc.) certain elements and connecting them. The same element can, of course, be "related" to multiple others. That is why a bunch of photocopies makes such work easier. I usually want to see where there are connections made in my data and where there are not, as well as memo the actual contents of the discourse. Silences can thus be made to speak.

These relational maps help the analyst to decide which stories—which relations—to pursue. This is especially helpful in the early stages of research when we tend to feel a bit mystified about where to go and what to memo. A session should produce several relational analyses with the situational maps and several memos. Of course, such careful attention to the messy situational map will likely lead you to change that map and then you will need new photocopies and then . . . you are really analyzing!

At early stages of analysis, memos can and usually should be partial and tentative, full of questions to be asked and answered about the nature and range of particular sets of social relations, rather than being answers in and of themselves. Such memos thus help plan theoretical sampling strategies. They can also act as analytic "placeholders" to remind the analyst to return to particular relational questions later in the research process and to then "complete" the memos through further analytic work if it then seems worthwhile. One would answer the questions that remained both unanswered and interesting. Relational analyses using situational maps are not particularly exotic, but rather provide a systematic, coherent, and potentially provocative way to enter and memo the considerable complexities of a project laid out in a situational map.

In doing relational analyses, then, we start by asking what these nurses had to say about all the other elements. I have circled what seemed to be the most significant relations—which are many and complicated. The most interesting and important would be memoed. Questions would be asked. Data needed to answer them would be specified. Relations of nurses not only to patients but also to hospital managers, consultants, patients' families and friends, and to discourses *about* nursing would all be examined.

Looking at Figure 3.7, the first general impression is of the centrality of the nurses in the situation. And they could be viewed as related to other elements too (though not as strongly). Second is the wide range of elements to which they relate. Third, the analysis looks a bit chaotic. This is interesting in that the mapping strategy as a mode of analysis is reminding us of the disorderliness of providing nursing care in the hospital and the many elements that must be juggled.

The key relationship on which the research is predicated is that between nurses and patients. This certainly deserves early and ongoing memoing. I think of certain memos as "feeder memos" to which I return again and again, noting with a date all new entries. This first relational memo on Bone's data would be such a feeder memo.

The part of Bone's study addressed here is tightly focused through the gathering of interview data exclusively from experienced nurses recognized by their peers as highly skilled at and valuing of emotion work. Looking at Figure 3.8, the first general impression is of the much smaller size of the web of relations. Not at all tiny but more focused. And it is not only "the usual suspects" that are webbed together relationally here but also "work design strategies" and "information technologies" along with "nurses as angels." What *are* the relations between angels and infotech? What did the nurses interviewed have to say about this?

Furthermore, in doing relational analyses with situational maps, we would *not* be limited to focusing only on nurses' relations to other elements. One would work through the relational analysis exercise and see if there are other relations that seem very important for the analyst to grasp. There is,

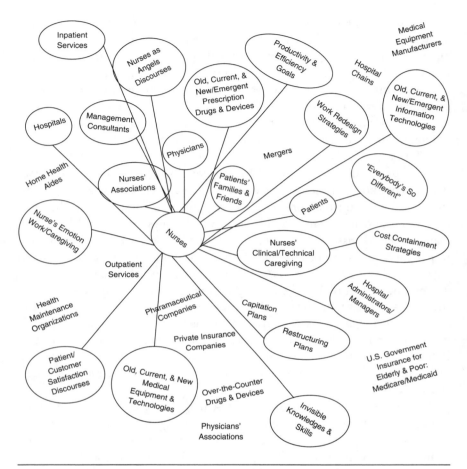

Figure 3.7   Relational Analysis Using Situational Map: Focus on Nurses'
Work Under Managed Care

after all, a vast secondary literature on health care that can help us answer such questions accurately in the research. For example, if changes in Medicare insurance coverage of the elderly were about to occur, allowing improved coverage of home health aides, the analyst would want to read about those changes as well as track how the nurse respondents discussed them. Such questions would commonly be used to direct theoretical sampling and/or refocus the interview questions. For Bone's study, if such changes were perceived to be salient to emotion work, it would be important to ask subsequent participants explicitly about these changes. I would do

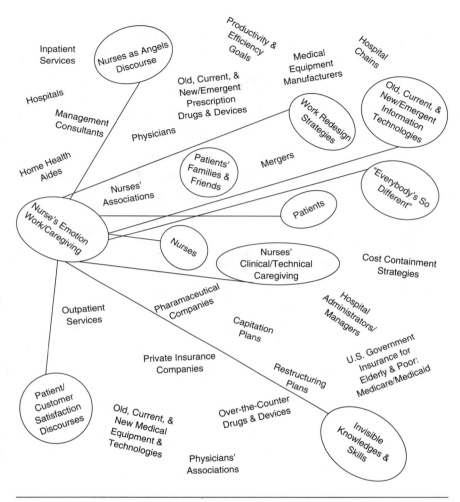

Figure 3.8   Relational Analysis Using Situational Map: Focus on Nurses'
Emotion Work

so toward the end of the interview to first allow them the opportunity to
initiate discussion of these changes as salient. This in itself would affirm the
value of further pursuit of the topic.

Our second exemplar, Shim's research, is quite complex. I have focused on
the two main actors in the relational analyses offered here, but there are many
other analytic drawings possible. Figure 3.9 focuses on epidemiology (see
solid-line relations) but also slightly/gently deconstructs it to also analyze the
relations of social epidemiology (see dotted-line relations) that seem to extend

Figure 3.9   Relational Analysis Using Situational Map: Focus on
Epidemiology

beyond those of mainstream epi. The map shows that Shim's decision (discussed below) that mainstream and social epi were both part of epi (rather than separate social worlds) works well here in terms of the analysis showing how social epi is bringing new relations to bear on mainstream epi. Social epi extends the overall web of epi to new relational sites, even if the ties seem weaker. But those ties may seem strong indeed to the social epidemiologists who have worked for decades to build them (e.g., Granoveter 1983).

Looking at Figure 3.10, again we see a smaller and weaker web of relations, much less formally organized, especially concerned with media and various historical discourses of injustice. Here, for example, a line connecting the historical and symbolic event "The Tuskegee Experiment"

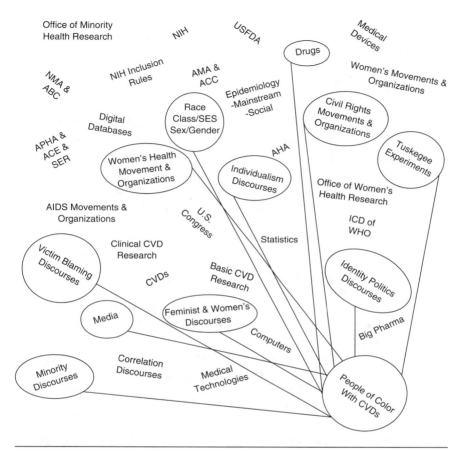

Figure 3.10   Relational Analysis Using Situational Map: Focus on People of Color With CVDs

with the people/patients of color Shim interviewed would be an important relation to memo. The Tuskegee Experiment allowed "Negro" men suffering from advanced syphilis to go untreated for decades after antibiotic treatment was available and would likely have dramatically improved the quality and length of their lives. The U.S. government sponsored the withholding of appropriate treatment as an "experiment" to see what would happen to their bodies (especially their brains at autopsy). Dramatically uncovered in the 1970s (Jones 1981/1993; Reverby 2000), this case of experimental human subjects abuse explains and symbolizes aspects of the deep lack of trust of many African Americans in the U.S. medical system today. Intense and often insensitive research on the effects of radiation was also done among survivors of the nuclear bombings of Japan by the United States after World War II (e.g., Lindee 1997). Did any of the people/patients mention these? Did any of the epidemiologists mention it? Given her study, Shim certainly needs at least a memo on such events and on any mentions of such events by study participants.

In doing her relational analyses, Shim also runs smack into an absence. Although her project is concerned with the meanings of race, class/SES, and sex/gender, no discourse about social class or SES is evident in the situational map. There is also no social movement explicitly organized around class or class-related issues. There is silence on class. How American! What are the implications of these absences for the ways in which Shim's epidemiologists and people/patients make meaning about class/SES? Does it affect their meaning making around race? Sex/gender? Could the concept of race be doing double duty as a proxy for class in American culture? In epidemiology? This certainly deserves a memo!

In sum, then, relational analysis using the messy situational map should get the analyst up and moving into the data, into the analysis, and into memos. At the early stages, some memos clearly need to be written, as the topics need to appear in final reports anyway (e.g., Tuskegee). As a practical matter, doing the situational map and then the relational analysis it organizes can be tiring and/or anxiety producing. The issue is to work until you feel stale and then take a break. This is not the same order of work as entering the bibliography. The fresher you are, usually the more you can see. Glaser (1978:18-35) also cautions against prematurely discussing emergent ideas—that we might not necessarily benefit from talking about everything right away, but rather from reflection—and memoing before talking. I strongly agree, especially about early even if quick and dirty memoing. But we all must find our own ways of working best. For most, the work of this map occurs over time and through multiple efforts and memos. Again, the memos are the invaluable products of all the analytic work.

Final Comments on Situational Maps

What is a good enough situational map and how do you know when you have one? The key word here is saturation—from classical grounded theory (Strauss & Corbin 1998:143-162, 212, 292). You have worked with your map many, many times, tinkered, added, deleted, reorganized. You can talk at some length about every entry and about its relations to (many if not most) other entries if there are any relations that "matter." It has been quite a while since you felt the need to make any major changes. You don't think you have missed much of anything. You think these are the most important elements. (Of course, there are many others, but they don't seem to "make a difference" to the stories you would tell about the situation—your project.) If some virus wiped out your computer files and your notes, and all you had left was this piece of paper, could you work your way back into all the major stories you want to tell about this situation?

As the research proceeds, returning to all three maps can be analytically useful. Don't throw away earlier even if very messy versions. Often you want to go back because something was there that was important but now you are unable to remember.

Doing Social Worlds/Arenas Maps

> *The Use of Concepts. Throughout the act of scientific inquiry concepts play a central role. They are significant elements in the prior scheme that the scholar has of the empirical world; they are likely to be the terms in which his problem is cast; they are usually the categories for which data are sought and in which the data are grouped; they usually become the chief means for establishing relations between data; and they are usually the anchor points in interpretation of the findings.*
>
> —Blumer (1969:26)

Social worlds/arenas/discourse analysis is deeply rooted in symbolic interactionism. It was presaged theoretically but not elaborated methodologically as such by Anselm Strauss and others, including myself (see Chapter 2). Much of sociology, especially that which is concerned with "variables," suffers from problems of conceptual blindness because it uses the individual as the unit of analysis and frames the notion of the "social" itself as aggregate. In sharp contrast, symbolic interactionism in general and social worlds/arenas analysis in particular focus instead on meaning-making social groups—collectivities of various sorts—and collective action—people "doing things together" (Becker 1986). Social worlds are defined as "universes of discourse" (Strauss 1978). Questions of power enter and lead us to also ask how people organize themselves in the face of others trying to organize them differently, and how they organize themselves vis-à-vis the broader structural situations in which they find themselves and with which they must come to grips, in part through acting, producing, and responding to discourses. The task here is to upset the binary between modernist conceptions of knowing subjects and objects as having "essences," and the extreme end of postmodernist conceptualization that argues that all is fragmented, unrelated, and falls into nothingness. There are intermediary and relentlessly social spaces and places (e.g., Lather 2001a, 2001b; Law 2002), and social worlds/arenas/discourses analyses seek to frame them.

Abstract Social Worlds/Arenas Maps

The tremendous strength of grounded theorizing after the postmodern turn lies in its meso-level analytic frameworks of which social worlds/arenas maps are key. Here the meso level is the level of *social* action—not an aggregate level of individuals, but where individuals become social beings again and again through their actions of commitment to social worlds and their participation in those worlds' activities, simultaneously creating and being constituted through discourses. This is the analysis of social/symbolic interaction. It is not high modern macro-level grand theoretical abstraction, ungrounded or inadequately grounded in empirical worlds. Rather, we can "see" collective action directly, empirically. We can also see individuals acting both as individuals and as members of social worlds; we can see social worlds, arenas, regimes of practice, social formations, and discourses produced and circulating in them. The maps themselves allow the fluidities and actions among structures and agencies to become visible and, thus, theorized and memoed.

To make a social worlds/arenas map, one enters into the situation of interest and tries to make *collective* sociological sense out of it, starting with the questions: What are the patterns of collective commitment and what are the salient social worlds operating here? The analyst needs to elucidate which social worlds and subworlds or segments come together in a particular arena and why. What are their perspectives and what do they hope to achieve through their collective action? What older and newer/emergent nonhuman technologies and other nonhuman actants are characteristic of each world? What are their properties? What constraints, opportunities, and resources do they provide in that world?

While some actors (individuals, collectivities, and even worlds) might prefer *not* to participate in a particular arena, their dependencies (usually but not always for resources) often coerce their participation. This reluctant participation of some actors further distinguishes arenas theory from many organizational theories. Social worlds are actor-defined, permitting identification and analysis of collectivities construed as meaningful by the actors themselves (Clarke 1991; Strauss 1993:209-260).

Looking at Figure 3.11, my current Abstract Map of Social Worlds in Arenas (cf. Figure 2.5), let me first and foremost emphasize the dotted lines as indicating usually porous boundaries. This porousness is what gives social worlds/arenas analysis its flexibility, its plastic capacity to take change and heterogeneous perspectives into account. In an empirical study, if boundaries turn out to be very rigid, this is usually noteworthy. Second, there are multiple social worlds, and some overlap, demonstrating visually that some people and collectivities are participating in more than one. Similarly, certain social worlds are shown as participating in more than one arena, a common occurrence. As usual, we the researchers must delimit our stories to those that we can tell coherently. That is, the social worlds/arenas map commonly portrays what Park (1952), as noted above, called "the big news" about the situation of concern. It is highly unlikely that the final reports of a given research project, even one focused particularly on social worlds and arenas, will tell even all the "big stories" framed by the social worlds/arenas map. Rather, the map should help you determine which stories to tell.

The researcher should seek to specify difference(s) and variation(s) of all kinds within worlds as well as between worlds. The feel this has in process

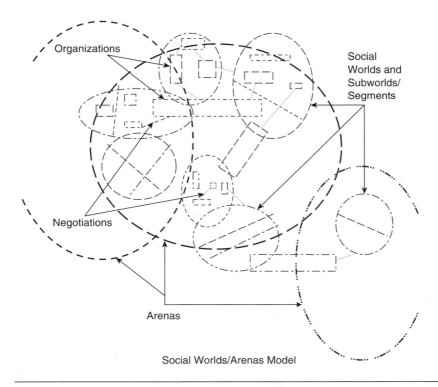

Figure 3.11   Abstract Map of Social Worlds in Arenas

is of both mapping contradictions and not having to commit oneself analytically quite yet precisely because of the variation(s). It can mean that we are unsure when/whether there are different social worlds because of the depth of different perspectives of participants themselves *within* what may be one deeply polarized or balkanized world or several different worlds. Thus there can be both frustration and relief on the part of the researcher. *Specifying the key social worlds is the major analytic task for this map.* There are also extant concepts in social worlds/arenas theory that allow and even feature such ambiguities, such as Bucher's (1962, 1988) concept of *segments* of social worlds. Such segments can be social or reform movements within a particular world, or parts of worlds deeply committed to different facets of the world's work, and not valuing other facets very highly unless or until their utility or unity is questioned by outsiders. Laying out the segments of a world frames the key interior differences. One is always juggling and trading off, back and forth, among similarities, differences, boundary placements, and negotiating conflicting subgroup perspectives in doing these maps.

In addition to segments, I discussed in Chapter 2 the basic conceptual toolbox to date of the social worlds/arenas theoretical framework. These sensitizing concepts may be of help in creating social worlds/arenas maps, in locating the stories of particular interest vis-à-vis social worlds in your data, and in analysis.

Social Worlds/Arenas Theory Conceptual Toolbox[10]

Universes of discourse	Entrepreneurs
Situations	Mavericks
Identities	Segments/subworlds
Commitments	Reform movements
Shared ideologies	Bandwagons
Primary activities	Intersections
Particular sites	Segmentations
Technology(ies)	Implicated actors and actants
Specialized knowledges	Boundary objects
More formal organizations	Work objects
Going concerns	Discourses

For those interested in studying social worlds qua worlds as the key units of analysis—situated meso-level action, structures, and discourses—certain analyses are particularly helpful. Activities within all social worlds and arenas include establishing and maintaining *boundaries* between worlds and gaining social *legitimation* for the world itself (Strauss 1982b). These processes involve the social construction of the particular world and a variety of *claims-making activities* (e.g., Aronson 1984). Indeed, the very history of the social world is commonly constructed or reconstructed in the discursive process (Strauss 1978). Of course, individual actors compose social worlds, but in arenas, they commonly act as *representatives* (Becker 1982) of their social worlds, performing their collective identities. For example, in a medical staff meeting at a psychiatric hospital, psychiatrists committed to a somatic/biological ideology of etiology and treatment will both be viewed as, and often view themselves as, representing that tradition, taking pains to distinguish their perspective from that of, say, psychotherapeutics (Strauss et al. 1964). In addition, personal interests are at stake and may be predominant in a given situation.

The analytic focus on commitment to action as boundary setting between or among social worlds (rather than function or geographic area) permits *empirical* determination of who—which collective entities or social worlds—is in the arena. Thus analytic focus can be on action as process, the classic "basic social processes" of grounded theory, *and/or* the units of action—the collective social worlds and arena(s) entities present in the situation. The kinds of action characteristic of a particular world and/or of an arena—the nature of the basic social processes—are empirical questions. The meanings of the actions in the arena are to be understood by developing a dense understanding of the perspectives taken by all the collective actors, the social worlds involved in that arena. What are the meaningful commitments of the social world and how are these collectively acted upon in the situation? What is happening between particular worlds? Here structure/process is enacted in the flows of people and nonhuman objects doing things together. Structure is action and action is structure and everything is perspectival.

Data that address these questions can be generated in heterogeneous ways: from interviews, organizational documents, historical as well as contemporary archives, observations at meetings or other gatherings of key actors, secondary data (previous historical and contemporary research on the topic, media imagery and discourses), and so on. As a researcher, you need to think through what kinds of data you want, what you can realistically obtain, and, eventually, the adequacy and trustworthiness of the materials gathered and analyzed. Further data gathering may well be necessary.

That is, data may point to the presence of social worlds not yet noted or noticed, and further research on them may be necessary to determine their salience to the stories you want to tell. The social worlds/arenas map may well elaborate over the course of the research.

Discourses per se are not explicitly represented on social worlds/arenas maps. This is not because they are not present in worlds and arenas but because social worlds *are* universes of discourse (Strauss 1978) in arenas—constituted and maintained *through* discourses. Instead, the focus of social worlds/arenas maps is on *collective social action*. Attention to collective action—meso-level analysis—is often profoundly inadequate, especially in qualitative research. Few people really grasp "the social" and the ways in which collectivities and their discourses of various kinds organize us all, day after day. One major analytic map is requisite to ensure that collective action analysis is adequately undertaken. This way, the collective actors are vividly clear at least somewhere in the project's analysis, whether or not they end up in final products. At least they will have been framed, explicated, and given systematic analytic consideration.

However, in the initial memos on each major social world, the key discourses of that world should certainly be at least noted and briefly narrated. The more important they seem, the more they should be elaborated. These narrations will be based on your grounded theorizing analyses of the discursive materials produced by the various worlds. Positions taken in such discourses are analyzed in the positional maps discussed below. Full-scale discourse analysis maps can be made later—if and when you decide to pursue an in-depth discourse analysis of some kind. Mapping and analyzing extant narrative, visual, and historical discourse materials are discussed in Chapters 4-7. But for this initial effort, making the social worlds/arenas map is complex enough in itself.

Next we come to the problematics of relative size and power and placement on the map. When you have a working draft of the social worlds/arenas map, you can start tinkering with it a bit, if it seems worthwhile, to attempt to represent such differences. This can be done by enlarging or diminishing the graphic size of particular social worlds, the type size they are named with, color codes, the thickness of the dotted lines around them, and so on. I have only used relative size in the maps included here, and I have not tinkered a lot with placement. My usual pattern in placement is generally to place like with like and to try and loosely represent conflictful/oppositional relations by placement on opposite sides of the page.

Spending considerable time on such tinkerings would only be worthwhile if you planned to use your social worlds/arenas map as a project map or as part of such a map—as a representation for public use in presentations and/or publications. Here we are predominantly concerned with doing maps as analytic exercises. But there are ways to do this as needed. Computer graphics will eventually make this easier and likely much more fun as well. In terms of temporality, if you are mapping social worlds/arenas at more than one historical moment, please see Chapter 7.

Once the basic social worlds/arenas map is done for your situation of inquiry, it becomes the basis for other forms of entering/interrogating the data. *The next task is describing each major social world in a memo in enough detail to meet your needs:*

- What is the work of each world?
- What are the commitments of a given world?
- How do its participants believe they should go about fulfilling them?
- How does the world describe itself—present itself—in its discourse(s)?
- How does it describe other worlds in the arena?
- What actions have been taken in the past and are anticipated in the future?
- How is the work of furthering that social world's agenda organized?
- What technologies are used and implicated?
- Are there particular sites where the action is organized? What are they like?
- What else seems important about this social world?

I think of these memos as analytically walking round and round and through and across the worlds and staring relentlessly until their commitments, ideologies/discourses, work organization, technologies, and so on can be specified. Put in these memos whatever you currently think is important on the different social worlds and add to them later as needed.

Similarly, one needs to memo a description of the arena or arenas in which the social worlds of concern are involved or implicated—situating them appropriately:

- What is the focus of this arena?
- What social worlds are present and active?
- What social worlds are present and implicated or not present and implicated?
- Are there any worlds absent that you might have expected?
- What are the hot issues/contested topics/current controversies in the arena's discourses?
- Are there any surprising silences in the discourse?
- What else seems important about this arena?

In many ways, the social worlds/arenas maps offered here are very crude drawings, especially in attempting to "represent" relative size and power of different worlds in relation to one another. But even crude drawings like these work well in at least three ways. First and most important, doing them forces you—the analyst—to actively draw the social worlds/arena(s) map. You must figure out how best to conceptualize and represent collective actors—the social worlds and arenas in your study. *The process of producing the map is analytically important in itself.* Second, even crude representations are often quite adequate to grasp the limited and simplified stories that we can actually tell in an article—or even a book. They suffice far more than one would imagine at first glance as they become the *conceptual infrastructure* of the project at hand, undergirding many of the analytic stories later told. Last, once you have tried to produce such a map, you often remain engaged with it, seeking to improve it, make it better represent your interpretation of your data. These kinds of engagements help sustain interest and deepen the analysis in the research process over time. They set up ongoing interrogations of the self as analyst.

Once the basic social worlds/arenas map and memos are done, the analyst has a working big picture of the structuring of action in the situation of inquiry. Where to go next is a decision or set of decisions to be made by the analyst (now or later). There are many possible foci through which to further pursue social worlds/arenas analysis, discussed shortly. But first I want to emphasize that the analyst may want to move next to the positional maps before going further with social worlds/arenas analysis. That is, by now you are already fairly deeply into the social worlds/arenas analysis, and going further would usually be done based on a decision that one of the directions is really interesting, should be pursued, and may well become part of research reports—one of your main "stories." Moving next to positional maps delays this decision making—often quite appropriately.

Possible directions for going more deeply into social worlds/ arenas analysis if you so choose include (but are far from limited to) the following:

- An intense focus on the work of a particular social world
- An intense focus on a technology a social world uses or produces and how it travels within and among worlds
- An intense focus on actions taken by particular worlds on particular issues
- An intense focus on boundary construction processes between worlds by different worlds in the arena and discourses about them
- An intense focus on discourses produced by a world or worlds within the arena
- An intense focus on the arenawide discourses (which may also implicate other arenas)

The direction needs to be decided by the analyst based on interest, availability and accessibility of data, and many other concerns.

Social Worlds/Arenas Maps: The Exemplars

The exemplars on emotion work in nursing and on race, class, and gender in cardiovascular epidemiologies are continued here.

Social Worlds/Arenas Map Exemplar I: Bone's Project

Looking at Figure 3.12, we see a wide array of social worlds in the hospital arena, itself in a much broader U.S. health care domain (which, of course, has multiple other arenas in it).[11] We can think of this hospital arena as both constituted of the several hospitals where the nurses Bone studied worked and as an exemplar of smaller to mid-sized, nonuniversity-based American hospitals. Giant and university-based American hospitals are rarer and would be more complex, and Bone sought instead to portray mainstream hospital nursing work under regimes of managed care. Many of the social worlds in the hospital arena in Figure 3.12 are business related (management consulting, hospital management, public and private insurance companies). Many are professional (nurses, physicians, other health professional worlds). Patients are present but not as collective actors. Rather, they dwell in spaces "in between" physicians and nurses and their families and insurance coverage. But they are also implicated actors, discursively constructed by many other worlds in the hospital arena— including business-oriented worlds. Interestingly, all the social worlds and patients themselves simultaneously have a presence in the broader U.S. health care domain outside the hospital arena as well. The hospital is thus only one of several arenas that these social worlds are active in, tracking and monitoring them all.

Figure 3.12 helps us to see that there are a number of other very powerful social worlds in the hospital arena potentially constraining and differentially enabling the situated actions of nurses. While nursing work, including emotion work, is central to hospital work, it is far from the only work done there and, furthermore, may not be the most symbolically valued work. That is, if hospitals are places where very ill people go to be treated, then symbolically the work of physicians of various kinds and the effects of medical technologies, drugs, and devices may, in the minds of many (but not all), trump that of nursing. The business of running the hospital at a profit (or not at a loss) will occupy

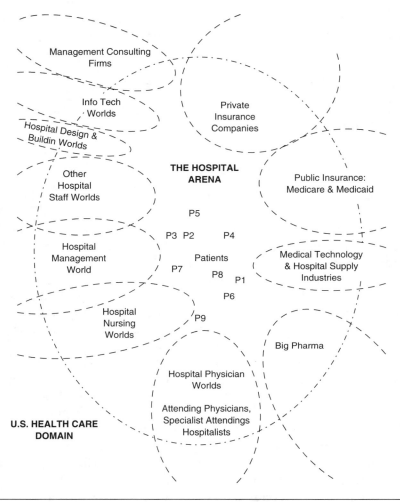

Figure 3.12   Social Worlds/Arenas Map: Nursing Work in the Hospital Arena

many others—and so on. Nurses in hospitals are, as Bone has ably documented, "feeling squeezed," and the social worlds/arenas map helps us see how and why and its complexities. Furthermore, most nursing work is squeezed, not only emotion work. This situates nurses' emotion work itself more clearly in this situation.

Let me emphasize here the distinctive analytics of constructing the big picture through the social worlds/arena analysis. Describing the big picture requires the analyst to take several steps back from the phenomenon of interest. The goal of arena analysis is to locate the research project in its broader situation, not to focus narrowly on the project per se. For example, for Bone's project, we have located nursing and nursing work in the broader hospital arena where it is undertaken. Emotion work is but one part of nursing work—and even nursing work and the hospital are here situated much more broadly. We might be tempted to do a map that is focused much more closely, for example, on a particular hospital unit, and look at the many different kinds of work going on around and with a particular patient. These would not be "bad" maps, but they would be project maps—focused on particular aspects of the project per se—rather than a social worlds/arenas analysis. The social worlds/arenas analysis is intended to reveal certain broader conditions—constraints, opportunities, and resources—that may well otherwise go unnoted. It is a key part of situational analysis that replaces the conditional matrix.

Social Worlds/Arenas Map Exemplar II: Shim's Project

Figure 3.13 on Shim's project situates expert cardiovascular epidemiologies and people/patients diagnosed with CVDs in the United States today in an arena focused around CVD, itself within a much broader domain of health care that includes multiple other arenas. Inside that CVD arena (but often extending beyond it as well into other arenas in the broader health care domain) are a number of quite large and complicated social worlds that have key segments or subworlds pertinent to her project. Shim's project centers on U.S. research largely sponsored by the federal government, so the first major worlds are composed of those related agencies and organizations: the U.S. Congress, the NIH, and the Offices of Research on Minority and Women's Health in the NIH. By virtue of their gate keeping and control over access to funding resources, these entities retain considerable bureaucratic and regulatory power to shape the agendas, methods, and conduct of epidemiologic work. Also in this arena is a huge private nonprofit nongovernmental organization (NGO)—the American Heart Association (AHA)—a social world unto itself with local, national, and international suborganizations. By positioning the AHA as a large and similarly significant world to the NIH vis-à-vis CVDs, this map signals that this nonprofit organization is continuous/coconstitutive with the governmental organizations in highly significant ways. The map thus constructs what might be considered a "cardiovascular disease enterprise," parallel to what Estes (1979) called "the aging enterprise"—a broad network of major players who have tremendous powers and influence over most aspects of the CVD arena—including but far from limited to the world(s) of cardiovascular epidemiological research. Such enterprises typically have long and consequential histories.

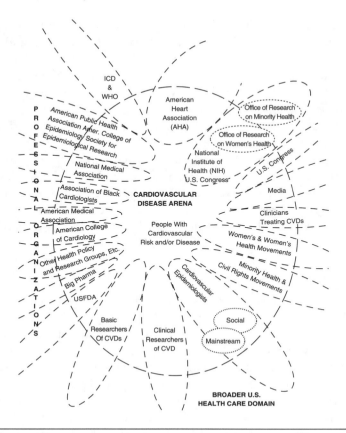

Figure 3.13   Social Worlds/Arenas Map: The Cardiovascular Disease Arena

The next major social world in this map is that of epidemiologists and their professional associations. When considering the concept of individualism discussed earlier, it quickly became clear to Janet Shim that the discipline of epidemiology seems in actual practice to be divided into (at least) two subgroupings or segments: mainstream epidemiology and social epidemiology. Mainstream/conventional epidemiologists tend to focus on cardiovascular risk factors as *individual* phenomena, while social epidemiologists tend to conceptualize sex/gender, race, and class as more complicated *social/cultural* processes. After some months of research and a lot of thought and analysis, Shim decided that these were segments of a single social world rather than separate worlds for several reasons.

Both groupings still identify professionally as epidemiologists and are in the same professional organizations. Both use many of the same methods and share many other disciplinary trappings. While the research agendas and questions raised by social epidemiologists differ from those of mainstream epidemiologists, this is more in degree than in kind, and mainstream epidemiology itself is characterized by divergent agendas as well. Social epidemiologists are definitely critical of many mainstream research assumptions. Yet, given their as yet still somewhat marginalized status within the discipline and vis-à-vis funding organizations, and so on, and the many possible contestations over their research agendas, Shim sees them as relatively modest in their critiques. She finds that social epidemiologists are arguing now that epidemiology merely needs to expand its lens, to pursue research at multiple different levels, *including* the social. This is not arguing for a totally different kind of epidemiology. Thus we can view the social epidemiologists as constituting a "reform movement" inside the social world of epidemiology (e.g., Bucher 1962). Shim has further noted that this segment is having some successes as more social epidemiologists are being hired into major U.S. departments and are chairing more such departments. The professional associations of epidemiologists are also on the social worlds/arenas map (e.g., the American Public Health Association, the American College of Epidemiology, and the Society for Epidemiological Research).

The nonmonolithic nature of this social world highlighted for Shim an important theoretical sampling issue: In interviewing epidemiologists, she should attend scrupulously to their categorization of their own work as conventional or social epidemiology. She could get even more specific by asking herself—and asking her informants and data—questions such as: Why are there seemingly two groups of epidemiologists? Where did they come from? Are there other debates between them? What perspectives on data collection, conceptual models, measurability do they share or disagree about? What are their relationships to funders and regulatory agencies? Are there other groups?

In the cardiovascular arena, there are in addition several loosely bounded social worlds of the clinicians of various kinds who treat CVDs. These range from M.D. epidemiologists (who are *both* clinicians and clinical researchers) to general practitioners, internists, hospitalists, nurse practitioners, and other health professionals. Another loosely bounded world is composed of basic and medical scientists who do basic scientific research on CVDs and their underlying biological processes, usually using animal models or computer models rather than human subjects. The professional associations of clinicians are also on the social worlds/arenas map. These include the American Medical Association, the American College of Cardiology, and the National Medical Association (a predominantly African American organization founded in 1895 when "Negroes" were not allowed to join the AMA) and its Association of Black Cardiologists.

In sharp contrast, any set of people diagnosed with particular conditions and patients in general are not *collective* actors, the special focus of social worlds/arenas analyses. This absence of collective identity and commitment to act together among patients has been a key aspect of understanding many medical practices historically, especially how patients are situated differently from medical professionals (e.g., Alford 1972).

Yet people (who are some of the time also patients) often have their own understandings, thoughts, and beliefs—"lay" knowledges—about their health conditions. Such "knowledges" are rarely recognized by medical professionals and, even then, are usually marginalized, in contrast to the centrality of "official" knowledge production regarding cardiovascular health and disease. Lay actors in medical arenas are rarely given active voice and participation in the production of authoritative knowledge. As such, they are more often "implicated actors." However, under certain conditions, people diagnosed/patients can become collective and agentic actors in health care arenas—when they organize themselves into social movements concerned with health issues generally (such as the women's health movement) or into "patients' movements" around particular conditions/diseases (AIDS, Alzheimer's movements). Such groups are becoming increasingly common and today are changing the dynamics in many arenas in the health care domain quite powerfully in the United States and elsewhere.[12]

Unsurprisingly, then, another major set of social worlds in Shim's social worlds/arenas map are social movements of various kinds. Those diagrammed here include civil rights/antiracism movements, women's movements, women's health movements, and AIDS movements. Not only did Shim find that these social movements were extremely consequential in structuring what "differences" epidemiologists should attend to, and who should be included in their research, but they also raised larger concerns about the public credibility and social status of U.S. health research in general and about epidemiology as a field of professional expertise in particular.

Yet another social world in Shim's analysis is the media, who increasingly consider it their responsibility to translate new scientific findings to the public to implement the claims of epidemiologic science regarding cardiovascular risk and disease prevention. Health and illness are "news," and coverage of medical topics by the media has expanded dramatically, as well as extensive direct-to-consumer advertising of pharmaceuticals. Big Pharma, the current term for the vast international network of major pharmaceutical companies, is also quite present as a social world. The CVD arena is particularly important to them, as many people diagnosed with such diseases, especially in the first world, take *daily* medications for them—the backbone of pharmaceutical profit making. Yet another world or set of worlds present in the cardiovascular arena are health policy, public health, academic health, and other groups who attend to developments in this arena, including Shim and myself as researchers!

Looking at this social worlds/arenas map, Shim can ask: What is possible in the world of cardiovascular epidemiology now? Given the situation(s) in which they are located, where do researchers think the discipline should go and how do they think they can get there, given possible path options? How do these research directions relate to the conceptions of race, class, and sex/gender held by epidemiologists? And by people of color diagnosed with CVDs?

In sum, we can see in the Bone example that even if one's research project is using in-depth interviews to focus on individuals' lived experiences of something, the phenomenon of interest will be embedded in social worlds and arenas—scenes and sites of collective action. These social structural elements deserve articulation in project narratives, as they are fully present and quite consequential *in the situation* that the individuals are describing and in which their specific (inter)actions that are the focus of the research take place. In her research, Bone was focused specifically on the perceptions and interpretations of *only* the expert nurses in this complex hospital arena. Thus hers is a study from the perspective(s) of only one segment of a social world in the arena. But, as we have clearly seen, the presence of all the other worlds was pervasively experienced and consequential for all the nurses. Moreover, the views from that one world were far from monolithic.

Similarly, Shim pursued the perceptions and interpretations of people in one social world—epidemiologists—and those of people who are not collectively organized—patients/people of color diagnosed with CVDs. These people are themselves varyingly aware of and involved with the social worlds and arenas in which their CVDs are studied, but those worlds are highly consequential for them. They are, then, implicated actors in those worlds. By and large, epidemiology seems unaware of and unconcerned about the perspectives of the people/patients with CVDs.

Shim's study thus works beautifully for her explicit comparative purposes. She can compare and contrast the meanings of race, class, and gender constructed by epidemiologists (who constitute a highly focused if highly segmented professional social world and who frequently communicate with one another across multiple venues) with the meanings held by people of color diagnosed as having the disease (who are not in communication with one another, nor with the epidemiologists). Here, as is often the case, there are considerable differences *within* particular groups as well as *across* "different" groups. Such studies help us deconstruct difference as essential.

Final Comments on Social Worlds/Arenas Maps

What is a good enough social worlds/arenas map and how do you know when you have one? The first indicator is that no new major social worlds have appeared in your arena(s) of concern for some time. Data may have revealed related arenas and their worlds, and some of those worlds and arenas may be active in terms of the one you are focusing on, but their primary arena(s) are not yours. The related collective entities that you have wondered whether they were social worlds on their own or segments of other worlds have resolved into one or the other. Alternatively, the fact that they have not done so has been interpreted as their being at a turning point in the history of that entity to be further tracked. If there are implicated actors, you have found, described, and analyzed their constructions by various worlds in the arena. You have described and analyzed the major constructions of the non-human implicated actants and their consequences as well.

If you are historically minded, you have some glimpses of how the arena might have appeared some years ago—a strong sense of the changes that have happened—and you have pursued sufficient data to be able to explicate the situation. You may glimpse how two previously distinct social worlds intersected and became one by the present moment, or how one former world became two or more through segmentation processes. If you are studying emergent or rapidly changing worlds and/or arenas, you have noted particular sites where segmentations and/or intersections might occur and marked them to return to prior to publishing anything.

Because social worlds/arenas analysis attempts to represent most if not all of the major social worlds in a given arena, it is a much more democratic "regime of representation" (Latour 1988b) than many other analytic approaches. This grew out of and fits well within a Deweyian pragmatist/symbolic interactionist approach. It also challenges functionalist models based on normal/deviant, core/periphery, or substructure/superstructure distinctions. Significantly, in the very act of representing the key social worlds, the analyst grants greater power to the less powerful worlds—the democratizing move discussed in Chapter 2.

In many ways, social worlds/arenas analyses are figure/ground relations—multiple simultaneous legitimate analyses are possible at the same time. They can be slippery to do, but one can use this to analytic advantage. One social world can itself be teased out and analyzed as an arena itself as a means of deconstructing it, determining its segments, their positions, commitments and agendas, the implicated actors, nonhuman actants and their constructions, and so on. The porous nature of the boundaries of worlds and arenas and their plasticity are vital, as it is through these that changes enter the situation of inquiry. Social worlds/arenas analysis is a form of organizational analysis, dealing with how meaning making and commitments are organized. The boundaries of social worlds may crosscut or be more or less contiguous with those of formal organizations. This element fundamentally distinguishes social worlds theory from most organizations theory (Clarke 1991; Strauss 1978, 1982a, 1982b).

For example, some of the organizations in the diagram of Shim's project are represented as social worlds unto themselves (the NIH and the AHA). Because they are themselves so vast, they may well require a focused sub-analysis. They overlap and interlock with other organizations and worlds so complexly that it is like watching morphing Russian dolls running amok. Here, at the same time that the elasticity of the social worlds/arenas concepts is advantageous, it can be quite challenging.

To proceed in the face of such challenges, I would like to draw attention to what has happened here, through this discussion. In struggling to make the social worlds/arenas map of Shim's project, we have confronted and are still involved with coming to grips with how to think about these very large and very powerful actors in the cardiovascular arena. This, I would argue, is an *analytically* useful and worthwhile place to be as researchers. We will not have answers to everything. But pointing out and pointing at particularly important complexities such as this is part and parcel of a strong situational analysis. The take-home lesson here is that often when we run into big, thorny problems during the analysis, especially conundrums that do not fit comfortably into our analytic categories and/or our expectations, and that do not go away over time, they may be among the Big News findings of the situational analysis.

Last, there are ways in which social worlds/arenas analysis can work analytically to smooth over differences, especially within particular worlds but also at times between them, that the analyst should be aware of and attempt to guard against. In some part, the risk is heightened because it takes a lot of space simply to narratively lay out the worlds and arenas, and we often stop short of full elucidation of them—thus representing them in simplified form. In some senses too, narratives of differences can be suppressed in favor of fuller representation of social worlds' perspectives/ideologies/discourses as articulated by participants themselves. We can and should certainly struggle against such smoothing and oversimplification. But it is precisely such differences that we can still seek through the positional maps discussed next.

Doing Positional Maps

Both within and against conventional notions of social science research, the goal is not so much to represent the researched better as to explore how researchers can "be accountable to people's struggles for self-representation and self-determination."

—Visweswaran (quoted in Lather 1999:140)

Positional maps lay out most of the major positions *taken in the data* on major discursive issues therein—topics of focus, concern, and often but not always contestation. Issues, positions on issues, absences of positions where they might be expected (sites of discursive silence), and differences in discursive positions central to the situation under study are the focus of positional maps. That is, positional maps are analytic tools applied here to the discursive materials gathered through fieldwork, participant observation, and interviewing. (Such maps can also be used for studies of extant discourse data, discussed in Chapters 4-7.)

Here there is no such thing as a "negative case"—no "normal" versus "deviant" position. That would require the researcher to be committed to the perspective of particular discursive position(s). Instead, here there are just *other positions,* perhaps outlier, less common, or more marginal positions. And it is fine to note this, as indeed we do seek to analyze power in all its fluidities. The goal is to *represent the positions articulated on their own terms.* These are not necessarily the terms of the researcher but rather the researcher's best effort to grasp and represent the positions taken in the discourse. Thus this is based in a more insistently democratic theory of representation as noted earlier.

Perhaps the most important and radical aspect of positional maps after the postmodern turn is that *positions are not correlated/associated with persons or groups or institutions.* Instead, we are seeking here to begin moving with Foucault (1973:xiv) beyond "the knowing subject." *Positions on positional maps are positions in discourses.* Individuals and groups of all sorts may and commonly do hold multiple and contradictory positions on the same issue. Positional maps represent the heterogeneity of positions.

I cannot overemphasize the importance of *not* seeing these maps as "representing" individuals or groups. Positional maps do *not* seek to represent individual or collective voices or experiences "in their own terms" in depth. Other qualitative approaches such as various narrative, feminist narrative, autoethnographic, and phenomenological approaches do this very well.[13] Rather, in positional maps, various social sitings are captured and represented through the mapping process. Emphasis here is on the map rather than particular positions. A focus on particular position(s) can, of course, be developed downstream in the research if that is deemed appropriate. If so, a full-scale discourse analysis should be considered.

Why analyze positions separately—on their own? How can they be properly framed without connecting them to social worlds or organizations or individuals? It is important precisely because the centralizing tendencies and the stereotyping inherent in social science focused on similarities rather than differences constantly deletes heterogeneities from our vision. We are constantly blinded by binaries. It is difficult to see that which one does not expect. It is even more difficult to see that which one does not grasp or understand! And yet even more difficult to hear silences (see note 5). I am ironically arguing that articulating positions independently of persons, organizations, social worlds, arenas, nonhuman actants, and so on allows the researcher to ultimately, downstream, see *situated positions* better. Contradictions abound and positional maps enable us to see the broader situations, as well as specific positions, better.

The concept of positionality here creates an important "space between." The researcher can (at least temporarily in the research process) attempt to step outside the politics of representation that tend to routinely and at times tediously imbricate us in various politics of identity. These are very hot political areas in the United States and elsewhere, and tendencies are toward oversimplification. Instead, analytically focusing on the space between actors and positions can allow fresh analyses. I see this space between as a post-modern space; it is not naive, but rather highly reflexive and analytic. Such spaces can allow us to see what happens to the empirical materials themselves in our own visions of them as the analyses begin to merge, and to see what other shapes they might flow into or might flow into them. Such spaces allow us to articulate doubts and complexities where heretofore things had appeared "unnaturally" pat, sure, and simple. As Massumi (2002:8) has asserted, "[P]ositionality is an emergent quality of movement."

Should you later decide to write about or otherwise articulate and represent the positions of individuals or groups, social worlds in an arena, on particular issues, this is of course completely legitimate. In fact, one of the exemplars used here, Shim's project, compares the positions taken in the data from two different sets of respondents. Furthermore, one can always articulate positional maps with the social worlds/arenas maps if that seems a valuable pursuit. I have certainly done so myself, seemingly productively in a paper on RU486 used as the exemplar for Chapter 5 on narrative discourse analysis (Clarke & Montini 1993). In doing such work, I would argue for as nuanced a portrayal as possible, delineating intraindividual and intragroup differences at least as enthusiastically and elaborately as interindividual and intergroup differences. Of course, such representational projects are commonly highly politically charged. Representationally handling those politics with great care is crucial.[14]

It is often radically democratic to represent the major positions taken in a situation *on their own terms*. It is, in fact, a form of relativism, a term that requires some discussion. Relativism is often *mis*interpreted to mean that if you represent multiple positions, this equals valuing all such positions equally, or that you yourself value such positions equally. Most interactionists find such an interpretation ludicrous, asserting that we always have operant values that lead us individually and collectively to different valuations, and that valuation is rarely if ever genuinely "equal." We have also asserted that representing *all* positions on their own terms is a democratizing move, a *politics of the acknowledgment of presence* instead of fascist denial and repression of diversity. Certainly, many of us have been deeply moved by feminist theory in this regard.[15] Many silences still need to be broken.

Abstract Positional Maps

To do positional maps, one first seeks to elucidate from the data what the basic (often but not always contested) issues are in the situation of inquiry about which there are different positions, and array these dimensionally in some fashion. While this sounds simple, it of course quickly gets complicated in the empirical world. And furthermore, one may come across what seems to be a position and not know what issue(s) it speaks to. Thus, in practice, the analyst weaves back and forth from elucidating issues and axes to positions and vice versa.

Figure 3.14 offers an Abstract Positional Map that portrays positions on a particular issue in the larger specific situation of concern. There are two main axes, and an infinity of positions is possible. The analyst tries to lay out the axes in terms of "more versus less," if this seems to work. Otherwise, alternative means of clearly articulating the axes could be pursued. Analytic fracturing—basic grounded theory coding and situational and social worlds/arenas mapping—opens up data for positional analyses. Heterogeneous positions and other aspects of difference(s) and variation are usually manifest during coding. Coding allows the analyst to see and ultimately carefully name the different positions held down in the data.

Positional Maps: The Exemplars

The first exemplar of a positional map is from Bone's project on the emotion work of nurses under managed care.

Positional Map Exemplar I: Bone's Project

In Figure 3.15, Positional Map: Clinical Efficiency and Emotion Work in Nursing Care, we see four basic positions articulated through her data. At the top left is the position that clinical efficiency is the most important work in hospital nursing care. The top right position holds that both clinical efficiency and emotion work are important in hospital nursing care. And the lower right

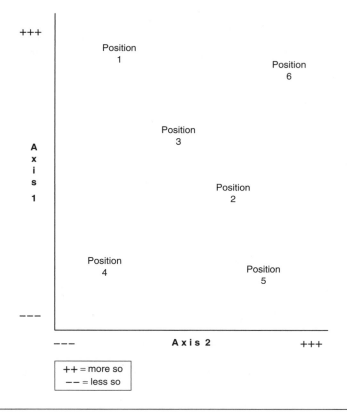

Figure 3.14   Abstract Positional Map

position is that emotion work is most important in hospital nursing care. Yet another position further held that what is most important is an empirical situational question for the nurse(s) involved to address! That is, what is important actually varies with the needs of the specific patient and is thus *situation specific*. Because it did not fit easily on this map, I placed this position in the center of the map. Although this is a bit awkward, it works well enough for us to see the full range of positions taken and not taken in this situation. Its awkwardness works to highlight its distinctiveness. Missing in Bone's data was the position that *neither* clinical efficiency nor emotion work is important in hospital nursing care. While this position did not present in Debora Bone's research, and would be expected to be very rare, it still might exist.

What should certainly be clear is that disarticulating positions from persons and institutions (individually and collectively) is important in allowing complexities and differences to be more fully represented. Through such mapping

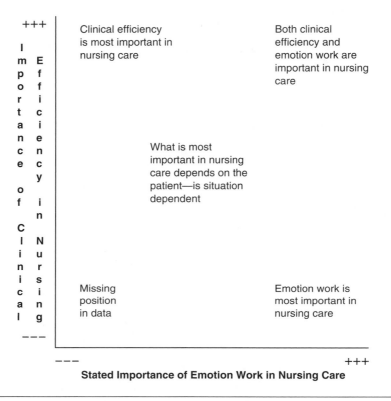

Figure 3.15   Positional Map: Clinical Efficiency and Emotion Work in Nursing Care

and careful articulation of the multiple positions, no set of actors becomes or remains monolithic and unnuanced. Of course, we can critique this map as not sufficiently distinguishing between the two axes—as clinical efficiency can certainly be argued to include sufficient emotion work to "get the job done well." But that does remain a different position than asserting that emotion work is the most important kind of work in nurses' caregiving in the hospital.

Positional Map Exemplar II: Shim's Project

The second exemplar is Shim's research on race, class, gender, and cardio-vascular epidemiologies. In Figure 3.16, Positional Map: Race in Expert Cardiovascular Epidemiology, we see three major positions held down. Working from the top right, the first position holds that race is very significant

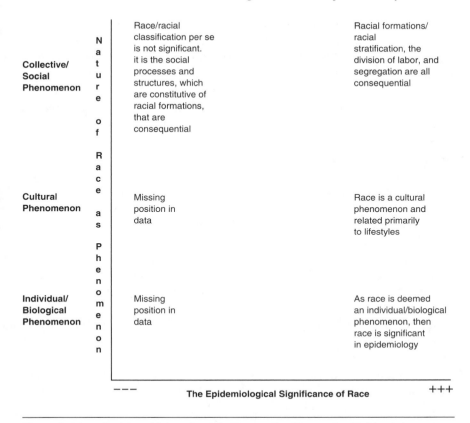

Figure 3.16   Positional Map: Race in Expert Cardiovascular Epidemiology

epidemiologically and that race is a *collective/social phenomenon*. Specifically, racial formations and racial stratification as manifest in the division of labor, institutional and geographic segregation (e.g., from housing to region in the United States), and so on are all consequential for cardiovascular health. The second position is that race is an epidemiologically important *cultural phenomenon* and manifest in lifestyle practices that are consequential for cardiovascular health. This, Shim finds, is a more middle-of-the-road position on race in contemporary epidemiology, especially insofar as it constructs race as more than an individual, biological, and perhaps genetic attribute. The third position holds that race is an epidemiologically significant *individual/biological phenomenon*. (I should also carefully note that the concepts "biological" and "race" are handled quite complexly both within epidemiology and in Shim's work in ways I am *not* detailing here.)

All but one position predicated on race *not* being epidemiologically significant were missing from Shim's data. This is not to say they do not exist within epidemiology, but that after years of research, they did not appear in her data. The one position that did appear, on the top left, is very nuanced. Here it is argued that it is not race in and of itself that is consequential (read it is not race *biologically* that is important). Rather, it is the social processes and structures that constitute racial formations that produce ra*cism*. The position is that ra*cism in its many guises* impacts people of color and has negative consequences for their cardiovascular health.

In sum, in Shim's study, race seems to be a significant variable to most if not all cardiovascular epidemiologists but for different, if sometimes overlapping, reasons. The most nuanced position disarticulates race per se as a property of individuals from the practices of racism. While I will not offer the positional map on class/socioeconomic status for Shim's project, the patterns were essentially the same as for race. Historically, much of epidemiology has been the study of the consequences of the effects of poverty on health, today captured in the new language of "social disparities in health" and "population health."

Figure 3.17 is another positional map of Shim's work, focused this time on sex/gender in expert cardiovascular epidemiology. The left axis on the nature of sex/gender as a variable makes the classic if still problematic social science distinction between sex as a biological category and gender as a performative social category on which various kinds of stratifications systems are built. These include paid employment, work undertaken in families, and other kinds of segregations and stratifications. In between is "sex/gender" as a hybrid nonfungible social category—the elements of which cannot meaningfully be separated. Neither Shim's epidemiologists nor the individuals of color she studied took up this category. It is present in this positional map because it is present theoretically in the social constructionist social sciences today where the assumption that biology is, after all, "really" "underneath it all" is refused. Instead, the relations between what we usually deem "social" and "biological" are viewed as inseparable, coproduced and coconstitutive. In this instance, then, the researcher has clearly stepped into the analysis in terms of constructing the *possible* categories on the positional map. This position was added because it is available to epidemiologists as a conceptual resource in related social science research. This position on sex/gender is also close to the nuanced position on ra*cism* articulated above. The fact that the epidemiologists did not take *any* related positions is quite interesting. This is another way of helping the data speak to silences.

Se*xism* and its consequences are not understood similarly to ra*cism* even among social epidemiologists. Shim's data were actually quite bifurcated here. Most epidemiologists, social and mainstream alike, would support the position that sex as a biological category is fundamentally central to the

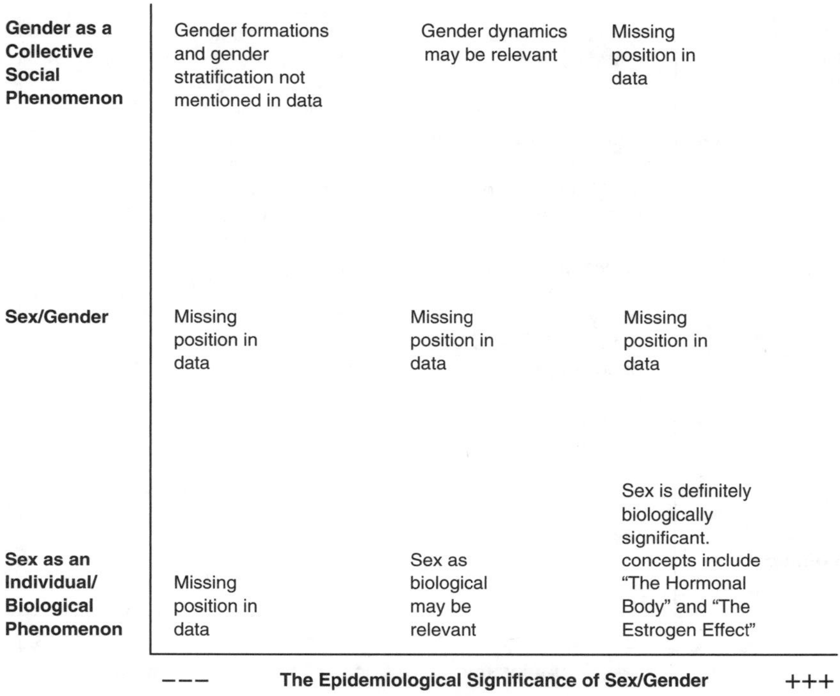

Gender as a Collective Social Phenomenon	Gender formations and gender stratification not mentioned in data	Gender dynamics may be relevant	Missing position in data
Sex/Gender	Missing position in data	Missing position in data	Missing position in data
Sex as an Individual/ Biological Phenomenon	Missing position in data	Sex as biological may be relevant	Sex is definitely biologically significant. concepts include "The Hormonal Body" and "The Estrogen Effect"

‒ ‒ ‒   **The Epidemiological Significance of Sex/Gender**   +++

Figure 3.17   Positional Map: Sex/Gender in Expert Cardiovascular Epidemiology

study of CVD. There is very little doubt in their minds that hormonal and other physiological differences between the categories of persons deemed women and men are significantly responsible for differences in CVD incidence. However, a few epidemiologists question whether gender—that is, power relations and social processes predicated on socially constructed assumptions of difference and hierarchy—might not *also* have effects on cardiovascular risk, the position represented at the top middle site on the positional map. Also, the upper right position, that gender formations and discrimination are consequential, is actually missing in epidemiologists' accounts, and hence missing here. Shim carefully noted, however, that this last position was common in the narratives of the people/patients of color diagnosed with CVD who she interviewed.

Figure 3.18, Positional Map: People/Patients on Causes and "Cures" of CVDs, is a different positional map of Shim's work than the last two and needs some introduction. In examining constructions of "difference" across the "expert"/"lay" divide, Shim found some general differences. The people

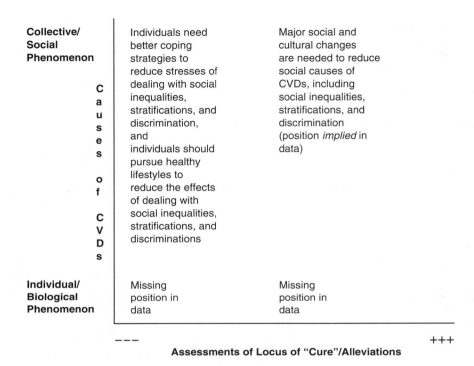

Collective/
Social
Phenomenon

Individuals need better coping strategies to reduce stresses of dealing with social inequalities, stratifications, and discrimination, and individuals should pursue healthy lifestyles to reduce the effects of dealing with social inequalities, stratifications, and discriminations

Major social and cultural changes are needed to reduce social causes of CVDs, including social inequalities, stratifications, and discrimination (position *implied* in data)

C
a
u
s
e
s

o
f

C
V
D
s

Individual/
Biological
Phenomenon

Missing position in data

Missing position in data

– – –   +++

Assessments of Locus of "Cure"/Alleviations

Figure 3.18   Positional Map: People/Patients on Causes and "Cures" of CVDs

of color she interviewed, when providing causal/etiological accounts of their CVDs, implicated complex and interlocking structural social processes. These included the racial and sex/gender divisions of paid and unpaid labor they confronted in their lives, the educational and employment opportunities they did and did not have, and the institutional and personal discrimination they observed and personally experienced. Thus lay epidemiology tended to be very social in its level of conceptualization. That is, for these people/patients, the causes of their CVDs were understood to lie in the highly racially stratified and discriminatory ways in which daily life and broader opportunities to make one's way in life are routinely organized unequally. To them, the concrete and deeply stratifying practices of ra*cism* and sex*ism* were highly consequential for their health.

Looking at the figure, we see first that this map is part of the analysis of the discourse of individualism in Shim's project. It is based on Shim's ironic finding that at the same time some of her participants—the people/patients of color diagnosed with CVDs—viewed the causes of their cardiovascular conditions and diseases as social, they also viewed themselves and their own individual actions as the sole source of improvement or "cure." That is, they articulated a position that *individuals* need better coping strategies to reduce the effects of stress on themselves from dealing with *social* inequalities, stratification, and discrimination. In that upper left position, there was in fact an intense discourse among participants regarding health promotion, healthy lifestyle, educate yourself, and self-awareness—all to be taken up on the *individual* level to counter *social* inequalities, stratification, and discrimination. On the upper right, the need for major social changes to reduce the social causes of CVD was only implied in the data, present but really only hinted at, according to Shim. The other two possible positions were missing from the data.[16]

In contrast, Shim found that the "expert" epidemiologists tend to define "difference" in largely *individualistic* terms: race as *cultural* difference, sex/gender as a *biological* distinction, and to most often conceptualize social class in terms of *individualized measures* of socioeconomic status (occupation, income, and educational attainment). Historically, such conceptions have been widely routinized in epidemiologic research. Shim found that there is a fair amount of controversy and acknowledgment that these interpretations are methodologically and conceptually inadequate in many ways, articulated especially by social epidemiologists. However, despite these controversies, a multitude of other conditions in the broader epidemiological research situation support and facilitate the continued standardization of race, class/sex, and sex in those historic ways in epidemiologic work today. These conditions include regulatory requirements regarding racial and gender representation that emerged from the complex influence of identity politics on late-20th-century U.S. health research; economic and research sponsorship constraints that structure what kinds of theoretical models and raw data—the tools of epidemiologists—are available; funding concerns; and criteria for scientific credibility that circumscribe possibilities of interdisciplinary work. In Shim's project, this story thus links many of the elements of the social worlds/arenas and positional maps together.

Again, we can see in the positional map exemplars the advantages of disarticulating positions from persons and institutions (individually and collectively) in terms of representation of the full range of variation—of differences both within and across groups of actors.

Final Comments on Positional Maps

What is a good enough positional map and how do you know when you have one? First and foremost, the key word again is saturation—from classical grounded theory. Here, saturation means that no hot new issues, axes, or major positions are popping up in new data. You have done positional maps of everything that you think deserves them. Importantly, you have also done memos about the maps as well. Researchers should anticipate doing multiple versions of each positional map—multiple ways of representing a particular issue and positions taken on it—before successfully creating one that is really adequate to the representational tasks of the research. Because the wording is so distilled, capturing nuance and/or detail can be most challenging. Some details and conceptual refinements will, of course, be presented only in the narrative.

Furthermore, any one study will likely produce a number of different positional maps depending upon how many contentious issues there are in the situation of concern. Of course, not all such maps will earn their way into final research products. The researcher's anguish will, as usual, center on which ones to pursue among the (hopefully) dense data. To me, one of the most important aspects of doing positional maps is that they allow the researcher to see possible positions that are *not* taken in the data, positions that remain unarticulated. These possibly silent or silenced positions should trigger theoretical sampling (further data collection) if it seems worthwhile, or at least be otherwise noted in memos. The presence and/or absence of articulations of particular positions in various sites is itself information that aids in the analysis and in situating research more broadly. Silences can be made to speak. Noting silent positions is "speaking" them.

Positional maps may initially seem (too) procedural, formal, or even for-mulaic. Creating them—determining the axes and thinking about possible positions in relation to the actual data—does tend to ease such concerns. They *are* very systematic modes of interrogating data, and systematic approaches do risk rigidities. Yet given the difficulties of thinking about what is *not* there, gaining the ability to explore silences and to articulate positions missing in data make the risks worth taking.

The positional maps I have framed here can also be made using discourse rather than ethnographic data: documents, texts, and images of various kinds. They can also be done comparatively. I discuss such possibilities in Chapters 4-7.

Final Products: Project Maps

> *Undoubtedly, the most difficult skill to learn is "how to make everything come together"—how to integrate one's separate, if cumulative, analyses.*
>
> —Strauss (1987:170)

Project maps are maps of particular projects that may draw upon the three kinds of maps described here and/or traditional grounded theory diagramming but may or may not be identical with them (see note 1). They are no longer maps furthering one's own analysis but instead are maps tailored to explicate particular aspects of a specific project to intended audiences. Thus doing project maps involves developing representational practices that can travel well. The politics and mechanics of representational practices have been of profound importance in qualitative research since the postmodern turn (e.g., Denzin & Lincoln 1994, 2000; Lather & Smithies 1997; Visweswaran 1994), and project maps need careful attention. Here the crossings between text and fieldwork, the narrative and literariness of fieldwork data, and the final papers and book(s) produced from them are foregrounded.

In terms of doing project maps, it is very unlikely that actual situational maps would be used as published project maps. A situational map does not tell an analytic story but rather frames that story through mapping the broader situation as a whole and all the elements in it at a more general and abstract level. In contrast, a relational analysis using a situational map might well be the basis for a project map. Social worlds/arenas maps are also analytic and are very common project maps. They work well at quickly and easily providing research audiences with a big picture into which a narrative portrait can be placed and well situated.

There is no such thing as an "abstract project map," so I cannot offer one. I also cannot use Bone's or Shim's research here, as neither did a project map and I am unwilling to attempt one on a project not my own. The social worlds/arenas/discourses maps I did of their work could, of course, be used as project maps. Positional maps can also work well as project maps and are especially useful where the situation is very complicated and the positions very nuanced. For example, the positional maps we developed around Janet Shim's research would work as good slides or overheads for audiences to ponder while she orally elucidated and illustrated the nuanced positions she found in her data.

Here I briefly present two project maps developed by other students in their dissertation research. Sara Shostak (2003a, 2003b) recently completed a very ambitious dissertation at UCSF titled *Locating Gene-Environment Interaction: Disciplinary Emergence in the Environmental Health Sciences, 1950-2000*. In it she analyzes three emerging social worlds in the environmental health sciences numbered on Figure 3.19 as small circles (1), (2), and (3). Number (1) is molecular epidemiology, (2) is environmental genomics, and (3) is toxicogenomics. Each of these worlds or subworlds is developing a distinctive new technology that is radically changing the nature

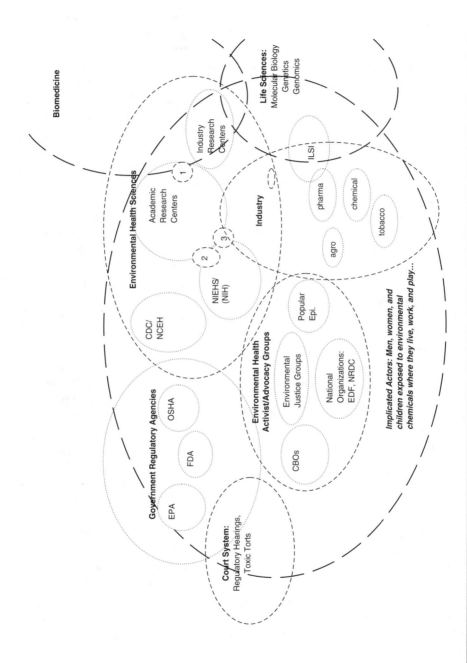

138

Figure 3.19   Shostak's Project Map: The Arena of Environmental Health in the United States

of knowledge production in these specialties and beyond, and Shostak tells these stories in her project. She uses Figure 3.19 to provide an accessible background framing for these stories and to help audiences to understand the intersectional character of these emerging disciplines. While this is a complicated project map, she needs to tell complicated stories, and has found that the map works quite well, especially when left up for the audience to stare at while she speaks.

In another project map example, Carrie Friese, a doctoral sociology student at UCSF, is interested in journalistic/print media discourses about cloning and new reproductive technologies and their production. Her initial project (Friese n.d.) is a content analysis of articles on sex preselection in major American newspapers from circa 2000 to 2004. She has also (Friese 2003) initiated an interview-based study of journalists who have produced in-depth articles on cloning, the focus here. She asks questions about the public understanding of science, the work of the print media in producing such understanding, and the conditions of work and production inside the media that may shape print media discourses on reproductive technologies. For example, does the fact that many newspapers now routinely run advertisements for infertility clinics affect reporting on cloning and stem cells? What are the consequences of the organization of science writers into different departments (business, science/medicine) in newspaper organizations? What are the consequences of the science training sessions (offered by universities, medical schools, and industry, often collaboratively) for science journalists in terms of producing ideoscapes?

Please look at Figure 3.20, Friese's Project Map: Reporting Cloning—Journalists' Perceptions About Relationships Between Science, Media, and Publics. The reporters interviewed essentially mapped their own positions as "in the middle," somewhere between science with its deep governmental linkages and many different publics. They discussed "translating" science to the people—and also discussed how they had to translate it quite similarly to their editors in order to get their articles in print! This is an effective project map that nicely captures how the reporters see the discursive worlds in which they dwell.

I also offer project maps elsewhere in this book. In Chapter 5, there is one based on my narrative discourse analysis. In Chapter 7, I present the project map from my historical discourse analysis of the organization of scientific research materials discussed above (see also Radnofsky, 1996).

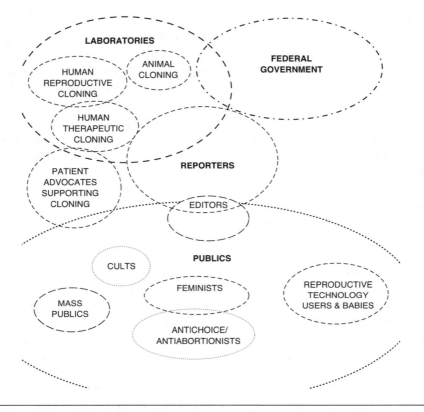

Figure 3.20   Friese's Project Map: Reporting Cloning—Journalists' Perceptions
About Relationships Between Science, Media, and Publics

Provisional Conclusions

*It is important to move away from formulaic criteria for the
adequacy of research. . . . Glaser and Strauss do discuss various particular procedures. But these should not be regarded as
constituting a hard and fast set of recipes.*

—Atkinson et al. (2003:158, 151)

In sum, the three forms of situational maps and analyses elaborated here—
situational maps used for relational analyses, social worlds/arenas maps,
and positional maps—provide new means of entering and mapping data,

situating individuals and collectivities, nonhuman actants, discourses, organizations, and so on. They offer new modes of interrogating data analytically, demanding careful consideration and considerable reflexivity on the part of the researcher. They can supplement and complement "basic social processes" analyses generated through traditional grounded theory. The series of three situational analyses also go beyond basic social processes to structurally situate whole projects in ways that capture fundamental elements of the situation of inquiry. Echoing Atkinson and colleagues' epigraph, these maps are not intended as formulas for analysis, but as directions through which to begin and deepen analytic work, as sites of engagement.

While the format of this chapter features each of these mapping strategies one at a time, they can and usually would be pursued together, some aspects being constructed simultaneously. That is, later in the research process, it is often easier to have all three maps out at the same time, as in working on one of them, ideas for the others will emerge. It is fine to move back and forth among them, so long as a memo is done at the end, characterizing major changes and any new directions for each map.

I also discussed in this chapter that making these maps should make connections in our data that surprise us. The ways we are surprised by some results of our work often demonstrate covert assumptions we have had that we were blind to. Such assumptions had to be revealed to us through counterintuitive results that we were finally somehow able to "see." Certainly we have assumptions we are aware of upon entering the research. Those we can usually be made to articulate through asking ourselves or being asked a few choice questions. What I am trying to point at here is that there are conscious and/or unconscious assumptions as well. I am always very happy when a student discusses being surprised at some outcome because it usually means they are working very hard analytically, confronting themselves as well as the data in seriously reflexive ways. I want to emphasize that surprise at grasping some new position or way of "seeing" something indicates openness to unanticipated data, analyses, and difference(s)—*not* stupidity for not having "seen" it before. Though the very process of analysis strives to open things up, partialities-r-us.

I have also written at length about mapping differences. Yet at the same time as we may target our analysis to seek differences, it remains important to problematize our own concepts and categories. In short, try not to take your own categories for granted but interrogate them as much as you do the categories provided by participants/informants. This involves asking yourself "What do *I* mean by X?" as assiduously as you might ask a participant "What do *you* mean by X?" At such junctures, a working analysis group is invaluable.

Final products using the approaches developed here should show some aspects of what Park (1952), as noted above, called "the big news" and some close-up shots. To do this, one needs to construct the full map(s) sufficiently to at least fully frame the smaller segments selected to be blown up as close-up shots. The TV documentaries by Ken Burns often use this visual strategy with historic photos—starting with a close-up of a person or thing and then pulling far back to show the entire photo—the wider situation. The various exploratory cartographies performed should find their way into memos of various sorts, which can then act as analytic holding places for return visits after the features for "blowing up" have been selected. The next generation of researchers will likely do these maps with specially designed computer graphics programs. All of the diagrams in this book were originally created in MS Word.

Through these mapmaking processes, one is forced to think about the nature of various relationships in the data that otherwise might be unthought and unarticulated. *All mapping strategies are at base relational.* This is a radical aspect of the approaches offered here compared to "normal" social science and positivist approaches that are at base atomistic, based on supposedly isolable "variables," and intentionally decontextualizing (for lack of a better term).

Of course, while the three modes of situational analyses offered here do certain kinds of analytic work very well in terms of structurally situating qualitative projects, they have their own partialities. Some partialities are addressed next, in Chapter 4, where we grapple more explicitly with "the society of the spectacle" (Debord 1967/1999)—the explosion of discourses that constitute the cultures of consumption, the seas of narrative, visual, and historical discourses in which we are all routinely awash. Grounded theorizing after the postmodern turn can be used to more fully address and integrate analyses of many kinds of discourses. The three modes of situational analyses presented here can also be expanded in a variety of interesting and provocative ways, including making linkages to coding diagrams or maps and producing project-specific maps that capture and articulate these analyses.

Notes

1. On coding, see especially Glaser and Strauss (1967:21-43, see also chs. 3 and 5), Glaser (1978:55-82), Strauss (1987:22-109), Strauss and Corbin (1998:55-181), and Charmaz (1995b, 2000, 2001, 2002b, 2003b, 2005, in press). On diagramming, see especially Strauss (1987:130-230) and Strauss and Corbin (1990:195-224, 1998:217-242). For examples of diagrams, see, e.g., Miller (1996) and Kearney, Murphy, Irwin, & Rosenbaum (1995).

2. On memoing, see especially Glaser and Strauss (1967:105-113), Glaser (1978:83-92), Strauss (1987:109-130, 184-214), Strauss and Corbin (1998: 217-242), Charmaz (1995b, 2000, 2001, 2002b, 2003b, 2005), and Charmaz and Mitchell (2001).

3. On theoretical sampling, see especially Glaser and Strauss (1967:45-78), Glaser (1978:36-54), Strauss (1987:16-21, 38-39, 274-277), Strauss and Corbin (1998:201-216), Charmaz (1995b, 2000, 2001, 2002b, 2003b), and Charmaz and Mitchell (2001).

4. On silences, see Poland (1998), Charmaz (2002c), Schoenberg and Drew (2002), Star (1991a), Trepagnier (2001), and Zeruhavel (2002).

5. There is no adequate language for what I am trying to get at here. First, second- and third-world rhetoric at least describes some orderings of power, distributions of capital, and other resources. The terms "less developed," "developing," "more developed," "developed," and "overdeveloped" are highly evaluative in linear, overgeneralizing, and other ways I find problematic, and do not take stagnancy into account, much less the moving toward (sliding back to ?) "less developed" status that is increasingly common. First, second, and third world language also allows one to discuss the complexities of regions, locales, or neighborhoods of third world cultures, lifestyles, and political economies that exist in first and second world nations and regions, and vice versa.

6. These include Moore's (1997) on sex workers and safer sex, Casper's (1998a, 1998b) on fetal surgery, Timmerman's (1999) on CPR, Kearney's (1998; Kearney et al. 1995) on pregnant women using crack cocaine, Wiener's (2000a, 2000b) on accountability in hospitals and (1991) on careers and arenas, Miller's (1996) on new mothers reentering the work place, and all the studies in Strauss and Corbin's edited grounded theory research book (1997).

7. Bone completed the PhD in sociology in 1997. Virginia Olesen chaired her dissertation committee. See Bone (1997, 2002). See also Olesen and Bone (1998) and Bolton (2001) on the United Kingdom. Bone is currently associate professor of nursing at Cabrillo College.

8. Shim's dissertation committee was chaired by Howard Pinderhughes. See Shim (2000, 2002a, 2002b). This writing on her research is based in part on a group analysis session done much in Strauss's (1987) working group tradition with Jennifer Fishman, Jennifer Fosket, Laura Mamo, Janet Shim, and myself on November 2, 2000. Shim is currently on the faculty at UCSF.

9. These are also known as HMOs. Like preferred provider organizations (PPOs), these are private health insurance organizations. They are usually local or regional. Primary care physicians in HMOs do not collect a fee-for-service from each patient but instead are usually on salaries or, more commonly in the United States, are in capitation plans. Here, primary physicians receive a set amount of money that is "capped" for caring for each patient per year, no matter how much or how little care that patient needs or actually gets. The burdens of efficiency management vis-à-vis patient care outside the hospital thus fall in significant proportion on primary care physicians. This is one manifestation of the de facto "rationing" of health care services in the United States today. In PPOs, patients can often go

outside the main providers list, but if they do so, they typically incur greater out-of-pocket costs (copayments). Specialists too confront capitation. Surgeons, for example, may only receive $X for a particular surgery under Insurance Plan A, while Plan B might pay more or less for the identical surgery, depending upon the contract between the specific company and the physician. See also Wiener (2000a).

10. On universes of discourse, see Mead (1927/1964, 1934/1962), Strauss (1978), and Shibutani (1955, 1962, 1986). On situations, see Thomas and Thomas (1928/1978), Thomas (1923/1978), Mills (1940), and this book. On identities, see, e.g., Charmaz (1991), Lal (1996), Coffey (1999), and Zavella (1996). On commitments, entrepreneurs, and mavericks, see Becker (1960, 1963, 1967/1970, 1982). On shared ideologies, see Strauss et al. (1964, 1985/1997). On primary activities, particular sites, and technology(ies), see Strauss (1978) and Strauss et al. (1985/1997). On going concerns, see Hughes (1971). On subworlds/segments and reform movements, see Bucher (1962, 1988), Bucher and Strauss (1961), Bucher and Stelling (1977), and Clarke and Montini (1993). On bandwagons, see Fujimura (1988). On intersections and segmentations, see Strauss (1984) and Clarke (n.d.). On implicated actors and actants, see Clarke and Montini (1993) and Chapter 2. On boundary objects, see Star and Griesemer (1989) and Bowker and Star (1999). On work objects, see Casper (1994, 1998b). On discourses, see Chapters 4-7 herein.

11. The concept of domain here is used in the Straussian sense (see Strauss 1993:240) and Clarke (n.d.), not in the sense Spradley (1979) used it.

12. Patient movements are forms of "biosociality" (Rabinow 1992), often organizing around new "technoscientific identities," identities only determinable through technoscientific means (e.g., medical tests) (Clarke et al. 2003). There is considerable interest in such movements today because of their growing power, including movement organization sponsorship of their own research. See, e.g., Epstein (1996), Brown et al. (2004), Rabeharisoa and Callon (1998), and Ganchoff (2004).

13. See, e.g., Behar (1993), Benner, Tanner, and Chesla (1996), Bochner and Ellis (2001), Chesla (1995), Riessman (1993, 2002), Messias and DeJoseph (n.d.), and Traweek (1999).

14. On representation of difficult situations, see Ellis (1995), Kitzinger (2004), Van Maanen (1995), Fine (1994), Fine, Weis, Weseen, and Mun Wong (2000), Lather (2001a, 2001b), Lather and Smithies (1997), and Bloom (1996, 1998).

15. See Butler (1993) and Star (1995) on "Why I Am Not a Nazi." See also Becker (1967/1970), and on kinds of relativism, Hollis and Lukes (1982).

16. Shim had one caveat here. She did not explicitly ask nor did participants volunteer ideas on how to alleviate CVDs. Thus the upper right position is only implied in their accounts of what they think the causes of their CVDs were, and her asking about race, class, and gender and analytically arguing for a connection. She also carefully notes that sometimes the participants did not make connections between these dynamics and their health. The individual as the site of "cure"/alleviation is so intensely present because the participants all talked about how they managed their risks (or did not) when she asked them about what they thought their risk factors were.

4

Turning to Discourse(s)

*The highest goals of discourse analysis are to support the freedom
of access to knowledge through discourse and to help in revealing
and rebalancing communicative power structures.*

—de Beaugrande (1994:209)

Today the qualitative research enterprise is moving beyond field notes
and interview transcripts to include discourses of all kinds. We dwell,
in postmodern times, in "societ[ies] of the spectacle" (Debord 1967/1999)—
explosions of images, representations, and narrative discourses that constitute cultures of consumption as well as production, of politics writ a million
ways, of diverse individual and collective social and cultural identities,
including racial, ethnic, gendered, religious, and subcultural identities, of
dense histories, of old and new technologies and media from television to the
Internet, and so on. Because *we and the people and things we choose to
study* are all routinely both producing and awash in seas of discourses, analyzing only individual and collective human actors no longer suffices for
many qualitative projects. Increasingly, historical, visual, narrative, and
other discourse materials and nonhuman material cultural objects of all
kinds must be included as elements of our research and subjected to analysis because they are increasingly understood/interpreted as both constitutive
of and consequential for the phenomena we study. Chapters 4-7 therefore
address the postmodern turn to discourse in qualitative research and how
grounded theory and situational analysis can be used to analyze the increasingly heterogeneous forms of data pertinent to qualitative research projects.

145

Current research trends of studying new forms of data and including multiple kinds of data in one study—now called "multisite research"—are cutting across all the social sciences, history, and varied professional domains. Disciplines themselves are being reconfigured and new disciplinary formations established. "Borrowing" new kinds of data and methods across disciplinary boundaries has become common, producing hybrid multi/transdisciplinary projects, and the study of documents, media, and visual materials of all kinds is everywhere taken up. Yet in terms of research on discourses, one problem is that "[t]he dominance of quantitative methods has resulted in an underdeveloped theory of qualitative textual analysis" (Manning & Cullum-Swan 1994:463). Thus the need for new theory/methods packages for qualitative discourse analysis also cuts across the social sciences, humanities, and professional domains.

In drawing grounded theory/situational analysis around the postmodern turn in these chapters on analyzing discourses, I therefore go far beyond saying "just do it"—just go ahead and use grounded theory and situational analysis with extant historical, narrative, and visual discourse materials. Instead, I offer in-depth introductions to discourse studies in general and to all three specialty areas, including overviews of extant theoretical and research approaches and lots of examples. I do so because I suspect that most who will find their way to this book will not have strong training in any of these intellectual terrains. Nor did I. But over the past two-plus decades, I kept finding myself doing grounded theory research with historical, narrative, and visual materials. And I needed the very kind of introductions I am supplying here to facilitate entrée.

Moreover, I see grounded theory and situational analysis as analytic tools that can be used on their own with discourse data and/or along with and complementing other theoretic and analytic approaches already in use. That is, I see qualitative analysis after the postmodern turn as the proper work of bricoleurs (Denzin & Lincoln 1994:2). Bricoleurs assemble project-appropriate tool kits from a broad repertoire of available concepts and approaches—selecting what they believe are "the right tools for the job." We need to keep in mind, of course, that the "tools," the "job," and the "rightness" are all constructions, always already emergent and changing (Clarke & Fujimura 1992/1996). There is no "one right way," and as I stated in Chapter 1, I am not interested in purity. Rather, pragmatist to the core, I am interested in developing interesting and *useful* methods of analysis, useful tools with which to approach a wide array of research projects with quite heterogeneous forms of data. It is the *combination* of the groundedness of interpretation with the systematic handling of data that makes grounded theory and situational analysis robust approaches in qualitative research.

Including narrative, visual, and historical discourse materials in research is part of my project of pushing grounded theory around the postmodern turn through situational analysis. It was, of course, especially Michel Foucault who offered new framings, emphasizing how discourses are produced and how we are constituted through them. This section of the book thus deepens the engagement between interactionism and the work of Foucault discussed in Chapter 2. Here I am "following in Foucault's footsteps" (Prior 1997) and taking grounded theory and situational analysis into sites of his serious theorizing.

There is a fundamental difference between analyzing interview and ethnographic field data and analyzing extant discourses. Historically, the social sciences have been by and large predicated on "'grasp[ing] the native's point of view, his relation to life, to realize *his* vision of *his* world' (Malinowski 1922:25)" (cited in Prior 1997:64; Prior's emphasis). That is, for over a century, focus has been relentlessly on "the knowing subject" in *both* quantitative and qualitative research. However, again in Prior's (1997:64) words:

> This dependence of the social sciences on the knowing subject . . . has itself been consistently questioned during the final decades of the twentieth century. . . . [L]ittle of such introspection, self-reporting, and questioning touches the core of social life because social life is established on mutual social relations of various kinds. That is . . . it is established on forms of collective activity or praxis. . . . [S]ocial science . . . has to look at something that lies beyond . . . individuals.

Prior is amplifying Foucault's call for a focus beyond the knowing subject. Specifically, Foucault argued that his analysis was to be based not on a theory of the knowing subject but rather on a theory of discursive practice. And much of his own work examined discursive rules through which knowledges come to be produced, framed, and displayed.

Interestingly, Prior (1997:65) notes that some sociologists have in fact taken this less trodden route and specifically credits Anselm Strauss as a qualitative sociologist who gave texts pride of place in the sociological study of interaction. Strauss drew, of course, from the long Chicago tradition of analyzing documents of all kinds (Bulmer 1984:89-108). Strauss's project of understanding "the social" assumed that most things of sociological interest were not produced by single individuals but rather by people "doing things together" (Becker 1986), such as producing discourses. Discourses are relentlessly social phenomena. Producing discourses is a form of *social* action: "Discourse is language use relative to social, political and cultural formations—it is language reflecting social order but also language shaping social order, and shaping individuals' interaction with society. This is the key factor explaining why so many academic disciplines entertain the notion of discourse with such commitment" (Jaworski & Coupland 1999a:3).

It is important to grasp the very different issues and projects that proceed under the shared banner of discourse analysis. This chapter therefore continues with an in-depth introduction to discourse analysis as practiced to date. It offers an overview of the major kinds of discourse analysis and short exemplars of each. I then discuss multisite research, focusing on issues of research design and the two modes of using situational analysis in such research.

Introducing Discourse Analysis

> *"Discourse" is now generally used to designate the forms of representation, conventions and habits of language use producing specific fields of culturally and historically located meanings.*
>
> —Brooker (1999:66-67)

But what do I mean by discourse? At minimum, one can say "analysis of discourse is, necessarily, the analysis of language in use" (Jaworski & Coupland 1999a:1). Yet discourse is not limited to language but also includes visual images (e.g., art, film, family photos), symbols (e.g., logos, flags, other icons), nonhuman things/material cultural objects (e.g., chairs, coffee mugs, computers, buildings), and other modes of communication (e.g., nonverbal movements, signals, sounds, music, dance). In any given discourse, multiple modes are typically combined. All of these modes are, as Brooker notes in the epigraph above, "culturally and historically located." All are open to discourse analysis.

Thus we need to start by thinking of the concept of discourse writ large: communication of any kind around/about/on a particular socially or culturally recognizable theme—contemporary and/or historical. Discourse includes "word choice, arguments, warrants, claims, motives, and other purposeful, persuasive features of language, visuals and various artifacts"; discourse frames debates, influences perceptions, and creates objects of knowledge (Lay, Gurak, Gravon, & Myntii 2000:7; see also Chalaby 1996). Discourses are, of course, forms of representation, and Tuchman (1994: 315-316) provides a rich theoretical framing:

> The term representation invokes specific theories. It means much more than depiction, illustration, image or portrayal. Rather, it serves as a referent to postmodernist theories, which see both written documents, [images] and mundane

activities as "texts." Initially based in the ideas of linguist Ferdinand de Saussure, these theories argue that the assumptions of an era (an époque) are both inscribed and embedded in (documentary or lived) texts. Texts are to be analyzed as parts of webs or systems of signification that may be viewed as a "set of language systems." Because language systems are characteristic of an era (place, class or **situation**), one can analyze any particular text in relationship to other texts; that is as part of a *structure* of meaning. Indeed the analyst's . . . task is to elucidate that structure. . . . Poststructuralist notions of representation follow this idea to its logical conclusions. [Bolded emphasis added]

Thus discourses are dense and complex sites for analysis.

Discourse theory has many roots. I focus here on two: (1) social constructionism and ethnography (specifically including symbolic interactionism) and (2) the analytics of power (specifically including Foucault) (Dillon 1994:211). First, discourse concerns *constructions* of meanings—meaning making—by those somehow involved. It includes the communication of such meanings through discursive representations of diverse kinds and, thereby, the discursive constitution of the realms of the possible—"reality." In their canonical *The Social Construction of Reality* (1966), "Berger and Luckman argue that our everyday sense of reality is the product of an ongoing negotiation over the meaning[s] of objects, events, and actions. *In order to understand our construction of the sense of reality, we should . . . concern ourselves . . . with the processes by which that 'reality system' is produced"* (Bazerman 1994:115; emphasis added). We can pay close attention to the production of realities—how the "conditions of possibility" are framed—through discourse analysis.

The second focus of discourse analysis is the analytics of power. Foucault (1972, 1973) moved discourse analysis away from formal linguistic emphases toward framings of discourses as bodies of knowledge constituting sets of practices, distinctive disciplinary formations through which power/knowledge (power as knowledge/knowledge as power) operates. Foucault (1972:80, cited in Jaworski & Coupland 1999a:2) said, "Instead of gradually reducing the rather fluctuating meaning of the word 'discourse,' I believe I have in fact added to its meanings: treating it sometimes as the general domain of all statements, sometimes as an individualizable group of statements, and sometimes as a regulated practice that accounts for a number of statements." All these meanings are in play here.

Discourse analysis has come to the fore since the 1970s—since the postmodern turn hove into view in the social sciences, humanities, and beyond, and the "power/knowledge question" raised by Foucault and others was asked more widely:

> The rise in importance of discourse has coincided with a falling off of intellectual security in what we know and what it means to know—that is, a shift in episte-mology, the theorizing of knowledge. . . . The question of how we build knowl-edge has come more to the fore. . . . [L]anguage ceases to be a neutral medium for the transmission and reception of pre-existing knowledge. It is the key ingre-dient in the very constitution of knowledge. . . . This is the shift often referred to as the "linguistic turn" in the social sciences. (Jaworski & Coupland 1999a:3-4)

If knowledge is power in the Foucaultian sense, attending to the ways in which knowledges are produced, legitimated, and maintained through language/through discourses/through discursive practices becomes central in analyzing power of all kinds.

In research broadly speaking, "Discourse analysis offers a means of exposing or deconstructing the social practices which constitute 'social struc-ture' and what we might call the conventional meaning structures of social life" (Jaworski & Coupland 1999a:6). It is usually (but not always) the analysis of particular sets of texts or narratives chosen because they are *pro-duced by* a particular group or social world in which the researcher is inter-ested, or because they are *about* a particular group or social world or thing(s) in which the researcher is interested. In essence, a discourse claims to properly and adequately describe how X is (or should be) in the world, and a strong discourse analysis would deconstruct and analyze *both* the descriptions and the claims. The conceptual tools of discourse analysis are brought to bear on this data.[1] For example, feminist and antiracist scholars often study how women and people of color are constructed in various pro-fessional discourses (medicine, psychiatry, the law) or in the media, compar-ing these discursive constructions with other, usually rather contradictory, forms of knowledge about the group in question.

Critical discourse analysis "examines the structure of spoken and written texts in search of politically and ideologically salient features, which are con-stitutive of the (re)produced power relations without often being evident to participants" (Jaworski & Coupland 1999a:497; see also Fairclough & Wodak 1997). This is predicated on a Foucaultian analytics of power wherein power is potentially productive as well as controlling and destructive, and cir-culates at every level of action and interaction—preventing, enabling, serving as a resource, flowing sometimes wildly about. I have argued in Chapter 2 that this framing of power overlaps extensively with Strauss's (and others') assumptions about power found in some interactionist frameworks, espe-cially social worlds/arenas and negotiated ordering. Following Mead and others, Strauss (1978) defined social worlds as "universes of discourse." Foucault (1973, 1975, 1979) similarly focused on institutional discourses involved in disciplining (e.g., the clinic, the prison, the human sciences) but also (1975, 1988) on subject making through disciplining. For Foucault, discourses are constitutive of subjectivities; for Strauss, social worlds/arenas are constitutive of their members' identities and ideologies. In taking up discourse, they pointed in similar directions, and both are drawn upon here.

We also need to remember that the social sciences are themselves discourses producing "'regimes of truth'—sets of understandings which legitimate particular social attitudes and practices" (Cameron, Frazer, Harvey, Rampton, & Richardson 1999:141-142). Disciplines are implicated in projects of social control, including by the state, the professions (including education, medicine, etc.), and other agencies that ultimately serve the interests of dominant groups. Of course, not only the social sciences but all disciplines and professions are constituted by and through particular discourses that privilege and marginalize varied sectors. Discourse analysis provides tools to deconstruct and analyze such regimes of truth—discourses through which we ourselves are varyingly disciplined and constituted as people and as scholars. Reflexivity has many faces.

Why Analyze Discourses?

A number of key arguments have been made about the importance of analyzing discourses. Fairclough (1999:203-205) broadly states that discourse analysis should become "part of the methodological armoury of social science" for several reasons. His theoretical reason is that discourses "constitute one important form of social action." The work that language does in the world is worthy of understanding on its own terms. His methodological reason is that "texts constitute a major source of evidence for grounding claims about social structures, relations, and processes." Fairclough's historical reason is that "texts are sensitive barometers of social processes, movement and diversity, and textual analysis can provide particularly good indicators of social change." That is, careful attention to the historical timing of the emergence of new discursive elements and changes in old ones can reveal both the timing and contents of proposals for new ways to construct reality. Last, Fairclough's political reason comes from the critical project: "It is increasingly through texts (notably but by no means only those of the media) that social control and social domination are exercised (and indeed negotiated and resisted)."

Among interactionists who have focused on analyzing media, Altheide (2003:658) considers "the mass media to be our most important social institution" precisely because they are so ubiquitous and powerful in producing "the definitions of situations in social life"; understanding the discursive work of the media is thus "relevant for any attempt to understand 'power in society.'" Denzin (1991) agrees and further argues that the primary commodity that the media produce is audiences that consume discourses.[2] Discourse analysis is valuable precisely because it allows us to connect media representations to people, discourses to our daily practices of subject making (including the resistant). Farnell and Graham (1998:414) similarly argue that

> discourse-centered approaches . . . seek to dissolve the long standing dilemma in Western social theory of how to connect "social structure" and/or "culture" with individual human agency. . . . When . . . persons are viewed . . . as causally empowered embodied agents with unique powers and capacities for making meaning, discursive practices emerge as the means by which social action, cultural knowledge, and social institutions are achieved and enacted.

Analysis at such sites is exciting and valuable.

In an important paper on analyzing documents as discourse, Atkinson and Coffey (1997:45, 47; emphasis added) offer yet another key reason for studying discursive materials:

> [I]t is important to realize the extent to which many cultures and settings are *self-documenting*. . . . [R]esearchers continue to produce ethnographic accounts of complex, literate social worlds as if they were entirely without writing. . . . [T]extual communicative practices are a vital way in which organizations constitute "reality" and the forms of knowledge appropriate to it.

We ignore such data at our analytic peril. Atkinson and Coffey further point out that organizational documents are evidence in their own right of the ways in which organizations seek to present themselves to particular audiences (e.g., annual reports, Web sites). That is, the goal of including such evidence in research design is not to triangulate for the "truth" of interview or ethnographic data, but rather as additional data sources about the world(s) in which you are interested.

Prior (1997:66) elaborates on this point of taking discourse "on its own terms":

> We should treat each text as coherent simply because it is there, lying before us as a unified object. The task of the researcher is therefore to investigate "archeologically," as Foucault might say, the innumerable accidents and myriad twists and turns of human practice that have brought the text to its present form. Qualitative research in this context then, is not so much a question of deciding what a given text or textual extract might mean to a thinking subject as a matter of analyzing

the origins, nature, and structure of the discursive themes by means of which the text has been produced.

The questions become: Where did this text come from? What work is it intended to do in the world? How so?

But texts and images are not all we need to take into discursive account. Nonhuman material cultural objects are also "often of significance because, being disregarded as trivial, they were often a key unchallenged mechanism for social reproduction and ideological dominance. . . . The key theories of material culture developed in the 1980s demonstrated that *social worlds were as much constituted by materiality as the other way around*" (Miller 1998:3; emphasis added). This has led to studies of objects of material culture as analogous with text, certainly including consumer goods as discursive objects. We can study "the social life of things" (see, e.g., Appadurai & Kopytoff 1986; DeGrazia & Furlough 1996; DuGay, Hall, Janes, Mackay, & Negus 1997). And certainly we can study how people deploy things discursively. Studies of fashion, culture, and identity (e.g., Crane 2000; Davis 1992; Kaiser 1990), and subcultures (e.g., Gelder & Thornton 1997) are classic examples. It is important to remember that discourse analysis engages across all of these and there are multiple ways to pursue such questions.

Yet studying discourses can be difficult, as Farnell and Graham (1998: 412) note:

> Analyzing discourses can be challenging on several grounds. One is that they do not stay still. Discourse-centered work emphasizes the heterogeneous, multifunctional, and dynamic character of language use and the central place it occupies in the social construction of reality. . . . According to a discourse-centered framework, culture is an emergent dialogic process, historically transmitted but continually produced and revised through dialogues among its members. It is constantly open to new associations and interpretive moves.

Discourses are, nevertheless, consequential. "They are at one level always already a 'play of signs'; yet at the same time, they are a 'real, effective presence'" (Bolter & Grusin 1999:19). And some discourses are more widely consequential than others, such as those shaping war, elections, and social policy.

Another problem to be aware of vis-à-vis discourse analysis is not being credulous to overly broad claims. Discourses operate at different levels of scale: Families usually have established discourses and so too do organizations, disciplines, nation-states, corporations, and so on. But some argue that there can be "[s]*ocietal-level* analysis of discourse, such as of anti-drunken-driving messages," and that in such analysis, *society is seen as* a "speaker" (Manning & Cullum-Swan 1994:465-466; emphasis added). While I agree that *society* can be *seen as* a "speaker," I would, with Hall and McGinty (2002:303), argue that "[w]ords like society, the state, bureaucracy, and group mask contradiction, complexity, ambiguity and incompleteness." To me, there is no such thing as "society," but rather mosaics of social worlds, arenas, and discourses—some at quite large scales with vast audiences—but never everyone. Even the largest arenas do not extend everywhere. One important task of analyzing discourses is noting their limits.

Moreover, using such a monolithizing term as "society" itself risks hegemonizing dominant discourses as the only possible discourses (vertently or inadvertently). Hegemony, in Fraser's (1997) words, is "Gramsci's term for the discursive face of power, . . . the power to establish the 'common sense' or 'doxa' of a society, the fund of self-evident descriptions of social reality that normally go without saying." So, instead of muttering vaguely about some mythic "society," we need to remember that analytically the "nature and degree of social organization" to which a given discourse pertains "must be an empirical question" (Hall & McGinty 2002:303). Discourses can be dangerous places to get lost.

Genres and Foci of Discourse Analysis

Refer the discourse not to the thought, to the mind, or to the subject which might have given rise to it, but to the practical field in which it is deployed.

—Foucault (1978:15)

As the range and heterogeneity of discourses elaborate, so too does the analysis of discourse. I next introduce an overview framework that I find particularly helpful (see also Lieblich, Tuval-Mashiach, & Zilber 1998). Jaworski and Coupland (1999a:7) assert that "[d]iscourse analysis can range from the description and interpretation of meaning making and meaning understanding in specific situations through to the critical analysis of ideology and access to meaning-making systems and discourse networks." They focus on how different kinds of discourse analysis foreground one or another *substantive feature* of discourses. Their reader in the field (1999b) is organized around four main foci and some particular methods of discourse analysis used to address them. I expanded on their framing here:

- *Sequence and structure of speech and conversation: A focus on form.* The formal organization of speech and conversations is the research object. Methods include conversation analysis, ethnomethodology, anthropological linguistics, and some forms of narrative analysis and feminist narrative analysis (see also Jaworski & Coupland 1999a:215-220).

- *Negotiating discourses in social relationships/interaction: A focus on discursive interaction.* How discourses actually enter into social action/interaction is the research object here. Methods include ethnomethodology, studies of ritual interaction, grounded theory, Goffmanian and related dramaturgic approaches to face-to-face interaction and performativity, and studies in politeness theory (see also Jaworski & Coupland 1999b:291-301).
- *Producing identities and subjectivities through discourse: A focus on subject making.* How particular discourses are taken into account in changing identities and subjectivities is the research focus. Methods include some forms of narrative analysis, including feminist versions, phenomenological approaches, content analysis, grounded theory, and Foucaultian approaches (see also Jaworski & Coupland 1999b:407-414). And last,
- *Producing power/knowledge, ideologies, and control through discourse: A focus on the situation of production.* How discourses are produced, by whom, with what resources, and under what conditions are the research foci. Methods include critical analyses (e.g., Chaplin 1994), Foucaultian discourse analyses, grounded theory, content analysis, and so on (see also Jaworski & Coupland 1999b:495-501).

I am not pursuing here any of the approaches that focus on form. These are distinctive projects with their own elaborate and complex methodologies.

Situational analyses can be done that pursue the remaining three areas of substantive focus: (1) negotiating discourses in social relationships/interaction; (2) producing identities and subjectivities through discourse; and (3) producing power/knowledge, ideologies, and control through discourse. Thus situational analysis is one option within an array of other analytic possibilities that address discursive materials, including narrative analyses, Foucaultian discourse analyses, material cultural analysis, content analysis, and so on. Furthermore, content analysis can also be done using categories generated inductively through grounded theory.[3] Situational analysis may also be used along with other approaches in a complementary fashion to foreground a focus on the situation itself, on the social worlds in the situation and the arenas in which they participate, and/or on positions taken and not taken in the discourses analyzed.

Let me next discuss and give brief examples of research pursued in each of the three areas of substantive focus. But first some caveats. One is that each area should be understood as a large umbrella category containing many and diverse kinds of projects. Furthermore, hybrids are more than possible—they are likely and unavoidable. A study focused on negotiation in interaction will also be concerned with the production of identities and subjectivities. That is, *discourses qua discourses are typically doing all three kinds of work more or less.* What varies is what is foregrounded in the analysis—what the researcher is choosing to feature, to attend to most, to write most about.

Second, one can also read these three areas of focus as describing/operating at different levels of analysis. Studies of negotiating social relationships in (discursive) interaction largely take up discourses produced in and through face-to-face interaction. Studies of producing identities and subjectivities through discourse center on sites where individuals and discourses meet—often where institutions and persons intersect, particular sites of traction for symbolic interactionists historically and today. Studies of producing power/ knowledge, ideologies, and control through discourse typically center on more elaborate and complex social formations that produce their own discourses. Such studies may also engage their interactions/negotiations with related social formations through and about discourse. Since access to many such sites is often limited or restricted, researchers may well be "studying up" when pursuing such sites. Third, discourse analysis can draw upon multiple forms of discourse—narrative, visual, historical, and in varied combinations/ hybridities.

Negotiating Social Relationships in Discursive Interaction

A wide range of studies pursues how social relationships are negotiated in interaction—how discourses actually enter into social action/interaction situations. Here, "[i]nvestigators are interested in how individuals gain rights to particular modes of transforming discourse, or are denied such rights, and [how] the signifying acts of those with status and power achieve performativity (that is, are effective) while those of others fail" (Farnell & Graham 1998: 413). Classic examples include Erving Goffman's studies, such as his work on the presentation of self in everyday life as negotiated interaction (e.g., Goffman 1963a, 1963b) and his work on stigma as interactionally produced through active stigmatizing processes (1963b). As we shall see in Chapter 6, Goffman was also interested in visual discourse analysis.

Another example is Moore's research on the narrative discourses of safer sex. In one paper from this research, Moore (1997) focused intensively on the narratives of sex workers about their in-practice relations with various technologies of safer sex—material cultural objects from male and female condoms to saran wrap and sex toys. Her problematic centered on how public discourses of safer sex (e.g., from sex manuals, CDC public service announcements, and the media) entered into the doing of sex work per se. Her research was done during the early years of the AIDS epidemic, and sex workers were themselves intent upon figuring out how to incorporate safer sex strategies into the sexual activities they offered to clients without disrupting erotic flows. Moore examined the transformative technoscapes of sexuality they produced using latex in innovative ways at the same time that considerable practicality was manifest. One sex worker said of latex: "It's like you use pots and pans to cook. It's the tool." The sex workers needed to learn to use these tools well themselves and to enable their clients to do so also. Moore describes the discursive verbal and choreographic sexual interactional strategies they created to accomplish this.

A classic set of interpretive studies in this genre take up the *performativity* of gender, race, and other forms of difference. In a series of papers that ended up as an important volume (Fenstermaker & West 2002), Fenstermaker, West, Zimmerman, and others studied how the discourses of gender, race, and other social differences enter into the actual doing of interactions of various kinds. Their approach is a kind of ethnomethodological performativity analysis. They wrote: "Rather than a property of individuals, we conceive of *gender as an emergent feature of social situations:* both as an outcome of and a rationale for various social arrangements, and as a means of legitimating one of the most fundamental divisions of society" (Fenstermaker & West 2002:xiii; emphasis added). Racialization and other forms of differentiation are also viewed as interactionally emergent in given situations—and hence open to discursive study. Fenstermaker and West (2002:xv-xvi; emphasis in original) and others were interested in researching "*how* systems of domination operated to produce the outcomes of inequality chronicled so often." That is, playing on the words of the Thomas's dictum, for gender, race, or other difference to be consequential in a given situation, it first needs to be produced/performed in that situation. They therefore did empirical research on how inequality is literally "done" in concrete situated discursive practices—(re)created, enacted, performed, enforced, locally inflected, internalized, sustained—and changed. Studies included recruitment to gender identities, gender and the division of labor, sex and sexuality, cosmetic surgery, affirmative action, and adoption.

A narrative discourse study drew upon talk between medical professionals to focus on the particular kinds of work such discourses perform. Atkinson (1995) concentrated on "doctor-doctor" interactions between hematologists to discover how they produce representations of hematological disorders in actual practice. He captured the polyphony of such interactions by suggesting that medicine is simultaneously expressed in several voices that may conflict, such as the voice of science contrasting with the voice of experience. Atkinson describes much of such talk as a "ritualized liturgy," borrowing a "sensitizing concept" from religious rhetoric to capture how talk about medical cases is a discursive means of affirmation of professional membership—"talking the talk."

Research on negotiating social relationships in discursive interactions is an important area of effort in the social sciences, especially in sociology.

Producing Identities and Subjectivities Through Discourse

Discourses are also the means through which "the pressure of broad social or institutional norms is brought to bear on the identities and classifications of individuals" (Jaworski & Coupland 1999a:6). Discourse analysis can reveal how such systems operate. Here the problematic is how discourses are taken into account in situations where identities and subjectivities are on the line—at issue. These may be experienced as positive or neutral, though my examples are largely negative.

Major sites wherein identities and subjectivities are produced through discourses are the vast and elaborating labyrinths of "people-processing organizations," from medicine to social work to immigration, education, and beyond. Herein individuals are subjected to various kinds of assessments, ratings, certifications, diagnostic classifications, needs assessments and so on, all producing myriad forms of documentation (Atkinson & Coffey 1997:46). Prior (1997:75), for example, analyzed the actual interactions through which psychiatric diagnoses are made, studying both patient-provider interactions and the narrative medical records thereby produced. As texts, these discursive objects "fixed and stabilized [a patient's] biography—[and] followed him wherever he went" (Prior 1997:76). This is one instantiation of what Weber (1946) meant by the term "the iron cage of bureaucracy"—which are now shifting from paper to digital means that can travel fast and far (e.g., Timmermans & Berg 2003).

Bowker and Star (1999), fusing interactionist and Foucaultian approaches, studied classification systems as sites where individuals are constructed through discourses. One of the systems they analyze is the discourse and practices of racial classification under apartheid in South Africa—where a classification system and individuals' biographies met. The discourse was that of apartheid—the legally required spatial, geographic, and social separation of "the races" under white supremacy. Bowker and Star found that in the racial classification system that apartheid instantiated and enforced, there was a "stubborn refusal of 'race' to fit the desired classification system" in concrete practice (Bowker & Star 1999:196). They focused on both the making of the actual classification system (discussion of which would belong below as a study of the production of a discourse) and its application and consequences for the identities of individuals who legally contested their classifications. Actual classifying of people by race was done on the basis of *both* "ideal types" of what the different races "are" and extant forms of practical social reasoning such as routine police practices of classifying by race. Many instances of contested classification were due to the lack of fit between these two modes that positioned certain individuals in situations of "torque" wherein a particular body and its multiple identities, communities, and lived experiences cannot be aligned with the classification system(s). People's "lives [we]re then broken, twisted and torqued by their encounters with classification systems" as they were not allowed by law to live where or with whom they believed they belonged, based on their lives to that point (Bowker & Star 1999:26). Classification can be a brutal element of discursive identity and subjectivity formation.

Research on discourses and individual lived experiences is especially liminal and vivid around contested and/or ambiguous and uncertain diseases/conditions (Bell 2000). One example from the patient's perspective is Susan Greenhalgh's (2001) book on being misdiagnosed as having fibromyalgia and struggling with the disease discourse, illness, and identity issues ad nauseum, including Web site data. Another example from women's/patients' experience is Lather and Smithies's (1997) book about and for women living with HIV/AIDs that creatively uses a split-text format to "give voice" to different participants (often as they negotiated how they were being discursively constructed by others) and to themselves as the researchers.

Kristen Karlberg (2000) has studied medical professionals in genetic counseling wherein patients (and later their relatives) may totally unexpectedly find out they are carriers of genetic disease—emergent technoscientific identities that must somehow be negotiated (Clarke et al. 2003). Karlberg found that two major work ideologies were implemented by the professionals to handle the notorious ambiguities and uncertainties of genetic diagnosis: assessing the patient and tailoring the information given to the patient based on that assessment. Thus the professionals' discourse is not "the same" for different individual patients.

Media studies are major sites of discourse analysis "where individuals and discourses meet" (Hughes 1971). There are long research traditions in cultural studies, communications studies, and related areas that focus in two main directions. The first direction analyzes media products (from newspaper stories to movies to ads, etc.), and these studies usually fall in the category discussed below on "producing discourses." The second direction media studies often take is research on audiences of various kinds (their perceptions, reactions, interpretations, etc.). Of course, there is considerable focus group and market research at this intersection, but there is also serious recent interest in grasping the heterogeneities of "spectatorship." This has focused on whether there are distinctive differences within and across particular groups of spectators (e.g., female, male, working-class, racial, queer, etc.), though it is now assumed that one need not be a member of a particular group to occupy that group's spectator position (e.g., Kress & van Leeuwen

1999; Sturken & Cartwright 2001:367). Today, many if not most media combine visual with narrative discourses, and I discuss this in greater detail in Chapter 6.

Different media produce not only different discourses but different modes of discourse—ways of communicating with combined visual, narrative, and audio elements that themselves construct new "communications identities and subjectivities." One such mode is called the "e[lectronic] audience" producing new "information technology personas" (e.g., Altheide 2002a; see also Altheide 1996). Online research projects pursue studies of "online" personas in various game and chat discourse situations, study individuals in relation to Web site construction and use, and individuals in relation to various online networks (e.g., Heath et al. 1999; Jones 1999; Lyman & Wakeford 1999). Race discourses in cyberspace have been a recent focus (Kolko, Nakamura, & Rodman 2000).

Sites where individuals and discourses meet and identities and subjectivities are produced will continue to elaborate and increasingly be sites of significance for qualitative research.

Producing Power/Knowledge, Ideologies, and Control Through Discourse

Here we are concerned with discourse/text as product: Who made it, how, and with what goals and consequences? "A representation should be understood not as a true and accurate reflection of some aspect of an external world, but as something to be explained and accounted for through the discursive rules and themes that predominate in a particular sociohistorical context" (Prior 1997:70). Foucault (1972) argued further that a given discourse not only sets limits and restricts that which can be said about a phenomenon but also, in the positivity of power, empowers certain agents to speak and make representations, while also disempowering others from doing so. That is, discourses are forms of knowledge that set "conditions of possibility." This framing of the project of discourse analysis guides us toward studies of social worlds authorized to produce certain kinds of representations through studying the discourses they produce. Such studies are particularly congruent with the analytic tools of situational analysis.

Discourses are typically produced by and representative of particular social worlds and arenas and the conflicts and contradictions within them. One can actually do a "gestalt switch" and view arenas not as composed of social worlds but rather as arenas of related (and usually competing) discourses. To enter any arena is to plunge into a sea of discourses. Whether one "leads" analytically with social worlds or discourses (which can be viewed as "flip sides"), things quickly become more complex. Social worlds themselves are not monolithic but typically contain multiple segments (Bucher 1962) and positions, and even one segment can contain differences and contradictions. Hence even one world in an arena can and usually does produce multiple and conflicting discourses focused on the same topic. Thus pursuing a discourse analysis of an arena is a complicated project. Meanings are often layered as well as multivocal and contingent on the situation (e.g., Star & Strauss 1998). Long-lived discourses—discourses with histories—are commonly quite multilayered.

Another concept that is significant in critical discourse studies is "ideology." Jaworski and Coupland (1999b:496) "understand the term *ideology* as social (general and abstract) representations shared by members of a group and used by them to accomplish everyday social practices: acting and communicating. . . . These representations are organized into systems . . . which are deployed . . . 'in order to make sense of, figure out, and render intelligible the way society works'" (Hall 1996:26). This definition, citing cultural studies theorist Stuart Hall, overlaps extensively with Strauss (1978) and Becker's (1982) framing of social worlds as always having ideologies of some sort because ideologies are requisite to organize the practices and work of that world. "As meanings collect under an ideological canopy, unpacking them becomes more complex and problematic" (Manning & Cullum-Swan 1994:467).

Foucault and many others also assert that some aspects of discourses "never surface directly as texts" (Jaworski & Coupland 1999a:7). "[T]he visibility required by a discourse in the field of representation is directly proportional to the invisibility of what the discourse is intended to exclude from that field; showing more in order to hide better is the principle" (Apollon 1996:xxiv). For example, in a study that tracked relentless media-generated discourses of fear and crime in the United States when crime rates were actually dropping dramatically, Altheide (2002b:184) asks: "What happens to other discourses—of trust, community, and fellowship, for example—in the face of the discourse of fear?" Specifying such discursive displacements and repressions is an important part of the analysis of such materials. Thus the positional maps done as part of situational analysis are very useful here.

For example, working in the Foucaultian tradition, Lindsay Prior (1997:67) is interested in how "[t]extually ordered knowledge packages and stabilizes the order of things as they appear within a wider realm of discourse. Indeed a text instructs us how to see the world, how to differentiate the parts within it." Prior does a historical discourse analysis of the World Health Organization's classification of causes of disease and death—the International Classification of Diseases (ICD) as a set of texts. It is, he found, a very Western set of documents, framed largely within the discursive categories of Western biological and medical sciences of the individualized body and Judeo-Christian frameworks of causality: "There is thus no reference to ill-luck, malfeasance, or misfortune, nor to more mundane ideas such as poverty or old age or exhaustion here," although there were in past versions of the ICD. Prior (1997:67) therefore genealogically traces the disappearance of some categories and the appearance of others over time. Today, one is not allowed by the ICD to die of sorcery or witchcraft. Nor, interestingly, can one die of a nuclear accident such as Chernobyl. Thus one can read the development and spread of the use of the ICD as a major activity in the globalization of Western medicine, one that began in the 18th century (Foucault 1975). Here we see how a discursive representation can be stunningly consequential both at the level of the historical organization of the nation-state and also, closer to home, in the coroner's office, where the causes of individual deaths are "determined"/constructed (e.g., Bowker & Star 1999; Timmermans 2002, in press). Many other studies of medical diagnostics have been done that take up differential diagnoses according to gender and race, especially but not only in psychiatry.

A recent project on sexology by Jennifer Fishman (2003) follows the discourse and categories in "reverse" direction. Through her work on Viagra, Fishman discovered that a group of medical professionals (especially but not only urologists) are reorganizing the diagnostic categories of sexual "diseases" based not on research on diseases of sexuality per se but rather on new drugs and their areas of effectiveness. That is, new discourses of "disorders of desire" in both men and women are being created as diagnostic categories (usable for insurance coverage) that correlate with new drugs as the drugs become available to prescribe. The research is organized as clinical trials for the drugs rather than as clinical research on disease. Capital is thus "driving" medicine in new discursive directions.

Nancy Naples and Herb Gottweis have taken critical discourse analysis into social movement and policy domains. Naples (2003:9) combines a materialist feminist approach with Foucauldian discourse analysis "to reveal how the shifting patterns of gender, race, class, region . . . shape whose voices are represented and heard within the process of social movement framing of 'community control.'" She was interested in how, despite initially successful progressive framing of particular social issues, the critical feminist and/or other progressive elements soon "get lost" in the discourse, displaced by others' elements. In policy domains, Naples studied the U.S. Congress's dismantling of welfare "as we knew it" through discursive strategies such as the privileging of narrative individualist and coercive behavioral strategies and the silencing of social structural analyses of the causes and consequences of impoverishment. Gottweis (1998:3), a political scientist, uses discourse analysis strategies to create a new and exciting form of poststructuralist science and technology policy analysis: "For social scientists, the most important analytic message of poststructuralism may be the need to pay careful attention to the complicated ways in which language and discourse are used to constitute social, economic, scientific or political phenomena, to endow them with meaning, and to influence their operation." Drawing upon historical as well as contemporary visual and narrative materials, Gottweis combines the study of important political actors with the discourses they produce in the areas of genetic engineering and stem cell research, including comparative international work. These are the new discourses of "life itself" (N. Rose 2001), important sites for research.

Hybrid Examples

Few studies fit neatly into the three categories above. Some researchers actually combine studies at different levels of analysis in one project. For example, Van Dijk (1999) studied narrative denials of racism as integral parts of racist discourse in face-to-face interaction, in the press, and in parliamentary debates. He found that the more racist the discourse, the more denials of racism were articulated. "Besides positive self-presentation and negative other-presentation, such discourse signals group membership, white ingroup allegiances and, more generally, the various conditions for the reproduction of the white group and their dominance in virtually all social, political and cultural domains" (Van Dijk 1999:542). Denials of racism in essence do the work of maintaining racist discourse interpersonally, in politics, in the media, and beyond. They keep racist discourses "alive and well."

Another excellent hybrid example is Press and Cole's (1999) *Speaking of Abortion: Television and Authority in the Lives of Women.* They comparatively examine visual television portrayals of social class in relation to abortion (where economically needy women predominate over middle-class women in seeking abortion) and everyday women's narrative discourse on the same topic generated through focus groups of friends who watched a television show about abortion together. While the television portrayals were narrow and predictable, they found an incredible diversity of positions among the women in the focus groups—across class and race.

A final example that stretches across categories is the Gay and Lesbian Alliance Against Defamation (GLAAD) Dissertation Fellowship Program (see www.glaad.org). This relatively new and intensively discourse-focused program "solicits proposals for original, creative, and rigorous research on the cultural, institutional, economic, social, and political dimensions of gay, lesbian, bisexual, and transgender *representations,* and the ways in which such representations are generated, interpreted, mobilized, and contested in a variety of genres and contexts, including historical and cross-cultural work." Their Web site offers examples of possible research topics, most if not all of which center on the analysis of visual and narrative discourses. In reading through this list, I suggest you keep in mind that one could substitute *any* particular community/social grouping for "lesbian, gay, bisexual, and transgender," including disciplines, professions, and industries such as defense or pharmaceuticals in the following possibilities:

- Ways in which the economic and social organization of media industries influence representations of lesbian, gay, bisexual, and transgender people
- The formation and development of independent media sectors by and for lesbian, gay, bisexual, and transgender people
- The reception of lesbian, gay, bisexual, and transgender television characters by a range of audience groups
- Public opinion on lesbian, gay, bisexual, and transgender issues
- The development of and political intervention by antigay media campaigns
- The social and cultural significance of the erotic press for lesbian, gay, bisexual, and transgender people
- Media coverage of state and/or federal legislative reform in contemporary and historical contexts
- Media images of AIDS activism and of people with AIDS/HIV
- Representations of lesbian, gay, bisexual, and transgender minorities in entertainment or news media
- The ways in which lesbian, gay, bisexual, and transgender issues of equity and diversity have been addressed in contemporary or historical media contexts
- Youth-oriented images of lesbian, gay, bisexual, and transgender people, including such educational materials as textbooks and classroom videos
- Queer cultures in cyberspace

These heterogeneous examples of narrative, visual, and historical discourse studies (GLAAD's list and the others discussed in this section) should provoke interesting ideas for discourse studies of many kinds. All can be pursued using grounded theory and situational analysis. Let us turn next to key issues in multisite research.

Multisite/Multiscape Research

Multisite research "arises in response to empirical changes in the world and therefore to transformed locations of cultural production."

—Marcus (1995:97)

Situational analysis addresses the increasing need for what is now being called multisite research—projects that examine multiple kinds of data from a particular situation of inquiry, including discourses. This involves diverse approaches that move us away from single-site, intensive, immersed ethnographies or interview studies of the past. Today we seek to better capture the increasingly complex, diffuse, geographically, discursively, and/or otherwise dispersed aspects of research topics of interest to scholars in the social sciences, humanities, and professions.

George Marcus (1995:97), the anthropologist who initially wrote about multisite research, captures the fundamental basis for such projects: "Empirically following the thread of cultural process itself impels the move toward multi-sited ethnography." But one can also argue that multisite/multiscape research is not new, more newly named and (re)framed.[4] Many if not most ethnographies have been multisited, if not with the breadth we are now seeing. What is different today is that the researcher, at design and later research stages, explicitly designates an array of possible sites the study of which would contribute to both a broad and deeply *empirically* grounded understanding of the phenomenon of interest. Given that anthropology has pursued projects all over the world, including phenomena that themselves have traveled the globe, it is not surprising that anthropologists have pioneered multisite research.

In one of the more ambitious attempts to address global processes, Arjun Appadurai (1996:33-35) has argued that "[t]he complexity of the current global economy has to do with certain fundamental disjunctures between economy, culture and politics that we have only begun to theorize." He then proposes five dimensions of global cultural flows that can help us to explore such disjunctures. The suffix "scapes" in each indicates that these are highly perspectival, hence multiple. Heterogeneous views exist discursively and await our analysis:

- *Ethnoscapes:* The fluid and increasingly heterogeneous landscapes of persons, identities, and subjectivities that constitute the shifting worlds in which we live
- *Mediascapes:* The expanding distribution of electronic capabilities to produce and disseminate information (from print to television to films and emergent forms) and the varyingly inflected images of the world thereby produced
- *Technoscapes:* The fluid global configurations of technologies, and the ways in which both high-tech and low-tech, mechanical and informational, modes move at high speeds across heretofore uncrossed boundaries into/producing new scapes
- *Financescapes:* The disposition of capital through a global grid of currency speculation and capital transfer flows along with the production and distribution of more kinds of things through ever more dispersed landscapes

- *Ideoscapes:* Concatenations of images and ideologies, like mediascapes, but usually having to do directly with politics, including the ideologies of states, of movements seeking to capture state power, often using the terms "freedom," "welfare," "rights," "sovereignty," "citizenship," "representation," and "democracy"

All these new scapes and others unspecified here are building blocks, mutually imbrocated, of the *imagined worlds* in which we live—"[m]ultiple worlds constituted by the historically situated imaginations of persons and groups spread around the globe" (Appadurai 1996:33). I find Appadurai's scapes to be provocative tools to think with in terms of designing multisite or multiscape research. These five elements are fundamental to many if not most research questions, and may open up how we think about designing a project to include analyzing pertinent discourse(s) from the outset.

In another provocative move, Steiner Kvale (1996) framed modern and postmodern knowledge production processes by contrasting a mining metaphor with a traveling metaphor. In modernist mining, knowledge is buried, waiting to be uncovered by human research via the individual inter- view, purified through transcription, and then conveyor-belted to validity via correlation with others. In postmodern traveling, knowledge consists in heterogeneous discourses gathered by the traveling researcher, entering into conversations, noticing sites and images along the way, gathering stories and available "collectibles"—stuff of all sorts. The researcher wanders about asking questions and reconstructs the answers as new stories to be told of his or her adventures. Postmodern knowledge is validated through prac- tice(s). The postmodern is complicated, impure, messy, full of different kinds of "stuff" that the researcher collected and now must somehow handle— rather like life itself. "The ethnographer must, like a surrealist, be . . . open to objects trouvés, after arriving in the field. This approach invariably affects the subsequent interpretation and analysis" (Okely 1994:19). Kvale also noted that "interview only" studies were becoming less common and are increasingly viewed as less adequate to the research task. Multisite/ multiscape projects produced through traveling are multiplying.

Obviously, such projects challenge extant data-gathering strategies that must now be expanded. The goal is to gather appropriate data for multi- site/multiscape projects, including the nonhuman, historical data, visual data, and other narrative discourse data. Data sources must be specified explicitly, then enter the research design, and be collected. Importantly, multisite research does *not* mean that any single research project has covered/researched *all* the sites that could help one understand a given phenomenon. But living with the tension between density and chaos that characterizes multisite work will likely be an ongoing part of the research experience.

Multisite/multiscape research challenges us with a host of questions and decisions. First, how do we decide what kinds of data are important to gather? Then, how do we collect and handle heterogeneous data sources and do so with some version of a reasonably systematic approach in order to use those data productively? If the approach is too rigid, we will likely miss gathering important "collectibles," and if too sloppy, we will likely end up unable to adequately defend some of our (likely favorite) arguments due to inadequate data, inadequate documentation, and/or inadequate analysis. The often challenging major research design task for multisite/multiscape research, then, is deciding which among the multiple possible sites are most worth exploring, will fit together relatively coherently, will provide valuable data, "make sense" together, and so on. One must, of course, reserve the right to add and/or delete additional sites later. In fact, doing so should be understood as a form of theoretical sampling specific to multisite/multiscape research. It is rare that one can determine "all" the "proper," "best," "possible/feasible" sites in advance. But, thoughtful, careful, initial multisite design is best and can help avoid costly misadventures.

An Exemplar of Multisite/Multiscape Research: Rapp's *Testing Women/Testing the Fetus*

> *Our ethnographic work is continuously relocated in practice as we incorporate an appreciation of lack of holism, nonclosure, and self-positioning into the representations of the phenomena we study.*
>
> —Rapp (1999b:12)

Among the most ambitious recent exemplars of multisite/multiscape research is the work of Rayna Rapp (1999b) on the emergence of prenatal genetic testing offered as part of public health screening to all pregnant women in New York City. Rapp initially got into this project through personal experience, having chosen to have amniocentesis for a pregnancy when she was older, gotten a diagnosis of a Down syndrome fetus, and then chose to have an abortion despite very much wanting a child at that time. Rapp wrote about this experience in *Ms.* magazine in 1984 as a feminist advocate of reproductive rights personally confronting an anguished situation. She had such extensive and intriguing responses from readers that she decided to undertake a full-blown research project. It took 15 years and transformed her life. Rapp's (1999b) multisite/multiscape research project ultimately included the following:

- In-depth interviews with 155 women from multiple health clinics, of highly heterogeneous racial/ethnic backgrounds (ethnoscapes in Appadurai's terms; and we might add genderscapes)
- In-depth interviews with 15 of the male partners of these women (also ethnoscapes; and genderscapes)
- Extended ethnographic observations and interviews in a city laboratory where the prenatal tests—amniocenteses—were processed (technoscapes)
- Extended ethnographic observations and interviews with members of a Parents of Down Syndrome Children Group (both ethnoscapes and ideoscapes)
- Extensive interviewing of about 50 genetic counselors (ethnoscapes, technoscapes, and ideoscapes)
- Extended ethnographic observations of genetic counseling and related professional association meetings (ethnoscapes, technoscapes, and ideoscapes)

I am using Rapp's work as an extreme exemplar here, as her project was much too ambitious for most researchers to be able to undertake. But in her publications, Rapp is beautifully reflexive on the research process. She vividly articulates (Rapp 1999a, 1999b) how the pieces of her research both fit together and fail to do so, worked wonderfully, abysmally, and ultimately at least satisfactorily, how the research process can easily bleed into everyday life, and what is gained—and lost—through multisite research. The book is clearly the work of a mature scholar, profoundly instructive about the research process as well as its products. Reading her work would probably constitute the best possible preparation for multisite/multiscape research design and execution.[5]

While I am not at all suggesting that Rapp should have done so (and would have counseled against it if asked, given the project as laid out above), let us now use her work as an exemplar to look briefly at some historical, visual, and narrative discursive materials that could have appropriately been included in this project. One of the key findings of Rapp's research was that women undergoing prenatal testing today are "moral pioneers" as they enter a new social, cultural, and technoscientific territory—a new technoscape—and do so largely on their own. But they are also parts of distinctive familial configurations and ethnoscapes that shape their ways and means of pioneering. This new territory/social space has been produced through technoscientific innovations recently translated into a state-sponsored public health screening program for detecting genetic fetal abnormalities offered to *all* pregnant women in New York City as part of routine prenatal care (a field of practices). The tests themselves are far from perfect: Both false negatives and false positives are possible. The only "treatment" for a diagnosed fetal abnormality as yet available is abortion. The genetic counselors who work in such programs are usually trained within intense "information-based" and "client-as-decision-maker" frameworks. And there are few guidelines for pregnant women's decision making about the complex moral issues involved in possibly terminating a pregnancy that might (or might not, if the diagnosis is wrong) result in a disabled baby. Thus regardless of their own desires, the pregnant women are constituted as "moral pioneers" through having to deal with the offer of this new technology—they are forced to accept or refuse it, and also to somehow address the consequences of their decision.

Yet (some) women have always had babies. A historically oriented approach to research design here might ask whether there has been earlier research about how pregnant women have engaged other new technoscientific innovations that might be consequential for their pregnancies (e.g., the use of massage and other techniques to reposition the fetus for a safer birth; the use of pain medications in delivery; the shift from using midwives as experts in pregnancy and birth to using physicians). This would, of course, mean seeking out extant historical research (the secondary historical literature) and possibly primary (original source) materials.[6] There are also contemporarily executed projects that retrospectively explore older women's experiences of mothering when they were young, such as Jacquelyn Litt's (2000) *Medicalized Motherhood: Perspective From the Lives of African-American and Jewish Women*. Litt sought to understand how her participants related to the new discourse of "scientific motherhood" that was rife in the 1930s and 1940s. They had mothered during these years as Dr. Spock became the guiding cultural voice of modern expertise in a new technoscape—producing a new professionalized discourse on good mothering that has disciplined and (re)constituted mothers and others ever since.

But, interestingly, today such historical research efforts on a particular project could also include a review of the pertinent social science research done across the 20th century. That is, we now have about a century's worth of published social science research, and such works can themselves now be treated as primary historical data on how social scientists approached these issues in past eras. The research reports have themselves become historical cultural documents. Analytic questions could include: What forms did the research discourse take? How were pregnant and nonpregnant women discursively constructed by the researchers? Were the risks of having a disabled baby articulated or not? How were fetuses and babies differently or similarly constructed? How were different disabilities discursively constructed? That is, rather than view such projects as "outdated research" not worth bothering with, they should be seen as rich historical artifacts in themselves, now open to analysis *qua historical discourses*. Taking up this literature involves doing a historicizing literature review. It is, of course, revealing of the history of social science, reminding us of Saussure's point that the assumptions of an era are inscribed in its texts—in its discourses.

In terms of the possible contributions of a visual cultural studies/media-scape component to Rapp's project, several can be conceptualized. Certainly a study of the images on all the materials distributed to the pregnant women in New York City about prenatal genetic testing would be a likely pursuit. Were there logos and other similar symbols situating the testing endeavor in commercialized discourses, as is now common in recruitment materials for participation in clinical trials (Fosket 2002)? Were there photographs or images of people? Who was imaged and how? Who was not imaged? Were disabilities imaged in any ways? How? Were there diagrams about the procedures? Graphs of possible results? How was the test "marketed" to pregnant women overall? Other companion studies of related visual images could take up mass-media portrayals of prenatal testing, for example, in movies, television soap operas, sitcoms, or Web sites.

Grounded theory has also been known as "the constant comparative method" wherein comparison cases are explicitly sought out and used rhetorically by the researcher to provoke analysis (e.g., Glaser 1969). One contemporary discursive comparison case for Rapp's work could be infertile women. One of the fascinating findings regarding infertility is that infertile women's and men's deep commitments to using reproductive technologies that aid in conception and "treat" infertility are sustained despite the fact that significantly more babies conceived through in vitro fertilization themselves turn out to have health problems and disabilities than babies conceived through intercourse (Jackson, Gibson, Wu, & Croughan 2004). In Becker's (2000; Becker & Nachtigall 1994) work on infertility, she found that *none* of the infertile couples she studied talked about the risks of having a disabled child, even when they did talk about risks. In Rapp's study, pregnant women are offered the means to avoid some of the risks of having a disabled child, while in Becker's work, nonpregnant women undergoing infertility treatment are apparently willing to take those risks, if those risks are even "visible" to them.

Any of the possible additions to Rayna Rapp's project that I have sketched out here could easily turn out to be not worth pursuing very far or could make a great addition to that project. Actually trying out multiple sites may be necessary to see which may be worth pursuing further. It is important to remember that abandoning a selected site should not be viewed as failure.

Rather, this trying out of sites should be viewed as theoretical sampling where you seek out particular kinds of data in order to analytically explore some idea. Let us now turn to some related issues in situational analysis of discourse.

Issues in Situational Analysis of Discourse(s)

Frames are like the border around a picture that separates it from the wall and from other possibilities.

—Altheide (2002b:176)

Thus far in this chapter we have examined the field of discourse analysis and the wide range of research pursued under that rubric. We have also examined the emergent mode of qualitative research as multisite/multiscape, often drawing ethnographic/interview research together with research on discourse sites in the same project. The rest of this chapter begins to relate these to doing situational analysis of discourse(s). I focus on the three main differences one confronts as a reflexive researcher in doing situational analysis of discourse materials: (1) issues of research design and data gathering, (2) differences between situational analysis and most other modes of discourse analysis, and (3) how situational analyses themselves can be pursued across multiple sites.

Research Design: Selecting (Multiple) Sites/Scapes

This calls for both a responsible intersubjectivity and for an itinerant methodological approach that traces connections.

—Heath et al. (1999:452)

Multisite/multiscape research opens up what constitutes the research situation. It brings us closer to the messy complexities that constitute "life itself." But it also places additional burdens of design, data gathering, analysis, and accountability on us as researchers and can be quite daunting. The understanding that all understanding—and research—is partial and provisional can allow us to continue in the face of such uncertainties. Let us now turn briefly to questions of what sites one might want to consider including in a multisite/multiscape study, what data to gather, which discourses might be of interest, how much interest, and so on.

Many if not most of the topics of research interest to scholars in the social sciences and humanities are associated with historical, visual, and a variety of narrative popular cultural and other discourses. In designing a major research project today, say, for example, for a doctoral dissertation or an academic book, the researcher might well want to include the analysis of specific related historical, narrative, or visual discourses as one or two chapters, in addition to interview and/or ethnographic research. Or for a smaller project, one might want to analyze the visual culture of a particular social world (e.g., Web sites on a particular women's health issue), or the popular cultural discourse around a particular social problem (e.g., homelessness) in a particular locale. Situational analysis of the discourse data can be most useful here.

A key issue is research design: careful, strategic, and thoughtful selection of the discourse data to analyze. One is usually choosing from among a wide variety of possibilities, but the data may be more or less available, thorough, accessible, detailed, and so on. One might also want to set careful boundaries to delimit the domain of discourses to be addressed to avoid biting off more than one can conceptually chew! Few of us could successfully complete a study as ambitious as Rayna Rapp's even without the possible extensions I sketched. But we can certainly complexify our projects productively through adding discursive sites of inquiry and analyzing them integratively and/or comparatively (discussed below).

Let me give some examples, starting from a minimalist approach. Two of my students, Mamo and Fishman (2001), analyzed combined visual and narrative promotional materials for Viagra, one among many new pharmacological technologies often dubbed "lifestyle drugs" that promise to refashion the body with transformative, life-enhancing results. Specifically, Viagra enables most men to have stronger and longer-lasting erections. Fishman and Mamo looked *only* at print and television advertisements and the materials put out by the company itself—Pfizer—including its Web site. They found that the Viagra materials perform cultural/ideological work through *both* discursive scripts and visual images. That is, the scripts and images worked together to reinforce and augment the inscription of dominant cultural narratives onto material bodies, particularly narratives of hegemonic masculinity and heterosexuality. Yet they also found that, through both subtexts and imaged signals, Viagra advertising strategies simultaneously seek to undermine narratives of conventional heterosexual coupledom to transgressively create a more open market for heterogeneous (off label) users, including gay men and any and all women. That is, the intent of the ads was to generate "complex spectatorship"—to allow and encourage a wide range of viewers, here as potential consumers (discussed in Chapter 6). This study led one of the students, Fishman (2003), to pursue a dissertation noted earlier on the biomedical construction of new "disorders of desire."

Moore's (1996) dissertation research focused completely on the production and content of narrative (and some visual) discourses about safer sex toward the goal of prevention of HIV/AIDS generated through three "sites": (1) the public service announcements of the U.S. Centers for Disease Control about HIV/AIDS and safer sex; (2) recently published sex manuals, focusing on the sections about HIV/AIDS and safer sex; and (3) sex workers' narratives about practicing safer sex from in-depth interviews (noted earlier). She used a combination of grounded theory and content analysis to analyze each of these discourses separately, and offers comparisons of the different discourses.

A key element constantly represented in all three of Moore's discourses was sperm in all its sexual travels. This has now led Moore (2002, 2003, n.d.; Moore & Schmidt 1999) to take up such representations much more broadly. Her new project examines social, cultural, and scientific visual and narrative representations of human semen from the reproductive sciences, the Internet, children's "facts of life" books, forensics transcripts, and sex workers' narratives. Semen representations, she finds, are distinctively related to gender, especially changing social positions of men, masculinities and constructions of male differences, and, of course, to HIV/AIDS. In secular children's books, sperm carry the responsibilities of cultural reproduction, while in Christian children's books, God assumes this role. Moore's analyses of the drawings of sperm in children's books are fascinating and chilling.

As another example, in any study of poverty in the United States since at least 1900, the researcher would need to consider the current and historical discourses on "welfare rolls," "welfare mothers," "bums," "hobos," the "culture of poverty," and so on that have been ubiquitous in the United States, intensifying in distinctive mediascapes during economic downturns such as the Great Depression of the 1930s and during election campaigns. Today these discourses are, in fact, elements of identity construction *for* welfare mothers themselves—they must be negotiated by women on welfare in their own processes of personal identity construction in their daily lives. With "the end of welfare as we knew it," engineered by the Clinton administration, the gender lens on U.S. poverty recently refocused on the homeless, who are mostly (but far from all) male. Moreover, the homeless are very differently constructed in discourses produced in different locales—*particular* cities or neighborhoods. Thus there may be very different local issues in terms of both individual identity construction and maintenance, and in homeless policy development. This is a site where local histories are hugely consequential and are ignored only at a researcher's peril (e.g., Bogard 2001; Bourgois, Lettiere, & Quesada 1997; Collins 1999; Snow & Anderson 1995). Often discourses such as those on "welfare mothers" or "the homeless" do the work of "othering"—making particular individuals and groups separate, different, and "lesser" beings for political and moral reasons. Asking what work a discourse is doing in the world is usually a useful point of entrée. Materials for such a discourse analysis would be available in local newspapers, on Web sites of local homeless and related organizations, in local agency policy documents, in local legal codes, and so on. One could pursue this discourse analysis on a single genre of data or as a multisited project.

These examples should provide some ideas for discourse projects or, alternatively, for extending classic interview/ethnographic projects to include multisite/multiscape analysis of related historical, visual, and/or narrative discourses. Researchers should feel encouraged to pursue innovative designs that include discourse data *for your own purposes*. We can now turn to what can be done analytically with such discursive materials as they are gathered using situational analysis.

How and Why Situational Analysis of Discourse(s) Is Different

In my project for this book of pushing grounded theory around the postmodern turn in part through an integration of Foucaultian discourse analysis, I am tinkering with both approaches. This tinkering is especially vivid vis-à-vis actually analyzing discourses per se. That is, critical Foucaultian discourse analyses usually (re)represent and analyze only *one discourse in a situation*—that with the most power in that situation. "To analyze 'regimes of practices' means to analyze programmes of conduct which have both prescriptive effects regarding what is to be done . . . , and codifying effects regarding what is to be known" (Foucault 1991:75), how discourses set the terms of "the conditions of possibility."

In his own work, Foucault pioneered in analyzing the discourses of major institutional regimes or discourse formations across long historical periods: the (bio)medical regime through *Madness and Civilization* (1965), *The Birth of the Clinic* (1975), and the development and elaboration of the clinical gaze; the state and its inherent interests in governmentality to *Discipline and Punish* (1979); the human sciences as a regime/formation of the academy that organizes *The Order of Things* (1973). In each, the featured discourse is that of "the powers that be." In part, this is because Foucault's key point was that discourses per se have social power autonomously from individual or collective human agency: "Discourse—the mere fact of speaking, of employing words . . . is in itself a force. Discourse is, with respect to the relation of forces, not merely a surface of inscription, but something that brings about effects [un operateur]" (Foucault [1976], quoted in Davidson 1997: 4-5). Discourses organize what is to be known and understood and what is not. Discourses have agency (see Chapter 2). Foucault's work here was and remains deeply theoretically innovative.

Yet a number of critiques of Foucault (including some feminist, materialist, and interactionist critiques) have centered on the absence of agency that itself allowed the absence of resistance to discourse in his work.[7] That is, for Foucault in these works, human (and other) subjects were constituted through discourse but either did not respond to it (were unagentic, were paralytic in the face of discourse, and/or were discourse itself) or their responses were not noted or included by Foucault. Later in his career, likely provoked in part by such critiques and others, the question of agency comes more to the fore in his work and in his published interviews and conversations. In addition to constituting knowledge practices (power/knowledge), discourses are also then described by Foucault as "technologies of the self," repertoires of possibility drawn upon and potentially not drawn upon in the self making of subjectivities. Agency was problematized.

In very sharp contrast, in situational analysis, analyzing discourses through situational mapping instead seeks to represent *all of the major discourses related to the situation* of interest—not just what could be called "the master discourse," that which usually trumps the others.[8] This is radically different. By *not* analytically recapitulating the power relations of domination, analyses that represent the full array of discourses turn up the volume on lesser but still present discourses, lesser but still present participants, the quiet, the silent, and the silenced. Such analyses can amplify not only differences but also resistances, recalcitrancies, and sites of rejection of a discourse per se. Moreover, some voices/discourses will be empowered through these representational processes that recognize and acknowledge their contributions. Others may metaphorically be forced out of the closet—having intentionally sought silence, and possibly the protections of silence. Conflicts and withdrawals are rendered visible, along with enrollments and acquiescence. I believe these analytics of power in its varied fluidities offered by situational analysis are congruent with both later Foucaultian and Straussian interactionist approaches.

Of course, with this analytic "opening up" to the range of discourses in a given situation, it becomes even more important to carefully analyze power in that situation: "It is these games of power that one must study in terms of tactics and strategy, in terms of order and of chance, in terms of stakes and objective" (Foucault, quoted in Davidson 1997:4). It also means that as researchers who tinker with the volume controls, *we* risk being "had up on charges" of such tinkering. That is, especially by *our* representing the heretofore silent/silenced, we risk being accused of supporting and/or attacking them! Removing veils can have its price, and like it or not, we may well be interpolated in terms of credibility (e.g., Becker 1967/1970). But we may also run into situations that we ourselves do not want to make public/publicize through research because of the damage we might do—the risks we might be placing others at rather than ourselves.[9] I return to these concerns in the remaining chapters.

Integrative and Comparative Mapping

The three modes of situational analysis (situational maps, social worlds/arenas/discourse maps, and positional maps) work exceptionally well with multisite/multiscape research in two main ways: via integrative mapping and analysis and/or via comparative mapping and analysis. First, in *integrative mapping and analysis,* the same modes of analysis (grounded theory coding and analytic memoing, doing the three kinds of situational maps, and analytic memoing) are used across all the different data sources *together,* asking what all of these data sources have to say about the phenomenon of interest. Codes are generated in/through all of the materials, sifted and coalesced into categories in traditional grounded theory fashion. The three kinds of maps and analytic memos based on them are done using all the materials simultaneously as "the data." The maps generated thus represent the "situation" of all the data together. The stories then told in publications thus also represent the varied data sources as constituting "a whole situation."

But grounded theory and situational analyses offer another set of possibilities—*comparative mapping and analysis* of the different data domains. Here, each data source is grounded theory coded, situationally mapped and analyzed *separately,* and then the results are *compared.* For example, one would do the three kinds of maps separately on interview and ethnographic data, and/or on a movie(s) on the topic, and/or other visual discourse materials, and/or mixed media such as magazine articles, and so on. What different elements are deemed present in the situation in the various domains? What are absent in some and present in others? What discourses appear in some analyses and not in others? What different positions are articulated in some but not in others? What similar positions? Such comparisons can assess which codes emerge where—and which do not, where there are silences, articulations of difference, and so on.

For example, in comparing popular discourse materials and interview data, one can see which elements of a particular discourse are taken up by real live people and which are not and vice versa. As mentioned above, Press and Cole (1999) analyzed a television film about abortion and later watched that film with focus groups of women who already knew one another. The popular culture television show discourse generally allowed for only two quite narrowly and rigidly constructed positions to be articulated—"pro-choice" or "pro-life." In contrast, Press and Cole's analysis of the women's own discourses found that while they did use rhetorics of "pro-choice" and "pro-life," their narratives were much more complicated, layered, deeply situational (carefully focusing on and analyzing *particular* pregnant women's decision-making situations regardless of legality), and even comfortably contradictory. The women (but not the television show) also talked about how it is necessary for women to confront authority figures (at least symbolically and sometimes literally) in order to obtain an abortion. The differences between the two discourse domains are very interesting and revealing, among other things, of the intense simplification that characterized popular television discourse and of the nuanced and personal empirical situational ethics frameworks generated and used by everyday women.

Last, theoretical sampling should also play a part in the analytic process of collecting and handling these discursive materials integratively or comparatively. If you lack the data you think you need for theoretical reasons, even late in the research process, it should be pursued if at all possible. In a deep sense here, *from a grounded theory perspective, data are data, open to grounded theory basic social process analyses and to situational analyses alike.* But you need to take serious responsibility for design and data collection adequate to the project's analytic goals.

Turnings

> As long as we believe that "discourse" is an authority or an infrastructure, as long as we ask what relation of causality that authority may have to social or economic evolution . . . we have not yet understood [Foucault].
>
> —Veyne (1971/1997:182)

This chapter has framed and provided many examples of discourse analysis and facilitated access to other useful and interesting analytics in the literature. It should be very clear how important it is for the future of grounded theory and situational analysis to be used with discourse materials. Agency is not enough. Interaction is not enough. The planet is full to overflowing with all kinds of things, including discourses, produced by and consequential for people and for the nonhuman as well. It is time to move beyond "the knowing subject" to *also* analyze what else is there in social life—materially and discursively. Going beyond "the knowing subject" constitutes both theoretical and methodological innovation.

A major part of my project in bringing grounded theory around the postmodern turn is relentlessly emphasizing the social, and the relentlessly social nature of discourses insists on the import of analyzing them. But there are also particular challenges to the researcher: "The 'undecidable' or the uncertainty in meaning that arises . . . is an irreducible and a given in all texts [discourses]. One must accept the difficulty" (Manning & Cullum-Swan 1994:467). We need to learn to live with the ambiguities of discursive analysis to even begin to stagger around the postmodern turn.

Situational analysis offers flexible and elastic *empirical* tools (situational maps, social worlds/arenas maps, and positional maps) with which to deconstruct "society" into mosaics of arenas organized around and through different kinds of discourses and action. Situational analysis also (inspired by but also contra Foucault) intentionally seeks to represent *all* the social worlds and discourses in an arena, amplifying the silent and silenced, specifying implicated actors and actants, and seeking out their (usually quite marginalized) discourses. These are the radically democratic—and not undangerous—features of situational analysis. "It is precisely the angst attending our recognition of the hidden powers of discourses that leaves us now at the threshold of postmodernism and that signals the advent of questions that will leave none of us untouched" (Denzin & Lincoln 2000:xiv).

Next we turn to "how to" analyze narrative (Chapter 5), visual (Chapter 6), and historical (Chapter 7) discourses as "texts" that complicate our understandings—and "trouble" our analyses (Lather 1996).

Notes

1. For entrée into discourse analysis, see Jaworski and Coupland (1999a, 1999b) and Van Dijk (1997a, 1997b); for organizational and management studies, see Phillips and Hardy (2002); on frame analysis, see Goffman (1974); on discourse tracking (following issues, words, themes, and frames over time and across media), see Altheide (1996, 2002b). On content analysis, see, e.g., Ball and Smith (1992:ch. 2), Prior (1997, 2003, 2004), G. Rose (2001:ch. 3), and van Leeuwen and Jewett (2001:ch. 2).

2. See also Altheide (1996, 2000, 2002a, 2002b), Balsamo (1996), Clough (2000), Denzin (1992, 1996a, 1997, 2000, 2001a, 2001b, 2001c).

3. This is performed by initially coding the data using grounded theory approaches. Then a subset of these inductively generated codes is selected—for analytic/theoretical reasons. Last, quantitative or qualitative content analysis using these codes is pursued. See note 1.

4. The term "multisite research" is also used to indicate that the same kinds of data were gathered at multiple sites (e.g., clinical trials, policy research). See Marcus (1995, 1998) and Gupta and Ferguson (1997).

5. The reflexive methods paper (Rapp 1999a) appears essentially as Chapter 1 in the book (Rapp 1999b).

6. Loosely speaking, we can view secondary sources as books and articles written by historians, social scientists, or critics within the past 50 years. But the distinction between primary and secondary sources is not always clear and simple. See, e.g., Tuchman (1994:esp. 317-321). Entrée into the secondary historical literature that might be relevant for Rapp's project could be through Apple's (1990) feminist historical handbook.

7. See, e.g., Burchell et al. (1991), Castellani (1999), Jones and Porter (1994), Davidson (1997), Fraser (1989), Dreyfus and Rabinow (1983), Sawicki (1991), and Veyne (1971/1997).

8. I am playing here on Everett Hughes's (1971) important concept of "master status," a particular social status that essentially trumps all others one might possess and requires "marking" in interaction—for example, a *woman* physician or pilot, a *male* nurse, a *black* actor, a *trophy* bride.

9. There are ongoing debates: See especially Lather's work, Wacquant (2002), and Kitzinger (2004).

5

Mapping Narrative Discourses

Attempting to be accountable to complexity, thinking the limit becomes the task, and much opens up in terms of ways to proceed for those who know both too much and too little.

—Lather (2001a:202-203)

P ostmodern theorist Jacques Derrida (1978) argued that in the West, speech has long been valued over the written word, and that we ignore the written word at our peril. This is precisely why analyzing discourse materials is particularly important in pushing grounded theory around the postmodern turn through situational analysis. Given the stunning elaboration of written, digitalized, and media discourses over the past century, discourse analysis can today be said to be a necessary tool for daily life. It allows us to see and better understand the world around us that is also producing us/in us (Foucault 1988). Analyzing pertinent discourses also helps produce better research regardless of whether the research project is wholly focused on discourse.

Narrative discourses, the focus of this chapter, are parts of most situations, and situations need to be analyzed inclusively. I focus here on narrative materials that have already been produced when we seek them out as data/research materials. The researcher does not coproduce such narrative materials, as you would interviews, but instead selects them from extant sources. Furthermore, I focus here especially on analyzing the content of discourse materials, though how they are produced, used, and travel may also be examined.

The research literature on narrative discourse commonly distinguishes among several kinds of materials that can be data for research. First, personal narratives are produced by individuals about themselves for whatever reasons (e.g., diaries, memoirs, autoethnographies). They center on "the knowing subject" and "typically take the perspective of the teller rather than that of the society" (Manning & Cullum-Swan 1994:465). Analysis of the content of such discursive materials is usually done using one of the more phenomenological approaches to narrative centered around lived experience, of which there are many.[1] But personal narratives often appear to float unanchored to the planet. Here, situational analysis as a new form offers the ability to deeply contextualize and situate personal narratives per se. Such a situational analysis would analytically explain what the specific personal narrative taken up is a "case [study] of" where it comes from and why it matters. This analytic work too often remains inadequate in case studies today (Baszanger & Dodier 1997). This is an example of how situational analysis can be used complementarily with other approaches.

Second are narratives produced by individuals about something else we are interested in, centering our focus on that topic. Here, situational analysis could be undertaken of a selected set of "narratives about X." For example, there is an ambitious literature of illness narratives centering on what it is like to live with X disease or condition. One could design a discourse study to examine all the books and articles in certain popular media venues produced before and after the availability of a particular new technological innovation that changes how that disease or condition affects people. Or one could compare how gender, class, and race seem consequential or inconsequential in a set of such narratives. There are many possibilities.

Some individually authored narrative discourse materials may be aural instead of textual. Farnell and Graham (1998:420-424) discuss identifying, collecting, and recording live situated discourse as a "soundscape." Such materials are handled like interview tapes—transcribed (if verbal), listened to again while annotating the transcription, and stored for later reference (see also Poland 1995). An excellent example here is Angela Davis's (1999: xi, xiii) transcription and analysis of African American women's blues songs from the mid-20th century. She pursued this as "an inquiry into the ways their recorded performances divulge unacknowledged traditions of feminist consciousness in working-class black communities." While it is understandable that "black social consciousness has been overdetermined by race, . . . there remains a paucity of research on the class-inflected character of historical black feminism," and the oral blues tradition offers "a vast body of musical texts and a rich cultural legacy" for analysis. Davis (1999:xvii) concluded that through the blues "as a privileged discursive site," working-class black women achieved both expression of their own sexuality and enhanced authority over it, an authority not available to middle-class black women who lived under the repressive constraints of middle-class respectability.

The third main genre of narrative materials that can be data for research is produced by collectivities and takes the form of documents of many sorts. Using documents as data sources has a long tradition in symbolic inter-actionist research, dating back to the early-20th-century Chicago ecological studies discussed in Chapter 2 (Bulmer 1984:89-108). Then, documentary data were "just another kind of data" collected as part of fieldwork/ethnography. Today, after the postmodern turn, such data are taken up much more reflexively. Today we emphasize the deeply social nature of the production and maintenance of discourses of all kinds. "[T]he modern world is made through writing and documentation, a point that was emphasized, above all, in Max Weber's perceptive analysis of 'bureaucracy'" (Prior 2003:4). Thus all major social institutions have reams of documents (e.g., medical histories, school records, court records, criminal records) that, along with Web sites per se, are increasingly digitalized and hence increasingly facilitate analysis.

I thoroughly introduced and gave extensive examples of the three main modes of analysis of discourses in Chapter 4: (1) negotiating discourses in social relationships/interaction, (2) producing identities and subjectivities through discourses, and (3) producing power/knowledge, ideologies, and control through discourses (Jaworski & Coupland 1999b). Therefore we next turn directly to the nitty-gritty issues of doing situational analysis of narrative discourse materials. I begin with the major concerns and complexities of the design stage and then move quickly into a concrete situational analysis using one of my own projects as the exemplar.

Designing a Narrative Project

> [T]extual experiments are not so much about solving the crisis
> of representation as troubling the very claims to represent. If, as
> Foucault states, we are freer than we feel, how can we feel freer
> in this space?
>
> —Lather (2001a:201)

Designing a narrative discourse project first poses the problem of deciding what kind of narrative discourse study you want to pursue—what kind of study best addresses your interests and research needs. There are literally millions if not an infinity of narrative discourses "out there" awaiting analysis.

Social scientists, including historians, are usually interested in discourses where there are multiple perspectives and what we term "interesting" and "important" conflicts—such as a local discourse on homelessness, a national discourse on health care insurance coverage, the discourse on download-ing music for free/music piracy, and so on. Alternatively, we can follow in Foucault's footsteps: "While Foucault does not say much about the selection of his archive, it is clear that his preference is for what we might call 'pro-grammatic' texts, writings that try to impose a vision or spell out most clearly a new way of conceptualizing a problem" (Kendall & Wickham 2004:144). An example here is the Bowker and Star (1999) chapter on the laws of apartheid as "programmatic" texts in Foucault's sense and the problematics of their implementation (discussed in Chapter 4).

Which Narrative Materials?

Designing a narrative discourse project starts from your own extant knowledge of the situation. The grounded theory/situational analysis approach does not assume that the researcher is a tabula rasa, but rather that you are already quite knowledgeable about the substantive area you have decided to pursue. Moreover, you likely have a certain theoretical and methodological sophistication about how to proceed and the nature of your commitments in this domain. The importance of this prior/extant knowledge will soon become clear.

Once you have decided what broad situation or discursive terrain you want to examine, the next step is to do a very sketchy and very preliminary discourse/arenas map. The flip sides of social worlds/arenas are discourses/arenas. Here you roughly map out all the kinds of discourse materials you believe are in that situation. Ultimately, you need to determine what dis-courses exist and are feasible to study, which discourse(s) to focus upon, and who/what contributes to and participates in their production, maintenance, and distribution. So, begin by laying out what narrative discourse materials you believe are in the situation of interest, the arena(s) writ large. The main goal here (and in subsequent reworkings) is to make sure you capture and provisionally name *all the major extant discourses in the situation* on this map and any minor ones you think are significant. You will not pursue them all, and usually only a few. But as they are all continually changing in rela-tion to one another—the "field of discourse"/"arena" is a negotiated order—you need to know what is in that field/arena. This is yet another way that situational analysis situates your work: You will be able to defend your selection of discourses to examine by articulating those you chose not to pursue and why.

Analytically, situational analysis starts from the assumption that we seek to represent *all the major narrative discourses related to the situation* in which we are interested, at least in our analyses, if not in our publications. Thus we must also begin from the assumption that *we do not know* what narrative discourses are actually in the situation. That is, we will likely know what some but not all of them are, and not much about their interrelations. This can have the experiential sense of feeling one's way in a very dimly lit space, especially at the outset.

Locating, Collecting, Tracking, Situating

The next step, with rough and dirty map in hand, is to determine what kinds of extant data exist, how accessible they are, and how "good" they initially appear to be. That is, data for a narrative discourse study could consist solely of extant documents if these offer ambitious representations of all the key features of the discourses/elements of the situation. Or, alternatively, there might be adequate discursive documentary data from and about certain social worlds in this discursive arena but not on others. Then one would consider making the multisite move to also acquire interview/ethnographic data as needed to flesh out data sources on *all the key elements* to some degree. You might choose to focus on only a few, but you need to know what else is there and why you will not pursue it.

Of course, in wonderful contradictory qualitative fashion, at the initial stages of research, you will likely *not know* what "all the key discourses" are. Thus, as noted above, it is very likely that you may be patching together data sources in the later stages of some projects. This is a form of theoretical sampling in that the analytic/theoretical salience of the element emerged late. But it still needed to be pursued through theoretical sampling—through your gathering new data that speak specifically to the theoretical point. Again, as the French would say, "It's normal."

In short, the materials should be the best range of discursive materials you can obtain related to the situation that you have chosen to research. If you are pursuing a multisite project, the narrative discourse materials should articulate well with the other sites you are examining (e.g., an ethnographic/interview site or a visual discourse site or a historical discourse site). By "articulate well," I mean that the materials allow you to reasonably address the same areas of focus or appropriately conflicting ones, and so on. The most challenging part can be bounding the data to be collected "systematically enough." Returning to Kvale's metaphors of mining versus collecting, casually amassing interesting discourse materials is not enough. For a discourse study or discourse site within a multisite study, the data should offer both depth and range of variation. Using the grounded theory concept of saturation, narrative discourse data collection itself should continue until *nothing analytically useful* is being collected—until further analysis is no longer provoked by the new materials.

Very, very careful tracking (dating, sourcing, and otherwise situating) each discourse document is highly important. Collecting and tracking are fussy, tedious tasks, important to get right the first time. If you don't, the capacity to publish something may disappear. Depending on what you are collecting, it may best be done where there is space to spread out and a handy photocopier, as it might involve making working copies and preserving originals in files or binders. Tracking narrative materials can be crucial if you want to publish something for which written permission is required—and it usually is required, unless the materials are in the public domain.[2]

For some projects, some kind of log should be maintained that tracks the "provenance" of all the narrative materials—where they came from in terms of "who, what, where, when, how, how much," and so on. In addition, you may need to attend to confidentiality issues with great care if the documents are not "public" materials. For example, using and certainly publishing non-public documents of an organization you are studying would require written permission from that organization. Such permissions can be notoriously difficult to obtain.

Overall, the very design of a narrative discourse study using situational analysis (the three main kinds of maps and memos) involves the researcher in tacking back and forth between situational elements, the discourses, the social worlds/arenas, and the positions taken in the discourse(s) throughout the project. In many ways, doing the research is (re)doing the design. Experienced grounded theorists will likely find this familiar territory. I am trying to be very clear about it here especially for relative neophytes. I seek to reassure you that suddenly discovering downstream in the project yet another discourse produced by a heretofore invisible social world in the arena is an indicator of successful use of the methods and not personal analytic failure! Moreover, you might even "find" it through doing a positional map and finding a "new" position articulated.

I find discourse data collection especially challenging. It is usually the case that one is unable to collect "all" of the discourse data on anything. Challenges for the researcher are then to assess the adequacy of what has been collected, to come to tolerate its partialities, to determine how to explain its partialities in publications, and to focus on doing a strong analysis of the materials you have.

Doing Situational Maps of Narrative Discourse

One has to proceed by progressive, necessarily incomplete satura-
tion. And one has to bear in mind that the further one breaks down
the processes under analysis, the more one is enabled and indeed
obliged to construct their external relations of intelligibility.

—Foucault (1991:77)

As with mapping interview and fieldwork data, basic grounded theory coding of the narrative materials should be pursued first. What are these data about? What is going on here? What are these stories of? The usual solid coding will ground you, the analyst, in the discourse and allow you to pursue the situational maps.

Because collecting extant documents is very different from doing interviews and observations, the initial basic coding time, energy, and memos may be even more important. That is, there is a lot of "invisible work" happening in interview processes. We experience the doing of interviews and observations as active participants, consciously, unconsciously, and semiconsciously developing dense visual, narrative, and emotive memories and ideas about the situations in which we find ourselves. As we move along, these often produce much more elaborate analytic contributions than we knew at the time. We are always processing and analyzing information on the move, as we go. In sharp contrast, in analyzing discourse documents, much of this work may be missing. The initial grounded theory reading and coding may well be your first serious immersion in the data. The key point is that you must know your data to map it. Coding produces knowing. Also, then, simply reading the narrative materials as you gather them, rather than merely tucking them into files, can be very important, often invisible work.

The classic questions for doing the situational map with narrative discourse materials include: What are the discourses in the broader situation? Who (individually and collectively) is involved (supportive, opposed, providing knowledge, materials, money, what else?) in producing these discourses? What and who do these discourses construct? How? What and whom are they in dialogue with/about? What and who do these discourses render invisible? How? What material things—nonhuman elements—are involved in the discourse? How are they constructed? How do they configure the human actors? Were there implicated/silent actors/actants? What were the important discursively constructed elements in the situation? What historical and other contemporary cultural symbologies are evoked in the discourse? What work do these discourses do in the world? What are some of the contested issues in the discourse? Specifying these anticipates the later need for issues and axes to develop positional maps. It can be helpful to think of a discourse itself as an arena from social worlds/arenas theory. Who/what is in that arena and what do they have to say about it? Who is engaged and debating with whom in/through this discourse?

Flipping back and forth from social worlds to discourses provokes in-depth analyses and the deconstruction of social worlds into segments with their own (sub)discourses. This elasticity of social worlds/arenas analysis makes some people very anxious. But therein lies its power—it keeps you analyzing more and more and works against formulaic usage.

Introducing the Narrative Discourse Exemplar: RU486 Discourse Project

I use my own work here as an exemplar of a study of producing power/knowledge, ideologies, and control through discourse. The caveat is that it was not pursued with explicit use of situational analyses but with an incipient form that relied on social worlds/arenas analysis. Furthermore, this project did not start out as a discourse analysis though it surely ended up as such. It began impetuously in 1989 when a member of the board of supervisors of the city of San Francisco where I live made the morning papers, arguing that San Francisco should be a test site for the U.S. Food and Drug Administration (FDA) approval of the use of RU486, widely known as "the French abortion Pill," in the United States. Actually a set of pills to be taken in a specified timed sequence, RU486 is the first "medical" abortion technology (in contrast to surgical abortion technologies that remove the conceptus, a very early fetus, from the uterus). After taking RU486, the woman's body expels the conceptus similarly to having a very early miscarriage. Approved and used in France since 1982 and in many other European nations, the contested nature of abortion in the United States considerably delayed and complexified its approval here.

I began the project as a brand-new assistant professor, planning it as an interview/ethnographic endeavor to follow the FDA approval process "in practice," assuming there would be some "local" involvement, given extensive local scientific, medical, feminist, and women's health infrastructure—and the enthusiasm of that supervisor. Special protocols for early FDA approval of AIDS drugs had even been developed and utilized locally. I was hopeful and excited about my new project. I began gathering data from the media, from involved organizations, attending conferences, collecting papers from the medical literature, and so on. Several years later, because San Francisco clinics were not involved, that supervisor had disappeared, and

FDA approval was so delayed, my third research assistant on the project (Theresa Montini) and I "ended up" doing a discourse analysis focused on the main social worlds involved in the RU486 arena (Clarke & Montini 1993). RU486 was actually not FDA approved until September 2000 (Joffe & Weitz 2003:2353).

I can frame this exemplar as a classic grounded theory project with the "basic social process" as "constructing RU486." We actually titled the paper "The Many Faces of RU486" as a play on the old Nunally Johnson movie about multiple personalities titled *The Three Faces of Eve*. In certain ways, I have always thought of this paper as largely a methods paper—a precursor of situational analyses—because it is organized around an explicit social worlds/arenas analysis of narrative discourse. Analytically, we examined the discursive constructions of RU486 put forward by most of the key social worlds (and some subworlds) that had committed themselves to action of some kind in the abortion arena regarding this abortion technology. We focused largely but not exclusively on the United States, and especially on reproductive and other scientists, birth control/population control organizations, pharmaceutical companies, medical groups, antiabortion groups, pro-choice groups, women's health movement organizations, politicians, the U.S. Congress, and the FDA.

We also examined what little research existed on women users/consumers of RU486 itself as a narrative discourse.[3] I conceptualized these women as "implicated actors"—actors who are either not actually present and/or denied agency in the situation, but for whom the action in the situation is or likely will be consequential (discussed in Chapter 2). There were also silent implicated actors in this situation—actors with sufficient power and resources to "act" but choosing not to do so "for their own reasons." Despite laying out the quite heterogeneous discourses of this wide array of actors, we also acknowledged the partiality of the glimpses of the different worlds we were able to offer in one paper.

This was a multisite study with a nonhuman object—a new abortion technology—at the center. Our data included published materials, interviews with key players, documents produced by involved organizations, and observations of some (but not all) key events. (Today we would use Web sites as a means of access to pertinent organizational discourses.) We regularly accessed materials listed in Med Line, the *Readers Guide to Popular Literature,* the *New York Times,* and other major news media. In fact, investigative journalists were some of the major document makers/contributors to the debate. Interviews were conducted by both of us. Dr. Etienne-Emile Baulieu, the key scientist behind the development and use of RU486, was especially generous with his time (he won the prestigious Lasker Prize in 1989).

Situational Map Exemplar: RU486 Discourse Project

See Figure 5.1 for the Messy Situational Map: RU486 Discourse Project. I have not entered the specific names of the many different organizations involved but rather have categorized them under general rubrics here (e.g., feminist organizations, women's health movement organizations) for a simpler and more easily readable map. Particular organizations are discussed in the published paper. In the situational map, then, we can see the varied collective actors concerned about abortion, committed to act and to producing discourses in that arena. The main nonhuman actant is RU486. Anyone familiar with U.S. abortion politics will note that "all the usual suspects" are gathered

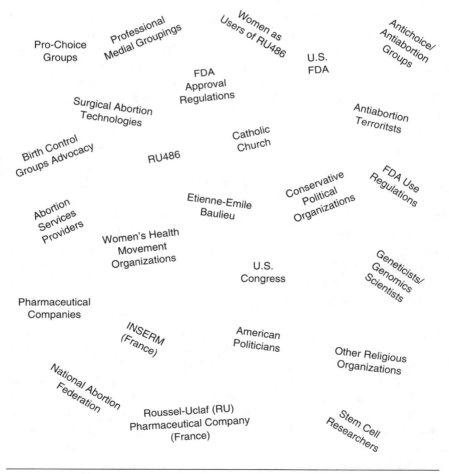

Figure 5.1   Messy Situational Map: RU486 Discourse Project

here. I do note one particular organization, the National Abortion Federation, the only national organization of abortion care providers. Established in 1976, it seeks to improve the safety of and access to abortion care for all women, serving as a national abortion technical training unit and information clearinghouse. It also serves as a main bulwark of defense against the ongoing domestic terrorism that has been directed at abortion clinics, workers, and physician providers for many years, including the murders of seven members of the abortion-providing community to date: three physicians, one escort, two receptionists, and one off-duty policeman (www.prochoice.org).

In addition to women users of RU486 as implicated actors, there are also two sets of silent scientific collective actors. Both are concerned with reproductive phenomena and are constituencies for whom abortion is of considerable importance but who seek to keep the proverbial "10-foot pole" between themselves and the white heat of the current U.S. abortion controversy. For both, RU486 has distinctive meanings. First are geneticists and others active in human genomics (e.g., the Human Genome Initiative) and/or clinicians involved in any and all aspects of prenatal genetic screening. Since there are no therapeutic interventions for most of the conditions current and anticipated screening will find, abortion remains the only therapeutic alternative. Enhanced access to and options for abortion for women who wish to terminate such a pregnancy, such as those provided by RU486, would seemingly be central concerns for these actors. Yet abortion was then and remains largely absent from their public discourse.

The second silent collective scientific actor is fetal tissue researchers—a category that includes what are now, over 10 years later, called "stem cell researchers." This research has since become a very serious and growing segment of the biotechnology industry, especially in the United States and the United Kingdom. Since the 1980s, when the fetus emerged as a significant cultural icon in abortion politics, scientists have assiduously attempted to discursively construct fetal tissue research as essentially unimplicated in abortion politics (Casper 1994, 1998b). They have done so despite the almost universal use of fetal tissue from induced abortions as requisite materials for certain scientific research. While a ban on U.S. federal support of such research has been in place on and off since 1988, privately funded research has not been interrupted. Increased numbers of RU486 abortions might negatively impact scientists' access to abortion materials in the United States because the aborted materials are expelled at home, rather than collected through vacuum aspiration in the clinic and potentially donated to research.

Readers may have noted that I was actually doing situational analyses here. As a feminist researcher, I knew about these silent actors and I put them on the map—a map where they would likely rather not appear. This illustrates the importance of the analyst's own knowledge of the situation in situational analysis as well as the legitimacy of using that knowledge "up front." The analyst uses their knowledge to help design data collection and does not wait quietly for magically appearing data to speak! That is, the analyst needs to anticipate what data should be gathered in the initial design, as well as use theoretical sampling appropriately downstream.

See Figure 5.2 for the Ordered Situational Map: RU486 Discourse Project. The ordered map reveals one significant individual, Etienne-Emile Baulieu, the scientist primarily responsible for its development, who also fully accepted the additional role of public sponsorship and advocacy. There were many significant collective actors organized by and large into recognizable social worlds. This map also clearly demonstrates the importance of the history of politics generally to the history and politics of abortion in the United States—temporal elements. In the 1980s and 1990s especially, abortion as an issue was used by the Republican party and other conservative groups in the United States to recruit and organize segments of the populace previously not politically engaged or committed. (The issue of gay marriage is being discursively deployed similarly today.)

But the most important new point to emerge through doing the ordered map concerns attending to spatial elements. A key feature of RU486 as a medical abortion technology is that it potentially could be distributed where there are no abortion clinics. Fully 84% of U.S. counties do *not* have abortion services (Joffe & Weitz 2003:2354)! RU486 could legally put abortion services in the offices of primary care physicians and gynecologists in all of those counties. This element was and continues to be key in the politics of RU486 (discussed further below). The *New York Times Magazine* article that discussed this property of RU486 was titled "The Little White Bombshell" (Talbot 1999)—a vivid narrative discourse statement/in vivo code indeed!

Doing Social Worlds/Arenas
Maps of Narrative Discourse

Ultimately material culture always has to be interpreted in relation to a situated context of production, use, discard, and reuse.

—Hodder (2000:706)

Social worlds/arenas maps of discourse data do the same work as such maps of other data—provide a portrait of the meso-level actors in the situation— producing, contributing to, and maintaining the discourses. I should also note that one can do such maps perspectivally—from the perspective of one particular social world in the arena. (I return to this point at the end of the section.)

INDIVIDUAL HUMAN ELEMENTS/ACTORS

Etienne-Emile Baulieu

NONHUMAN ELEMENTS/ACTANTS

RU486
Surgical abortion technologies
FDA regulations for approval
FDA regulations for use

**COLLECTIVE HUMAN
ELEMENTS/ACTORS**

U.S. FDA
U.S. Congress
Pro-choice groups
Antichoice/antiabortion groups
Birth control advocacy groups
Women's health movement groups
Abortion services providers
National Abortion Federation
Professional medical groups

**IMPLICATED/SILENT
ACTORS/ACTANTS**

Women as users
Genetic/genomic scientists
Genetics/clinicians
Stem cell researchers
Antiabortion terrorists

**DISCURSIVE CONSTRUCTION(S)
OF HUMAN ACTORS**

Social world constructions of others
Social world constructions of Baulieu
Social world constructions of FDA

**DISCURSIVE CONSTRUCTION
OF NONHUMAN ACTANTS**

Social world constructions of RU486
Social world constructions of abortion
Constructions of approval regulations
Constructions of use regulations

**POLITICAL/ECONOMIC
ELEMENTS**

Access to abortion
Costs of abortion
Political party concerns re abortion

**SOCIOCULTURAL/SYMBOLIC
ELEMENTS**

Morality of abortion
Morality of unwanted children
Pill for abortion as "magic bullet"

TEMPORAL ELEMENTS

Lateness of U.S. approval compared
  to Europe
Rise of religious right in U.S. politics
  since 1970s

SPATIAL ELEMENTS

Potential ease of wide geographic
  availability of RU486
Lack of abortion services in 84% of
  U.S. counties

**MAJOR ISSUES/DEBATES
(USUALLY CONTESTED)**

Safety of RU486
Safety of abortion
Morality of abortion
Morality of unwanted children

**RELATED DISCOURSES
(NARRATIVE AND/OR VISUAL)**

Abortion discourses
Birth control discourses
Sex/gender/feminism discourses
Sexuality discourses

Figure 5.2   Ordered Situational Map: RU486 Discourse Project

Social worlds shape and are themselves shaped through their active participation with other social worlds in their arena(s) of concern. One of the key ways in which this shaping is done in practice is through the production and promotion of competing discourses and/or particular elements of the broader discourse. I thus start my discursive maps with the questions: What were the patterns of collective commitment and what were the salient social worlds operating here? What were their discourses and what did they hope to achieve through their production and distribution? What were the discursive constructions of nonhuman actants as well as of individual and collective human actors? How did the various worlds "see" and constellate one another through their contributions to the overall discourse? What were their relations and how can I best map these visually?

Social Worlds/Arenas Map
Exemplar: RU486 Discourse Project

Doing the social worlds/arenas map is more complex than one might imagine. It provokes the ever-present but now more pressing problems of scale, scope, position, and context particularly intensely. Do RU486 and the social worlds involved in this discourse constitute an entire arena? Or, would it be "better"/"more accurate" to situate the RU486 Discourse Project in the broader arena of abortion in the United States? To me, the answer when I find myself asking such a question is "do both," and I have.

Social worlds/arenas analytics are elastic. They can be stretched wide to encompass considerable complexity and "context"/"situatedness" (see Figures 7.3 and 7.4, the social worlds/arenas maps for the development of modern contraceptives). And they can also be pared down to a simpler version—eminently articulable and coherent as a publishable story in one paper. One social world can itself be analyzed as an arena or subworlds/segments—each having its own distinctive discourse. One of the things to be learned in doing situational analyses is how to both expand and contract social worlds/arenas analysis to address the needs of the project at hand—to get comfortable using its elasticity for your own analytic and downstream representational purposes.

See Figure 5.3 for the Social Worlds/Arenas Map: RU486 Discourse Project. This map situates RU486 and the social worlds involved with it and producing discourse about it in the larger U.S. abortion arena as it intersects with both political and medical arenas. The full complexity of these arenas is clear here. RU486 is relatively "small potatoes"—insignificant—in this broader, highly politicized, cultural, medical, and political situation.

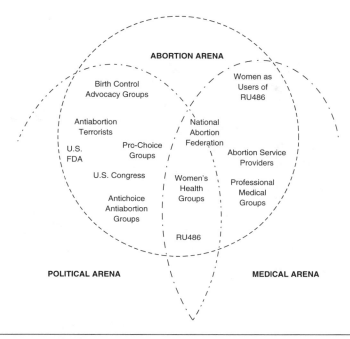

ABORTION ARENA

Birth Control
Advocacy Groups

Women as
Users of
RU486

Antiabortion
Terrorists

National
Abortion
Federation

U.S.
FDA

Pro-Choice
Groups

Abortion Service
Providers

U.S. Congress

Women's
Health
Groups

Professional
Medical
Groups

Antichoice
Antiabortion
Groups

RU486

POLITICAL ARENA

MEDICAL ARENA

Figure 5.3   Social Worlds/Arenas Map: RU486 Discourse Project

Studying RU486 when we did was a discursive opportunity, rather like a photo opportunity or sound bite, a very small story inside a very complicated big saga. Looking at this map when I initially did it well over a decade ago, I realized that one article could not capture such complexity. I would have to decide whether or not to aim for the "full saga" book-length version. I was very hesitant to do so because so much had already been written, including excellent feminist work. I kept hearing Strauss's injunction to "study the unstudied" echoing loudly.

My second set of concerns centered on RU486 as a technology. I have long been interested, as a feminist medical sociologist, in technologies that affect large numbers of women around the world—masses of women—such as contraceptives and the Pap smear (the main screening method for early detection of incipient cervical cancers). RU486 was, I believed, going to become such a technology. But RU486 qua special technology would get lost—be a minor player—if I went down the "full saga" path and wrote about the abortion arena as a whole. I therefore decided to feature that

Figure 5.4   Project Map: RU486 Discourse Project

technology *analytically,* and produced a project map that did this work. See Figure 5.4, Project Map: RU486 Discourse Project.

This map can be read as a close-up or zoom lens version of a social worlds/arenas map wherein the major social worlds and arenas discursively involved with RU486 are much enlarged. It can also be easily and coherently narrated in one paper. In that paper, we drew on the broader social worlds arenas map (Figure 5.3) to help construct our narrative, to discursively situate RU486 more broadly. But we organized the paper itself, section by section, through this zoom lens "project map" (Figure 5.4). After a short introduction, we literally started in the middle of this diagram with a history of the development of RU486 (problematizing that as well). We then worked our way around the circle, (re)representing the discourses on RU486 produced by each of those social worlds and some of their subworlds.

This is a classic social worlds/arenas study "played on the flip side," largely using narrative discourse data about a nonhuman object—a material cultural object—with which all the social worlds were concerned. The paper literally centers on the discursive constructions of that object made by each of those worlds (reproductive scientists, birth control/population control organizations, pharmaceutical companies, medical groups, antiabortion groups, pro-choice groups, women's health movement groups, politicians, Congress, the FDA, and women users/consumers of RU486). While the organization of the paper mirrors the project map, our narrative also focused on the heterogeneities of these groups' discursive constructions. The discourses, like the social worlds, were not monolithic. We also addressed how they deployed their discourses to convince others of the validity of their own perspectives, to create alliances, to denigrate enemies, and to further their own (rather heterogeneous) interests.

This analysis demonstrates rather vividly that there are not "two sides" but rather N sides or multiple perspectives in any discourse—even abortion in the United States! It is very rare for more than two sides to be represented about anything in the United States, not just abortion. Simplification (Star 1983) into two "sides" is not necessarily benign, and delimiting representation of contestation to "two sides" may in itself be a hegemonic strategy to intentionally silence other actors/actants and perspectives/discourses. Power analytics are very important. Here they particularly raise the possibilities of implicated actors and actants in the discourse under study. In fact, as noted above, there are two sets of implicated scientific/clinical actors whose discursive silences are both interesting and significant.

Doing Positional Maps of Narrative Discourse

> *Marginality and subordination are conditions lived by social actors. But they are also inscribed in categories, classifications, texts and treatises.*
>
> —McCarthy (1996:109)

To do positional maps of discursive data, one first seeks to elucidate from the data what the basic (often but not always contested) issues are in the discourse about which there are different positions, and to array these two-dimensionally in some fashion. It is important to remember that positions here are not correlated with persons or groups. The goal is to elucidate *all* the seemingly important positions taken in the discourses. There may therefore, of course, be multiple positional maps.

Ideally, having done the situational maps (both messy and orderly versions) and the social worlds/arenas map, by now the researcher is deeply familiar with the data. This usually makes doing the positional maps easier. Sometimes one grasps from discovering a particular position in the data what the axis is or could be. That is, each axis is likely to interact with more than one other axis. Playing with this analytically can be most useful. Furthermore, the very doing of the positional maps will reveal those positions not taken in the data gathered to date and trigger theoretical sampling. That sampling may or may not find heretofore silent positions articulated.

Positional Map Exemplar: RU486 Discourse Project

See Figure 5.5 for Positional Map I: RU486 Discourse Project—Constructing RU486 viz. Safety and Morality. It takes up two major contested elements of the discourse on RU486 that are related to each other—safety and morality. There are multiple positions taken on the safety of using RU486 for abortion, including differences among and within women's health groups. Certainly there are differences on the morality of abortion using whatever technology. There are also positions especially against using RU486 for abortion. I am not going to detail these substantive issues here (see Clarke & Montini 1993; Joffe & Weitz 2003).

Interestingly, one position *not* taken in the data was that RU486 is safe but is not moral. Unsafeness and immorality go hand in hand in this discourse. Thus one of the fascinating insights that emerges from this positional map is that both the "regulatory science" (Jasanoff 1990) of the FDA and the basic science, clinical research, and epidemiology regarding the safety and efficacy of both medical and surgical abortions are contested in the discourse. Science itself is discursively implicated. This is actually becoming increasingly common in controversial arenas where science "matters." Classic examples include tobacco, nuclear and other forms of power, most anything concerning the environment, and so on. In fact, within the scientific establishment itself, RU486 was designated a "Runner-Up Molecule of the Year" by *Science* magazine for 1989, not surprisingly at the top of the "Most Controversial [Molecule]" category! The natural sciences, which had been considered inviolate—fully/wholly separate from politics and social life—no longer enjoy such "exemption" from the sociology of knowledge, including among lay-people.

Figure 5.6 offers Positional Map II: RU486 Discourse Project—Constructing RU486 viz. Safety and Access. Here the safety axis from Figure 5.5 intersects with another axis—access to the technology for abortion

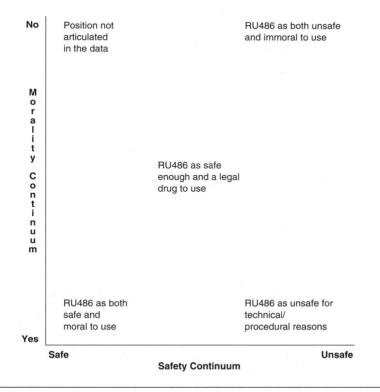

Figure 5.5   Positional Map I: RU486 Discourse Project—Constructing RU486 viz. Safety and Morality

purposes. At one end of the access continuum is the position that access should be wide (via primary care physicians and obstetrician/gynecologists as well as established abortion care providers), while at the other end is the position that access to it should be limited to established abortion care providers (available in only 14% of U.S. counties). Predictably, antichoice/antiabortion groups have sought the narrowest access. In sharp contrast, many positions were and are held down by the groups that support a woman's right to choose to have an abortion. These positions turned on perceptions of drug safety, whether local hospitals would provide adequate and reliable backup surgical services, whether primary care physicians and obstetricians/gynecologists would provide adequate and quality abortion counseling and services, and so on. Unusually, there was no absence of positions taken in the positional map. There was, in Foucault's (1978) terms, considerable "incitement to discourse" among the pro-choice worlds. In fact, the discourse examined here in the early 1990s continues. Today it centers around FDA regulations for use of the drug

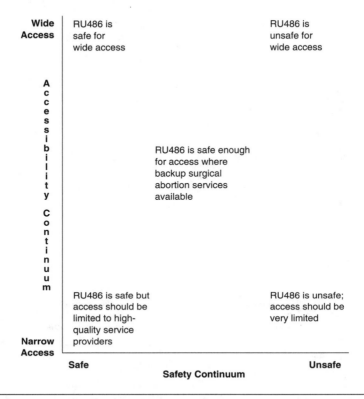

Figure 5.6   Positional Map II: RU486 Discourse Project—Constructing RU486
viz. Safety and Access

where safety concerns have particularly loud voices (see, e.g., Joffe & Weitz
2003). I doubt it will disappear in my lifetime.

I noted above that one can do a social worlds/arenas map from the
perspective of one particular social world in the arena. See Figure 5.7 for an
Abstract Perspectival Project Map. I have called it "The Arena According to
Social World X." In making such a map, one would first proceed as above,
(re)representing the discourses of *all* the major social worlds in the arena.
One would also seek out and represent the discourses of any minor worlds
noted by X world in its discourse, and any others you think worthwhile pursuing. Then, *in addition,* one would articulate the discursive commentary
and evaluations of the discourse(s) of all the other worlds offered by social
world X. The latter narrative would be "the arena according to social world
X." But to be of any interest, the perspective of X world would need to be
compared to those of the other worlds (which you laid out first) to see what

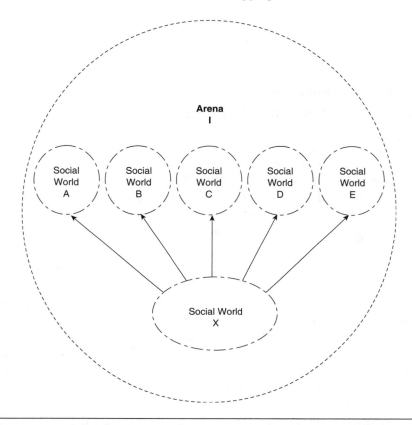

Figure 5.7   Abstract Perspectival Project Map: The Arena According to Social
World X

in particular makes the discourse of social world X distinctive and worthy of being featured analytically. It is the comparisons that matter most here.

Obviously, doing such a map and analysis is of most use if you really want to understand social world X in depth. For example, in the RU486 arena, all the social worlds today have an interest in having a very clear understanding of how the Bush administration (or any other political administration, for that matter) constructs their worlds. That is, each world needs to regularly discursively (re)position itself vis-à-vis the current administration's distinctive stand on abortion and on RU486 in general, but also on themselves qua organizations/social worlds in particular. A presidential administration has sufficient power in the situation that the other social worlds might well not only seek to reconstellate their own discourse but to do so vis-à-vis those of the other worlds in the arena. Perspectival project maps are especially useful in the study of long-lived arenas, and may of course be usefully done for more than one world in an arena.

Final Comments: Situational Analysis of Narrative Discourse

> *The interpretation of mute material evidence puts the interaction-ist view under pressure. How can an approach that gives consid-erable importance to interaction with speaking subjects . . . deal with material traces for which informants are long dead or about which informants are not articulate? . . . Although the evidence cannot "speak back," it can confront the interpreter in ways that enforce self reappraisal.*
>
> —Hodder (2000:710)

In this epigraph, Hodder reminds us that contemporary and historical discourse analyses are quite different projects from those relying on "knowing subjects" who speak to us and may tell us where we have gone analytically astray. He reminds us that we need to take our confrontations with the data very seriously. While I have not nagged about memoing very much in this chapter, I want to do so now. Memos are the best way to confront discursive data—"mute material evidence"—and your own analyses. Memos are sites of conversation with ourselves about our data. Those conversations are even more important in the absence of speaking subjects who often inadvertently confront our hidden assumptions and cherished ideas. Doing collaborative projects and/or working and pursuing analysis in Straussian working groups can also expand conversational—and analytic—possibilities. But they do not replace memos!

In terms of selecting projects, Hodder (2000:714) further argues that "[t]he challenge posed by material culture is important for anthropological and sociological analysis because material culture is often a medium in which alternative and often muted voices can be expressed." As I wrote this book, I was also watching documentary histories of American jazz and blues music. It would be hard to think of any other medium in which the experiences, cultures, ideologies, perspectives of a broad spectrum of African Americans were more vividly expressed (e.g., Davis 1999)—"alternative and often muted voices" indeed.

Documents too provide entrée to special domains. But we must take care not to reify them: "[I]f we are to get to grips with the nature of documents then we have to move away from a consideration of them as stable, static, and pre-defined artifacts" (Prior 2003:2). Documents have agencies in the world. What is it a document of? What work is it doing? Where does it go? How is it changing? That is, in analyzing discursive materials, we need to analyze not only their contents but also how they are used, how they travel, and so on (see, e.g., Kendall & Wickham 2004; Prior 2003:21-26 and ch. 9). Any or all of these may be featured in our final products.

In sum, situational analyses of narrative discourse data not only can be fun and interesting but often immensely useful. They provide maps of a particular discourse of interest that ambitiously frame the entire discourse arena. They can flexibly allow the analyst to pursue one or another element of the discourse for further analysis—while holding that element clearly "in place" within the broader discourse arena as a whole. In sum, situational analysis provides big picture maps that enable the researcher to "see" better where they may—and may not—want to go in terms of smaller portraits and/or the use of wide-angle lenses. Situational analysis is thus very user friendly with diverse discourse materials.

Last, the accessibility and relative cheapness of access to certain kinds of discursive materials make such projects attractive as well. A lot of qualitative research is not supported by research funds. Finding good, very cheap but still highly worthwhile, interesting, and provocative projects is important—especially but not only for students.

Notes

1. On narrative analysis, see, e.g., Chesla (1995), Cortazzi (2001, 2003), Czarniawska (1998), Lieblich, Tuval-Mashiach, and Zilber (1998), Josselson, Leiblich, and McAdams (2003), Mishler (1995, 2000), Plummer (1995, 2001a, 2001b), and Riessman (1993, 2002). On feminist narrative analysis, see, e.g., Bloom (1998), Naples (2003), and Messias and DeJoseph (n.d.).

2. Permission to use materials for academic scholarly purposes is sometimes free and usually granted upon request—once you have located the right person or original publisher, whichever holds the copyright. However, some advertisers and other copyright holders will not grant permission; in such situations, careful narratives of the ads or other images must suffice and can be more than adequate. Copyright holders can also charge for use of their materials. In academia, authors rather than publishers are generally expected to bear these costs, which can be hefty. Obtaining permissions can be quite time consuming, and advance planning is best. Also, preparing materials for reproduction can be complex and costly, and is also usually done by authors.

3. Discursive constructions of end users of a technology are common. See, e.g., Woolgar (1991), Akrich (1992, 1995), Forsythe (2001), Oudshoorn (2003), and Oudshoorn and Pinch (2003).

6

Mapping Visual Discourses

[T]he postmodern is a visual culture.

—Mirzoeff (1998:4)

I have been provoked to extend situational analysis to visual discourse from many directions. Stafford (1996) has called for the encouragement of visual literacies. Evans and Hall (1999:1) have expressed concern that "'visual culture' has been somewhat overlooked in the rapid expansion of cultural and media studies throughout the past decade and a half." Harrison (1996:75) has contended, "[T]he value of visual imagery and visual methods . . . is such as to warrant a more central location in research training and research practice." And perhaps most important, Mirzoeff's epigraph insists that a method that seeks to engage the postmodern must engage the visual. There are visual materials in most if not all of the situations of inquiry that we research. We ignore them at our analytic peril. Instead, we can engage them, seek to understand how visuality is constitutive of those situations, and come to fuller terms with their rich and dense contributions to social life.

My goals here are to foster and support the analysis of *extant* visual discourse materials on their own and/or as a related part of an integrated multisite/multiscape research project within the broad domain of qualitative research undertaken in various disciplinary and professional venues. Thus I do *not* discuss producing new visual materials as part of a research project,[1] using visual materials in the research process itself (e.g., to solicit responses from participants),[2] or exploring perception or reception— how audiences "read" visual materials—but do refer you to works on these topics.[3] There exist vast literatures on visual materials,[4] including some strong social science research texts.[5] While still images are the main focus here, situational analysis can certainly be used with film, video, and other visual forms, including multimedia.[6]

As with historical and narrative discourses, visual discourse can be the focus of a small or large project, or a subpart of a larger project. The digital revolution is transforming making, altering, storing, and reproducing images while simultaneously lowering the costs of doing so. The inclusion of visual materials of all kinds in scholarly journals and books is becoming increasingly routine. Thus in addition to studying the un(der)studied, we will be able to publish research on visual materials in sites and ways that in the past could only be fantasized.

Because I suspect very few people who read this book will have been particularly exposed to studies of visual discourse, much less the vast scholarship on the visual, I begin by providing some historical and conceptual entrée that should be useful in actually doing analysis of visual materials. The remainder of the chapter focuses on doing grounded situational analysis of visual discourse using an exemplar from my own work.

Entering Visual Discourse

> *I argue for the need to recognize, and act upon, the occurrence of a profound and comprehensive intellectual revolution. This overturning affects all branches of daily life and even the more arcane reaches of humanistic and scientific research and practice. Simply put, it is the radical shift underway since the eighteenth century from a text-based to a visually-dependent culture.*
>
> —Stafford (1991:xviii)

Visual discourses have entered the domains of the social sciences and humanities as subjects of research by multiple routes and for multiple reasons, especially since the postmodern turn. This shift recognizes that historically there has been a truly dramatic increase in both the numbers and kinds of representations with which most humans on the planet live and in the number and kinds of things with which we visually dwell (Mitchell 1994). Material culture has elaborated and is deeply visual (Miller 1998). Most modern modes of display of visual representation can be traced to the 1820s and 1830s when the technologies of lithography, photography, and other modes of duplication of images allowed the mass production of representations for the first time. Walter Benjamin (1970) famously argued that this intense reproduction of art and images by mechanical or technological rather than human means of copying constituted the major turning point in the development of visual cultures to that date. And it was less than 200 years ago.

Advertising is perhaps the mass-produced visual discourse most "seen" in "modern social life." Early ads promoted personal services, books published, apprentices, horses and dogs, commodities available at particular shops, remedies for various bodily ills, and public carnivalesque events showing monsters, prodigies, and freaks. Interestingly, drug and toiletries advertising led the way, became and remain dominant today. Raymond Williams (1980:179) argues, "The half-century between 1880-1930 . . . saw the full development of an organized system of commercial information and persuasion, as part of the modern distributive system in conditions of large-scale capitalism." The combined use of visual and narrative discourses in advertising and the ways in which commercial information and persuasion cannot be meaningfully separated have made this a key site for visual discourse analysis for many decades (e.g., Barnard 1995; Goffman 1976). Advertising has also influenced other modes of visual representation.

In the 19th-century West, public visual displays of the rare and exotic, long a part of fairs and carnivals, were repackaged. Displays of exotic colonial cultures and their "exports" were routinely mounted for international exhibits in a pattern that is still alive and well, including "dioramas" of live people in their cultural habitats (e.g., Bennett 1995; Smith 1999). Since about 1900, photography and film/video have been important in ethnographic anthropology. Many early visuals were efforts in "salvage ethnography," attempting to save remnants of "disappearing" cultures (Marcus & Fischer 1986). However, such visuals have also been sites of major recent critiques centered on how such visuals can work in complicitous ways in "exoticizing" and "othering" native peoples, much like the living dioramas are all too reminiscent of zoos. Today, globalized tourism routinely displays exotic local cultures for visual (and aural) consumption (e.g., MacCannell 1976). While visual ethnography remains vital in anthropology (e.g., Pink 2001), there has recently been a shift to the ethnography *of* indigenous media as well as of new intentionally transnational/diasporic indigenous media forms (Ginsberg 1999; Ginsberg et al. 2002).

Among sociologists, Georg Simmel (1903/1964, 1908/1970:150) was the first to highlight the significance of the visual in modern culture: "The rapid crowding of changing images, the sharp discontinuity in the grasp of a single glance, and the unexpectedness of onrushing impressions." Urban life "shows a great preponderance of occasions to *see* rather than to *hear* people." In the early 20th century, he saw people becoming visual objects in new ways, including through consumption (DeGrazia & Furlough 1996; Solomon-Godeau 1996).

Photography and the visual then played a serious role in two strands of early American sociology—social reform and Chicago social ecology. The social reform strand used photography for advocacy inside sociology and academia but publication of such visuals in sociology journals was abandoned by circa 1915 as scientism gained ground (Harper 1994). The Chicago social ecology strand produced what Denzin (1991:100) has called "the incipient cultural studies tradition and agenda, focused on communications [that] has always lurked inside interactionism." This strand, though never extensive, followed on from Simmel in taking the visual seriously, and is continued in this book.[7] It extends today to cultural studies topics such as tattoo, fashion, Las Vegas, video and teletechnology, film studies, media studies, and projects on visual cultures in science and medicine studies.[8] Across the 20th century, the development of film, television, electronic media, the Internet, and so on have each added waves of new visual materials and technologies to our cultural heritage. We are routinely awash in the mass media and new media. "The new information technologies turn everyday life into a theatrical spectacle; into sites where the dramas that surround the decisive performances of race, ethnicity, gender, sexuality, and age are staged" (Denzin 1991:8).[9]

What I would argue is that recently the second major turning point/ rupture in the development of visual culture has occurred—the capacity to change photos and other images electronically. "Digitalization techniques seem to permit an unprecedented enhancement and manipulation of pictorial representations . . . [now] more a matter of computing proficiency than camera, darkroom, or editing skills" (Ball & Smith 2001:313). Widely democratized as desktop computer technologies, this manipulability is dramatically changing how visual media are to be understood (e.g., Harper 2000; Lister 1995).

Realisms and Gazes: Concepts and Studies

> *Visual studies is poised to become one of the most interesting and conceptually challenging subjects that has emerged in academic life in the last several decades.*
>
> —Elkins (2003:vii)

How, then, can we think about the rise of the visual theoretically? Chaplin (1994:159) makes a distinction between what she calls the critical and empirical paradigms in visual cultural studies:

The critical paradigm focuses attention on the unequal relations between social strata, and analysis is informed by a vision of a more equitable society. Such an analysis is therefore also an argument for change; it is concerned with what *should* be. The empirical paradigm, on the other hand, has classically not been concerned with what should be; one of its tenets has been that social inequalities have first to be empirically established. Its proponents want to explore what human society is actually like.

Chaplin asserts that these two paradigms have been held apart too long. I concur. To do strong visual analyses, one needs to be familiar with both. Therefore, I next briefly frame some of the key concepts in the critical paradigm that can be of use in empirical work.

Freud actually coined the psychoanalytic term *scopophilia* to capture the drive to look and the pleasure of looking, arguing that this is characteristic of humans (Sturken & Cartwright 2001). It is important to note that the rise of visual discourse in the West was parallel to the rise of capitalism and consumption. This rise of visual discourse was and remains integral to imperialism, colonization, globalization, and democratization—travels of people, material things, ideas, practices, maps, and sundry representations. And since the turn of the 20th century, it has been especially linked to corporate and transnational capitalisms (Williams 1980). In "the society of the spectacle" in which we live, Debord (1967/1999:98) argued, "The spectacle is *capital* to such a degree of accumulation that it becomes an image," mediating social relations in ways that serve the needs of capital but obscure its power.

Because so many visual discourses are put to work in the service of capitalism, the state, and other forms of "the powers that be," many social theorists are highly critical of the visual. One area of concern centers on problematics of realism. Analytically, visual materials are particularly important precisely because of the *claims to realism* they usually convey and their consequences in particular situations.[10] This has been especially true of photography. Called photorealism or documentary truth, there is a gripping "myth of photographic truth. . . . The medium itself is considered transparent" (Sekula 1982:86). To interrupt this myth, viewers must think reflexively about how images are made—acts of posing, framing, capturing—and about viewing per se. Yet even then, "viewers engage in the work of decoding. Viewers *project* wholeness, coherence, and identity onto a depicted scene, refusing an 'impoverished reality in favour of an imaginary plenitude'" (Burgin 1982:147; emphasis added). "Usually this takes place instantaneously, unselfconsciously, and apparently naturally" (Bell 2002:9). That is, whether or not we consciously *intend* to flesh out an image, our eyes/mind have been so trained as users/consumers of the visual that they tend to do it "for us"/"to us."

This point is wonderfully captured in the famous surrealist painting of a pipe by Rene Magritte done circa 1928 that has written across the bottom "This is not a pipe." The painting is also titled to rupture our viewing: *The Treachery of Images* (Sturken & Cartwright 2001:15). Magritte is reminding us that this is a *picture* of a pipe—assuredly *not* the "real thing."[11] The visual is surreal and in need of critical analysis. Today technology allows us to move easily beyond the real in visual discourses through many forms of electronic creation and manipulation. The "myth of photographic truth" has been ruptured—but unevenly and unstably. In fact, the tendency to assume stability and authenticity remains very strong in terms of many genres of visual culture such as family photos, school photos, documentary films, and so on, while dubiousness reigns more commonly vis-à-vis advertising, political and celebrity images, and entertainment. But the boundaries leak (Minh-Ha 1989:94).

In terms of the visual as suspect, all visual modes can be implicated, not just photography. The issue is the power of what has been called "the gaze."[12] Who gets to look? At whom or what? Who is in control of seeing? Who/what is the object of the gaze? With what consequences? As discussed in Chapter 2, "the gaze" is an important concept for situational analysis. Perhaps the most important formulation is that of Michel Foucault (e.g., 1975, 1979). Foucault means by the concept not merely looking or seeing but the production of power relations *through* looking or seeing—through the *practices* of "the gaze." The gaze manifests a power relation between gazers and gazees. There is a sense of being objectified, subordinated, or threatened by being the object of the gaze—by being stared at. Power and privacy are deeply related. Voyeurism is often part of the gaze. Here gazers can gaze to their heart's content, as the gazee cannot "look back"—cannot "return" the gaze as a subject but only as an object to be looked at, consumed.

Foucault was particularly interested in the relations of knowledge/power produced when a collectivity of some kind such as a discipline gains jurisdiction over broad domains of life through use of a disciplinary gaze. That is, the gaze can be a collective/institutional authority to stare as well as individual. For example, Foucault famously argues (1975) that since the 18th century, the clinical gaze of medicine in the hospital both with and without scopic technologies (see also Cartwright 1995a, 1995b, 2000; Kevles 1997) has become a relentlessly disciplining gaze focused on illness and disease. My own work with colleagues has followed this gaze into the 21st century and the biomedicalization of health (Clarke 2003). An institution such as the state gains power through the disciplinary gaze of the panopticon of the prison (Foucault 1979:ch. 2), and more recently via photo and other forms of ID, bodily and property "screening" technologies for "security purposes" (Tagg 1987).

Let us turn now to some exemplary research projects that have used these and other concepts to analyze visual discourses. Taking off in part from Berger's (1972:47) comment that in the classic Western tradition of images, "men act, women appear," Laura Mulvey (1975/1989) framed the concept of "the male gaze." This is the exercise of male authority in visual domains (as elsewhere) such that the gazer is usually assumed to be male/masculine (unless otherwise clearly noted), while the gazee is female/feminine. That is, who or whatever is gazed upon is feminized (read disempowered) by the gaze itself. Women typically become *sexualized* objects of the gaze, exhibiting a distinctive "to-be-looked-at-ness" (Mulvey 1975/1989:19).

Working at the same time Mulvey was theorizing the male gaze as part of second-wave feminism, Erving Goffman (1976), an interactionist heir of Simmel, produced one of the earliest studies of power in visual materials in the social sciences. While he focused especially on gender and especially on advertising photographs, his mode of analysis is much more broadly generalizable and useful across visual discourses.

Goffman teaches us some basics of "reading"/analyzing visual materials. He focused on six main ways in which power is commonly expressed, illustrated, and normalized in visual discourse. I have selected one image to illustrate each here (there are dozens in his book). Figure 6.1 illustrates Goffman's analysis of relative size in the image: Larger is more powerful. Figure 6.2 shows ritualistic touching and pointing compared to utilitarian touching and pointing: The utilitarian is more powerful. Figure 6.3 shows function ranking whereby the more powerful party is seen as holding an executive role, as the doer rather than the done to. Figure 6.4 illustrates how family scenes with appropriate age/gender configurations often frame women (but not men) in the category of children: Men *and boys* are typically more powerful. Figure 6.5 illustrates what Goffman called the ritualization of visible subordination. This is usually accomplished through positioning such as lowering the body as in bowing and through deferential facial gestures. These can visually—and quite silently—"naturalize" gender, racial, and other hierarchies of power. Last, Figure 6.6 shows expressions of horror, shame, and/or vulnerability as more commonly female, feminizing and disempowering in the situation imaged. If you plan to analyze visual discourse, Goffman remains a basic entry-level primer that can accompany more contemporary introductory works such as Sturken and Cartwright's excellent text (2001).[13]

Quite obviously, there are many other visual gazes of power, perhaps most importantly in terms of race and ethnicity, produced through Western imperialism and colonization after circa 1500, an early wave of globalization.[14] The "imperial gaze" is that of the colonist upon the colonized, and is famously captured in Edward Said's (1978) concept of "orientalism." He

Figure 6.1   Goffman: Relative Size

SOURCE: Goffman (1976:82). Reprinted by permission of HarperCollins Publishers Inc.

Figure 6.2   Goffman: The Feminine Touch

SOURCE: Goffman (1976:30). Reprinted by permission of HarperCollins Publishers Inc.

Figure 6.3   Goffman: Function Ranking

SOURCE: Goffman (1976:32). Reprinted by permission of HarperCollins Publishers Inc.

Figure 6.4   Goffman: The Family

SOURCE: Goffman (1976:38). Reprinted by permission of HarperCollins Publishers Inc.

Figure 6.5   Goffman: Ritualization of Subordination

SOURCE: Goffman (1976:43). Reprinted by permission of HarperCollins Publishers Inc.

Figure 6.6   Goffman: Licensed Withdrawal

SOURCE: Goffman (1976:58). Reprinted by permission of HarperCollins Publishers Inc.

refers to centuries of relations between Europe/the West and Asia/the East as based in the Western presumption of Western superiority. Western power and authority were achieved not only militarily but also through a relentlessly disciplining gaze that, since circa 1500, has continually portrayed the East as exotic, indolent, devious, and untrustworthy. (I wrote this after reading a morning newspaper report describing the U.S. occupation of Iraq that performed all four of these modes of othering in two short paragraphs.) Orientalism is an ongoing project, an outcome, and a continually remediated product of Western imperialism (see also Marcus 2001).

The globalizing imperial gaze was, of course, not only directed at the East but also at the South. This gaze emphasizes racialization—the stratification of races and ethnicities produced by and through colonization and its various forms of domination, beginning with but far from limited to the many forms of slavery. The racializing gaze places marked cultures as remote, far away, "at the edge of the world," carefully establishing boundaries (Mbembe 2001). Various visual formats perform the colonizing gaze of racialization—past and present (see note 16). Early anthropology offers a classic example:

> [C]olonial discourses and power relations provided a context in which photographs of possibly sensitive matters could be taken and reproduced with little fear of censure by those observed. . . . Evans-Pritchard's [1940] *The Nuer, . . .* a well-known text . . . , contains close-up pictures of completely naked (black) men and women with visible genitalia. Some of these people are obviously in their early teens. It is an interesting thought-experiment to consider what would happen if equivalent images were to appear in a sociology text dealing with western, white subjects. (Emmison & Smith 2000:15)

This tradition of bare-breasted and otherwise bared "natives"—open to Western/Northern visual inspection but never vice versa—has been ably sustained and brought into public culture in museums, another site of the racializing gaze. For example, Teslow (1998:72-73) studied the Chicago Field Museum of Natural History's visual display on the science of racial classification. Titled "Races of Mankind," it was on show from 1933 to the mid-1960s, and consisted of 101 life-sized, realistically diverse bronze sculptures. "The predominant message of the [original] exhibit was clear: racial groups exist in nature . . . within a hierarchical scheme that relegated 'black' and 'yellow' races to primitive status on the margins of the civilized 'white' races." Later, after the racial classification apparatus had been seriously critiqued within the sciences, the sculptures were displayed on their own. Thus across the 60 years of their display, these sculptures have been "read" in quite varied ways—as a scientific hierarchy, as institutionalized racism, and most recently as celebration of the "glorious diversity" of race. More contemporarily, eminent Afro-Caribbean cultural studies scholar Stuart Hall (1990:230; emphasis in original), who works in England, is concerned that not only "were we constructed as different and other within the categories of knowledge in the West by those regimes. They [also] had the power to make us see and experience *ourselves* as 'Other.'" That is, such visuals can be constitutive of objectified people's *own* identities/subjectivities. Hall views visual cultures as significant elements of those disciplining regimes, especially in diasporic situations where one's visual cultural roots can be thousands of miles away and can themselves be experienced as alien. In her book *Black Looks: Race and Representation,* bell hooks (1992) takes off from Hall's analyses in seeking to decolonize the gaze—to learn how to "look back" defiantly and resist. Her goal is to assist in developing a critical "oppositional gaze" that can displace degrading white supremacist readings and visuals with more race-positive and complex discussions about visual materials.

An example that combines orientalism and racialization with the male gaze is Gifford-Gonzales's (1993) analysis of women's "positions" in recent dioramas of "Early Man" in anthropological museums. In these often life-sized, three-dimensional visual displays usually intended as educational, the bodies are mostly bronze and black, and only partially clothed. The women are commonly seated or on their knees cooking or child-tending, or leaning over animal skins to tan and otherwise prepare them as hides for clothing, bedding, and so on. The men are commonly imaged in a scattered but clearly coordinated group pursuing large beasts on foot in a pastoral yet threatening wilderness. She titled her paper, ironically if not subtly, "Women Can Hide But They Can't Run."

In a book that tries to take the nonhuman quite seriously, I want to also point out that there are very similar, but also different, "othering" processes that address the nonhuman, especially animals and plants. Donna Haraway's (1989) *Primate Visions: Gender, Race, and Nature in the World of Modern Science* and her other work (1991a, 2003) take this up quite vividly. The symbolic conquering of the animal world through trophy hunting and its imagery of both mounted "heads" and pictures of "great white hunters" with a conquering foot on a very big, very dead animal are classic visual manifestation of such "othering." The scientific version collects living and dead specimens for zoos, museums, and research purposes (e.g., Mitman 1996). In fact, one of the major companies that used resources from German colonies before World War II focused on three activities: catching animals for live export, displaying exotic people at exhibitions, and making the Munich zoo (Rothfels 2002). Perhaps most dramatic, a famous early moving picture was the staged *Electrocuting an Elephant,* capturing its falling and slow death (Edison Manufacturing Co. 1903, quoted in Cartwright 1995b:19). The photohistory of redwood logging in the Pacific Northwest of the United States is similarly rife with dramatic differences in size—tiny humans versus giant trees. Visual mastery over (large) animals is complemented with visual mastery over (large) nature. The most popular show ever mounted at the San Francisco Museum of Modern Art was a 2002 retrospective of the photography of Ansel Adams, who specialized in vistas of the American West—demonstrating how nature too has become a visual spectacle for our consumption.

Most of the initial analyses of othering through visual means that I have discussed—concepts of the gaze, the male gaze, orientalism, racialization, and other visual forms of dominance—have now been seriously critiqued and theoretically complexified. One key point is that we need to take into account the social and historical contexts of both the production of the images and the social and historical contexts of spectatorship—expectations of viewing. In the postmodern, multiple gazer and gazee positions are possible. For example, Linda Williams (1989) studied hard-core pornography as a means of challenging a simplistic reading of "the male gaze." She argued that while most heterosexual pornography may well be produced by males, directed at males, and consumed by males, audiences can actually be diverse and the subject position of viewer is open to any who choose to view. Obviously, some lesbians can comfortably partake of the male gaze in this visual form. But if sexual and gender identities are no longer understood as rigid, bounded, and permanent, then most anyone might find pleasure through occupying the male position, including the pleasures of male privilege (however temporary). The same holds true for gay porn; it has its targeted audiences/consumers, but others are possible and more than likely.

I have argued that "[i]n postmodernity, capital has fallen in love with difference" (Clarke 1995:146). Intentionally transgressive advertising also strategically attempts to work simultaneously across seemingly contradictory categories of potential consumers. The advertising of Viagra (discussed in Chapter 4) is an excellent example (Mamo & Fishman 2001; see also King 2002). Usually designed to appeal explicitly to older heterosexual men, in these ads there are also subtexts and keyed visual signals inserted to alert other possible consumers such as gay men and any and all women to the possibility of taking Viagra. Across multiple venues today, from advertising to popular culture, males are also being increasingly displayed for consumption and expectations of their appearance are similarly rising. Especially given metrosexuality, gay men are no longer the major consumers of male versions of "to-be-looked-at-ness." Everyone and everything can be constellated as objects in intensely visually mediated cultures of consumption.

"[V]isual images which surround us in everyday life must be viewed as actively at work in constructing the world how it has to be, and not just reflecting how it is" (Harrison 1996:80). They tell us who we "should" be and what we "should" do, and often "how to" do it and the products to use in the process. They are ever disciplining and never innocent. Analytically, then, we need to be alert to the many kinds of work visual materials can be doing in a given situation—including (in a doubled reflexivity) in the situation of our own research. Visual materials can be colonizing, racializing, gendering, sexing, classifying, stratifying, fetishizing, deceiving, authenticating, mesmerizing, transgressing, clarifying, stunning, muting, distracting, subjecting, cherishing, preserving, cluttering, and so on. And, most challenging analytically, they can be doing multiple and contradictory things at once. Again, this pertains to all visual discourses including high art, television, advertising, family photos, print media, the Internet, and so on.

The key summary point vis-à-vis all these modes of othering through the visual—the critical paradigm of the gaze, the male gaze, orientalism, racialization, victory over nature, and other forms of marking—is that in engaging in the analysis of visual materials, one realizes in a particularly vivid way that there is no space outside of power and discourse. When viewed with a critical eye, the baldness, the "in-your-faceness" of visual representation—the facticity of its having been produced, distributed, preserved, and looked at, usually again and again—insists on our learning how to take it seriously in research.

Disciplinary Gazes, Visual Cultures

> *This is a looking culture, organized in terms of a variety of gazes, or looks (tourist, investigatory—medical, social science, television, religious, political—artistic, photographic, and so on).*
>
> —Denzin (1991:9)

Despite the intense linkages of visual discourses to commercial capitalism and consumption, capitalism is far from alone in its intense visual relations. The use of the visual can also be in the service of many other social worlds and institutional forms. "It is hard to think of one institution in society that does not use reproduced images" and produce a visual discourse open to analysis (Evans & Hall 1999:2). I use the term "culture" here to specifically indicate shared collective forms of visuality. There exist many and heterogeneous "visual cultures" (e.g., Evans & Hall 1999), "scopic regimes" (e.g., Foucault 1975; Jay 1993), "regimes of representation" (Latour 1988b, 1990), "art worlds" (Becker 1982), and so on. Visual cultures are produced through particular disciplines and discourses (Foucault 1975), or social worlds (Strauss 1978), and/or subcultures (Gelder & Thornton 1997). That is, visual cultures are distinctively *situated* in institutional/discursive realms, and we begin to make sense of visual cultures by taking this situatedness into account (e.g., Haraway 1991b). In Becker's (1998:84) concise wording: "It's (almost) all a matter of context."

Each discipline, social world, subculture has its own specific discourse, including rhetorics (e.g., Bazerman & Paradis 1991), technological apparatus (Strauss 1978), and distinctive visual imagery—its visual culture(s) (Evans & Hall 1999). Within a particular world, signs, symbols, and cues will work in particular ways in its own conventions of visuality that frame meaning making (Becker 1982). Foucault (1975, 1979) further argues that disciplinary gazes organize the world, producing "the order of things." They frame apprehension and perception—we can only "see" and understand the world and "the conditions of possibility" through gazes we have learned/ internalized/been disciplined by. Thus institutional locations and their visual cultures are important features of most situations under analysis. Disciplines are social worlds—communities of shared practices, universes of discourse. The term "discipline" can be used literally for scholarly disciplines such as sociology, anthropology, education, nursing, social work, communication, management, and so on or metaphorically for an institutional formation.

One of the interesting changes in analysis of visual materials since the postmodern turn is the increasing frequency of studies of the visual cultures of particular disciplines and other social worlds. In the past, it was assumed that an image "reflected" the world in which it was made in a mirrorlike, more or less realistic fashion. In contrast, today we tend to look at visual materials as "produced in and by" particular social domains for particular purposes. Visual images are then analyzed as *discursive cultural products* of particular worlds or disciplines (Pryce 1996:99). No mirroring, or realism, or authenticity is assumed (Rorty 1979), and a more than skeptical stance may be taken toward the images. Thus today analyzing a visual is predicated to some degree on understanding the world that produced it.

Another focus of analyzing a visual culture in relation to its production world concerns images used in that visual culture in the past. There are two important concepts here: referencing and remediation. *Referencing* usually takes the form of including particular elements that symbolically refer to earlier images or events in a newly produced visual discourse. These symbols usually point out something important, valued, and so on. Referentiality is rife across all visual media. It is at the heart of both creating art and producing art history. But referencing is also common across many if not most other forms of discourse. In music, for example, phrases of other composers or musicians are often "quoted." Such quotation is at the heart of jazz improvisation, and the recognition of such quotations is a key part of jazz connoisseurship. As scholars, we are constantly referencing, quoting, and citing in patterned ways that situate our work in comparison with others. Learning to decode referentiality is part of learning visual discourse analysis.

Remediation is the concept Bolter and Grusin (1999:14-15) use to discuss how the actual contents or framings that older media cultures traditionally carry (including conventional forms of racism, sexism, etc.) are commonly imported unquestioned into new media. But, due to the newness of the mechanisms of delivery (e.g., the Internet or CD-ROMs), it *appears* as if the contents embedded in these new forms of representation are themselves new and innovative. Older visual cultures are commonly thereby technically gussied up while merely reinscribing old content and/or framings (see also Forsythe 2001). Again, learning about remediations in your situation of research inquiry is part of learning visual analysis.

To illustrate *disciplinary gazes, visual cultures,* and their study as part of visual discourse analyses, I next offer a couple of examples. First, the sciences and medicine have produced an array of distinctive visual cultures. Here the research studies by scholars from the social sciences and humanities are usually analyses of "practices of visualization" in a particular scientific discipline or specialty (Emmison & Smith 2000:22).[15] That is, much of the routine work of actors in many different sciences "requires visualization as a component of human thinking and problem solving" (Harrison 2002:857). "A scientific journal such as *Nature* depend[s] upon depictions: tables, graphs, scattergrams, maps, sketches and photographs. . . . The science that it reproduces would be impossible without visualization: depictions are *constitutive* of scientific production" (Fyfe & Law 1988:3; emphasis in original).[16]

In terms of the discipline of medicine and its visual cultures, Foucault (1975) alerted us to how the very founding of modern medicine in the 18th century was based on visualization—the birth of clinic was made possible *through* the medical gaze. In the clinic, the physician *observes,* rather than (or at least much more than) engaging with patients in speech, and one physician gets to observe many different patients. The body is understood to speak loudly to a skilled observer (including at autopsy)—especially when there are many bodies to compare. Foucault (1973) noted that a newly visualized "anatomical atlas" began to emerge (as the exemplar demonstrates below). Hospitals and asylums organized such comparative work institutionally, and their architecture—the built visual environment—furthered such carceral projects (Prior 1988). Historically, visual images of the medically incarcerated have been at the heart of medicine in its ambitious segregation and disciplining of the insane, the feebleminded, and the diseased—often by disease (e.g., Gilman 1985, 1996; Tagg 1987).

Enhancing and elaborating the medical gaze, enabling physicians to see inside the body through various technologies has been a central mode of biomedical innovation, and a number of scholars have examined these varied visual cultures of medicine.[17] Among the earliest "technologies of the gaze" were a wide range of anatomical visual images and models (from carved ivory "Venuses" to wax figures). There were also many collections of pathological specimens, and physicians from the Renaissance onward spent considerable time staring at items such as these (Roberts & Tomlinson 1992). Gradually, such visual cultural materials were organized by specialty (embryology, dermatology, cardiology, gynecology) and used as devices for medical training. Today many such collections are in museums, and some are being digitalized and organized online into Web sites and other new formats (being remediated as it were), fascinating sites for analysis of visual cultures.[18] Recently, public displays of plastinated corpses have also been controversial but well attended.

Western anatomy collections have typically featured sex/gender differences as fundamental. Unless a display was focused on race or racial classification such as the Field Museum exhibit discussed earlier, the convention has been to display only white bodies, making whiteness the standard here as in other sites. Jordanova (1989) argues that the visual discourses of anatomy *about* sex/gender have themselves been *constitutive* of the categories of sex and gender. The discourses have actively mapped these categories onto living bodies. Historically, the power of sciences to thereby *naturalize* hierarchical social relations has been considerable because of their increasingly privileged epistemological position as "official" knowledges since the 18th century. Anatomy in particular, she finds, is a science of transgression by invasion and public display. The exemplar from my work offered below follows up on Jordanova's points.

In concluding this incredibly brief and partial introduction to analyzing visual culture, I want to note that visual materials often seem quite different from other kinds of research data. They can appear to be dramatically more symbolic, historical, and referential in their content. The hackneyed phrase "A picture is worth a thousand words" points to this aspect. We often feel compelled to look—and are moved by looking. However, with Bell (2002:6), I want to "blur the distinction between verbal and visual narratives, drawing inspiration from photographers like [Jo] Spence who argue that attempts to 'purify' media—that is to clearly distinguish images and words, or verbal and visual narratives—are utopian modern projects." Words and images commonly flow into one another and, most importantly, are (re)presentations to be reflexively analyzed (e.g., Sava & Nuutinen 2003). Furthermore, even "the distinction between social analysis and visual representation is becoming less clear-cut, and . . . social analysis . . . *should* make more use of visual depictions" (Chaplin 1994:2). How to do this is discussed next.

Doing Situational Analysis of Visual Discourse

> *Kids know it better than the rest of us do. Words and pictures are primally bound. Watch any preliterate child or beginning reader with a book, and you see it immediately. Kids don't look at pictures as diverting illustrations or supplements to the text. They read the pictures avidly, mining them for every bit of information, mood, feeling, mystery, and nuance of the world fanning open before them.*
>
> —Winn (2003:E1)

What do I mean by visual data? What counts as visual data for possible analysis? With Emmison and Smith (2000:ix, xi, 1), I would argue for a very broad definition:

> Social life is visual in diverse and counterintuitive ways. Consequently, there are many more forms of visual data than the photograph, the advertisement and the television program. Objects and buildings carry meanings through visual means just like images. Clothing and body language are significant signs which we use to establish identity and negotiate public situations. . . . [V]isual data can be located in sources as diverse as wedding albums and pornography, living rooms and waiting rooms, living bodies and stony statues, august museums and playful shopping malls . . . drawings, maps, sketches, diagrams, . . . directional signs.

Situational analysis can be done with all these kinds of visual data and others. Emmison and Smith (2000:4) also assert that "the raw material for visual investigation must also be viewed, understood [and/]or placed in some analytical framework before they can be regarded as data." Our questions become: What project will be furthered or what question better answered by analyzing a particular set of visual images? What are the visuals data *for?* What *situation(s) of inquiry* do they speak from and to? This is the theoretical/substantive question that the analyst needs to address first.

For doing situational analysis of visual data, my recommendations combine the recording of initial impressionistic interpretations along with doing systematic memos. The goal is to open the visual data up for analysis. Here, as elsewhere in this book, researchers are expected to use their insight along with the methods specified rather than symbolically stand out of the way so that some heretofore repressed "voice" or other analytic can "emerge."

One thing is clear. Doing visual analyses requires us to stop and stare trebly hard in order to rupture the taken-for-grantedness of "good looking" (Stafford 1996), in which we usually (read "naturally") dwell. Perhaps the key point to remember is that there is no one "correct" reading of any image (e.g., S. Hall 1997). We need to do multiple readings and consider them at length. Making and keeping lists of possible interpretations of wholes, parts, particular things imaged, and so on can be exceptionally useful downstream.

Which Visual Materials?
Deciding, Locating, Collecting, and Tracking

Visual culture is what is seen.

—Gertrude Stein (quoted in Elkins 2003:4)

Four main steps are initially involved before analysis gets under way: deciding, locating, collecting, and tracking the materials. The first question the researcher must address is: Where shall the visual materials come from? Research design issues—aspects of deciding and locating—have been discussed previously (esp. Chapters 2 and 4). In short, the materials should be the best range of visuals you can obtain related to the situation that you have chosen to research. If you are pursuing a multisite project, the visual materials should articulate well with the other sites you are examining. For example, Fosket (2002) studied a large clinical trial of cancer chemoprevention drugs. While she mapped the trial with care, she could also have studied the visuals images printed on the paper materials on the trial that were given to participants, and the logo and other design elements of the various freebie items distributed, from sweatshirts to mugs, to tote bags, and so on. I assume the researcher will locate and gather particular materials of interest. The Internet also provides access to a stunningly rich array of visual images, and the number and kinds of such archives that can be used for visual discourse analysis projects grows daily.[19]

The next two steps, collecting and tracking visual materials, are often fussy, obsessive, and tedious tasks. And because collecting may well be distributed across the life of the project, tracking may well be also. Doing these tasks is very much like entering bibliography in that if you get it right the first time, *much* anguish is saved downstream. If you don't, the capacity to publish something cherished may disappear.[20] It is best done where there is space to spread out and a handy photocopier, as it typically involves making working copies and preserving originals (for later duplication).

Tracking materials can be crucial if you want to publish a visual for which written permission is required—and it usually is required.[21] Some kind of log should be maintained that tracks the "provenance" of all the materials—where every visual came from in terms of "who, what, where, when, how, how much" and so on. For some projects, a carefully labeled separate folder and computer file (hard copy as well as digital) *for each visual* with all the pertinent provenance information on it inside will be the safest way to go. A separate loose-leaf binder or folder of labeled copies of all the visuals is also useful to have, as you can easily flip around and compare images without going into the files or having to refile.

Entering and Memoing Visual Discourse Materials

[I]t is the act of describing that enables the act of seeing.

—Price (1994:5)

There are three main levels of analysis of an image (Ball & Smith 1992): (1) its content—what is given, (2) its referents—what it refers to, and (3) its context(s)—where it appears and what uses are made of it. These are not at all necessarily clear to the analyst, and can also be hard to hold apart meaningfully—they may blend together. The *content* can usually be described fairly well. You are looking at it and can describe it in more or less detail. In contrast, its *referents* may or may not be able to be "decoded" by people unfamiliar with the genre of the image (e.g., 17th-century Dutch master paintings, rap music videos, Irish weddings, butoh dance, French versus American versus Brazilian advertisements, etc.). You may well not even know that some element in the image carries symbolic weight—*is* actually referential. This is one of the most challenging aspects of visual analysis, as becoming expert in a genre means much greater ease of decoding the referents—but can take considerable time and effort. It can also be quite fun and exciting. All three levels are addressed in the memos.

Entering the visual discourse you have chosen to study is accomplished through writing analytic memos—producing various kinds of narratives about each visual. These memos require the researcher to articulate—to "put into words"—what you "see" and what you think about what you see in particular ways. Three kinds of memos are recommended:

1. Locating memo

2. Big picture memo

3. Specification memo

These are parallel acts to the word-by-word, line-by-line, segment-by-segment initial "open" grounded theory coding of interview and ethnographic materials (see also G. Rose 2001:ch. 2). You may well prefer to tape record these memos, as it allows faster pacing. Transcribing them later then becomes a reflexive revisiting and polishing of your preliminary ideas.

Locating Memo

> An image "presents merely the possibility of meaning. Only by its embeddedness in a concrete discourse situation can [it] . . . yield a clear semantic outcome.
>
> —Sekula (1982:91)

Situating the visual is extremely important and the focus of the first memo on each image. It should first describe how this image fits into the situation of inquiry that is your overall visual project focus. Then it should at least sketch the social world(s) that produced this visual: why you chose this world(s) and these visual materials; where the image came from; who in particular produced it (if you know); for what audience(s) (as far as you know); with what goals and intended uses; and so on. Enter now as much as you can about the situation from which your visual emerged. Then stop writing this memo for the moment. You will return to it later when you map the social worlds/arenas in your project.

Big Picture Memo

> Representation follows two laws; it always conveys more than it intends; and it is never totalizing. The "excess" meaning conveyed by representation creates a supplement that makes multiple and resistant readings possible.
>
> —Phelan (1996:2)

An important mode of entrée into visual discourse is to analyze what Robert E. Park (1952) called "the big picture"—what is going on overall in the visual. The big picture memo has three parts:

1. First impressions

2. The big picture

3. The little pictures

First impressions: Quickly, off the top of your head, what is this whole thing an image of? There can and should be multiple and even possibly conflicting answers—your own impressions of the overall image. I strongly advocate spending your initial time with the images memoing your first impressions on audiotape or in a computer file so that your own alternative/contradictory readings do not get lost—even if you do get lost (Lather 2001a, 2001b) for a while in reading the image(s). All too quickly an image can "resolve" into X or Y such that we cannot recapture our initial visual grasp when it was "other." What had been open closes. Quick and dirty bulleted notes about your main "takes," and how the image hits you, and so on are the goals for memoing first impressions.

The big picture describes the visual fully. The goal here is to make visual data more like other data while at the same time retaining its distinctiveness as visual and retaining our interpretations and analyses of it as visual. If a picture is worth a thousand words, you will likely write a lot to describe it adequately for analysis. The demands of actually writing a narrative description of the image(s) will make you "see" more clearly, elaborately, and precisely. In the words of Mary Price (1994:5), "[I]t is the act of describing that enables the act of seeing." Putting it into words also creates an intertextuality—a moving back and forth between words and images—that can rupture the taken-for-grantedness of either or both modes of representation (e.g., Graham 1992). It can shift "good looking" (Stafford 1996) into "good seeing."

The little pictures section of the memo does the same for the different parts of the image. You will need to divide the image up into sections either by quandrants, by moving systematically upward or downward, or by some other means that parallel taking textual segments one at a time. Having photocopies you can draw on to divide the image into segments may be helpful. The goal is to memo for each segment "what are these images of?" Your own words, your own takes on the images are all that is desired at this stage of analysis. For example, "I see X and Y. Funny—there is no Z!"

The goal is to describe in lush and vivid detail—purple prose is fine—what you see. Write all the impressions down; don't worry about perfect typing—just memo. Later, you can put questions to what you have described (e.g., "What is that yellow shoe doing there?"). Pretend you want to fully convey the image to someone who cannot see it. Begin by narrating the big picture and then the segments. These narratives tell us what has been framed—what *is* there.

Depending upon the kind and number of visuals you are dealing with, you may or may not need to do elaborate memos of every single visual. I return to this point later. The main risk of producing a narrative text is, in fact, premature bounding and closure on the readings. Next we break the frame as another means of analytic entrée.

Specification Memo

If there is a center to poststructural thought, it lies in the recurring attempt to strip a text, any text, of its external claims to authority. Every text must be taken on its own terms.

—Denzin (1995:41)

There are a number of ways to analytically "break the frame" so that we can "see" an image in multiple ways. The goal here is to get outside the frame through which we are *supposed* to view that image (likely as a member of the audience envisaged by the creator(s) of the image—but not always). Further deconstruction of an image can be accomplished through addressing each of the following topics in a *specification memo*:[22]

- *Selection.* What is represented? Why do you think X, Y, or Z was selected rather than A, or B, or C?
- *Framing.* How is the subject framed? What is included, excluded, cut off at the edges?
- *Featuring.* What is foregrounded, middle-grounded, and backgrounded but still present?
- *Viewpoint.* Is the image a close-up, medium shot, long shot, low angle, high angle? What difference(s) do these make?
- *Light.* How is light used in the image? What is featured through highlighting? Backgrounded? How does the variation in light direct your attention within the image? What is more or less obscured?
- *Color.* How is color used in the image? What is bright and vivid and what is not? How does the variation in color direct your attention within the image?
- *Focus/Depth of Field.* Is everything in sharp focus? If not, what is blurred? What is clear? How does the variation in focus direct your attention within the image?
- *Presence/Absence.* Given the topic/focus of the image, is everything there that you would expect to be there? What is absent that you might have expected? What is different than you expected?
- *Intended/Unintended Audience(s).* Can you determine whether the image was aimed at any particular audience(s)? More than one? Who is *not* supposed to look here? Who would likely be made to feel uncomfortable looking here in "mixed" company? "Mixed" in what ways?
- *Composition.* What is emphasized? What is juxtaposed? What is placed apart? What is balanced/imbalanced? Are there tilted images? Moving images?
- *Texture.* Are there areas of different textures? What are they? What work do these areas do in the overall image?
- *Scale and Format/Proportions.* How are these expectable? Unexpected? What is emphasized? De-emphasized?
- *Technical Elements.* Are there any distinctive techniques used such as a wide-angle lens, telephoto, flash-lighting, special photo processing? What difference(s) do they make?

- *Single or Multimedia.* What media are in the work? How are they positioned vis-à-vis one another? Is work in one medium echoing or referencing another? To what end(s)?
- *Relationship to Other Work in Same Media.* Are there differences or largely similarities? What, if anything, is distinctive?
- *References.* Are there symbolic or other references in the image that you can decode? What are they? Where do they come from? Why do you think they are there? What work do they do in the visual? Is there a consistent pattern of referencing across multiple visuals? If you are unsure if something is or is not a reference, note this and return to it later. You can ask others and even try Googling some symbols.
- *Remediations.* Are there "remediations" wherein new visual technologies such as computer graphics or the Internet present themselves as offering newly refashioned and improved versions of older media while merely reinscribing old content in a newer format? How is this done? Is it easy to see? How can you tell?
- *Situatedness.* How is this image situated historically, geographically, temporally? In terms of social worlds/arenas, related discourses?
- *Relations With Visual Culture(s).* How is this image related to past and/or contemporary or futuristic visual (sub)cultures/social worlds? What are its relations to past or contemporary sociopolitical situations?
- *Commonness/Uniqueness.* Is this image one of a kind, rare, common? What difference(s) does this make?
- *Work of the Image.* What work is the image doing in the world? What is implicitly and explicitly normalized? Naturalized/unnaturalized? Marginalized? Featured?
- *Injunctions to Viewers.* What, if anything, are viewers being told to do or think or be? Not to do or think or be?

Any or all of these can be important or not in your overall analysis. But systematically considering these issues, *after* you have worked with your initial takes on the image and memoed them in a narrative, certainly breaks frame and reopens the analytic moment. Once a particular point is made in your memo, you do *not* need to say the same thing five times. Do annotate or keyword files so that you can retrieve key points or codes.

Doing Situational Maps of Visual Materials

[T]he postmodern era is one where visual and spatial forces are coming to organize our social life in ways which defy easy comprehension.

—Emmison & Smith (2000:xi)

Before I discuss doing the situational maps, I want to emphasize that the situational, social worlds/arenas, and positional maps done vis-à-vis visual research materials can take you far beyond these discursive materials per se. They rely, perhaps more than with interview and ethnographic data, on the researcher's creative insight, logic, and reflexivity, as well as on the research materials. They rely especially on the knowledge the researcher has gained about the research area through the very doing of the research—the research processes per se. As in situational analyses of other materials, prior coding according to the precepts of basic grounded theory is requisite. The memos you have written serve as the narrative data to be coded. Code first.

The general tasks of doing situational maps and analyses of narrative materials can now be applied to the narratives and codes you have produced of the visual materials along with the visual materials themselves. *Your situational map should include all analytically pertinent human and nonhuman, material, and symbolic/discursive elements of a particular image.* It is likely that, over time, not all will remain of interest. As with other data, this first effort is usually intentionally very messy, and hence very accessible and manipulable. Some people will prefer to continue working in this fashion.

One of the challenges of mapping visual materials is their partiality. Parts—elements—may well be missing that you know as an intelligent analyst are "really" present in the broader situation of which this visual is a part. There may well be many *implicated* actors, actants, institutions, and so on. Your responsibility as an analyst is to try and specify these while also noting their *explicit* absence. That is, there is a particular delicacy and ethicality at play here: You do not want to argue beyond the evidence, but you also don't want to play dumb. Lather (1991) has talked about "getting smart," and one way to do so is to analytically point to *possible* implicated actors, actants, institutions, and so on in your memos You can clarify these points through theoretical sampling downstream. So, in the situational map, implicated elements can, if you like, be indicated as implicated—or not. Whether you ultimately find these interesting and worthy of further analytic pursuit remains at this juncture a wide-open question. But you have, smartly, marked your question down. As with other genres of data/materials, you should do both messy and orderly situational maps, carefully dating them and keeping old versions "in case."

Doing Social Worlds/Arenas Maps of Visual Materials

Any given photograph is conceivably open to appropriation, . . . each new discourse situation generating its own set of messages.

—Sekula (1982:91)

The visual materials you have gathered and begun analyzing may or may not allow you to portray what in the epigraph Sekula calls a "discourse situation" and do a social worlds/arenas analysis of them. More commonly, the visual imagery you have gathered will have been produced by a major social world in your situation of concern, and you may or may not be studying the entire arena. Thus you may have images of one particular social world representing itself, other worlds, human and/or nonhuman actors in the arena, and so on, or not. Ultimately, you will need to address such partialities, if they exist in your data, in your memos.

The issue of *perspective* is obviously key here. From whose perspective are the visuals constructed? For whom? What/who are the intended audience(s)? Do(es) the image(s) refer to collective action in any way? What kinds of action? Involving what social worlds? Are other social worlds represented, and if so, how? Is there an arena implicated by the pattern of social worlds visualized? How is it portrayed? Again, you do not want to venture too far beyond your data, but . . .

Doing Positional Maps of Visual Materials

[D]emystification is the permanent revolution.

—Lyotard (1984:29)

The narration of the images, especially those aspects generated through breaking the frame, should generate a listing of key issues and their axes in the visual data—or implicated by the visual data. These may or may not be interesting at first glance, but some should at least be there. The analyst can then simply proceed with making positional maps as described in Chapter 3. I would recommend persisting in the face of disinterest here for at least a little while. Positional maps allow the specification of absences—what is *not* there—and this can be especially useful in the analysis of visual materials that one cannot necessarily theoretically sample or further interrogate.

Let us move next to the exemplar.

Visual Discourse Exemplars: Moore and Clarke's Anatomies

Lisa Jean Moore and I have been studying anatomies since the early 1990s, using science studies perspectives that examine the contents of sciences and technologies as well as their institutional and other manifestations. We chose genital anatomies based on our prior knowledge of what we suspected were radical interventions made by two early feminist publications: *Our Bodies Our Selves* (Boston Women's Health Book Collective 1970/1998) and *A New View of a Woman's Body* (Federation of Feminist Women's Health Centers 1981/1995).[23]

We were interested in anatomy as a discipline because it is widely understood as a science that has been done, is essentially complete and stable. Figures 6.7 and 6.8 show the female and male side views produced in 1981 by the Federation of Feminist Women's Health Centers. Both show the genitalia at rest and erect/engorged. We found both to be very uncommon images, especially the female. In part, we wanted to see if the innovations of feminist anatomies had been taken up in other recent genital anatomies.

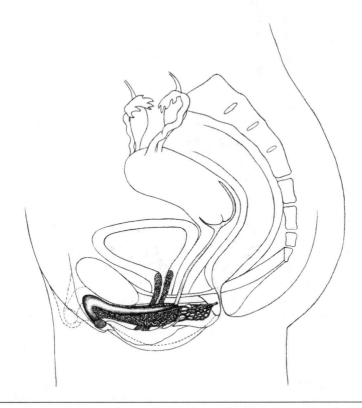

Figure 6.7   Federation of Feminist Women's Health Centers: Female Side View
SOURCE: Federation of Feminist Women's Health Centers (1981:48).

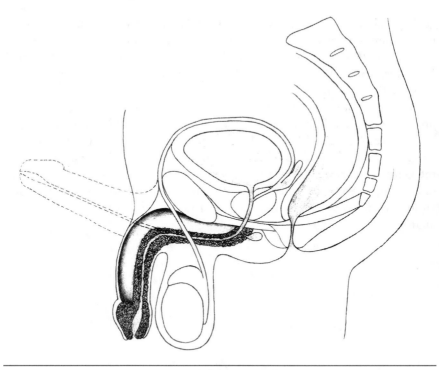

Figure 6.8   Federation of Feminist Women's Health Centers: Male Side View

SOURCE: Federation of Feminist Women's Health Centers (1981:49).

Which Visual Materials?
Deciding, Locating, Collecting, and Tracking

We began by casting a very wide net. In our work to date, we have examined images from medieval texts to the present, focusing on how different historically based visual cultures do the work of representation differently (Clarke & Moore n.d.). Our published work has centered on both anatomy texts and online "cyberanatomies" of human genitalia circa 1900-2000. We analyzed how anatomists represented, labeled, and narrated the various "male and female parts," focusing especially on what (if anything) counted as "the clitoris" (Moore & Clarke 1995, 2001). We use the term "genital" as our generic term to designate "what's down there" for specific historicopolitical reasons. Labels hold power: Whether the areas of the body where the clitoris and penis lie are labeled genital, sexual, or reproductive anatomy, or some combination thereof, is a meaning-making interpretation—part of the visual culture of anatomy itself. "Genital" is closest to a generic regional term, while the terms "sex," "sexual," "generative," and "reproductive" became our *analytic* categories.

Exemplar I: Furneaux Text Anatomy (circa 1904)

Locating Memo: Furneaux

I have chosen two sets of images from our published work to use here as exemplars. Although we did not explicitly use situational analysis as laid out in this book, I was using elements of it in my own work. I also wanted to use exemplars in this book from my own work with which I am most familiar. So, while I cannot reproduce for you a memo we wrote about any of the images per se, I can produce such memos for selected images. You can seek out our published work for greater detail on the project as a whole.

One exemplar is from medical texts published in Britain circa 1904, and the other is from a CD-ROM cyberanatomy produced in the United States in 1994. At the end of this section, I give the overall conclusions that Lisa Jean Moore and I have reached on our anatomies project to date. These exemplars document the conclusions nicely.

Big Picture Memo: Furneaux

I begin with my overall locating memo of Figures 6.9-6.10, the female "flap anatomy" (Furneaux circa 1904:back cover). I have included the male images here as Figures 6.11 and 6.12 for comparative purposes, but do not narrate them due to space limitations (see Furneaux 19??).

First Impressions. In Figures 6.9-6.10, I see drawings of a quite young-looking white girl/woman done in a very flat plane. She reminds me of cutout dolls that came in some coloring books when I was a child, though they were not bare-breasted. She also reminds me of Egyptian art with its full frontal imaging and some Greco-Roman figures. These impressions are reinforced by the fabric covering her genitalia, draped togalike around her lower torso and tucked in around the waist. This toga thing makes her feel culturally remote—"other." Her face looks somehow like a Victorian child, but she certainly does *not* seem British from the neck down!

The series of three connected images reminds me of the triptych format of three connected paintings (often literally connected by hinges) I associate with Renaissance and later Christian religious art, but likely having earlier origins. Triptychs typically show three aspects of the same event—such as the Annunciation or the coming of the Magi. This format evokes the long

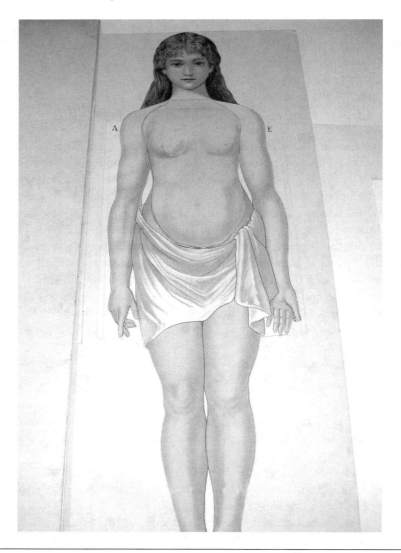

Figure 6.9   Furneaux Female Anatomy Front View: Flap Closed

tradition in both art and craft of visuals as narrative storytelling devices that are usually read left to right in the West. Looking at the series of anatomical images of this young woman overall, I can tell, given our prior knowledge of reading anatomies, that we are supposed to be seeing/reading "deeper and deeper" from left to right. I, at least, am always struck by the complexity—even of simplifications such as these.

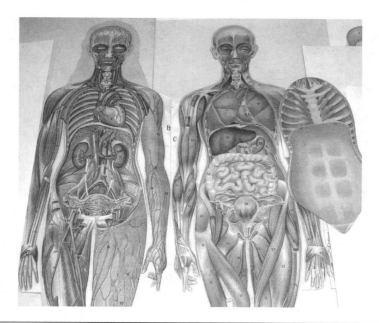

Figure 6.10   Furneaux Female Anatomy Front View: Flap Open

Big Picture. The young woman has long hair flowing below her shoulders (we cannot see how long). Her arms are at her sides. Her pointer finger on her right hand is in fact pointing downward in a clear way, seemingly instructing us to pay attention. Her left hand, in contrast, is turned palm facing us, perhaps to provide another view of the hand or to indicate its flexibility. Her bared breasts are high, and indicate by their shape that she has not breast-fed. Her abdomen is muscular and rounded. This is definitely a pre-Twiggy female: big, healthy, and athletic-looking.

The young woman looks at us seemingly directly but also straight ahead and seems not to see us. She is clearly *not* engaging us in the gaze, yet does not look away. She also does not look real. That is, she is not portrayed realistically but rather more abstractly and somehow symbolically. We are clearly not looking at a representation attempting to be the real thing. In fact, the effort seems to have been to be intentionally unrealistic through being somewhat artistic.

Little Pictures. In Figure 6.10, in the image labeled B, an overall flap seemingly constituting the skin and surface flesh has been drawn back to reveal circulatory and neurological systems/networks and major internal organs of the body (heart, kidneys, uterus, and fallopian tubes [both still

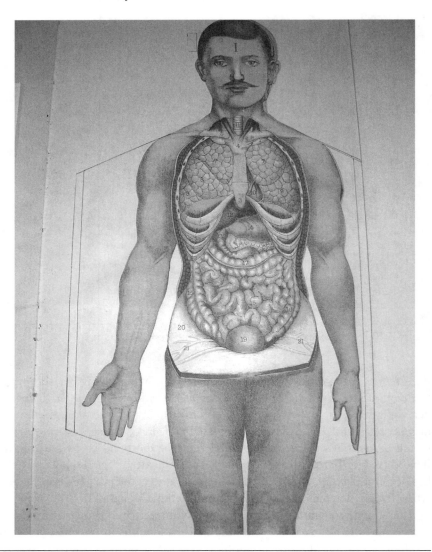

Figure 6.11   Furneaux Male Anatomy Front View: Flap Closed

sealed/whole]). Moving downward from the top of the image, we see that the shape of the hair is still there but the hair is not. The eyes are half dead and staring. The ribs are still in place except where (somehow) deleted to reveal the heart/lung(s). The anatomy of the two legs is different, revealing different bodily elements.

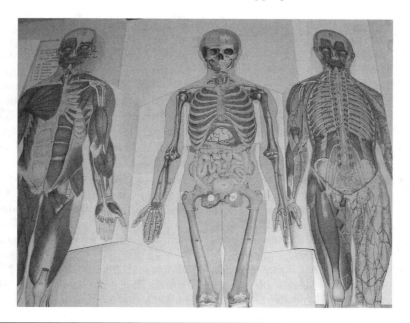

Figure 6.12   Furneaux Male Anatomy Front View: Flap Open

In the image on our right labeled C, two more flaps over the torso that have been drawn back are shown—the ribs and the abdominal musculature. The head looks almost fully skull-like with skeletal sockets without eyeballs. The body too is further reduced essentially to skeleton and some musculature in arms, legs, and shoulders, though the outline/shape of the original body remains (which it would not do in a dissection, one of the reasons dissections are challenging to see). Many areas are simply dark and murky, indicating that what was there has been removed. Some absences are thus indicated. The uterus and fallopian tubes/ovaries have been opened (dissected frontally), revealing a fetus in the uterus.

Specification Memo: Furneaux

The questions used to construct the specification memo are here *in italics* for clarity. There is no need to repeat oneself endlessly. The purpose of the specification memo is to push oneself to be very, very systematic in examining the visual. It is the *combination* of the groundedness of overall interpretation with the systematic handling of data that makes grounded theory and situational analysis robust approaches in qualitative research—applied to visual as well as other materials.

- *Selection. What is represented? Why do you think X, Y, or Z was selected rather than A, or B, or C?* The images are three anatomical views of a young woman done circa 1904—see above memo. I cannot determine why particular elements were selected, although I can theorize that both the unreality of the image and the presence of the fetus may have been intended to desexualize the anatomical model. I know from reading secondary sources that, by this historical moment, differentiation of anatomy as science from both art and pornography was very important (e.g., Jordanova 1989). Scientific visual cultures were emerging, being refined, and being gendered, raced, and so on.

- *Framing. How is the subject framed? What is included, excluded, cut off at the edges?* Beyond the medical book, there is no visual context whatsoever except for the indications of "cut-outness." And the handful of letter labels. The framing is essentially the triptych strategy, calling upon us to read the three images as of the same thing or event varyingly portrayed—here going deeper and deeper.

- *Featuring. What is foregrounded, middle-grounded, and backgrounded but still present?* There really is only a relatively flattened ground of the front of the body. The flap indicators highlight/foreground the torso area, de-emphasizing and marginalizing the head, arms, and legs, but not wholly. What is featured is the opening of the body to our view and the complex detailing of various innards. The labels are very minor compared to many other anatomies.

- *Viewpoint. Is the image a close-up, medium shot, long shot, low angle, high angle? What difference(s) do these make?* The flat frontal image seems conventional/canonic for basic scientific anatomies by this time, neither close up nor distant. This works to distinguish scientific images from both artistic images (typically three-dimensional and realistic at this time with dense background/context) and from pornographic images (also typically three-dimensional and realistic at this time with dense though usually different background/context) wherein "the gaze" is often seriously engaged by the object/gazee staring back seductively.

- *Light. How is light used in the image? What is featured through highlighting? Backgrounded? How does the variation in light direct your attention within the image? What is more or less obscured?* While the reproductions technically possible in this book are far from perfect, the stylistic strategy seems to be to use light to aid a clarity versus obscurity continuum of representation.

- *Color. How is color used in the image? What is bright and vivid and what is not? How does the variation in color direct your attention within the image?* Soft gentle colors were used with shading to denote clarity/obscurity and depth.

- *Focus/Depth of Field. Is everything in sharp focus? If not, what is blurred? What is clear? How does the variation in focus direct your attention within the image?* In a way, there is not much depth, although we are supposed to be seeing deeper and deeper. Again, the clarity/obscurity continuum is doing this work.

- *Presence/Absence. Given the topic/focus of the image, is everything there that you would expect to be there? What is absent that you might have expected? What is different than you expected?* The very absence of context here makes a serious point. In sharp contrast with much pornography which trades on its specificities, scientific anatomical representations are not local and contextualizable, but rather abstract, generalizable, and universalizable. They are intended to be able to travel and be easily inserted in new sites/contexts (Latour 1986, 1990; Star & Griesemer 1989). Furthermore, and most interesting, absence is used to direct an intense emphasis on presence. When parts of the body are removed, we are not to lament their loss, or even attend to their absence, but rather pay attention to what their removal has revealed underneath it all. It is a sort of corporeal striptease. This anatomy reveals the infrastructures of the body, flap by flap.

- *Intended/Unintended Audience(s). Can you determine whether the image was aimed at any particular audience(s)? More than one? Who is not supposed to look here? Who would likely be made to feel uncomfortable looking here in "mixed" company? "Mixed" in what ways?* Yes, the images are from a medical text aimed at medical audience(s). Given that access to such texts was quite narrow, usually defined by access to a medical library, very few were supposed to look. Medical audiences were mostly male, and viewing in mixed company would have been charged—especially genital anatomy and sexual organs.

- *Composition. What is emphasized? What is balanced/imbalanced? Are there tilted images? Moving images?* The torso area is emphasized as are major organs. The flaps in this flap anatomy move. No tilted or moving images. All in general balance.

- *Texture. Are there areas of different textures? What are they? What work do these areas do in the overall image?* Again, the texturing is used to do the clarity/obscurity work featuring different anatomical elements.

- *Scale and Format/Proportions. How are these expectable? Unexpected? What is emphasized? De-emphasized?* To Lisa Jean Moore and me in the early 1990s before digital anatomies were circulating with hypertexted click-and-see options, this format with doll-like female was fascinating, and the flaps revealing one level at a time were interesting visual devices. Proportions and scale seem relatively realistic, although the head seems a little small for the body.

- *Technical Elements. Are there any distinctive elements such as a wide-angle lens, telephoto, flash-lighting, special photo processing? What difference(s) do they make?* The doll-like aspect stood out among all the anatomies we viewed produced between 1900 and 1990. Flap anatomies per se have a long history, and parallel early versions were even done in ivory and other media as sculptures with removable organs.

- *Single or Multimedia. What media are in the work? How are they positioned vis-à-vis one another? Is work in one medium echoing or referencing another? To what end(s)?* This is a single medium of medical illustrator-drawn anatomy. It may well be referencing earlier print and sculptural versions with removable parts that were lifelike with wigs and so on.
- *Relationship to Other Work in Same Media. Are there differences or largely similarities? What, if anything, is distinctive?* The major difference is the doll aspect combined with more traditional flap style. (Please see our published work for more extended discussion here.)
- *References. Are there symbolic or other references in the image that you can decode? What are they? Where do they come from? Why do you think they are there? What work do they do in the visual? Is there a consistent pattern of referencing across multiple visuals?* While there is no "background" or context, several references jump out. First is how much the young woman's head looks like that of a Victorian doll—both childlike (especially compared to the man) and unreal. Second, the toga references Greece, and perhaps even the Greek Olympics, given her strong athletic body. The head would be familiar in a British setting, while the body seems to be from "far away" in ways Tsing (1993) would see as distancing, and Said (1978) might view as orientalizing or "othering." Interestingly, this can be read as either/both eroticizing and de-eroticizing.
- *Remediations. Are there remediations wherein new visual technologies such as computer graphics or the Internet present themselves as offering newly refashioned and improved versions of older media while merely reinscribing old content in a newer format? How is this done? Is it easy to see?* Actually it does feel like a remediation of the flap style in a newer doll-like body. Today, flap anatomies are actually reincarnated/remediated as "click" anatomies online. In terms of content, representing the female as pregnant goes back at least to medieval anatomies.
- *Situatedness. How is this image situated historically, geographically, temporally? In terms of social worlds/arenas?* This is a visual from the social world of Western medicine in Britain in the early 20th century.
- *Relations With Visual Culture(s). How is this image related to past and/or contemporary or futuristic visual (sub)cultures/social worlds? What are its relations to past or contemporary sociopolitical situations?* This image illustrates the emerging conventions of scientific anatomical illustration—biomedical abstraction. (This question is actually at the heart of our overall anatomies project—see summary below.)
- *Commonness/Uniqueness. Is this image one of a kind, rare, common? What difference(s) does this make?* As a scientific medical illustration from circa 1904, this was a rare and special image, challenging to access unless one was part of a medical world. Its rarity and relative obscurity makes the image more interesting to us even today.
- *Work of the Image. What work is the image doing in the world? What is implicitly and explicitly normalized? Naturalized/unnaturalized? Marginalized?* This

image is doing many kinds of work. First, it represents an established medical specialty—anatomy. At the time of its publication, circa 1904, anatomy was very important because of the rise of surgery, which could now more commonly be successful thanks to both anesthesia and asepsis, along with anatomical knowledge. Pregnancy is naturalized for females. A "medical gaze" is taking on new forms of representation of bodies that can travel easily in medical books and hence among medical worlds in different locations.

- *Injunctions to Viewers. What, if anything, are viewers being told to do or think or be? Not to do or think?* The unrealism and static nature of the image—its stillness and abstraction along with its complex detail revealed flap by flap—seem to tell us to stare carefully. I also think we are not supposed to see this young woman as erotic. But nor does she wholly refuse such a gaze—an interesting ambiguity.

I could, of course, be much more thorough in my responses to these questions, and at the early stages of a visual research project, there is nothing more worthwhile. The payoff from systematic looking *and writing* is exceptional. The questions themselves provoke analysis.

Situational Maps and Analysis: Furneaux

Let us now turn to the situational map, social worlds/arenas map, and positional map for these images. Looking at Figure 6.13, the messy situational map for the Furneaux (circa 1904) anatomy text visuals, we see many human and nonhuman elements—and most are medically related. These especially include medical illustrators and publishers, the history of anatomy and of anatomical illustration, the technologies of both producing the illustrations and publishing them, a handful of early scientific studies of sexuality and reproductive phenomena, urology, obstetrics and gynecology and their histories. What came before matters a lot. It has always already "schooled" the gaze of medicine, formatting anatomical illustrations into visual cultures of which this is one example. All the likely "audiences/consumers" are also on the map. Presences beyond medicine include print pornography, historical and contemporary art, historical and contemporary popular cultural representations of human bodies, the historical and contemporary politics of gender and sexuality, living females and female bodies available for dissection, and so on.

The ordered situational map in Figure 6.14 makes the medical orientation even more clear. There is quite a range of nonhuman elements. To me, the techniques and technologies of doing such illustration and the technologies available to reproduce them stand out.

Figure 6.13   Messy Situational Map: Furneaux Text Anatomy (circa 1904)

Social Worlds/Arenas Map and Analysis: Furneaux

Figure 6.15 presents the social worlds/arenas map for the Furneaux illustrations of circa 1904. The text is situated within the medical arena, primarily in medical education. The medical/biological publishing world, medical journal publishing world, and medical education world intersect with those of anatomy and medical/scientific illustration. Hospital/clinic

INDIVIDUAL HUMAN ELEMENTS/ACTORS

Medical illustrators
Living bodies
Practicing physicians
Other health care providers seeking
    anatomical knowledge
Others seeking anatomical knowledge
Others seeking knowledge of bodies,
    including sexual knowledge

NONHUMAN ELEMENTS/ACTANTS

Medical textbooks
Technologies of medical illustration
Cadavers for dissection
Print pornography
Historical and contemporary medical
    illustrations
Print popular cultural anatomies

COLLECTIVE HUMAN ELEMENTS/ACTORS

Historical and contemporary anatomy
    as a discipline
Medical textbook publishers
Academic medicine
Physicians in training

IMPLICATED/SILENT ACTORS/ACTANTS

DISCURSIVE CONSTRUCTIONS OF HUMAN ACTORS

Human sexuality/sexology
Human reproductive science
Representations of bodies

DISCURSIVE CONSTRUCTIONS OF NONHUMAN ACTANTS

Conservative and progressive
    constructions of sexual anatomy
Conservative and progressive
    constructions of nude body images

POLITICAL/ECONOMIC ELEMENTS

Economics of medical publishing
Historical and contemporary politics
    of gender and sexuality

SOCIOCULTURAL/SYMBOLIC ELEMENTS

See discourses

TEMPORAL ELEMENTS

Historical and contemporary politics
    of sex/gender
Historical and contemporary politics
    of sexuality

SPATIAL ELEMENTS

Wholly decontextualized body images

MAJOR ISSUES/DEBATES (USUALLY CONTESTED)

"Best" means of representations of
    anatomy of different body parts
Historical and contemporary politics
    of gender and sexuality

RELATED DISCOURSES (NARRATIVE AND/OR VISUAL)

Discourses about sex/gender
Discourses about sexuality
Discourses about bodies

OTHER KINDS OF ELEMENTS

Figure 6.14   Ordered Situational Map: Furneaux Text Anatomy (circa 1904)

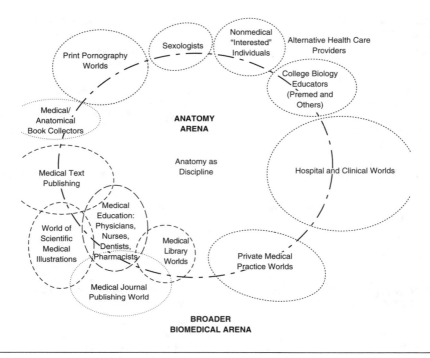

Figure 6.15   Social Worlds/Arenas Map: Furneaux Text Anatomy (circa 1904)

worlds are more tangential to this arena, as are private medical practices. Outside the medical arena are nonmedical interested individuals, including alternative health care providers who have an interest in anatomy and college biology educators who have an interest in anatomy and who teach premed students and others. Sexology as an emergent discipline is partially inside the medical arena and partially outside, as not all sexologists are medically trained.

The social worlds/arenas map also makes it clear how restricted access was to medical illustration at this time. These images reside almost exclusively inside the academic medical arena, especially in medical libraries. They may also be found (especially older or outdated versions) in hospitals, clinics, private physicians' offices, the libraries of private book collectors (especially those specializing in the history of anatomy and/or medical/scientific illustration, many of whom would be physicians), and in (likely medical) bookstores.

Positional Map and Analysis: Furneaux

Figure 6.16, the positional map I have drawn for the Furneaux illustration of circa 1904, is organized along two axes: (1) from obscure to clear and (2) from a reproduction emphasis to a sexuality emphasis. There were no labels, so the image stood on its own. I have placed the image in an intermediate position between obscure and clear in part because of the absence of labels naming and signaling body parts. Because of the fetus in utero, I have placed the image at the reproductive emphasis end of that continuum. Let me say that the act of conceiving the possible axes, deciding among them, and then placing the visual within this scheme feels very highly charged. Researcher reflexivity is intense here—as is interpretation. This is very much *my* map.

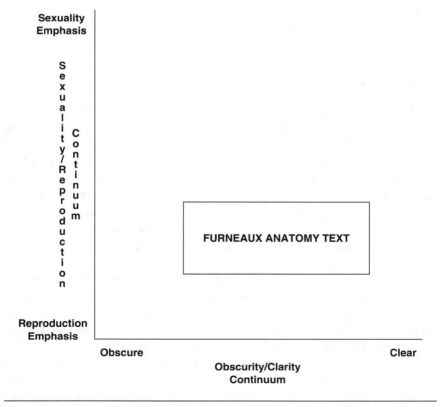

Figure 6.16   Positional Map: Furneaux Text Anatomy (circa 1904)

Exemplar II: BodyWorks 1994 Cyberanatomy

Locating Memo: BodyWorks 1994

> *Colorful, comprehensive graphics guide you on a journey through the body. With its vast database, BodyWorks Classic lets you study specific areas from head to toe, zooming in and out for a complete look at the world within you, and focusing on different internal systems such as the skeletal, muscular, cardiovascular, reproductive and more.*
>
> —CD-ROM Casenotes for BodyWorks[24]

I will be very terse here for reasons of space. In Figures 6.17-6.20, we have images from a CD-ROM produced by Softkey Multimedia in 1994. A "popular culture" general anatomy for the lay public and likely aimed at families with children, this CD contains line and color drawings, three-dimensional images, and movies with sound. BodyWorks cyberanatomy enables the user to click onto bodily systems from an icon-driven menu at the top of the screen.

Big Picture Memo: BodyWorks 1994

First Impressions. The cover image (Figure 6.17) is of an attractive young white woman looking sideways away from us. Her innards are shown where her breasts and abdomen would be. Images are not from a vivid realist visual culture such as photographs of cadavers, but rely instead on medical illustration techniques, largely from the visual culture of biomedical abstraction. Genital anatomy falls under the broad heading of "Genitourinary System," represented by the male and female symbols, and "includes the urinary and reproductive organs. Because these organs are located in the same area of the body, and share some functions, they're often treated together."

Visually, there are body parts and labels and no whole persons. After we leave the "Genitourinary System" with its buffed, athletic male silhouette (Figure 6.18) standing for both males and females in high modern universalist mode, the next click moves us immediately into the "Reproductive Systems" of the female (Figure 6.19) and male (Figure 6.20). While the female is labeled "Side View," no such instructions are offered with the male (also presented in side view). The labels do not stay still all at once. Our viewing skills are left to make sense of it all. Note that the icon for genital anatomy is a male symbol and a female symbol literally attached to each other. Moreover, using Goffman's power

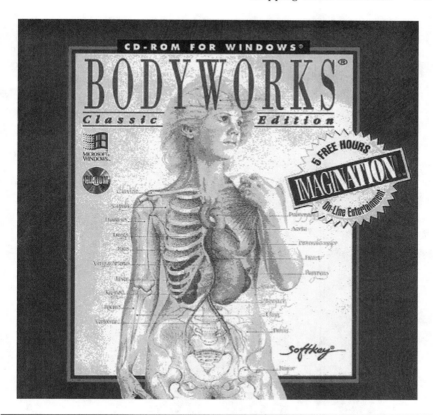

Figure 6.17   BodyWorks 1994 Cyberanatomy Classic Edition CD-ROM Cover

analytic on this icon, we see the male symbol portrayed as both larger and in the superior (higher) position.

Little Pictures. In keeping with many 20th-century representations, the male and female genitalia are unequally represented. Specifically, while the penis, glans of the penis, corpus cavernosa, and ejaculatory ducts of the male system are depicted, labeled, narratively defined, and hypertexted (all lighting up on the visual when the words are clicked on), the clitoris is not. The only mention of the clitoris is in the narrative listing of the parts of external organs of the vagina; it is not on the list of visual options. Nothing lights up. Male erection is described as part of sexual arousal, while the female reproductive system is exclusively portrayed, both visually and textually, as the site of conception and childbirth. The female body is a wholly nonsexual body. A Fetus

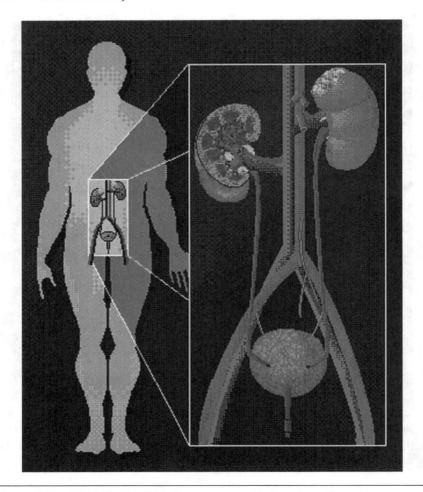

Figure 6.18   BodyWorks 1994 Cyberanatomy Genitourinary System Page

Icon provides entry into "The Living System" that "covers many of the processes of living including conception, pregnancy and childbirth."

It is difficult to memo this CD-ROM, as all the visuals I am referring to are not clear on the pages reproduced here. There is software that allows annotation for use with some visual materials. However, copyrighted products such as this might not be able to be imported into them for annotation. Therefore, when analyzing such materials, using the Print Screen function often and keeping the images with the memos are important. If analyzing a Web site, it is often also useful to download the entire Web site, if you can, and carefully date and archive it yourself. It is important to carefully date

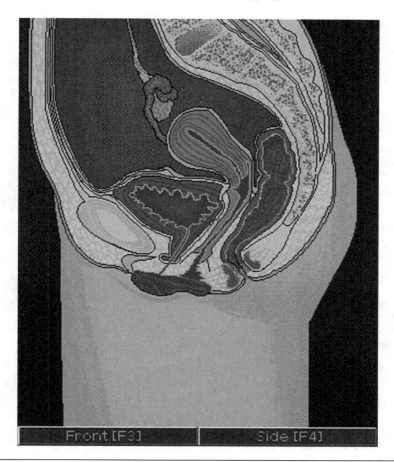

Front [F3]   Side [F4]

Figure 6.19   BodyWorks 1994 Cyberanatomy Female Reproductive System:
Side View

anything you print from any Web site, as there are usually no archives available online, and things tend to disappear.

I do not provide the specification memo for the BodyWorks cyberanatomy but move directly into an abbreviated situational analysis.

Situational Map and Analysis: BodyWorks 1994

Looking at Figure 6.21, the messy situational map for BodyWorks cyberanatomy, we see first that all of the elements in the situational map of the earlier text anatomy from c1904 are still present (e.g., medical illustrators, medical publishers, medical libraries). But there are many new elements as

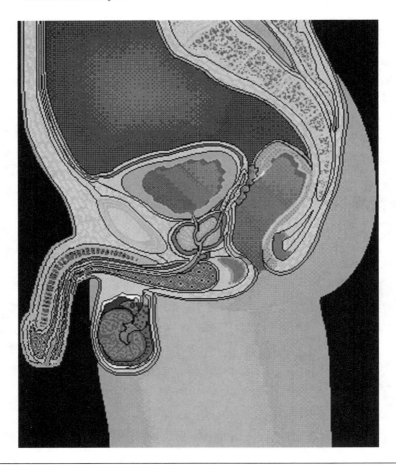

Figure 6.20   BodyWorks 1994 Cyberanatomy Male Reproductive System: Side
View

well. Some are expected such as computers and software. Others may be
more surprising such as medical illustration training programs (now in place
due to the increasing demand for such illustrations), and sex education as a
specialty field, which may be analytically important.

As usual, the ordered map is handy. See Figure 6.22.

Social Worlds/Arenas Map and Analysis: BodyWorks 1994

Looking at Figure 6.23, the social worlds/arenas map of BodyWorks,
we see that it appears in the sex education arena. Digital popular cultural

Figure 6.21 Messy Situational Map: BodyWorks 1994 Cyberanatomy

anatomies are situated at the intersection of software and computing industries with medical publishing worlds that extend into this arena from the medical arena itself. Print and digital medical anatomy illustration worlds also intersect and have similarly extended into the sex education arena from the medical arena. Two additional arenas of significance also impinge: the popular culture arena and the pornography/sex work arena (themselves increasingly overlapping).

INDIVIDUAL HUMAN ELEMENTS/ACTORS

Medical illustrators
Children, teens, families
Practicing physicians
Other health care teachers and providers
    seeking anatomical knowledge
Sex educators
Health educators
Others seeking anatomical knowledge

NONHUMAN ELEMENTS/ACTANTS

Medical textbooks
Technologies of medical illustration
Historical and contemporary medical illustration
Cadavers for dissection
Print popular cultural anatomies
Print and digital pornography
Computers
Software
Digital technical medical anatomies for health
    professionals (physicians, nurses, physical
    therapists, etc.)
Digital popular cultural anatomies

COLLECTIVE HUMAN ELEMENTS/ACTORS

Historical and contemporary anatomy
    as a discipline
Medical textbook publishers
Academic medicine
Physicians in training
Medical illustration training programs
Computer and software industries

IMPLICATED/SILENT ACTORS/ACTANTS

**DISCURSIVE CONSTRUCTION(S)
OF HUMAN ACTORS**

Human sexuality/sexology
Human reproductive sciences
Representations of bodies

**DISCURSIVE CONSTRUCTION(S)
OF NONHUMAN ACTANTS**

Conservative and progressive constructions
    of sexual anatomy
Conservative and progressive constructions
    of images of nude bodies

POLITICAL/ECONOMIC ELEMENTS

Economics of medical publishing
Historical and contemporary politics of
    gender, sexuality, and sex education
Historical and contemporary obstetrics
    and gynecology

SOCIOCULTURAL/SYMBOLIC ELEMENTS

Historical and contemporary popular culture
History of anatomy
Historical and contemporary anatomical
    representations
Historical and contemporary art

TEMPORAL ELEMENTS

Historical and contemporary politics of
    sex/gender
Historical and contemporary politics of sexuality
Historical and contemporary politics of
    sex education

SPATIAL DIMENSIONS

Available means of display of and access
    to anatomical dissection
Available means of display of and access
    to anatomical representations
CD-ROM click hypertext

**MAJOR ISSUES/DEBATES
(USUALLY CONTESTED)**

Historical and contemporary politics of
    sex education
Historical and contemporary politics of gender
    and sexuality
"Best" means of representation of anatomies
    of different body parts

**RELATED DISCOURSES
(NARRATIVE AND/OR VISUAL)**

Discourses of sex education
Discourses of sex/gender
Discourses of sexuality

OTHER KINDS OF ELEMENTS

Figure 6.22   Ordered Situational Map: BodyWorks 1994 Cyberanatomy

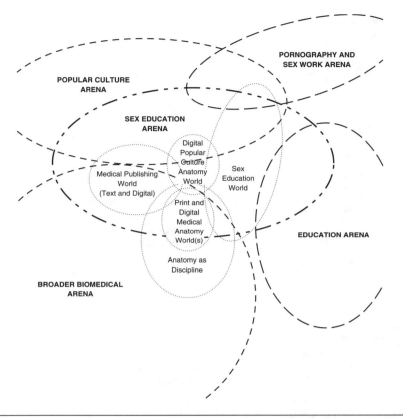

Figure 6.23   Social Worlds/Arenas Map: BodyWorks 1994 Cyberanatomy

Looking at the social worlds/arenas maps of both of the exemplars, we can see that major historical changes have occurred. The most significant for our purposes was the development of the sex education arena through which popular cultural anatomies such as BodyWorks are now both produced and consumed—at home and in schools. Keeping "appropriate" distance from the pornography/sex work arena, which has obvious interests in and commitments to sex education, is important to the developers of such products.

One of the most influential arenas for the development of a CD such as this is popular culture. Sex education products such as BodyWorks are in competition with all kinds of popular cultural products, from music videos to movies about/including sexual content. And children typically operate at the cutting edges of both new visual technologies and popular cultural trends. Creating and maintaining such a product as economically viable would be challenging.

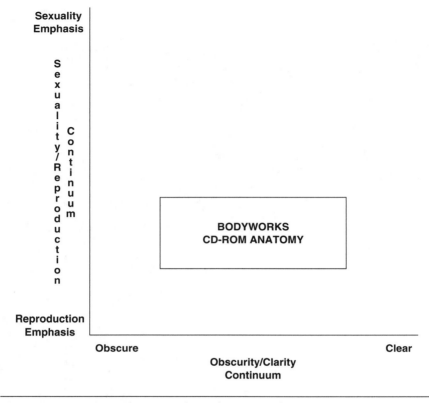

Figure 6.24   Positional Map: BodyWorks 1994 Cyberanatomy

Positional Map and Analysis: BodyWorks 1994

Finally, the positional map(s) will likely be particularly important in analysis of visual materials because these are discursive items, and the work they do—and don't do—in the world should be clarified by these maps. You will see that the similarities between the positional maps of both exemplars offered in Figures 6.16 and 6.24 constitute the heart of the analysis offered below in the summary.

Given the complete absence of female sexuality and the downplaying of male sexuality, in Figure 6.24 the BodyWorks CD is clearly positioned at the reproductive emphasis end of the reproduction/sexuality continuum. For the same reasons, I have positioned it between Clarity and Obscurity. What is there is clear, but highly partial. This is especially true given the incredible array of visual resources available to the producers—-almost a century's worth since the Furneaux anatomy of 1904. So, this positioning is deeply reliant upon the *researchers*—it is our vision based on our assessment of what was technically possible at the time of its production.

Analytic Summary of the Anatomies Project

The following are our conclusions to date regarding the anatomy texts and cyberanatomies we studied circa 1900-2000 (a much wider array than presented here) (Moore & Clarke 1995, 2001):

- Narratives and images often work together to render a discourse of external genital size as synonymous with physical superiority.
- In terms of images and/or labeling, the female may or may not have a clitoris, while the male always has a penis.
- When present, the clitoris is often presented as homologous (arising from the same embryonic cells) to the penis, but never vice versa.
- Clitoral agency or purpose (capacity for sensation and action such as engorgement) is rarely addressed, while the capacities and actions of the penis usually form a lively central narrative.
- Narratives of orgasm pertain *solely* to the penis except in explicitly feminist anatomies (of which there are, to date, really only the two noted above).
- The common scientific convention of singularity/unity of representation (using only one image of a female and one image of a male) and omission of variation continues to hold sway; we call this *anatomical essentialism.*
- Such essentialism is also manifest in the fact that only two sexes are ever mentioned, completely erasing sex variation (hermaphrodisms/intersexualities/transsexualities).
- Racism is also manifest in that the vast majority of anatomy figures, including cadavers, are imaged as white/Caucasian, and race is almost invariably an unmarked/unmentioned category.
- In most anatomies, heterosexuality is assumed, and conventions of heterosexualization inextricably link if not actually replace female sexual function with reproductive function in narratives and often also through visual representation of pregnancy.

In short, males are largely visualized as sexual, while females are reproductive.

Final Comments on the Visual Discourse Exemplars

I have offered here fairly thorough locating and big picture memos and one specification memo as exemplars, along with the situational analyses and maps of the two sets of exemplar images. You can easily imagine that being this thorough with every image you study would get more than tedious. What I recommend is selecting about half a dozen images from those you have collected that are as different as you can find and doing very thorough locating, big picture and specification memos, grounded coding, situational maps and analyses of all of them. These memos should provide the foundations of your analytic work. Subsequently, you can do abbreviated analyses of the remaining images, focusing especially on their *differences/innovations* compared to other images. Focus here should also be on similarities and differences with other images, seeking variation as a form of theoretical sampling in visual domains. Also, any image that jumps out at you for any reason deserves full systematic treatment.

Carefully situating the materials you have chosen to analyze in your written reports is also very important. The memos and maps are particularly helpful here. They should make you at least think through all the key relations, regardless of whether these are subsequently deemed worthy of further attention, analysis, and writing.

Final Comments: Situational Analysis of Visual Discourse

> *We should cease to be paralyzed by a heritage of claims about "realism" in visual data and accept the challenge they offer for sociological investigation into ways our social world is constituted, reproduced and experienced, in which seeing is as important as saying and doing, and visual depiction performs social work.*
>
> —Harrison (1996:91)

Thirty years ago, Howie Becker (1974:7) said: "Visual social science isn't new . . . but it might as well be." This chapter is long and detailed because Becker is still correct today, at least in terms of sociology, anthropology, nursing, education, and many other disciplines where qualitative research is pursued. At the same time, this chapter is superficial and oversimplified given the stunning density and theoretical sophistication of the literature that takes up analysis of visual discourse in art history and criticism, cultural studies, film studies, communications, visual studies, and beyond. My goal here has been to draw upon and refer you to that excellent work as well as perform situational analysis of visual materials in order to provoke inclusion of the visual in qualitative research projects.

I want to conclude by addressing the usual tension regarding using received theory versus grounded theorizing. Though one certainly does not want to slap on an extant analytic (Kendall & Wickham 2004), this does not need to be an either-or decision. Earlier I noted Chaplin's (1994:159) point about the critical paradigm and the empirical paradigm in visual studies (as elsewhere) having been too long segregated. I want to emphasize that hybrid approaches to visual analyses are possible, viable, and may well be most exciting. That is, grounded and situational analysis can be highly compatible, for example, with an analysis of how "the male or female gaze" or "the gaze of racialization" works in a particular image. Certainly after the initial stages of visual analysis recommended here (the locating, big picture, and specification memos, basic grounded theory coding, and the three situational maps and analytic memos), exploring where such concepts take one can be provocative. You will already have a well-grounded and situated empirical analysis.

While the sophisticated conceptual armamentarium of visual studies may not be familiar, it offers an established and elaborating set of tools not unlike social theory. As we might draw upon a century of social theory to explore identity or subjectivity issues in analyzing fashion,[25] analyzing *how* "the gaze" works in a particular visual does not predetermine any outcome! These tools are—or can be used as—what Blumer (1969) called "sensitizing concepts" that tell us directions in which to look but *not* what to see. Whether using such tools turns out to be as interesting as some other analytic point is an empirical question to be addressed by the researcher. The danger is, as always, not to be seduced by others' concepts and analyses and instead to keep working until you produce your own—but also not to waste time reinventing wheels or play dumb about other possible and even likely interpretations of your materials. After all, your own work will be situated in terms of them.

Given the elaboration of visual discourses and of their analysis, there is definitely not much "purity" of vision remaining. Elvis Mitchell (2003:AR1) recently argued that through recent DVD formats with directors' cuts, outtakes, talking-head commentary, and so on, "[e]veryone's a film geek now." I would argue that this is a broader phenomenon: Everyone is becoming a visual discourse geek now! Yet at the same time, major visual studies scholar W. J. T. Mitchell (1994:13) has said, "[W]e still do not know exactly what pictures are, what their relation to language is, how they operate on observers and on the world, how their history is to be understood and what is to be done with or about them." We can proceed and research the visual regardless, as long as we remember: "Interpreting images is just that, interpretation, not the discovery of their 'truth'" (G. Rose 2001:2).

Notes

1. See, e.g., Banks (2001) and his Web site, www.rsl.ox.ac.uk/isca/vismeth, Becker (1998), Harper (1994, 2000), Ball and Smith (2001), Chaplin (1994:ch. 5), Papademas (2002), Prosser (1998), and G. Rose (2001).

2. On using visual materials in interviewing, see, e.g., Ball and Smith (2001), Banks (2001), Bauer and Gaskell (2000), and Harrison (2002).

3. The extensive theoretical debates are reviewed by Chaplin (1994:1-158). On audience, reception, or spectatorship studies, see, e.g., Altheide (1996, 2002a) and Kress and van Leeuwen (1999).

4. For entrée, see Sturken and Cartwright (2001) and Chaplin (1994). The major readers offering the classic texts in visual studies are Evans and Hall (1999), Mirzoeff (1998), and Jones (2003). Elkins (2003) offers an advanced status report on the field. On compositional analysis, see, e.g., G. Rose (2001:ch. 2). On content analysis, see, e.g., Ball and Smith (1992:ch. 2), G. Rose (2001:ch. 3), and van Leeuwen and Jewett (2001:ch. 2). On symbolist and structural analyses, see Ball and Smith (1992:ch. 3). On semiology, see, e.g., G. Rose (2001:ch. 4) and van Leeuwen and Jewett (2001:chs. 5, 7, 9). On psychoanalytic approaches, see, e.g., G. Rose (2001:ch. 5). On cultural studies, see DuGay et al. (1997), van Leeuwen and Jewett (2001:ch. 4), Sturken and Cartwright (2001), and Evans and Hall (1999). Emmison and Smith (2000) organize their methods text by types of visual materials under study: two-dimensional (ch. 3), three-dimensional (ch. 4), built environment (ch. 5), and living forms such as bodies and identities (ch. 6).

5. Impressive volumes on analysis include Altheide (1996), Ball and Smith (1992), Emmison and Smith (2000), G. Rose (2001), and van Leeuwen and Jewitt (2001).

6. There exists a range of video annotating computer programs.

7. See Emmison and Smith (2000:5). For interactionist examples, see Park (1925), Zorbaugh (1929), Cressey (1932), Strauss (1976), and Lofland (1998). On the marginalization of the visual in the social sciences, see especially Fyfe and Law (1988) and Emmison and Smith (2000:10-20). On the history of uses of visual materials in sociology and anthropology, see also Ball and Smith (2001), Chaplin (1994), Denzin (1991, 1992, 1997), Harper (1994, 2000), Harrison (1996), and Prosser (1998).

8. See, e.g., Altheide (1996, 2000, 2002a, 2002b), Denzin (e.g., 1991, 1992, 1997), Clough (2000), Davis (1992), Fontana and Preston (1990), Gottdeiner, Collins, and Dickens (1999), Gottschalk (1995), Kaiser (1990), Moore and Clarke (1995, 2001), Moore (2003, n.d.), Peretz (1995), and Phelan and Hunt (1998). Denzin pioneered interactionist film studies.

9. On media studies, see especially Altheide (1996, 2000, 2002a, 2002b), Bolter and Grusin (1999), Denzin (1991), Dines and Humez (2002), Ginsberg, Abu-Lughod, and Larkin (2002), and Sturken and Cartwright (2001). On television, see especially Clough (2000:972), Gray (1995), and King (2002).

10. On realisms and visual materials, see, e.g., Burgin (1982), Ball and Smith (2001), Denzin (1997), Harper (1994, 2000), and Mitchell (1992).

11. Surrealism has offered a sophisticated critique of visual realism (e.g., Mundy 2001; see also the chart situating surrealism vis-à-vis other traditions in Western art circa 1890-1935 in Pollock 1988:51).

12. The concepts of "the gaze" and the "Other" as used in visual studies have roots in Jacques Lacan's psychoanalytic theory as well as in Sartre, Foucault, etc. For an introductory overview, see Sturken and Cartwright (2001:72-108) and Elkins (2003). For more theoretical elaboration, see Irigaray (1985) and Silverman (1996).

13. For a critique of Goffman, see Fenstermaker and West (2002:6-9). On sex/gender and sexuality in visual studies, see also, e.g., Solomon-Godeau (1996), Bloom (1999), Cartwright (1995a, 1995b), Dines and Humez (2002), Jones (2003), Smith (1999), and Treichler, Cartwright, and Penley (1998). See Irigaray (1985) on the feminine gaze.

14. On race/ethnicity in visual cultures, begin with Said (1978); see also Baker (1998), Bloom (1999), Dines and Humez (2002), Evans and Hall (1999), Gilman (1985), Gray (1995), Gunaratnam (2003), S. Hall (1997), Hammonds (1997b), Haraway (1989), hooks (1992), Kolko et al. (2000), Smith (1999), Teslow (1998), Twine and Warren (2000), and Van Dijk (1999).

15. Emmison and Smith (2000:50-54) take up scientific and medical visual studies comparing the United States and the United Kingdom. However, at least in the medical domain with which I am deeply familiar, they failed to cite several major works (e.g., Cartwright 1995a, 1995b; Treichler et al. 1998) as well as minor works (Moore & Clarke 1995; Waldby 1997), which appeared well before their book.

16. For entrée into visual studies of sciences, see, e.g., Chaplin (1994:ch. 4 for a review), Daston and Galison (1992), Fyfe and Law (1988), Haraway (1989), Latour (1986, 1988b), Lynch (1991, 1994), Lynch and Woolgar (1988), and Mitman (1996).

17. In medicine, see also Balsamo (1996), Cartwright (1995a, 1995b, 2000), Gilman (1985, 1996), Hammonds (1997b), Harrison (2002), Harrison and Aranda (1999), Jordanova (1989), Moore (2003), Tagg (1987), and Treichler et al. (1998).

18. See, e.g., http://nmhm.washingtondc.museum/collections/hdac/index.htm.

19. See, e.g., www.corbis.com; www.nytimes.com/nytstore; see also Swan-Jones (1999) and Evans and Evans (1996).

20. Advance inquiries to possible venues for publication are recommended. The currently operant rule of thumb is that as long as the author both covers the costs of the production work and provides the publisher with either camera-ready (scanable) or digital files along with appropriate written permissions for publication, images can be accepted like text. There are still usually some limits on numbers of images, and around the use of color as well.

21. Permission to reproduce visual materials for "academic scholarly purposes" is usually free and usually granted upon request—once you have located the right person or original publisher, whichever holds the copyright. Payment for permissions may also be required; authors rather than publishers are usually responsible (see also note 20). However, some advertisers and other copyright holders will not grant permission; in such situations, careful narratives of the images must suffice and can be

more than adequate. Obtaining permissions can be quite time consuming, and advance planning is requisite for timely publication.

22. Thanks for inspiration here from Deborah Loft's lecture and handouts on "Looking at Photographs," San Francisco Museum of Modern Art, Fall 1999.

23. See www.ourbodiesourselves.org and, for the Federation, www.fwhc.org/index.htm.

24. BodyWorks 4.0 is available from The Learning Company Web site: www.broderbund.com.

25. See, e.g., Simmel (1904/1971), Kaiser (1990), Davis (1992), Peretz (1995), and Crane (2000).

7

Mapping Historical Discourses

Fifty years ago we could not claim what we can claim now—that history has found a new, serious, and most likely permanent place in the ethnographic perspective.

—Brettell (1998:514-515)

Not only for historians but also for social science, humanities, and professional scholars who take the postmodern turn into account, the "unconditional present" is no longer enough. Taking history seriously is a key feature of postmodern work: At minimum, it historicizes. It understands what de Certeau meant when he wrote: "We never write on a blank page, but always one that has been written on" (cited in Lather 2001b:477-478).

This transdisciplinary shift to which Brettell refers in the epigraph was prompted from many directions. Sociologist C. Wright Mills (1959:158) famously noted, "We have come to see that the biographies of men and women, the kinds of individuals they variously become, cannot be understood without reference to the historical structures in which the milieux of their everyday life are organized." In his *Europe and the People Without History* about colonialism, Wolf (1982/1997) argued that to be without history is to be essentialized, fixed, and static. That is, dehistoricization was and remains a strategy of colonization—assuming that before "contact," or before "this research project," little had happened that mattered and, moreover, that those studied were not reflexive about themselves, their pasts, and their lives.

Taking history seriously is now common practice in the social sciences as well as the humanities and beyond because, as Tuchman (1994:306, 310; emphasis added) argues, history is *necessary:*

> [T]o wit, *adequate* social science includes a theoretical use of historical information. Any social phenomenon must be understood in its historical context. To grasp historical information, one must have a point of view, including an interpretive framework that includes some notion of the "meaning" of history. . . . The past continues to speak to the present. All that we take for granted as "natural" is a product of both historical and contemporary processes. *Our task as social scientists is to interpret those multifaceted meanings.*

The work of research is interpretation and analysis, whether the data are contemporary or historical.

But it can certainly be asserted that it has been Foucault who most assiduously reframed how we even think about history after the postmodern turn.[1] According to Veyne (1971/1997:181), Foucault revolutionized history: "The Foucault-style genealogy history . . . completely fulfills the project of traditional history; it does not ignore society, economy, and so on, but it structures this material differently—not by centuries, peoples or civilizations, but by practices. The plots it relates are the history of the practices in which men have seen truths and of their struggles over these truths." These are histories not of events but of practices, not of great men but of discourses that claim to tell truths, not of "wars and politics" but of how life is conceived and lived in daily practices. Significant social changes are constituted through changes in practices, in the ways in which living itself is routinely organized. Changes in practices cumulatively constitute changes in social formations, in "regimes of truth," and these are all worthy of research.

In history itself, those of postmodern bents have argued that empiricism is never enough. The postmodern turn has caused an important loss of "theoretical innocence" and a heightened appreciation of how theoretical assumptions undergird all history (Jenkins 1997:2, 10). One such feature of histories done after the postmodern turn is that they tend to take contingencies more seriously. Foucault used the term "history of the present," which "may be loosely characterized by its use of historical resources to reflect upon the contingency, singularity, interconnections, and potentialities of diverse trajectories of those elements which compose present social arrangements and experience. . . . [It] seeks to prevent anachronistic understandings of the past that make the present a necessary outcome of a necessarily continuous past" (Dean 1994:21). The major means of avoiding the present as "a necessary outcome" is problematizing how we have arrived at the present moment, seeking out those elements that each and all had to be in place for this present to "happen," and "how things could have been otherwise" (Hughes 1971).

> [W]hat Foucault, . . . following Nietzsche, called an "effective history" . . . sets itself against what might be called the colonization of historical knowledge [against appropriating history for other purposes]. . . . I would stress its status as a problematizing activity. Indeed, if the widely used term "postmodernism" is defined as the *restive problematisation of the given,* I would be happy to regard this type of history as an exercise of postmodernity. (Dean 1994:4; emphasis added)

Symbolic interactionism and Foucault converge around certain theoretical concerns such as the importance of contingency and related ideas about causality. According to Foucault (1991:76), contingency "means making visible a singularity at places where there is a temptation to invoke a historical constant. . . . To show that 'things weren't as necessary as all that.'" Foucault-inspired work attempts to reveal "the conditions of possibility" at a given historical moment. In interactionist terms, one seeks to show "how things could have been otherwise" (Hughes 1971) by explicitly laying out other possibilities and turning points, revealing the dense flotsam and jetsam of contingency in the historical moment (e.g., Strauss 1993).

Another set of shared concerns is the handling of causality. For Foucault (1991:76), this involves "rediscovering the encounters, supports, blockages, plays of forces, strategies and so on which at a given moment establish what subsequently counts as being self-evident, universal and necessary. In this sense, one is indeed effecting a sort of multiplication or pluralization of causes. . . . This . . . procedure means analyzing an event according to the multiple processes which constitute it." For grounded theorists and interactionists, assuming multiple complicated and problematizing contributory processes is also common practice (e.g., Lindesmith 1981).

The next question, then, is how to do history today? Brettell (1998:516) disquietingly argues that "[t]here are no mechanical recipes for proper methods." There are multiple strategies. The researcher must take responsibility for drawing these together, drawing upon the strengths of historiography.[2] Here I emphasize Foucault, grounded theory, and situational analysis.

Arguing for histories of the present in poststructuralist terms, Foucault moved away from traditional "total" history characterized by overarching principles and the accounts of particular persons. Instead he advocated what he termed "general" histories that are nonreductive, nontotalizing, and specify their own terrains (Dean 1994:93-95). Foucault (e.g., 1978, 1980) is known for two distinctive approaches to historical questions: archeology and genealogy. In archeological projects, which he pursued first, Foucault (1965, 1972, 1973) sought to understand knowledges, practices, relations, and so on that have stabilized. This is accomplished by focusing on "programmatic" discursive statements in the archive rather than on the authors of such statements or persons (Kendall & Wickham, 1999:22 ff., 2004:143).

Genealogies of discourses were at the heart of Foucault's (1975:xvi; emphasis added) later concerns: "We are doomed historically to history, to the patient construction of discourses about discourses, and to the *task of hearing what has already been said.*" In his later genealogical projects, through Nietzsche, Foucault (1978, 1979) proceeded by tracing changes in discourses (including the meanings of terms) back to their beginnings. Discourses of particular interest are those that seek to tell us what to see/ what can be seen and how to be.

Grounded theory approaches have been used on historical materials for many years but only by a fairly limited number of researchers. Grounded theory studies of historical materials to date have situated such projects both more theoretically and more organizationally and institutionally. Most of the historical projects have focused on the particular kinds of *work or practices* being done in the historical situation as the basic social process. Most have focused on technoscientific practices and used social worlds/arenas analysis (Clarke & Fujimura 1992/1996; Clarke & Star 2003).

This chapter next frames some of the key design issues in historicizing a contemporary project and in generating an historical project. I then use my own research as an exemplar of doing situational analysis with historical materials.

Designing Historical and Historicizing Projects

> *[Historical] material is not "raw" but already the result of other practices of conservation and organization.*
>
> —Dean (1994:15)

All of the situational maps and analyses can be used to do either fully historical work or to historicize contemporary research projects by including analysis of particular historical materials (perhaps as a dissertation chapter or book chapter, for example). That is, many qualitative research projects have historical dimensions that should be taken into explicit account to make better sense of a contemporary situation of interest. This is what I mean by "historicizing" contemporary research as compared to doing "full-on" history. I next offer several examples of historicizing projects and full-on historical projects.

Laura Mamo's (2002) recent dissertation on how lesbians who want to have a child manage to achieve pregnancy in the absence of heterosexuality included some historical research. She pursued primary and secondary historical materials on both the history of donor insemination (including biomedical and radical feminist approaches) and on the history of lesbian parenting in the United States. Each of these historicizing strategies revealed and highlighted key elements of the current situations of lesbians desiring pregnancy that productively informed her work. She concluded that the biomedicalization of reproduction is transforming lesbian as well as infertile heterosexual conception processes because, for many and varied reasons but mostly due to AIDS, lesbians today often resort to using infertility medicine to achieve pregnancy. Here we see the import of the history of infertility medicine, including the history of access to it, which is often denied to lesbians at certain historical moments and places. At the same time, the history of feminist health movements, with roots into the 19th century, was important in understanding contemporary feminist health traditions. These traditions center on do-it-yourself approaches to evade some medical interventions, and include "do-it-yourself donor insemination." Both traditional feminist approaches and queer community support are creatively enrolled by lesbians, at times to counter or subvert biomedicalization processes and/or consequences.

Another example of historicization of a contemporary project is Jennifer Fosket's (2002) research on the use of tamoxifen and raloxifene as chemoprevention drugs—treatments for the risk of breast cancer. Never before have such highly potent/toxic chemotherapy drugs been used for preventive purposes. Fosket studied the clinical trials of these drugs. For a coherent dissertation, she obviously had to situate the existence of these clinical trials. She therefore offers some history of breast cancer treatment: How did chemo*prevention* even get conceptualized? How did this particular trial come to pass? She also needed to grasp the history of clinical trials to situate the one she was studying. How is it similar? Different? Last, Fosket also needed to examine the history of using very strong drugs for other preventive purposes. The first major instance of this was, interestingly, the use of hormonal birth control pills for the prevention of pregnancy—which also had a controversial history (e.g., Oudshoorn 2003; Watkins 1998). None of Fosket's extensions into historical work constituted "primary research" in the historians' sense, yet her constellation of secondary source materials enriched the project, gave it a depth it otherwise would have lacked, and pointed her toward particular analytic questions that might have otherwise gone unasked.

In full-on historical projects, the social worlds/arenas framework elaborated in this book has also been used quite a bit, especially in the study of long-term controversies and studies of disciplinary and specialty emergence in academia and medicine.[3] For example, Garrety (1997, 1998) studied the history of the cholesterol controversy in public health over the past half century. She argues that the social worlds/arenas framework is exceptionally strong and useful for full-on histories, as many kinds of changes can be tracked over time along with the appearance and disappearance of social worlds and segments.

A wonderful hybrid example that comparatively analyzes four very different forms of historical discourse (a film, a popular book, a biography, and archival materials) is Graham's (1992) "Archival Research in Intertextual Analysis: Four Representations of the Life of Dr. Lillian Moller Gilbreth." A pioneer in the development of "scientific management" in industrial engineering, Gilbreth is more famed as the widowed mother of 12 who applied scientific management techniques to home management. Graham's (1992; see also 1998) interactionist study focused on deconstructing the myths about the Gilbreths articulated in the various materials. (Readers will likely be familiar with the 1950s movie and 2003 remake, *Cheaper by the Dozen.*) All historical projects depend heavily on designs that are adequate in terms of available materials.

Design Issues

In the same ways that situational analysis is intended to supplement basic grounded theory, it is also intended to supplement historiographic approaches in the study of historical discourse materials. Within the three-pronged framework of Jaworski and Coupland (1999a) focused on analyzing discourses in interactions, in the production of subjectivities/identities, and in producing power/knowledge (see Chapter 4), historical projects focus on the latter two and are oriented in more Foucaultian directions. Quite recently, there has been a flurry of books and papers attending to "Foucault's methods." Many of these can be quite useful in helping neophytes to design projects that meet their needs and goals. For example, Kendall and Wickham (2004:144-145; see also 1999) argue that there are four main elements in framing a Foucault-inspired historical project. First is asking a "how" question (rather than a "why" question) that centers the project on "how X came to be" or "how Y got to be the way things are done." Second is locating an archive of appropriate materials. Third is especially seeking "programmatic" texts, "writings that try to impose a vision or spell out most clearly a new way of conceptualizing a problem."

Last is making the commitment to "keep digging until one finds the relative beginnings of a practice. . . . We start with a known outcome but what we need to do is find the precursors that lead to this outcome." What were the conditions of possibility that led here? What were the sites of contingency?

Using situational analysis approaches, I recommend initiating design with historical discourse materials much as I recommended initiating the design process with narrative discourse materials—making a very preliminary messy map. That is, you first need to decide what historical terrain you want to examine. The next step is to do a very preliminary map that roughly lays out all the elements you think may be in that situation. The main goal here (and in the many subsequent reworkings) is to make sure you ultimately capture *all the major extant elements in the historical situation* on this map and any minor ones you think are significant. You will not pursue them all, and usually only a few. This map gives you a place to begin thinking through what historical research about this situation is possible, feasible, seemingly interesting, and worthwhile.

The next task is seeking out primary and secondary materials related to each of what you decide are the key elements. What materials are available? Are they dense and rich enough to support a project or subproject? Pulling together extant secondary works and examining their primary sources is often helpful. Using the wide array of historical databases available through university libraries and Googling are also appropriate early steps.[4] Public and accessible private document archives can also be excellent resources (see Prior, 2003, 2004). Through their professional societies, most specialty areas within history have now organized electronic resources vis-à-vis pertinent archives. I cannot walk you further through this stage here, aside from reiterating that using exquisite care now in organizing both your primary and secondary data is crucial (see discussion in Chapter 5).

Last, compared to contemporary social science, it is important to note that history is interpretation in the potentially complete absence of "knowing subjects" who are alive and interrogable. That is, historical discourse materials not only exist prior to the inception of your research project (unlike ethnographic and interview data), but you also may not have access to living persons or organizations with pertinent knowledge or experiences. (If you do have such access, seriously consider a multisite approach.) Thus the burdens of historical interpretation are considerable: "[A]ny one reading of a historical datum may coexist with other readings that are also 'true'" (Tuchman 1994:316). That is, good history will not resolve multiplicity into singularity. In fact, one may end up telling multiple possible stories/readings in history as elsewhere. In history as elsewhere, we seek to explore the "lived borders" between experiences and their representation

(Gubrium & Holstein 1997). And in history as elsewhere, we can seek to tell stories of the nonhuman—biographies of things as well as people, of technologies, discourses, and so on.[5]

Let us now move into doing full-on history and actually mapping some primary historical materials.

Doing Situational Maps of Historical Discourse

Historically constructed meanings become the raw materials for new cultural creation.

—Tuchman (1994:322)

Doing situational maps of historical data is basically like doing situational maps with contemporary ethnographic and interview data. The goal is to lay out as best one can all the human and nonhuman elements in the situation of concern of the research broadly conceived. The questions are: Who and what were in this situation? Who and what mattered in this situation? What elements made a difference in this situation? What elements were "invisibled" in the situation, and how was that accomplished? The key difference in doing situational maps of historical data is that one can and usually should do *multiple maps for different historical moments* in the research. Smaller differences include, first, the possible absence of desired data because it cannot be found, does not exist, or is inaccessible. While partiality is characteristic of all research, in historical work one sometimes knows exactly what is missing but cannot remedy this. Second is another possible partiality of data—that it may only hint at something rather than demonstrate it with sufficient evidence to make a strong argument. Whatever the problem, if relevant, it should be clearly described in the memos and research reports, as should surprising findings.

The basic guidelines for doing good history are also assumed to be followed here. For example, "(1) Historical documents should be read with a sensitivity to the social, political, and cultural context within which they were produced. (2) We must work not only to identify the ethnocentrism of the writer of a document but our own ethnocentrism as evaluators of that document" (Brettell 1998:518). Reflexivity, in short, is central to interpreting historical as well as contemporary materials. Similarly, the basic guidelines for doing good grounded theory coding and memoing are assumed to be followed here as well. Situational analysis of historical materials is intended to go beyond these, to supplement them analytically.

Historical Discourse Exemplar:
Developing Modern Contraceptives (circa 1915-1965)

I will not refer here in depth to my book *Disciplining Reproduction* on the development of the American reproductive sciences in biology, medicine, and agriculture (Clarke 1998), which is long, complicated, and unfamiliar territory to most people. Instead, for this exemplar of historical work, I draw here largely on two chapters from it (Chapters 6 and 8) and a paper I wrote (Clarke 2000) to tell stories about the development of modern scientific contraceptives circa 1915-1965. I used a wide array of data sources in what was very much a multisite/multiscape project before we had those terms: archival materials from four major sites, "insider" histories (written by participating research scientists and considered as primary rather than secondary sources), scientific literatures, interviews with scientists, and the extant secondary literatures.

I have clearly bounded the situation examined here historically (c1915-c1965) and substantively (focusing only on contraceptive development and not on the basic reproductive science or actual clinical use of contraception). The business of making new contraceptives got much more complicated after 1965, and I want a simpler story as an exemplar here, though it is far from simple—even limiting the stories as I do largely to those of the Pill and plastic IUDs. Such serious boundary making is often quite requisite in historical work, as commonly *one's project is telling as much of each significant story as you can without getting lost in too much detail.* Thus the researcher needs to know many, many stories in order to choose those most worthy of relating in print. Moreover, one must exercise considerable restraint in terms of detail or risk losing readers and/or not having space for other stories.

I can frame this exemplar as a classic grounded theory project with the "basic social process" of "developing modern contraceptives in the U.S. 1915-1965."[6] This is a dense historical study focused largely on collective action at the meso level of social organization. It examines the interactions of various key individuals and groups involved, over time, in the struggles around deciding what new kinds of contraceptives would be produced and around the actual production of two "modern scientific contraceptives" in the United States. Both the Pill and plastic IUDs were based on newly available nonhuman actants—synthetic sex hormones and plastics. These contraceptives were developed by some groups in the midst of opposition by yet other groups and their ongoing assertions of the illegitimacy of attempting to control reproduction through the use of "artificial" means (contraception rather than abstinence). The politics, then as now, were complicated.

Situational Maps Exemplar: Developing
Modern Contraceptives (circa 1915-1965)

My questions for the situational map include: Who and what were in the broader situation? Who was involved (supportive, opposed, providing knowledge, materials, money, what else)? What material things—nonhuman elements—were involved and required for contraceptive research and development? How were the prospective users of contraceptives present (or not) in the situation? How were users of these new technological devices conceived by the designers (discursively constructed) as they were making them?[7] What historical and other contemporary cultural symbologies and discourses were evoked by the topic of contraception? What social institutions were involved? How and why was it controversial and to whom? What were some of the issues? (This anticipates the later need for issues and axes to develop positional maps.)

I offer here my own messy map as Figure 7.1, Messy Situational Map: Developing Modern Contraceptives (circa 1915-1965). I think this is a perfectly reasonable way of working, especially at the outset of a project, but also to return to time and again. Once one gets farther downstream analytically, it is far too easy to lose sight of elements that might be important. Figure 7.1 offers a very dense situational map with many genres of actors and numerous actors within genres. This map collapses historical time—there is only one situational map presented here for the entire period 1915-1965. I could offer two or more maps (and do so below in the social worlds/arenas section), and I actually had multiple maps for my very historical work, using them to track changes over time. But it is also important to have a big picture situational map to remind you of what was, what is, and what may be there in the situation of action that you should check out. One could also annotate a version of the map with dates of first appearance of various elements.

Figure 7.2, Ordered Situational Map: Developing Modern Contraceptives (circa 1915-1965), shows the neat version. I find it useful to have both messy and orderly versions available to work with simultaneously. When I want to be sure I have not overlooked or forgotten some relation, the neatness of Figure 7.2 is helpful, as I can check through at a glance. With dense and complicated historical materials, the orderly map can also act as a placeholder for greater detail than can "fit" on the messy map. For example, the list of key individuals is extended. These are working maps to be modified to meet your own empirical and analytic needs.

Let me offer next a short analytic narrative that begins to tie some of these elements together. My analysis revealed that four often overlapping realms of controversy have plagued the reproductive sciences over the past century: (1) the commonly socially and culturally controversial status of issues of sexuality and reproduction; (2) the historical linkages of the

Figure 7.1   Messy Situational Map: Developing Modern Contraceptives (circa 1915-1965)

reproductive sciences to numerous instances of clinical quackery and controversial treatments and technologies; (3) the historical linkages between the reproductive sciences and several controversial social movements throughout its modern development (e.g., birth control and abortion movements); and (4) the capacities of the reproductive sciences to alter the "natural order" through its new technologies (e.g., infertility services, stem cell research), often seen as part of horrifying brave new worlds.

INDIVIDUAL HUMAN ELEMENTS/ACTORS

Margaret Sanger
Robert Latou Dickinson
John D. Rockefeller Jr.
John D. Rockefeller III
Frank Lillie
Gregory Pincus
M.C. Chang
Katherine McCormick
Russell Marker
Carl Djerassi
Frank Lippes
Lazar Marguiles

COLLECTIVE HUMAN ELEMENTS/ACTORS

Social Movement Organizations:

Feminist Birth Control
American Birth Control League (ABCL)
National Birth Control League (NBCL)
Medical Birth Control
National Committee on Maternal Health
Planned Parenthood USA and local clinic affiliates
International Planned Parenthood Federation
Eugenics
American Eugenics Society
Neo-Malthusians/Population Control
Population Association of America
Population Council

Major Funding Sources:

Bureau of Social Hygiene
Rockefeller Foundation
Carnegie Institution
National Research Council Committee
    for Research on Problems of Sex
Katherine McCormick
Ford Foundation
NIH NICHHD

Reproductive Scientists:

Biology, medicine, and agriculture,
    and their professional organizations

Regulatory Agencies:

U.S. Postal Service; U.S. FDA

Religious Groups:

Catholic Church
Other religious groups

Pharmaceuticals Companies:

Syntex, Searle, other companies

NONHUMAN ELEMENTS/ACTANTS

Galvanized rubber
Condoms
Diaphragms
Cervical caps
Spermicidal chemicals
Reports of prior clinical studies
Hormones as drugs
"The Pill"
Metal IUDs
Plastics (post-WW II)
Plastic IUDs

IMPLICATED/SILENT ACTORS/ACTANTS

Third world women as users
First world women as users

Figure 7.2   Ordered Situational Map: Developing Modern Contraceptives
          (circa 1915-1965)

(Continued)

DISCURSIVE CONSTRUCTIONS OF HUMAN ACTORS

Third world women as users
First world women as users
Constructions of other individual
   and collective actors

DISCURSIVE CONSTRUCTIONS OF NONHUMAN ACTANTS

Plastics as fantastic
Diaphragms and spermicides as "messy"
Condoms as "numbing"
IUDs as inherently dangerous
Hormones as powerful drugs
Pills as "magic bullets"

POLITICAL/ECONOMIC ELEMENTS

Histories of American race, sex,
   and class relations
1st-Era Social Movements: Civil Rights,
   Feminism, Women's and Children's
   Health, Eugenics,
   Neo-Malthusian/Population Control
Rise of medicalization

SOCIOCULTURAL/SYMBOLIC ELEMENTS

Children
Motherhood/femininity
Fatherhood/masculinity
Family/kinship
Nation statehood
Population "bomb"/"overpopulation"
Birth control as for "loose" women

TEMPORAL ELEMENTS

U.S. and European colonies
World War I
Great Depression
World War II
Ending of Colonial Era
Third World Nationalisms
U.S. War on Poverty

SPATIAL ELEMENTS

Reconfiguring of global interests
Organizing of first/second/third worlds
Puerto Rico as an American colony
American South as colony

MAJOR ISSUES DEBATED

Simple versus scientific contraception
Low-tech versus high-tech means
Safety of different means
Attributes of different women as users
Population growth: national and global
Legitimacy of using contraception

RELATED DISCOURSES

Sex/Gender: Women as reproductive
   bodies
Eugenics: "Better people through better
   breeding," "(White) race suicide," "Fit"
   and "Unfit" people, positive and
   negative eugenics and degeneracy
Birth Control: Family planning,
   contraception, planned parenthood,
   "Every child a wanted child"
Population Control: "Overpopulation/The
   Population Bomb"
Welfare: Class, race, gender, and poverty
Nationalism: Legitimating
   (post)colonialisms

In part, then, because of the controversial status of the reproductive sciences and contraceptive development, private philanthropy rather than government funding was essentially responsible for the production of modern scientific means of contraception. This occurred first through John D. Rockefeller Jr.'s support for basic reproductive sciences between World War I and II, given through the Bureau of Social Hygiene and later through the Rockefeller Foundation to the National Research Council's Committee for Research on Problems of Sex (not an official government agency) for distribution to researchers. Once established in 1921, the committee used biologist Frank Lillie's endocrinologically oriented basic research agenda as the basis for giving research grants instead of funding the psychological and social scientific studies of human sexuality originally envisioned. Basic scientific research clearly trumped social science research!

After World War II, because of the ongoing controversial status of the reproductive sciences and contraception, the U.S. government did not include the reproductive sciences in its expanding research agenda. Instead, to develop new contraceptives, a new wave of private philanthropists stepped forward (Ford, Macy, McCormick, and another Rockefeller). John D. Rockefeller III founded the Population Council in New York City where Drs. Jack Lippes and Lazar Marguiles then worked on a new plastic IUD ultimately called the "Lippes Loop." Katherine McCormick, a biologist, birth control advocate, and wealthy friend of Margaret Sanger's, supported biologists Gregory Pincus and M. C. Chang's work on the Pill at the Worcester Institute in Massachusetts. A few pharmaceutical companies also got involved, despite the risk of boycotts of all their products by religious and other opponents of contraception (e.g., Searle, and Syntex where Russell Marker and Carl Djerassi were located). Later, as part of the War on Poverty from circa 1965 to the late 1970s, the U.S. government did become a major funding source for contraceptive research through the National Institutes of Child Health and Human Development (NICHHD). Contraception was then viewed as a means of bringing down the welfare rolls and providing international aid to "developing" countries through "population control." The Ford Foundation also established new centers of reproductive and contraceptive research internationally, creating an ever more global and complicated "situation of inquiry" after circa 1965.

Looking at the two situational maps, Figures 7.1 and 7.2, we first vividly see people, organizations, companies, sex hormones, scientists, pills, labs, and monies. But we also need to ask what ideas, concepts, ideologies, discourses, symbols, sites of debate, and other cultural stuff may matter in this situation. For example, in most if not all studies of the biomedical sciences, the ideology/ discourse of the hierarchy of the sciences is important—which sciences and specialties rank highest and which lowest. In my own work, it was highly significant that the reproductive sciences in biology, medicine, and agriculture were at the low end of the status totem pole, while genetics was and remains high end. Reproductive scientists who had university positions were already situated close to the bottom rung of the status hierarchy; they did not want to slide any further down that ladder by participating in *applied* research on contraceptive development. Only maverick scientists participated in developing the initial modern products—the Pill and plastic IUDs. They were often themselves outcasts or refugees from academia, working in freestanding research shops and often hustling contract research work.

As a feminist paying serious attention to women as the usual downstream users of contraception, I viewed the prospective women users, especially third world women, as key *implicated actors* (see Chapter 2). Early developers of modern scientific contraception wrote about seeing poor third world women—in the streets of India or South Africa, for example—and wanting to "do something for" these women, to develop means of contraception for them, since they "obviously" had too many children. Thus *particular* women users were sometimes inscribed on/in *particular* kinds of contraceptives. The formal colonial era was just ending in the 1950s, nationalist movements were very much on the rise, and population control was one strategy to contain them. Specifically, due to usually tacit but sometimes vividly explicit racism, sexism, classism, and neoimperialism, those means of contraception that were less rather than more user-controlled were commonly inscribed as "for" third world women.

For example, Christopher Tietze described the mood of the group working on new plastic IUDs at the Population Council as follows:

> It was a very exciting period. . . . [W]e were working with something that had been absolutely rejected by the [American medical] profession [IUDs—because of risks of infection]. . . . There was such a feeling of urgency among professional people, *not* among the masses, but something had to be done. And this was something that *you could do to the people* rather than something *people could do for themselves.* So it made it very attractive to the doers. (Reed 1984:307; emphasis added)

This approach, seeking means of contraception "you could do to the people," which I generically termed "imposables," has guided much if not most subsequent research within the population control agenda. In sharp contrast, early feminists such as Margaret Sanger (c1915) and others initially desired improved spermicides, diaphragms, and other "simple contraceptives" that women could use or not use as they themselves saw fit. Their feminism guided them to seek "woman-controlled" birth control that was relatively simple and low tech. Meanwhile, most scientists, eugenicists, and population control advocates sought "modern *scientific* contraceptives" that they viewed as more elegant clinically, some of which were also potentially imposable.

From my research and studying my situational map, I then saw how third world women as end users were *implicated actors*. Neither their actual presence nor their vicarious participation was desired—at least not until the human testing stage.[8] Their discursive presence, created in grants and other narratives by contraceptive developers, helped raise research and development funds through a discourse of overpopulation, legitimating contraceptive research against opposing religious and other groups, and so on. Their *discursive* constructions thus did particular kinds of work for the developers. This is precisely how nonhuman actants can be quite agentic. *I* knew this as a feminist researcher, and had women on *my* map. But had I been following traditional grounded theory procedures and not attending to and iterating nonhumans in the situation—including discursive constructions of humans—I would have missed this completely.

As a feminist concerned with seeing the agency of women, I also analyzed how in concrete practices women have also pragmatically resisted, refused, flexibly reinterpreted, and reused some of those technologies for their own purposes. For example, women in Southeast Asia accomplished an early reinterpretation of birth control pills as abortifacients by using them differently than intended, a lay usage that presaged the morning-after pill.

In sum, the historical situational maps work very well as holding devices—allowing the analyst to see all of the elements simultaneously. While I offered here a single big picture situational map covering the historical period from 1915 to 1965, I told the big picture story more historically/chronologically. The stories I have told were produced through doing the relational analyses discussed in Chapter 3, tracing the relations among the elements over time. In the next section, I offer social worlds/arenas maps for two different times—1925 and 1965—and compare them.

Doing Social Worlds/Arenas
Maps of Historical Discourse

> *Written history both reflects and creates relations of power. Its standards of inclusion and exclusion, measures of importance, and rules of evaluation are not objective criteria but politically produced conventions. What we know as history is, then, the result of past politics; today's contests are about how history will be constituted for the present.*
>
> —Scott (1989:681)

Social worlds/arenas maps of historical data do the same work as such maps of contemporary data. Again, the difference is that you can and should do these maps for different historical moments, and I have done so in the exemplar below. I should also note that one can do such maps perspectively—from the perspective of a particular social world in the arena. (See Figure 5.7 for an Abstract Perspectival Project Map.)

Social worlds/arenas maps are at the meso level—the level of *social* action. These are not aggregates of individuals, but meaningful and meaning-making collectivities. Social worlds shape and are themselves shaped through their active participation with other social worlds in their arena(s) of concern usually but not only through producing discourses. I thus start my historical maps with the questions: What were the patterns of collective commitment and what were the salient social worlds operating here? What were their perspectives/discourses? Who were they in dialogue with? About what? What were their collective actions and what did they hope to achieve through them? What older and newer/emergent nonhuman technologies and other nonhuman actants were characteristic of each world? What were their properties? What constraints, opportunities, and resources did they supply to that world? How did the various worlds see and constellate one another?

Social Worlds/Arenas Map Exemplar: Developing Modern Contraceptives (circa 1915-1965)

As noted earlier, many different collective actors can be involved in an arena. For example, we see the broad arena focused on birth control in the United States mapped in Figure 7.3, Social Worlds/Arenas Map I: Developing Modern Contraceptives (circa 1925). The birth control arena intersects with three other related arenas—one focused on medicine/public health, a second on heredity/genetics, and a third smaller arena focused on the issue of control over the quantity of populations—population control (also then called neo-Malthusianism). Certain groups and organizations are situated in two or more of these arenas simultaneously. The medicine/public health, heredity/genetics, and population control arenas are only lightly sketched, as they are not *my* focus of analysis.

Looking at the birth control arena for 1925, we can see several major social worlds in it: The social worlds of birth control advocates and of philanthropists committed to birth control are fully in that arena. Also present are segments of the reproductive sciences world, segments of the clinical medicine and public health arena, segments of the population control arena, and last but not least, the "worlds of opposition to contraception." There were deep differences among the various segments of "the opposition worlds" qua worlds.

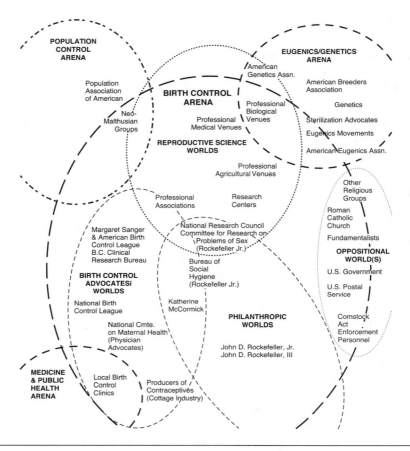

Figure 7.3   Social Worlds/Arenas Map I: Developing Modern Contraceptives (circa 1925)

It was composed of segments of the Roman Catholic Church, other religious groups and fundamentalist sects, and segments of U.S. federal, state, and local governments. Religious groups usually oppose(d) the use of birth control because they see it as intervening in divine processes/"God's way" and/or rupturing "the natural" with "the artificial." Governmental opposition began with the supposedly "antivice" Comstock Act of 1873, in force until at least 1936, which defined "the prevention of conception" as obscene and made it illegal to put through the mails any contraceptive advice, device, or information. The mails had been (and probably continued to be) the primary means of distribution of birth control information and devices (including abortifacients) for some decades. In addition to the Comstock Act, a variety of state and local statutes also prohibited distribution of contraceptive devices and information. Birth control advocates mounted many challenges to such laws (and are still doing so today), as well as seeking broad social and cultural legitimacy for the practice of contraception (also ongoing).

The birth control advocates' social world in 1925 included some physicians (some of whom had formed the National Committee on Maternal Health), two feminist organizations with different political strategies (Sanger's American Birth Control League and the National Birth Control League led by Mary Ware Dennett), and the producers of various contraceptives (such as spermicides, the diaphragm, and the cervical cap). Convincing physicians, especially the American Medical Association, of the clinical value of birth control was a major Sanger strategy. At the boundary where the birth control and philanthropic worlds met was the organization founded by John D. Rockefeller Jr. for his more radical philanthropic efforts, the Bureau of Social Hygiene. It was a major source of funding for birth control advocacy organizations and for early reproductive science through the NRC Committee for Research on Problems of Sex (as well as funding other controversial areas such as early sexuality studies).

Those segments of the clinical medicine and public health arena also in the birth control arena include some practicing medical personnel (physicians, nurses, other health care providers, public health personnel), and their various professional organizations, some of which took positions in support of contraception. Also, clinicians of various sorts were active as individuals in birth control advocacy organizations and in the many local birth control clinics all over the United States that grew out of this movement. While such clinics were the primary social movement strategy of the American Birth Control League, they were local organizations sometimes having a national affiliation, mapped separately. Many became affiliates of Planned Parenthood U.S.A. The reproductive sciences world overlaps with four arenas (only three are so diagramed): medicine/public health, heredity/genetics, population, and birth control. Inside reproductive scientists' world are their varied professional associations, research centers, and the professional venues in which they worked in circa 1925: university-based departments and schools of biology, medicine, and agriculture. At the boundary where reproductive science worlds meet and overlap with the heredity/genetics arena stood the American Eugenics Society, committed to "better people through better breeding," and the American Genetics Association. At the boundary where the reproductive sciences and philanthropic worlds meet is the National

Research Council's Committee. It provided both financial support and social legitimacy for the development of the modern reproductive sciences (c1921-1962), which in turn provided the knowledge base for the development of modern contraceptives. Not yet significantly present in this arena were the pharmaceutical and medical industries, as the production of contraceptives at that time was essentially a cottage industry.

Figure 7.4, Social Worlds/Arenas Map II: Developing Modern Contraceptives (circa 1965), represents the arena 40 years later. I won't recount this map as precisely as I did the earlier one, but rather point out some major changes. First we see two new freestanding research shops engaged with contraceptives: the Worcester Institute and the Population Council. In terms of the birth control movement, Sanger's group has succeeded, and there are Planned Parenthood clinics all over the United States and the International Planned Parenthood Foundation based in London (housed with the British Eugenics Society). Two pharmaceutical companies are now actively present in the arena: Searle and Syntex. The U.S. government is actively involved in the distribution of contraceptives nationally (usually through county-based family planning clinics, bringing contraception to rural areas often for the first time) and internationally (through the U.S. Agency for International Development—USAID). Margaret Sanger and her friend Katherine McCormick have become the "mothers" of the birth control Pill (through sponsoring it while in their 70s), while reproductive scientists Pincus, Chang, Marker, and Djerassi are its "fathers."

But let me add a cautionary aside: Even the best of maps cannot necessarily help us see. Despite my writing seriously about the controversial nature of doing reproductive science, I now believe I gave too short shrift to the significance of religious opposition to the development of modern scientific contraceptives in my work. I lost sight of this opposition on my map in ways that birth control advocates themselves did not and still do not today.[9] I was seeing religious opposition as related mostly to abortion, a view based in my own époque. But I now believe that was/is just the tip of the iceberg. Living through the Bush administration's and Catholic Church's ongoing opposition to contraception as well as to abortion, reading a new book on whatever happened to the male Pill (still unavailable after 40-plus years of the female Pill) (Oudshoorn 2003), and following recent morning-after pill and stem cell debates have been bringing this point home to me most powerfully. A postmodern stance, attempting to step outside the fog induced by Enlightenment conceptions of historical "progress," also helps.

In sum, maps are configurations, and looking at the social worlds/arenas maps for two different times vividly demonstrates the reconfigurations that have occurred—as well as helping us to see the relatively unchanging

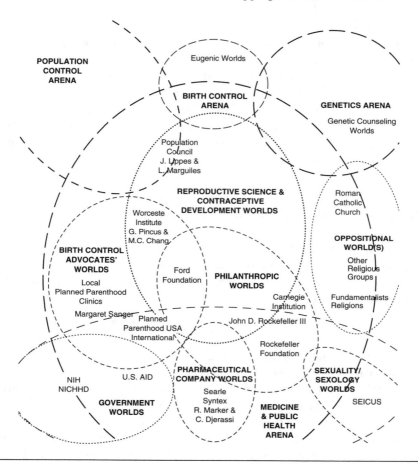

Figure 7.4   Social Worlds/Arenas Map II: Developing Modern Contraceptives (circa 1965)

elements. The researcher is certainly not compelled to tell each story, but the very *doing* of the maps (which I can find quite hard going) forces one to think about what happened to X and to Y and to the relationship with Z in analytical ways that simply telling stories/producing narratives does not. The value of these maps, then, is perhaps greatest in their provocation of further analysis after the researcher has managed to pull together some sort of narrative history, provoking among other things further theoretical sampling to determine "whatever happened to Z." The maps can help rupture our own premature and/or ill thought through analyses.

I also ended up using my social worlds/arenas maps of different eras to help me organize my (1998) book. Part I focused on the emergence era of the American reproductive sciences. It had an overview chapter on the science and a chapter on what I decided was the most important other social world in that era—the external funding source. Part II focused on the coalescence era. It too had an overview of the science, and the chapter on the most important other social world focused on the development of modern contraceptives. Thus social worlds/arenas maps can be useful organizationally as well as analytically.

Doing Positional Maps of Historical Discourse

> These theories also imply that the historian's account is an assembled text. It, too, is multivocal and bespeaks the context of its production. It, too, is an assemblage that bespeaks the historian's époque.
>
> —Tuchman (1994:316)

To do positional maps of historical data, one first seeks to elucidate from the data what the basic (often but not always contested) issues are about that there are different positions *in the same time period,* and to array these two-dimensionally in some fashion. This quickly gets complicated empirically, and the analyst has to be very careful vis-à-vis the historical data. That is, we can through our own interests too easily raise the horizon on particular topics that were not so lively in the era under examination. This can be intentional (seeking the history of X) or inadvertent (unwittingly reflecting ourselves and our own époque).

It is important to remember that the concept of positions here—with the ever-present possibility of multiple simultaneous and even contradictory positions being held by an individual, group, or nonhuman actant—creates an important space between. In such spaces we can, however briefly, attempt to step outside the charged politics of direct representation. Such spaces can allow us to see what is happening in the discourse itself and in our own visions of it as the analyses begin to merge. What other shapes might it flow into or might flow into it? Positional maps can allow us to articulate doubts and complexities where heretofore things had perhaps appeared "unnaturally" sure and simple. That is, positional maps may seem not to work, and that not working may turn out to be an important analytic point.

Positional Map Exemplar: Developing Modern Contraceptives (circa 1915-1965)

Here I focus on one substory in the development of modern contraceptives—the IUD development story. I offer two positional maps on IUD development for two different historical times to show changes.

As a feminist women's health advocate, I knew when I began my dissertation project in 1982 that, since the 1970s, physicians had been (at least somewhat) rightly blamed for many of the ills suffered by women from the use of IUDs. Apparently the worst was the Dalcon Shield, withdrawn from the U.S. market because of extensive mortality and morbidity and "dumped" for final product consumption in the third world. It was, then, quite a surprise to me during my research, and an interesting and important *analytic* complication, to understand that historically some practicing physicians involved with and committed to contraceptive development in the United States were so deeply opposed to IUDs that fears of infection were discussed at length at birth control conferences in the 1920s and 1930s. It was so controversial that there were no reports by physicians who had used IUDs allowed to be published in Western medical journals.

In Figure 7.5, Positional Map I: Developing Modern Contraceptives—American Physicians and IUDs (circa 1935), one axis is the (positive to negative) assessments of IUD safety offered by American physicians involved somehow with contraception. This axis is played against the (positive to negative) advocacy of using IUDs for contraception put forward by American physicians. On the positional map are the three main positions held at that time. The majority position was that IUDs were not safe due to risks of infection. Remember, this was before the existence of antibiotics, and infections could be fatal. There were two minority positions articulated in the data: that IUDs *are* safe enough, and that IUDs *may be* safe enough (and that their safety should be assessed through clinic-based research). I also note on the map that the position that IUDs are unsafe but should be used regardless was not articulated in 1935.

Later, as the explicit development of modern scientific contraceptives got seriously under way during the 1950s and 1960s, the entrance of two new nonhuman actants—antibiotics and plastics—changed this situation dramatically. A plastic IUD, it was argued, because it was softer and more flexible, would be less likely to injure uterine tissue than the metal IUDs previously used, and thus less likely to trigger infection. After World War II, antibiotics were routinely available, and IUD advocates pointed to this fact to help shift medical opinion. Had I done two different situational maps (one early and one late), antibiotics and plastics as relevant nonhuman actants

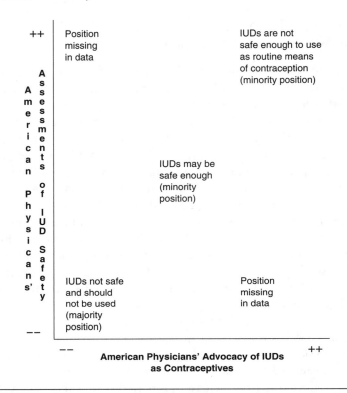

Figure 7.5   Positional Map I: Developing Modern Contraceptives—American Physicians and IUDs (circa 1935)

would have appeared only on the second map. These snazzy new nonhuman actants did a lot of work here, including the symbolic work of making IUDs very "modern," as plastics were "hot" in the 1950s.

There were multiple other positions articulated in my data, for which I am not providing maps, on kinds of contraception desired—"simple" or "scientific," kinds advocated and rationales, and so on. Note too the near complete absence of consumers/users and their desires and concerns. We must always ask: Who and what are *not* there that the analyst thinks might be there or should be there? Silences can thus be analytically made to speak.

Looking at Figure 7.6, Positional Map II: Developing Modern Contraceptives—American Physicians and IUDs (circa 1965), we see that the physicians' new majority position both assesses the IUD as safe and advocates its routine use. In the two positional maps on IUDs for 1935 and 1965 (Figures 7.5 and 7.6), then, a major shift of position is clear. Physicians'

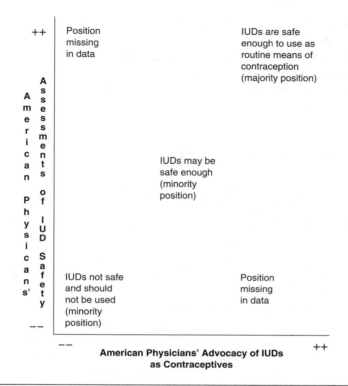

Figure 7.6   Positional Map II: Developing Modern Contraceptives—American Physicians and IUDs (circa 1965)

support of IUD use as routine birth control increased dramatically. The new *plastic* IUD became a successful "modern scientific contraceptive," with "modern scientific antibiotics" as the clinical safety backup technology. Later, the Dalcon Shield product recall in the United States drastically reduced physician advocacy due to very high rates of morbidity (commonly producing infertility) and some mortality due to infection, despite the availability of antibiotics. Sadly, in many places where IUDs have been made available, especially but not only in the third world, antibiotics are not available or are unaffordable.

IUDs are still available today and new versions are still being produced. Also, assessments of risk—professional, feminist activist, and lay/patient— have become much more complicated during this time. That is, most if not all individuals and groups in the birth control arena have come to understand contraception as complex and difficult, *both* technically and socioculturally. The fantasy of a single contraceptive as a magic scientific bullet ebbed across the 20th century along with other modernist fantasies, such as "one size fits all."

But do note that the maps do not capture the whole historical story. Maps point to stories but do not fully articulate them. As you can tell from my stories from the historical field, the research uncovered dense and complicated materials.

Project Map of Historical Discourse

As in some other chapters, in addition to the extended exemplar just detailed, I next offer a project map. Such maps are very similar to the diagrams advocated by Strauss and Corbin (Strauss 1987; Strauss & Corbin 1990, 1998), but also draw upon the mapping strategies of situational analysis.

Figure 7.7 offers the Project Map: Organizing Research Materials for the Reproductive Sciences. I discussed this project quite a bit in Chapter 3. At the beginning of my study of the emergence of the reproductive sciences in the early 20th century, I read the autobiography of one of the major scientists, George W. Corner, a historian of medicine by avocation. He told story after story about how hard it was to get hold of the materials he needed to do his research on ovarian hormones and to maintain access for the duration of a project. He also described organizing the very first primate research colony in the United States circa 1920. Trained by Strauss in the sociology of work, my ears were flapping madly. Organizing research materials was an unstudied aspect of scientific work—part of what Strauss was calling "invisible work" (Star 1991b; Star & Strauss 1998). I began to collect data on "research materials" wherever I went in my historical research (which was many archives, libraries, and interviews). Others described starting rat and opossum colonies (the latter were harder), the importance of having a slaughterhouse down the street from the lab for routine access to fresh specimens, having an assistant go by train for hours to get needed materials, and so on.

As I pursued the new reproductive sciences, I gained knowledge about the major shift then occurring in biology more broadly from predominantly morphological research (needing only a few good specimens, which would then be preserved) to experimental physiological research (with its ongoing demands for lots and lots of the same kinds of materials). This broader shift was the situational frame for understanding all the rat and monkey stories. The whole *situation* of biological research was changing dramatically, and scientists were hustling to get themselves organized to do the new kinds of research. Figure 7.7 is my organizatio*nal* map of this situation. It can be read as a conditional flow chart from top to bottom. At each level, the infrastructures of the previous level have become reliable and new kinds of

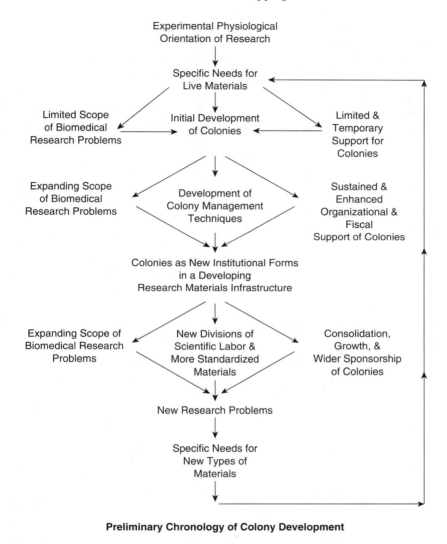

Preliminary Chronology of Colony Development

Figure 7.7   Project Map: Organizing Research Materials for the Reproductive Sciences

SOURCE: Clarke (1987/1995:328). Reprinted by permission of the American Physiological Society.

infrastructures are built on top of them. Then it happens all over again *if and only if* the conditions of demand keep flowing. One critique of Strauss's work, addressed here by my own, was that "he does not explicitly attend to how consequences become conditions" (P. M. Hall 1997:410). One answer is that consequences can become infrastructures that themselves become conditions for subsequent action (see also Bowker & Star 1999).

There were three unanticipated areas of theoretical payoff from this work for me in science and technology studies. First, the study of the actual day-to-day practices of science was just getting hot, and my work featured exactly this, framed as the sociology of work. Second, it also featured the nonhuman as important, also intellectually exciting at that time. Last, I could argue from my data that, contrary to the claims of the vast majority of the history, philosophy, and social studies of science literature, science is *not* always guided by theory. Once the scientists I studied had regular access to some material, they would instead figure out what other kinds of projects they could do using that material. Thus access to research materials was shaping the direction of some science.

Project maps are project-specific. A good map like a good picture or diagram can capture a lot of the story and make it visually more accessible.

Final Comments: Situational Analysis of Historical Discourse

> *[L]abyrinths may be important sensitizing devices, insisting— as they do—that both the historian and the qualitative social scientist are engaged in interpretive endeavors.*
>
> —Tuchman (1994:317)

What are good enough situational maps of historical discourse, and how do you know when you have them? The key word here again is saturation— from basic grounded theory. You have created maps of enough time periods, worked with your maps many, many times, tinkered, added, deleted, reorganized. You can talk at some length about every entry. You can easily discuss the maps comparatively. It has been quite a while since you have made any major changes. You think these are the most important elements. (Of course there are many others—partialities are ubiquitous—but they don't seem to make a difference to the stories you have decided you want to tell about the situation—your project.) You may want to produce simplified situational maps to include only those elements you intend to address in the final products of the research. These often become project maps—maps that display and feature various aspects of your project. This is fine, but, as always, don't throw away earlier, more complicated, even if very messy, versions.

Situational maps and analyses do particular kinds of work through mapping and framing historical as well as contemporary materials. Together they lay out the key actors and actants, key social worlds and arenas, key discourses, and key axes of conflict, specifying the positions taken *and not taken* in the data, implicated actors, silent actors, missing discourses, and so on. While potentially useful in most if not all research, situational maps and analyses can be distinctively helpful in taking on understudied or unstudied larger historical projects. In a bald sense, any map is better than no map. But beyond this, the maps proposed here are framing devices through which one can see what the possible (feasible vis-à-vis available and accessible data) historical stories are that one could tell. The maps also allow the researcher to say what is *not* feasible and, at least equally importantly, what they do not find particularly interesting or valuable. In short, these maps can clarify the situation in terms of research questions and directions for the project as a whole. And they can be invaluable in making the researcher return to the big picture—particularly important in historical research where getting lost in the interesting details is an ongoing risk. We need to remember that "[h]istory is what one makes of it. It has never stopped changing" (Veyne 1971/1997:182).

Notes

1. For useful entrée into history, see Jenkins (1997) and Breisach (2003). On Foucault's and Foucault-inspired historical methods, see Foucault (esp. 1972, 1980, 1991, 1995); and see Burchell et al. (1991), Cheek (2000), Dean (1994), Dreyfus and Rabinow (1983), Kendall and Wickham (1999, 2004), Jones and Porter (1994), Prior (1997, 2003, 2004), Schuerich and McKenzie (2005), Sinding (2004), and Veyne (1971/1997).

2. There are many conventional as well as currently debated historiographic issues I do not take up here, as others provide more than adequate guidance. See, e.g., Alberti (2002), Anderson (2004), Bonnell and Hunt (1999), Breisach (2003), Brettell (1998), and Scott (1989, 1992).

3. For varied examples of historical interactionist work, see Strauss's (1978) study of the American city, Star's (1989; Star & Griesemer 1989) studies of brain research and of a zoology museum, Fujimura's (1996) study of oncogene research, Casper's (1998a) study of the development of fetal surgery, Baszanger's (1998a) study of the development of pain medicine, and Shostak's (2003a, 2003b) study of the disciplinary emergence of ecogenetics/environmental genetics. Almost all of my own work is also historical. Foucault's influence is also apparent.

4. For example, Russell Maulitz has a regular feature in the *Bulletin of the History of Medicine* on electronic issues in historiography.

5. See Clarke (1987/1995, 1990a, 1990b, 1995, 1998, 2000) and Clarke and Montini (1993). I do not include citations from these works here but do cite a few important works published subsequently.

6. For historical careers and biographies of the nonhuman, see, e.g., Appadurai and Kopytoff (1986), Clarke and Fujimura (1992/1996), Daston (2000), DeGrazia and Furlough (1996), and Oudshoorn (2003).

7. Discursive constructions of end users of a technology are common among designers, engineers, developers, and scientists. See, e.g., Woolgar (1991), Akrich (1992, 1995), Forsythe (2001), Oudshoorn (2003), and Oudshoorn and Pinch (2003).

8. The concept of implicated actors emerged from this analysis. On Pill testing, see Briggs (2002), Oudshoorn (2003), and Watkins (1998).

9. Thanks also to Carol Joffe for numerous conversations over the years, wherein she tried to remind me.

Epilogue

FAQs and Conversations

[I] have come to this project to understand what it means to know more than we are able to know and to write toward what we don't understand.

—Lather (1999:152)

Situational analysis offers a new mode of doing grounded theory complementary and supplementary to the traditional approach focused on generating basic social processes. I have argued that new modes are requisite to push grounded theory around the postmodern turn and release it from remaining fetters of positivism toward a richer, more densely analytic constructionism. Situational analysis is itself grounded in Anselm Strauss's social worlds/arenas/discourse framework as an alternative conceptual infrastructure to that of basic social processes of action.

Situational analysis is an advanced qualitative method proposing innovations to an established, highly valued approach. It responds in part to some of the extensive critiques of that approach. I therefore explicitly framed the methodological innovations vis-à-vis both social theory and the history of grounded theory. I asserted that in its Straussian formulations, grounded theory and symbolic interactionism have constituted a theory/methods package that undergirds constructionist interpretive and analytic work. I then followed in Foucault's footsteps around the postmodern turn to explicitly push grounded theory and situational analysis beyond "the knowing subject" toward studies of extant narrative, visual, and historical discourses that increasingly permeate social life on the planet.

Pursuing situational analysis involves the making and analyzing of three kinds of maps—situational, social worlds/arenas, and positional maps—as means of opening up and analyzing data cartographically, emphasizing relationality and positionality. Like traditional grounded theory, it relies deeply on coding, theoretical sampling, seeking saturation, and extensive memoing. Unlike traditional grounded theory, it seeks to specify and map all of the important human and nonhuman elements in the situation of inquiry broadly conceived, the social worlds and arenas that organize the situation at the meso level of collective discourse and action, and the discursive positions taken and not taken in the situation, especially vis-à-vis debated and contested issues. To accomplish this, situational analysis makes demands on the reflexivity, accountability, and theoretical and substantive knowledges of the researcher.

Also largely unlike traditional grounded theory, situational analysis of extant narrative, visual, and historical discourses within the situation of inquiry are strongly encouraged, as well as ethnographic and interview projects. To facilitate entrée into the established worlds of discourse analysis, I provided introductory overviews of each of those territories—narrative, visual, and historical. Both short examples and lengthy exemplars of doing situational analysis with all the different genres of data were given.

Situational analysis also pushes researchers toward more reflexive and considered research design from the outset of a project. Because we now have a century of social science behind us that has already explored many if not most of the interesting sites of inquiry more or less, thorough literature reviews in advance of research are very strongly encouraged. These are undertaken in order both to avoid reinventing the wheel (one more study of X is *not* enough to make a serious academic or applied career) and to position the research project at the cutting edge of the substantive area as well as vis-à-vis contemporary theoretical engagements. The literature review should, moreover, help specify the heterogeneous forms of extant data that could be selected to address the topic of inquiry, allowing the researcher to pursue the less explored, to follow Strauss's injunction: "Study the unstudied!" Last, and very important to some, "In practice, you are unlikely to obtain research funding without having carried out a thorough literature review or having formulated some idea of the content of the data you are likely to collect" (Barbour 2001:115-117). This is increasingly true for both doctoral student as well as faculty research.

I have used, indeed leaned heavily upon, the metaphor of coming around the postmodern turn in this book. The power of postmodernism lies in its flexibility (Denzin 1996c:343-344), and I have argued here and elsewhere (Clarke 1991) that social worlds/arenas/discourses approaches as both analytic frame and root metaphor are similarly flexible. If empirical work is to move toward rather than away from difference(s) and complexities—to me, the heart of the postmodern project—we need tools that enable us to see difference(s), handle them analytically, and rerepresent them in fathomable ways that can travel. The various situational mapping strategies themselves offer means of translation across worlds. They offer symbolic vocabularies that can speak many languages. They (attempt to) speak the languages of those studied and to see the world through their perspective(s), as well as those of others, including those of researchers themselves as accountable and reflexive participants in joint endeavors to produce new knowledge. They attend to the nonhuman elements shaping and conditioning lived situations.

I have argued here for constructionist grounded theory and situational analyses that offer analytics and theorize rather than build formal theory. To me, the era of grand or formal theory is long over. Theorizing suffices in the postmodern moment. Theorizing invokes sensitizing concepts: "Whereas definitive concepts provide prescriptions of what to see, *sensitizing concepts merely suggest directions along which to look*" (Blumer 1969:147-148; emphasis added). Life on the planet is changing too quickly to claim permanence much less transcendence.

Across the disciplines today, literally millions of people are engaged in doing research and theorizing. This figure was likely in the thousands when grounded theory was originally formulated in 1967. Moreover, after a century of sustained and expanding work, the social sciences have gone far beyond the old disciplinary formations to include postcolonial, queer, diasporic, cultural, feminist, visual, disability, gender, and a host of other "studies." Today, sites of new knowledge production are increasingly (if not at all adequately as yet) recognized as global, distributed all over the planet (Canagarajah 2002). Situations of inquiry are stunningly heterogeneous. The very differences and complexities that situational analysis is intentionally designed to address are everywhere with us. Situational analysis is also pliant and flexible in ways that allow researchers to address the constraints, opportunities, and distinctive resources posed in their particular situations of inquiry. A good interpretive analysis of the situation of inquiry ideally produces new working sensitizing concepts or elaborates and refines old ones, integrates theoretical advances with grounded empirical work, and is explicitly located, situated, and historicized. It should also ultimately be useful in the world in some ways, capable of demonstrating its pragmatist roots.

At the end of Chapter 1, I offered a chart that mapped the directions in which I sought to push grounded theory around the postmodern turn via situational analysis. Here at the end of the book is a chart (Figure E.1) that summarizes the main areas of difference and similarity between traditional grounded theory and constructionist grounded theory and situational analysis.

TRADITIONAL GROUNDED THEORY	CONSTRUCTIONIST GROUNDED THEORY AND SITUATIONAL ANALYSIS
Positivist/realist	Constructionist/relativist
Master narrative	Modest contribution
"Knowing subjects": Interview and ethnographic data	"Knowing subjects" and extant discourses: Interview, ethnographic, narrative, visual, and historical discourse data
Universal truths and generalizations	Partial perspectives and situated knowledges
Simplification; difference as "negative cases"	Range of variation; differences and complexities as analytically central
Normativity/"normal curve"	Cartography/positionality
Researcher as tabula rasa	Researcher as knowledgeable about theory and substantive area
Literature review after analysis well under way/ complete	Thorough literature review prior to/part of project design
Project planning	Intensive and ongoing project design
Intensive grounded theory coding	Intensive grounded theory coding and situational maps and analysis
Theoretical sampling	Theoretical sampling
Theoretical sensitivity a goal	Theoretical sensitivity a goal
One basic social processand subprocesses	Multiple possible social processes and subprocesses possible
Substantive theory	Situational maps and analyses, social worlds/arenas maps and analyses, positional discourse maps and analyses
Formal theory	Substantive theorizing
	Sensitizing concepts and theorizing
Authority of author as expert	Accountablity of author as reflexive viz. research processes and products

Figure E.1   From Traditional Grounded Theory to Constructionist Grounded Theory and Situational Analysis

Frequently Asked Questions (FAQs)

> *[W]e do need an earthwide network of connections, including the ability to partially translate knowledges among very different—*

and power-differentiated—communities . . . in order to have a chance for a future.

—Haraway (1991b:187)

Approaches to methods tend to generate a lot of questions. I have, of course, tried to anticipate many of these in the previous chapters. I have also made an epilogue of FAQs and conversations provoked by students and colleagues.

Perhaps it would be better to stop doing social science research altogether?

Given the history of the social sciences and their contributions to producing and legitimating inequalities, this is a fundamental question (e.g., Cameron et al. 1999:142). It is a question I have debated with myself and others for many years, most especially as I began this book in 1995. Then, through deeply important conversations with Patti Lather, Katie King, and Kit Chesla, I was able to retire this question to the sidelines for the following reasons. Whether or not I contribute, the research machine—the vast and increasingly global technologies of knowledge production—will keep on turning (Spivak 1993). My hope is to shift the directions of that turning a bit. My interventions explicitly seek to challenge the status quo of research as focused on commonalities-as-core, to rupture the taken-for-grantedness of the normal curve, and instead to place differences, complexities, and silences at the analytic core. I hope to legitimate simultaneously attending to the social as well as to individual voices, to the nonhuman as well as to the human, and to producing further analytics of the discursive and interactive practices of power.

My "good" intentions can, of course, be perverted for other purposes. My interventions can, of course, be used to improve the panopticon's ability to monitor, assess, and discipline. We can and should, of course, struggle against this. Ultimately, as researchers, we need to continually assess the situations in which we pursue research and return again and again to the fundamental questions: Perhaps it would be better to stop doing this project? Who/what might be endangered by my doing this? And, perhaps I should stop doing social science research altogether?

What do you see as some theoretical issues and concerns here?

An excellent question. My major concern is that I may be read as appropriating the postmodern on behalf of the high/late modern—pushing around the *most*modern turn rather than the *post*modern turn. Patti Lather gave me the words to express this in her comments, for which I am grateful. That is, I know I will get feedback that I have gone much too far and feedback that I have not gone far enough. I am only worried about the latter, and there are several specific issues.

First, there is, I believe, inadequate understanding or even language for what I call here "the social"—spaces beyond individuals that are meaning making and world making. The situational maps and social worlds/arenas maps thus risk being read as more structural and modern analytically. Yet I am far from alone in seeing a deeper and broader understanding of the social per se as postmodern, as central to postmodernity, including issues of globalization and how things travel. To me, this is what Foucault was *about*, and hence my use of his work. Katovich and Reese (1993) raised this point about Strauss postmodernizing the social through grounded theory.

In situational analysis, it is the concept of the situation itself and the concrete practices of making the various maps and analyses that constitute a new post-structuralist/postmodern approach to inquiry. A "situation" is itself open, inde-terminate, changing, unstable, unfixed, tenuous, temporary. The maps can only be understood as analytic snapshots in time and space. I further see the social as central to the postmodern in situational analysis in that such indeterminacy and contingency are foregrounded, and attention centers on the organization*al*, institution*al*, and discursive *relationalities* rather than on organiz*ations* and institu*tions* per se. Local differences and hybridities are featured.

Moreover, precisely because of its empirical/conceptual elasticity and porous boundaries, I also see the social worlds/arenas/discourses framework as postmodern. Through actually using it with empirical materials, its fluidi-ties, indeterminacies, and serious instabilities become apparent. Then those very traits tend to make analysts anxious—actually an appropriate post-modern state! Analyzing extant discourses also works to decenter human agency in postmodern fashion, as does taking the nonhuman seriously. I am seeking to create postmodern spaces to articulate the social in research sites that can show its workings without having to carry the heavy weight and determinisms of received structural theory, but also with a stronger sense of history than usually borne by network and related poststructural theories. I suspect I will keep working on this for some time.

A second area of concerns centers on how differences, complexities, variations, silences, race, ethnicities, class, sex/gender, sexualities, (dis)abili-ties, and so on are handled in this book and in the situational analyses that it helps to produce. On the one hand, I worry about essentializing differences, reinscribing universalizing tendencies in the effort to challenge them: "In making room for something else to come about, how do we stop confining the other within the same?" (Lather 2001a:219). How do we speak of the particularities? On the other hand, I worry because "[t]he danger is to steal knowledge from others, particularly those who have little else, and use it for the interests of power" (Lather 2001a:221). I am banking a lot on the power of the positional maps as helping to work against such tendencies: their uncoupling of persons and groups from positions; their documentation of the multiplicity of positions, including contradictions; and perhaps most, their capacity to articulate the sites of silence, unoccupied positions. A method that does this can yank us around the postmodern turn—ready or not.

Last, I have written in several places here about the dark edges of the postmodern—or the darkness of the abyss at the edge—and people's (including my own) fears of falling off that edge into spaces where the very value of living is routinely questioned. In some senses, I have written reassuringly—that one can go to the edge and not fall off. But living in the United States at this historical moment feels like living at the bottom of the abyss. Not only because of this, but also because of it and for other reasons, I am beginning to understand the need to come to terms with the abyss as part of how one does come around the postmodern turn. Perhaps one does need to decide whether to do anything at all before one can do research after the postmodern.

For solace, I keep returning to this comment by Veyne (1971/1997:159): "[W]e cannot help but take a moment to breathe a melancholy sigh over the human condition, over the poor unconscious and absurd things that we are, over the rationalizations that we fabricate for ourselves and whose object seems to be chortling."

In Chapter 2 and elsewhere you discuss the importance of Foucault's work to situational analyses, yet you use interactionist language. Why?

I use the Straussian terminology because I believe it is more helpful in grounding situational analyses in both the interactionist concept of the situation and the Straussian social worlds/arenas/discourses framework, the conceptual infrastructures of this approach. I want to be able to see the grounding in actions and practices *in addition to* the Foucaultian flows of power in discourses. More specifically, I find that research describing flows and circulations of things and power too often (though certainly not always) glosses over particulars—glosses over what is going on in the situation and leaves it un(der)analyzed. Flows and circulations are of considerable import, but I *also* and particularly want to "feel" the drag of history and "see" what is being dragged along, the sites of traction and sources of friction. The point is not either/or but both/and. I think the Straussian language pushes that analytic further and makes the linkages between grounded theory and situational analysis clearer. But I am also happy to and do routinely use concepts from Foucault, Haraway, Deleuze, Gramsci, Hall, Star, Appadurai, Lather, Latour, Bowker, Rapp, Spivak, and many others. Concepts are the tools of scholarship, and situational analysis encourages both the generation of new and the creative use of extant sensitizing concepts.

How would you map the classic concepts of structure and process and the issues of agency onto situational analysis as compared to the conditional matrix?

Strauss refused the structure/process binary, and I do as well, though I do use terms such as structural, processual, micro, meso, and macro. To me, these are matters of analytic emphasis and we need the language to point with—to specify how we are emphasizing. *Structures are frozen processes/means of relating and organizing practices. Melting happens.* In Latour's words (1991), "Technology is society made durable," and we well know how quickly and consequently technologies change. All the new mapping alternatives framed here are *simultaneously* structural and processual, ultimately working against this binary. Most fundamentally, like pragmatism and symbolic interactionism, they are antideterministic vis-à-vis causality. There are no one-way arrows, but instead attempts to delineate processes of coconstitution through specifying conditions and relationalities. Situational analysis works against the structure/process binary by promoting analysis of the situated conditions of action and discursive representation. *Situations, then, are particular configurations of conditions—temporal, geographic, interactional, sentimental, and so on.* Structure/process is constitutive and, in Foucault's terminology, *are* the practices of discourse, existing in and through practices per se, constituting "conditions of possibility" in particular situations.

These questions also revisit the problematics of agency. By explicitly taking the nonhuman into account in situational analysis, we displace "the knowing/agentic subject." Agency is reformulated into something messy, "sticky," and "distributed" (Dumit 1997; see also Law 1999), varyingly animating all the elements that constitute a particular situation. But most important, agency is no longer a "property" of persons or groups, but instead is fluid, situational, and contingent—to be conditionally analyzed rather than assumed, much like the positivities of power in Foucaultian approaches.

The main difference between the conditional matrix and situational analysis is that the conditional matrix placed the conditions of actions *outside* the action (see Chapter 2 for diagrams). In very sharp contrast, situational analysis places both actions and conditions *inside the situation* and demands analysis of the *situation as a whole*. There are strong echoes here of the ways in which "Blumer embraced Mead's belief that reality exists *as* situations in relation to one another" (Morrione 1998:198). If social life can be conceptualized as an overlappingly layered mosaic of social worlds, arenas, and discourses in constant movement, it can also be conceived as an overlappingly layered mosaic of situations open to analysis.

Why is another form of grounded theory needed at all? Isn't this diluting grounded theory instead of enriching it?

I have several responses. First and foremost for me, the Straussian conditional matrix failed to adequately situate the phenomenon of interest. While I wholly endorse its conditionality (the relentless specifying of "under what conditions" does X happen), the specificities of the conditional elements were/are not enough. Situational analysis was developed and this book written to address this fundamental problem in grounded theory, and also to do so poststructurally, acknowledging and incorporating varied insights of the postmodern turn. Second, while grounded theory had been used with discursive materials, including using grounded theory to construct the categories for content analysis, this was rare. I seek to promote grounded theory and situational analysis of extant discourses, decentering the knowing subject as relentlessly as conditions have been specified.

Third, I have been deeply disturbed by how few self-proclaimed grounded theory studies take the situation into account. Many if not most do not even take up the conditional matrix with any degree of analytic seriousness. They do not even specify where in the world they did the research or when in history it was done. The "unconditional present" suffices for them. Not for me. The time has come to be much more explicit in situating one's research—temporally, geographically, and so on. Not to do so today reeks of unacknowledged imperialism. It is quite challenging to adequately situate research, and I think situational analysis can be particularly helpful here as more global aspects of situations would appear as elements *in* the situation and need to be analyzed as such.

There are many kinds of mapmaking strategies already in existence. Why create another?

Yes, of course. But none are linked to grounded theory as a mode of qualitative data analysis. Situational analysis was created by Strauss (social worlds/arenas maps) and me (situational maps and positional maps), and shares epistemological roots in Meadian and Blumerian interactionisms and (especially Foucaultian) poststructuralisms. Other kinds of mapping strategies (e.g., clustering, cognitive, conceptual modeling) may have different epistemological/ontological roots and do other kinds of work in the world. They are beyond my scope here and I leave it to others to compare them.

Historically, developing a basic social process through grounded theory was done through narratives. What differences does mapping make in the process?

Doing situational maps can work like narrative storytelling as a mode of generating analysis. Having a working analysis group helps, of course. One of Strauss's great gifts was in listening forth stories. In our working analysis groups, Anselm would sit back, get comfortable, bend his head down a bit, peer over his glasses, and say to the individual who was up that day, "So, tell us, what is this a story of?" The heretofore mute voice of the novice analyst would then use the most familiar of narrative forms to unblock analytic paralysis: "This is a story about . . ." To get someone going, I can remember our joking: "Okay, okay! Once upon a time . . ." Stories are a special genre. They are not lists of codes or categories. They are not frequencies. They are not decontextualized intellectual objects. Nor are maps. Anybody can tell a story or draw a quick and dirty map and talk about it.

Maps and stories both "cohere." They have threads that can be woven together—however unevenly and episodically. Their patterns end up linking codes, categories, themes, and other elements that become an analysis. Maps and stories are just different fabrics of life. You do not have to be a high theorist to tell a story or make a map. You just need a place to begin and a place to go that includes some interesting sites and observations along the way. In the presence of a skilled listener or alone at the computer, one can comfortably and informally learn the art of pulling fractured data and relational maps into analytic codes and categories, producing a new analytic story. Mapping provokes analysis in similar ways to the "once upon a time" narrative strategy. While grounded theory initially did not push making diagrams, Strauss later did so. One can read such diagrams as maps just as one can read situational maps as diagrams (see also Soulliere, Britt, & Maines 2001). Analysis is the goal.

You have noted that situational analysis is likely to be used across many disciplines. What do you worry about when methods travel? Is special attention to epistemology needed?

Borrowing both theory and methods across disciplines and interdisciplines is requisite and common practice today. There can be no disciplinary ownership of theory and methods that travel well. Crucially, however, this does not mean divorcing a method from its epistemology/ontology.

Epistemology/ontology constitutes the bedrock, the foundation of a method, rather than the precepts of the particular discipline in which it is being utilized. Situational analysis is clearly and deeply rooted in the epistemologies and ontologies of symbolic interactionism, pragmatist philosophy, and Foucaultian discourse analysis. This is a theory/methods package (see Chapter 1). My extended attention to theory in this book itself demonstrates this.

But researchers may well want to pull in concepts from elsewhere, tweak a map to do some other kind of work. The issue then becomes making things very explicit. As Riessman (2002:706) has stated: "Some fancy epistemological foot-work is required. . . . [Borrowing and/or] [c]ombining methods forces investi-gators to confront troublesome philosophical issues and to educate readers about them." That is, such philosophical problems deserve to be put on the table/discussed in our books and papers. We may well not be able to "solve" them, but coming to terms with the limits, constraints, and partialities they may place on our analyses is important reflexive work.

This does not mean that grounded theory and situational analysis cannot be used for quite disciplinary projects. They certainly can. Disciplines are, in essence, ways of organizing questions about the world. Some questions become canonic: such as the nature, meanings, and practices of culture in anthropology; the nature, meanings, and practices of social order in sociology; the nature, meanings, and practices of caring for nursing; the nature, mean-ings, and practices of learning for educators; the nature, meanings, and prac-tices of space for geography. Such questions are canonic precisely because they are worth revisiting over time as ways of rethinking disciplines. Using new tools such as situational analysis to analyze such questions can be provocative.

As scholars, we are also participants in constructing discourses as well as being constituted through them. We are parts of the knowledge production machinery that circles the globe that also constitutes inequalities in what counts as knowledge, whose knowledge can count, which knowledge can become canonic, and so on. There is *A Geopolitics of Academic Writing* (Canagarajah 2002) that centralizes some and marginalizes others. We need to attend to this more seriously as our belated understandings of globalization reshape our understanding of the workings of global knowledge machines. There is no place to stand outside of discourse(s) *including our own.*

Recently it has been argued that grounded theory is particularly good for use in third-world sites (Samik-Ibrahim 2000). Is the same true of situational analysis?

Even more so. Precisely *because* situational analysis specifies the elements of the situation itself, it can be used in many and heterogeneous situations to provide greater clarity *about that particular situation.* Moreover, the reasons for doing research are often to decide how to intervene in a particular situation to improve conditions of some kind. Knowing the key elements in the situation—the specific configuration of *local* conditions—would be very useful. Doing situational analysis produces flexible working maps of local conditions. To boot, grounded theory and situational analysis are cheap to do. The researchers' time, energy, and transport if needed, possibly along with some transcription and copying costs, are the main expenses. Situational analysis, because it engages the researcher more explicitly in project design issues from the outset, can improve the utility of grounded theory where traveling is difficult and return research trips highly unlikely.

Some years ago I had the pleasure of having several nurses from Botswana in my qualitative research courses, and it is through them and their doctoral work that I have engaged these traveling issues. Seboni, Shaibu, and Seloilwe have pursued several grounded theory studies there.[1] In small team field research projects, they collected data during the day, coded and analyzed it together during the evening, and then decided what else they needed to do and what additional data to gather before moving to the next field site on the following day. One of the projects concerned health needs assessments across a wide and very geographically diverse region. This involved not only learning what people needed and wanted to address those needs but also making sure that whatever the intervention was, it would work in the *specific local situation.* This is particularly important in designing interventions when funding is scarce. For example, in some areas, access to clean water was problematic, but not in others—a major difference in situation. Situational maps and analysis feature making such differences explicit.

Seboni, Shaibu, and Seloilwe also commented to me later that the dialogic approach of grounded theory—the goings back and forth between researchers and the people they were studying—was culturally insisted upon in Botswana because there was little or no prior experience of research there. It was not yet an "interview culture" (Gubrium & Holstein 2002). This meant that they themselves were actively interrogated and challenged as part of the field research process, for which they were at least somewhat prepared by our analysis groups. Working with these nurses pushed me further into creating situational analysis precisely because the specific conditions in their situations were strange to me. I could see the different conditions better— and see the value of the situation as a whole as the unit of analysis more clearly. I hope to hear from researchers who use situational analysis across many different situations about both the pleasures and problems of doing so. (The situational analysis Web site will include such users' accounts. See www.sagepub.com/clarke and www.situationalanalysis.com.)

Have you considered constructing a computer program that would facilitate doing situational analysis, especially the maps?

Yes, and I hope this can happen. Meanwhile, all the maps printed in this book were originally done with the basic techniques of Microsoft Word, so it is certainly possible to do them easily without a special program. But let me also say that there are clear and present dangers of using specialized programs. The obvious danger is of using the method formulaically—filling in the blanks and using the initial outcomes as terminal analyses. But there are also ways in which computerized programs are too neat. You have to put things here and not there, and it can take much good energy and time to get it to the "right" place in virtual space that you might want to change in 2 minutes. It is hard *not* to get lost in doing the program rather than doing the analysis, especially if you are an anxious analyst. Pencil and paper will remain useful, and best of all are working analysis groups.

This is an odd book. It has a lot of theory and a lot of method—perhaps too much of both.

Yes, it is an odd book, but it is the book it needed to be. It is a book that can push a grounded theory grounded in symbolic interactionism around the postmodern turn and explain the whys and wherefores as well as all the how-tos. All methods are theory/methods packages (Star 1989)—usually with the theory left out or only tacitly acknowledged. (This, of course, is a key source of the hegemony of positivism—it has been constructed to appear theoryless/atheoretical.) But if one sets out to change an established method or to expand it in new directions as I have done here, the theoretical and epistemological rationales for doing so need to be made clear.

In this case in particular, because grounded theory is so very popular and has traveled all over the planet, the whys and wherefores especially need to be discussed. Thousands of people have used grounded theory and thought about it intently as they did so and subsequently. There are many critiques of grounded theory. In fact, it was my agreement with many of these critiques that in part stimulated me to develop situational analysis. Many critics will understand exactly what I am up to. For example, over dinner with a French colleague who studies the history of Chicago sociology and its methods, I explained situational analysis in a couple of paragraphs. Without my mentioning the words, he leaped in and said, "Oh, you're going to fix the conditional matrix!" Quite. And, I hope, more.

"FAQs and Conversations about Situational Analysis" will be continued on the book's Web site found through www.sagepub.com/clarke or www.situationalanalysis.com.

Final Words

The most important thing I have learned is the doubled need for hope when the languages of hope that we have are no longer broadly persuasive.

—Lather (1999:143)

Action is not enough. We need analytic maps to plot positions and their relative locations. We need improved methods for grasping the constructions of terrain—altitudes, topographies, scales, textures, and so on. One key property of new world orders is a shift from national to new and different transnational configurations and social formations. Another key property is travel—most everything travels and there is much traffic, movement, dis/re/ordering. We need maps. We need to methodologically simultaneously address actors in action and reflection and extant discursive constructions of human and nonhuman actors and positions and their implications. We need cartographies of the vast wealth of discourses—narrative, visual, and historical—in which we are constantly awash. This is not to say that splendid studies have not been produced through analyzing basic social processes. They have been and will be. Nor do I seek to end or replace processual approaches and action analyses using grounded theory. I do seek to address situational analyses to multiple audiences.

Many questions remain: How can we talk about research practices without doing premature closure? How can we better allow entrée into our work from multiple disciplinary as well as inter/transdisciplinary sites? How can we increase the circumference of the visible/knowable in new pedagogies for the transdisciplinary research classroom? How can we adequately map and represent the nonhuman in our situations of concern without reification? How can we have perspective and best represent others' perspectives simultaneously without essentializing? How can we decenter the subject, the object, and ourselves, and also find sites for ourselves to stand and "profess"? Not all questions can be answered.

Methods are tools for the production of knowledges. Foucault (1995:720) said: "All my books are little tool boxes. If people want to open them, to use a particular sentence, a particular idea, a particular analysis, like a screwdriver or a spanner . . . so much the better!" And, "In fact, Strauss was fond of using the metaphor of interactionism as a conceptual banquet from which guests could select and discard at will, assuring the heterogeneities of practice that he found so fascinating" (Baszanger 1998b:355). Situational analysis offers another toolbox from which researchers will likely take a little of this and a little of that. Tools are to be used. Have fun.

I end with a comment by Denzin (1995:45): "None of the above measures are completely satisfactory. They are all reflexive and messy. That is as it should be, for the world we encounter is neither neat nor easy to make sense of. Where do we go next?"

Note

1. See Seboni (1997, 2003), Seloilwe (1998a, 1998b), Ndaba-Mbata and Seloilwe (2000), Shaibu (2002), and Shaibu and Wallhagen (2003).

References

Abir-Am, P. (1985). Themes, Genres and Orders of Legitimation in the Consolidation of New Disciplines: Deconstructing the Historiography of Molecular Biology. *History of Science, 23,* 73-117.

Akrich, M. (1992). The De-Scription of Technical Objects. In W. E. Bijker & J. Law (Eds.), *Shaping Technology/Building Society. Studies in Sociotechnical Change* (pp. 205-224). Cambridge, MA: MIT Press.

Akrich, M. (1995). User Representations: Practices, Methods and Sociology. In A. Rip, T. J. Misa, & J. Schot (Eds.), *Managing Technology in Society: The Approach of Constructive Technology Assessment* (pp. 167-184). London: Pinter.

Alberti, J. (2002). *Gender and the Historian.* Harlow, UK: Pearson Education.

Alford, R. (1972). The Political Economy of Health Care: Dynamics Without Change. *Politics and Society, 1,* 127-164.

Altheide, D. L. (1996). *Qualitative Media Analysis.* Thousand Oaks, CA: Sage Publications.

Altheide, D. L. (2000). Identity and the Definition of the Situation in a Mass-Mediated Context. *Symbolic Interaction, 23*(1), 1-27.

Altheide, D. L. (2002a). Toward a Mapping of the Mass Media and the "E Audience." In J. A. Kotarba & J. M. Johnson (Eds.), *Postmodern Existential Sociology* (pp. 41-62). Walnut Creek, CA: Rowan & Littlefield.

Altheide, D. L. (2002b). Tracking Discourse. In K. A. Cerulo (Ed.), *Culture in Mind: Toward a Sociology of Culture and Cognition* (pp. 172-186). New York: Routledge.

Altheide, D. L. (2003). The Mass Media. In L. Reynolds & N. Herman-Kinney (Eds.), *Handbook of Symbolic Interactionism* (pp. 657-683). Walnut Creek, CA: AltaMira Press.

Anderson, W. (2004). Postcolonial Histories of Medicine. In F. Huisman & J. H. Warner (Eds.), *Locating Medical History: The Stories and Their Meaning* (pp. 285-308). Baltimore: Johns Hopkins University Press.

Annells, M. (1996). Grounded Theory Method: Philosophical Perspectives, Paradigm of Inquiry and Postmodernism. *Qualitative Health Research, 6*(3), 379-393.

Apollon, W. (1996). Introduction II. In W. Apollon & R. Feldstein (Eds.), *Lacan, Politics, Aesthetics* (pp. xix-xxvii). Albany: State University of New York Press.

Appadurai, A. (1996). *Modernity at Large: Cultural Dimensions of Globalization.* Minneapolis: University of Minnesota Press.

Appadurai, A., & Kopytoff, I. (Eds.). (1986). *The Social Life of Things: Commodities in Cultural Perspective.* New York: Cambridge University Press.

Apple, R. (Ed.). (1990). *The History of Women, Health and Medicine in America: An Encyclopedic Handbook.* New York: Garland Press.

Arrighi, B. A. (2001). *Understanding Inequality: The Intersection of Race, Ethnicity, Class and Gender.* Lanham, MD: Rowman & Littlefield.

Aronson, N. (1984). Science as Claimsmaking: Implications for Social Problems Research. In J. Schneider & J. Kitsuse (Eds.), *Studies in the Sociology of Social Problems* (pp. 1-30). Norwood, NJ: Ablex.

Ashman, K., & Barringer, P. (2001). *After the Science Wars.* London: Routledge.

Ashmore, M., & Richards, E. E. (Guest Eds.). (1996). Special Issue on "The Politics of SSK." *Social Studies of Science, 26*(2), 219-356.

Atkinson, P. (1995). *Medical Talk and Medical Work: The Liturgy of the Clinic.* London: Sage.

Atkinson, P., & Coffey, A. (1997). Analyzing Documentary Realities. In D. Silverman (Ed.), *Qualitative Research: Theory, Method, and Practice* (pp. 45-62). London: Sage.

Atkinson, P., & Coffey, A. (2003). Revising the Relationship Between Participant Observation and Interviewing. In J. Gubrium & J. A. Holstein (Eds.), *Postmodern Interviewing* (pp. 109-122). Thousand Oaks, CA: Sage.

Atkinson, P., Coffey, A., & Delamont, S. (2003). *Key Themes in Qualitative Research: Continuities and Change.* Walnut Creek, CA: AltaMira Press.

Atkinson, P., Coffey, A., Delamont, S., Lofland, J., & Lofland, L. (Eds.). (2001). *Handbook of Ethnography.* London: Sage.

Baker, C., Wuest, J., & Stern, P. (1992). Method Slurring: The Grounded Theory, Phenomenology Example. *Journal of Advanced Nursing, 17,* 1355-1360.

Baker, L. D. (1998). *From Savage to Negro: Anthropology and the Construction of Race, 1896-1954.* Berkeley: University of California Press.

Ball, M., & Smith, G. (1992). *Analyzing Visual Data.* Newbury Park, CA: Sage.

Ball, M., & Smith, G. (2001). Technologies of Realism? Ethnographic Uses of Photography and Film. In P. Atkinson, A. Coffey, S. Delamont, J. Lofland, & L. Lofland (Eds.), *Handbook of Ethnography* (pp. 303-319). London: Sage.

Balsamo, A. (1996). *Technologies of the Gendered Body: Reading Cyborg Women.* Durham, NC: Duke University Press.

Banks, M. (2001). *Visual Methods in Social Research.* London: Sage.

Barbour, R. (2001). Checklists for Improving Rigor in Qualitative Research: A Case of the Tail Wagging the Dog? *British Medical Journal, 322*(5), 1115-1117.

Barnard, M. (1995). Advertising: The Rhetorical Imperative. In C. Jenks (Ed.), *Visual Culture: An Introduction* (pp. 42-58). London: Routledge.

Bartlett, D. (2001). Grounded Theory. In J. Michie (Ed.), *Reader's Guide to the Social Sciences* (pp. 687-689). Chicago: Fitzroy Dearborn.

Bartlett, D., & Payne, S. (1997). Grounded Theory: Its Basis, Rationale and Procedures. In G. McKenzie, J. Powell, & R. Usher (Eds.), *Understanding Social Research: Perspectives on Methodology & Practice* (pp. 173-195). London: Falmer Press.

Baszanger, I. (1998a). *Inventing Pain Medicine: From the Laboratory to the Clinic.* New Brunswick, NJ: Rutgers University Press.

Baszanger, I. (1998b). The Work Sites of an American Interactionist: Anselm L. Strauss, 1917-1996. *Symbolic Interaction, 21*(4), 353-378.

Baszanger, I., & Dodier, N. (1997). Ethnography: Relating the Part to the Whole. In D. Silverman (Ed.), *Qualitative Research: Theory, Method, and Practice* (pp. 8-23). London: Sage.

Baszanger, I., & Dodier, N. (2004). Ethnography: Relating the Part to the Whole. In D. Silverman (Ed.), *Qualitative Research: Theory, Method, and Practice* (2nd ed., pp. 9-34). London: Sage.

Bauer, M. W., & Gaskell, G. (2000). *Qualitative Researching With Text, Image, and Sound.* London: Sage.

Bazerman, C. (1994). *Constructing Experience.* Carbondale: Southern Illinois University Press.

Bazerman, C., & Paradis, J. (Eds.). (1991). *Textual Dynamics of the Professions: Historical and Contemporary Studies of Writing in Professional Communities.* Madison: University of Wisconsin Press.

Becker, G. (2000). *The Elusive Embryo: How Women and Men Approach the New Reproductive Technologies.* Berkeley: University of California Press.

Becker, G., & Nachtigall, R. D. (1994). "Born to Be a Mother": The Cultural Construction of Risk in Infertility Treatment. *Social Science and Medicine, 39,* 507-518.

Becker, H. S. (1960). Notes on the Concept of Commitment. *American Journal of Sociology, 66,* 32-40.

Becker, H. S. (1963). *Outsiders: Studies in the Sociology of Deviance.* New York: Free Press.

Becker, H. S. (1967/1970). Whose Side Are We On? In H. S. Becker (Ed.), *Sociological Work: Method and Substance* (pp. 123-134). New Brunswick, NJ: Transaction Books.

Becker, H. S. (1974). Photography and Sociology. *Studies in the Anthropology of Visual Communication, 1,* 3-26.

Becker, H. S. (1982). *Art Worlds.* Berkeley: University of California Press.

Becker, H. S. (1986). *Doing Things Together.* Evanston, IL: Northwestern University Press.

Becker, H. S. (1998). Visual Sociology, Documentary Photography, and Photojournalism: It's (Almost) All a Matter of Context. In J. Prosser (Ed.), *Image-Based Research: A Sourcebook for Qualitative Research* (pp. 84-96). London: Falmer Press.

Becker, H. S., & McCall, M. (Eds.). (1990). *Symbolic Interaction and Cultural Studies*. Chicago: University of Chicago Press.

Behar, R. (1993). *Translated Woman: Crossing the Border With Esperanza's Story*. Boston: Beacon Press.

Bell, S. E. (2000). Experiencing Illness in/and Narrative. In C. E. Bird, P. Conrad, & A. M. Fremont (Eds.), *Handbook of Medical Sociology* (5th ed., pp. 184-199). Upper Saddle River, NJ: Prentice Hall.

Bell, S. E. (2002). Photo Images: Jo Spence's Narratives of Living With Illness. *Health, 6*(1), 5-30.

Benjamin, W. (1970). The Work of Art in the Age of Mechanical Reproduction. In *Illuminations*. London: Collins/Fontana.

Benner, P. (Ed.). (1994). *Interpretive Phenomenology: Embodiment, Caring and Ethics in Health and Nursing*. Thousand Oaks, CA: Sage.

Benner, P., Tanner, C., & Chesla, C. (1996). *Expertise in Nursing Practice*. New York: Springer.

Bennett, T. (1995). *The Birth of the Museum: History, Theory, Politics*. London: Routledge.

Benoliel, J. Q. (1996). Grounded Theory and Nursing Knowledge. *Qualitative Health Research, 6*(3), 406-428.

Benson, J. K. (1977). Innovation and Crisis in Organizational Analysis. *Sociological Quarterly, 18*, 5-18.

Berger, J. (1972). *Ways of Seeing*. New York: Penguin.

Berger, P., & Luckman, T. (1966). *The Social Construction of Reality: A Treatise in the Sociology of Knowledge*. Garden City, NJ: Doubleday.

Best, S., & Kellner, D. (1991). *Postmodern Theory: Critical Interrogations*. New York: Guilford Press.

Bhabha, H. (1994). *The Location of Culture*. New York: Routledge.

Bloom, L. R. (1996). Stories of One's Own: Nonunitary Subjectivity in Narrative Representation. *Qualitative Inquiry, 2*(2), 176-197.

Bloom, L. R. (1998). *Under the Sign of Hope: Feminist Methodology and Narrative Interpretation*. Albany: State University of New York Press.

Bloom, L. (1999). *With Other Eyes: Looking at Race and Gender in Visual Culture*. Minneapolis: University of Minnesota Press.

Blumer, H. (1958). Race Prejudice as a Sense of Group Position. *Pacific Sociological Review, 1*, 3-8.

Blumer, H. (1969). *Symbolic Interactionism: Perspective and Method*. Englewood Cliffs, NJ: Prentice Hall.

Bochner, A. P., & Ellis, C. (Eds.). (2001). *Ethnographically Speaking: Autoethnography, Literature, and Aesthetics*. Walnut Creek, CA: AltaMira Press.

Bogard, C. J. (2001). Claimsmakers and Contexts in Early Constructions of Homelessness: A Comparison of New York City and Washington, D.C. *Symbolic Interaction, 24*(4), 425-455.

Bogdan, R. C., & Bicklen, S. K. (2003). *Qualitative Research for Education: An Introduction to Theories and Methods* (4th ed.). Boston: Allyn & Bacon.

Bolter, J. D., & Grusin, R. (1999). *Remediation: Understanding New Media.* Cambridge, MA: MIT Press.

Bolton, S. C. (2001). Changing Faces: Nurses as Emotional Jugglers. *Sociology of Health and Illness, 23*(1), 85-100.

Bone, D. (1997). *Feeling Squeezed: Dilemmas of Emotion Work in Nursing Under Managed Care.* Doctoral dissertation in Sociology, University of California, San Francisco.

Bone, D. (2002). Dilemmas of Emotion Work in Nursing Under Market-Driven Health Care. *International Journal of Public Sector Management, 15*(2), 140-150.

Bonnell, V., & Hunt, L. (Eds.). (1999). *Beyond the Cultural Turn: New Directions in the Study of Society and Culture.* Berkeley: University of California Press.

Boston Women's Health Book Collective. (1970/1998). *Our Bodies Our Selves: A Book By and For Women.* New York: Simon & Schuster. Retrieved from www.ourbodiesourselves.org.

Bourgois, P., Lettiere, M., & Quesada, J. (1997). On Homelessness, Social Misery and the Sanctions of Substance Abuse: Confronting HIV Risk Among Homeless Heroin Addicts in San Francisco. *Social Problems, 44*(2), 155-173.

Bowker, G., & Latour, B. (1987). A Blooming Discipline Short of Discipline: (Social) Studies of Science in France. *Social Studies of Science, 17,* 715-748.

Bowker, G., & Star, S. L. (1999). *Sorting Things Out: Classification and Its Consequences.* Cambridge, MA: MIT Press.

Breisach, E. (2003). *On the Future of History: The Postmodernist Challenge and Its Aftermath.* Chicago: University of Chicago Press.

Brettell, C. B. (1998). Fieldwork in the Archives: Methods and Sources in Historical Anthropology. In H. R. Bernard (Ed.), *Handbook of Methods in Cultural Anthropology* (pp. 513-546). Walnut Creek, CA: AltaMira Press.

Briggs, L. (2002). *Reproducing Empire: Race, Sex, Science, and U.S. Imperialism in Puerto Rico.* Berkeley: University of California Press.

Brooker, P. (1999). *A Concise Glossary of Cultural Theory.* New York: Arnold/Oxford University Press.

Brown, P., Zavestoski, S., McCormick, S., Mayer, B., Morello-Forsch, R., & Gaisor, R. (2004). Embodied Health Movements: Uncharted Territory in Social Movement Research. *Sociology of Health and Illness, 26,* 1-31.

Bryant, A. (2002). Re-grounding Grounded Theory. *Journal of Information Technology Theory and Application, 4*(1), 25-42.

Bryant, A. (2003). A Constructive/ist Response to Glaser. *FQS Forum: Qualitative Social Research, 4*(1). Retrieved from www.qualitative-research.net.fqs.

Bryman, A., & Burgess, R. G. (1994). Reflections on Qualitative Data. In A. Bryman & R. G. Burgess (Eds.), *Analyzing Qualitative Data* (pp. 216-226). London: Routledge.

Bucher, R. (1962). Pathology: A Study of Social Movements Within a Profession. *Social Problems, 10,* 40-51.

Bucher, R. (1988). On the Natural History of Health Care Occupations. *Work and Occupations, 15*(2), 131-147.

Bucher, R., & Stelling, J. G. (1977). *Becoming Professional.* Beverly Hills, CA: Sage.

Bucher, R., & Strauss, A. L. (1961). Professions in Process. *American Journal of Sociology, 66,* 325-334.

Bulmer, M. (1984). *The Chicago School of Sociology: Institutionalization, Diversity and the Rise of Sociological Research.* Chicago: University of Chicago Press.

Burawoy, M. (2000). Introduction. In Michael Burawoy et al. (Eds.), *Global Ethnography: Forces, Connections and Imaginations in a Postmodern World* (pp. 1-40). Berkeley: University of California Press.

Burchell, G., Gordon, C., & Miller, P. (Eds.). (1991). *The Foucault Effect: Studies in Governmentality.* Chicago: University of Chicago Press.

Burgin, V. (Ed.). (1982). *Thinking Photography.* London: Macmillan.

Butler, J. (1993). *Bodies That Matter.* New York: Routledge.

Cameron, D., Frazer, E., Harvey, P., Rampton, B., & Richardson, K. (1999). Power/Knowledge: The Politics of Social Science. In A. Jaworski & N. Coupland (Eds.), *The Discourse Reader* (pp. 141-157). London: Routledge.

Campbell, M. L. (1998). Institutional Ethnography and Experience as Data. *Qualitative Sociology, 21*(1), 55-73.

Campbell, M., & Gregor, F. (2002). *Mapping Social Relations: A Primer in Doing Institutional Ethnography.* Aurora, Canada: Garamond.

Campbell, M., & Monicom, A. (Eds.). (1995). *Knowledge, Experience and Ruling: Studies in the Social Organization of Knowledge.* Toronto: University of Toronto Press.

Canagarajah, A. S. (2002). *A Geopolitics of Academic Writing.* Pittsburgh, PA: University of Pittsburgh Press.

Canguilhem, G. (1978). *On the Normal and Pathological.* Dordrecht, Netherlands: Reidel.

Canto, J., Allison, J., Kiefe, C., Fincher, C., Farmer, R., Sekar, P., et al. (2000). Relation of Race and Sex to the Use of Reperfusion Therapy in Medicare Beneficiaries with Acute Myocardial Infarction. *New England Journal of Medicine, 342*(15), 1094-1110.

Carey, J. W. (2002). Cultural Studies and Symbolic Interactionism: Notes in Critique and Tribute to Norman Denzin. *Studies in Symbolic Interaction, 25,* 199-209.

Cartwright, L. (1995a). Gender Artifacts: Technologies of Bodily Display in Medical Culture. In L. Cooke & P. Woolen (Eds.), *Visual Display: Culture Beyond Appearances* (pp. 218-235). Seattle, WA: Bay Press.

Cartwright, L. (1995b). *Screening the Body: Tracing Medicine's Visual Culture.* Minneapolis: University of Minnesota Press.

Cartwright, L. (2000). Reach Out and Heal Someone: Telemedicine and the Globalization of Health Care. *Health, 4*(3), 347-377.

Casper, M. J. (1994). Reframing and Grounding Nonhuman Agency: What Makes a Fetus an Agent? *American Behavioral Scientist, 37*(6), 839-856.

Casper, M. J. (1997). Feminist Politics and Fetal Surgery: Adventures of a Research Cowgirl on the Reproductive Frontier. *Feminist Studies, 23*(2), 233-262.

Casper, M. J. (1998a). *The Making of the Unborn Patient: A Social Anatomy of Fetal Surgery.* New Brunswick, NJ: Rutgers University Press.

Casper, M. J. (1998b). Negotiations, Work Objects and the Unborn Patient: The Interactional Scaffolding of Fetal Surgery. *Symbolic Interaction, 21*(4), 379-400.

Castellani, B. (1999). Michel Foucault and Symbolic Interactionism: The Making of a New Theory of Interaction. *Studies in Symbolic Interaction, 22,* 247-272.

Chalaby, J. K. (1996). Beyond the Prison-House of Language: Discourse as a Sociological Concept. *British Journal of Sociology, 47*(4), 685-698.

Chaplin, E. (1994). *Sociology and Visual Representation.* London: Routledge.

Charmaz, K. (1983). The Grounded Theory Method: An Explication and Interpretation. In R. M. Emerson (Ed.), *Contemporary Field Research* (pp. 109-126). Boston: Little, Brown.

Charmaz, K. (1991). *Good Days, Bad Days: The Self in Chronic Illness and Time.* New Brunswick, NJ: Rutgers University Press.

Charmaz, K. (1995a). Between Positivism and Postmodernism: Implications for Methods. *Studies in Symbolic Interaction, 17,* 43-72.

Charmaz, K. (1995b). Grounded Theory. In J. A. Smith, R. Harre, & L. van Longenhove (Eds.), *Rethinking Methods in Psychology* (pp. 27-49). London: Sage.

Charmaz, K. (2000). Grounded Theory: Objectivist and Constructivist Methods. In N. Denzin & Y. Lincoln (Eds.), *Handbook of Qualitative Research* (2nd ed., pp. 509-536). Thousand Oaks, CA: Sage.

Charmaz, K. (2001). Grounded Theory. In R. M. Emerson (Ed.), *Contemporary Field Research: Perspectives and Formulations* (pp. 335-352). Prospect Heights, IL: Waveland Press.

Charmaz, K. (2002a). Grounded Theory: Methodology and Theory Construction. In N. J. Smelser & P. B. Baltes (Eds.), *International Encyclopedia of the Social and Behavioral Sciences* (pp. 6396-6399). Amsterdam: Pergamon.

Charmaz, K. (2002b). Qualitative Interviewing and Grounded Theory Analysis. In J. F. Gubrium & J. A. Holstein (Eds.), *Handbook of Interview Research: Context and Method* (pp. 675-694). Thousand Oaks, CA: Sage.

Charmaz, K. (2002c). Stories and Silences: Disclosures and Self in Chronic Illness. *Qualitative Inquiry, 8*(3), 302-328.

Charmaz, K. (2003a). Grounded Theory. In M. L. Beck, A. E. Bryman, & T. F. Liao (Eds.), *The Sage Encyclopedia of Social Science Research.* London: Sage.

Charmaz, K. (2003b). Grounded Theory. In J. Smith (Ed.), *Qualitative Psychology: A Practical Guide to Research Methods* (pp. 81-110). London: Sage.

Charmaz, K. (2005). Grounded Theory in the 21st Century: A Qualitative Method for Advancing Social Justice Research. In N. Denzin & Y. Lincoln (Eds.), *Handbook of Qualitative Research* (3rd ed.). Thousand Oaks, CA: Sage.

Charmaz, K. (in press). *Constructing Grounded Theory.* London: Sage. Forthcoming.

Charmaz, K., & Mitchell, R. (2001). Grounded Theory in Ethnography. In P. Atkinson, A. Coffey, S. Delamont, J. Lofland, & L. Lofland (Eds.), *Handbook of Ethnography* (pp. 160-174). London: Sage.

Cheek, J. (2000). *Postmodern and Poststructural Approaches to Nursing Research.* Thousand Oaks, CA: Sage.

Chesla, C. (1995). Hermeneutic Phenomenology: An Approach to Understanding Families. *Journal of Family Nursing, 1*(1), 63-78.

Clarke, A. E. (1986, August). Using Grounded Theory With Historical Documents and Archival Materials. Paper presented at meetings of the Pacific Sociological Association, Denver, Colorado.

Clarke, A. E. (1987/1995). Research Materials and Reproductive Science in the United States, 1910-1940. In G. L. Geison (Ed.), *Physiology in the American Context, 1850-1940* (pp. 323-350). Bethesda, MD: American Physiological Society. Reprinted with an Epilogue in S. Leigh Star (Ed.), *Ecologies of Knowledge: New Directions in Sociology of Science and Technology* (pp. 183-219). Albany: State University of New York Press.

Clarke, A. E. (1990a). Controversy and the Development of American Reproductive Sciences. *Social Problems, 37*(1), 18-37.

Clarke, A. E. (1990b). A Social Worlds Research Adventure: The Case of Reproductive Science. In S. Cozzens & T. Gieryn (Eds.), *Theories of Science in Society* (pp. 15-42). Bloomington: Indiana University Press.

Clarke, A. E. (1991). Social Worlds Theory as Organizational Theory. In D. Maines (Ed.), *Social Organization and Social Process: Essays in Honor of Anselm Strauss* (pp. 17-42). Hawthorne, NY: Aldine de Gruyter.

Clarke, A. E. (1995). Modernity, Postmodernity and Human Reproductive Processes c.1890-1990, or "Mommy, Where Do Cyborgs Come From Anyway?" In C. H. Gray, H. J. Figueroa-Sarrier, & S. Mentor (Eds.), *The Cyborg Handbook* (pp. 139-156). New York: Routledge.

Clarke, A. E. (1998). *Disciplining Reproduction: Modernity, American Life Sciences and the "Problem of Sex."* Berkeley: University of California Press.

Clarke, A. E. (2000). Maverick Reproductive Scientists and the Production of Contraceptives, c.1915-2000. In A. Saetmam, N. Oudshoorn, & M. Kirejczyk (Eds.), *Bodies of Technology: Women's Involvement With Reproductive Medicine* (pp. 37-89). Columbus: Ohio State University Press.

Clarke, A. E. (2003). Situational Analyses: Grounded Theory Mapping After the Postmodern Turn. *Symbolic Interaction, 26*(4), 553-576.

Clarke, A. E. (n.d.). Intersections in Scientific Work. Unpublished paper.

Clarke, A. E., & Casper, M. (1996). From Simple Technique to Complex System: Classification of Pap Smears, 1917-1990. *Medical Anthropology Quarterly, 10*(4), 601-23.

Clarke, A. E., & Chesla, C. (2001). Syllabus for Qualitative Research and Analysis. In J. D. Ballard (Ed.), *Qualitative Research Methods: Syllabi and Instructional Materials* (3rd ed.). Washington, DC: Teaching Resources of the American Sociological Association. Retrieved from www.asanet.org.

Clarke, A. E., & Fujimura, J. (1992/1996). Introduction: What Tools? Which Jobs? Why Right? In *The Right Tools for the Job: At Work in Twentieth Century Life Sciences* (pp. 3-44). Princeton, NJ: Princeton University. French translation (1996): *La Materialite des Sciences: Savoir-faire et Instruments dans les Sciences de la Vie.* Paris: Synthelabo Groupe.

Clarke, A. E., & Montini, T. (1993). The Many Faces of RU486: Tales of Situated Knowledges and Technological Contestations. *Science, Technology and Human Values, 18*(1), 42-78.

Clarke, A. E., & Moore, L. J. (n.d.). Sex/Gender/Sexualities in Genital Anatomies from Medieval Texts to Cyberspace. Manuscript in preparation.

Clarke, A. E., Shim, J. K., Mamo, L., Fosket, J. R., & Fishman, J. R. (2003). Biomedicalization: Technoscientific Transformations of Health, Illness, and U.S. Biomedicine. *American Sociological Review, 68*, 161-194.

Clarke, A. E., & Star, S. L. (1998). On Coming Home and Intellectual Generosity. *Symbolic Interaction, 21*(4), 341-352.

Clarke, A. E., & Star, S. L. (2003). Symbolic Interactionist Studies of Science, Technology and Medicine. In L. Reynolds & N. Herman (Eds.), *Symbolic Interactionism* (pp. 539-574). Walnut Creek, CA: AltaMira Press.

Clifford, J., & Marcus, G. (1986). *Writing Culture: The Poetics and Politics of Ethnography.* Berkeley: University of California Press.

Clough, P. I. (1992). *The End(s) of Ethnography: From Realism to Social Criticism.* Newbury Park, CA: Sage.

Clough, P. I. (2000). *Autoaffection: Unconscious Thought in the Age of Tele-technology.* Minneapolis: University of Minnesota Press.

Coffey, A. (1999). *The Ethnographic Self: Fieldwork and the Representation of Identity.* Thousand Oaks, CA: Sage.

Cohen, J. (1993). The Conflicting Views of Symbolic Interactionists and Talcott Parsons Concerning the Nature of Relations Between Persons and Nonhuman Objects: A Sequel to "About Steaks Liking to Be Eaten." *Studies in Symbolic Interaction, 14*, 127-153.

Collins, H. M. (Guest Ed.). (1981). Knowledge and Controversy: Studies of Modern Natural Science. *Social Studies of Science, 11*, 1-158.

Collins, P. H. (1990). *Black Feminist Thought: Knowledge, Consciousness, and the Politics of Empowerment.* Boston: Unwin Hyman.

Collins, P. H. (1999). Will the "Real" Mother Please Stand Up?: The Logic of Eugenics and American National Family Planning. In A. E. Clarke & V. Olesen (Eds.), *Revisioning Women, Health and Healing* (pp. 266-282). New York: Routledge.

Conniff, R. (1991). Chicago: Welcome to the Neighborhood. *National Geographic* (May), 50-77.

Corbin, J. (1991). Anselm Strauss: An Intellectual Biography. In D. Maines (Ed.), *Social Organization and Social Process: Essays in Honor of Anselm Strauss* (pp. 17-42). Hawthorne, NY: Aldine de Gruyter.

Corbin, J. M. (1997). Anselm L. Strauss, December 18, 1916-September 5, 1996. *Qualitative Health Research, 7*(1), 150-153.

Corbin, J. (1998). Comment: Alternative Interpretations—Valid or Not? *Theory and Psychology, 8*(1), 121-128.

Corbin, J., & Strauss, A. L. (1990). Grounded Theory Research: Procedures, Canons, and Evaluative Criteria. *Qualitative Sociology, 13*(1), 3-21.

Cortazzi, M. (2001). Narrative Analysis in Ethnography. In P. Atkinson, A. Coffey, S. Delamont, J. Lofland, & L. Lofland (Eds.), *Handbook of Ethnography* (pp. 384-394). London: Sage.

Cortazzi, M. (2003). *Narrative Analysis*. London: Falmer.

Covaleski, M., Dirsmith, M., Heian, J., & Sajay, S. (1998). The Calculated and the Avowed: Techniques of Discipline and Struggles Over Identity at Big Six Public Accounting Firms. *Administrative Science Quarterly, 43*(2), 293-327.

Crane, D. (2000). *Fashion and Its Social Agendas: Class, Gender and Identity in Clothing*. Chicago: University of Chicago Press.

Cressey, P. G. (1932). *The Taxi-Dance Hall: A Sociological Study*. Chicago: University of Chicago Press.

Creswell, J. W. (2002). *Educational Research: Planning, Conducting, and Evaluating Quantitative and Qualitative Research*. Upper Saddle River, NJ: Merrill/Prentice Hall.

Czarniawska, B. (1998). *A Narrative Approach to Organization Studies*. Thousand Oaks, CA: Sage.

Daly, K. (1997). Replacing Theory in Ethnography: A Postmodern View. *Qualitative Inquiry, 3*(3), 343-365.

Dark Star. (2001). *Beneath the Paving Stones: Situationists and the Beach, May 1968*. Edinburgh, Scotland: AK Press.

Daston, L. (1992/1999). Objectivity and the Escape From Perspective. In M. Biagioli (Ed.), *The Science Studies Reader* (pp. 110-123). New York: Routledge.

Daston, L. (Ed.). (2000). *Biographies of Scientific Objects*. Chicago: University of Chicago Press.

Daston, L., & Galison, P. (1992). The Image of Objectivity. *Representations, 40*, 81-128.

Davidson, A. I. (Ed.). (1997). *Foucault and His Interlocutors*. Chicago: University of Chicago Press.

Davis, A. Y. (1999). *Blues Legacies and Black Feminism: Gertrude "Ma" Rainey, Bessie Smith and Billie Holiday*. New York: Vintage.

Davis, F. (1992). *Fashion, Culture and Identity*. Chicago: University of Chicago Press.

Day, R., & Day, J. (1977). A Review of the Current State of Negotiated Order Theory. *Sociological Quarterly, 19*, 126-142.

Dean, M. (1994). *Critical and Effective Histories: Foucault's Method and Historical Sociology*. London: Routledge.

de Beaugrande, R. (1994). Discourse Analysis. In M. Groden & M. Kreiswirth (Eds.), *The Johns Hopkins Guide to Literary Theory and Criticism* (pp. 207-210). Baltimore: Johns Hopkins University Press.

Debord, G. (1967/1999). Separation Perfected. In J. Evans & S. Hall (Eds.), *Visual Culture: The Reader* (pp. 95-98). London: Sage/Open University Press.

DeGrazia, V., with Furlough, E. (Eds.). (1996). *The Sex of Things: Gender and Consumption in Historical Perspective.* Berkeley: University of California Press.

Denzin, N. (1977). Notes on the Criminogenic Hypothesis: A Case Study of the American Liquor Industry. *American Sociological Review, 42,* 905-920.

Denzin, N. (1989). *Interpretive Interactionism.* Newbury Park, CA: Sage.

Denzin, N. (1991). *Images of Postmodern Society: Social Theory and Contemporary Cinema.* Newbury Park, CA: Sage.

Denzin, N. (1992). *Symbolic Interactionism and Cultural Studies: The Politics of Interpretation.* Oxford, UK: Basil Blackwell.

Denzin, N. (1995). The Poststructural Crisis in the Social Sciences: Learning From James Joyce. In R. H. Brown (Ed.), *Postmodern Representations: Truth, Power and Mimesis in the Human Sciences and Public Culture* (pp. 38-59). Urbana: University of Illinois Press.

Denzin, N. (1996a). The Epistemological Crisis in the Human Disciplines: Letting the Old Do the Work of the New. In R. Jessor, A. Colby, & R. Shwender (Eds.), *Ethnography and Human Development Context and Meaning in Social Inquiry* (pp. 127-151). Chicago: University of Chicago Press.

Denzin, N. (1996b). Post-Pragmatism. *Symbolic Interaction, 19*(1), 61-75.

Denzin, N. (1996c). Prophetic Pragmatism and the Postmodern: A Comment on Maines. *Symbolic Interaction, 19*(4), 341-355.

Denzin, N. (1997). *Interpretive Ethnography: Ethnographic Practices for the 21st Century.* Thousand Oaks, CA: Sage.

Denzin, N. K. (2000). Aesthetics and Practices of Qualitative Inquiry. *Qualitative Inquiry, 6*(2), 256-265.

Denzin, N. (2001a). *Interpretive Interactionism* (2nd ed.). Thousand Oaks, CA: Sage.

Denzin, N. K. (2001b). The Reflexive Interview and a Performative Social Science. *Qualitative Research, 1*(1), 23-46.

Denzin, N. K. (2001c). Theoretical Note: Symbolic Interactionism, Poststructuralism, and the Racial Subject. *Symbolic Interaction, 24*(2), 243-249.

Denzin, N. K., & Lincoln, Y. S. (Eds.). (1994). *Handbook of Qualitative Research.* Thousand Oaks, CA: Sage.

Denzin, N. K., & Lincoln, Y. S. (Eds.). (2000). *Handbook of Qualitative Research* (2nd ed.). Thousand Oaks, CA: Sage.

Denzin, N. K., & Lincoln, Y. S. (Eds.). (2005). *Handbook of Qualitative Research* (3rd ed.). Thousand Oaks, CA: Sage.

Derrida, J. (1978). Structure, Sign and Play in the Discourse of the Human Sciences (A. Bass, Trans.). In *Writing and Difference* (pp. 278-293). Chicago: University of Chicago Press.

Devault, M. L. (1996). Talking Back to Sociology: Distinctive Contributions of Feminist Methodology. *Annual Review of Sociology, 22,* 29-50.

Devault, M. L. (1999). *Liberating Method: Feminism and Social Research.* Philadelphia: Temple University Press.

Dey, I. (1999). *Grounding Grounded Theory: Guidelines for Qualitative Inquiry.* San Diego, CA: Academic Press.

Dey, I. (2004). Grounded Theory. In C. Seale, G. Gobo, J. Gubrium, & D. Silverman (Eds.), *Qualitative Research Practice* (pp. 80-93). London: Sage.

Dillon, G. L. (1994). Discourse Theory. In M. Groden & M. Kreiswirth (Eds.), *The Johns Hopkins Guide to Literary Theory and Criticism* (pp. 210-212). Baltimore: Johns Hopkins University Press.

Dines, G., & Humez, J. M. (Eds.). (2002). *Gender, Race and Class in Media: A Text-Reader.* Thousand Oaks, CA: Sage.

Dingwall, R. (1999). On the Nonnegotiable in Sociological Life. In B. Glasner & R. Hertz (Eds.), *Qualitative Sociology and Everyday Life* (pp. 215-225). Thousand Oaks, CA: Sage.

Dingwall, R., & Strong, P. M. (1985). The Interactional Study of Organizations: A Critique and Reformation. *Urban Life, 14*(2), 205-231.

Dreyfus, H. L., & Rabinow, P. (1983). *Michel Foucault: Beyond Structuralism and Hermeneutics* (2nd ed.). Chicago: University of Chicago Press.

DuGay, P., Hall, S., Janes, L., Mackay, H., & Negus, K. (1997). *Doing Cultural Studies: The Story of the Sony Walkman.* London: Sage.

Dugdale, A. (1999). Materiality: Juggling Sameness and Difference. In J. Law & J. Hassard (Eds.), *Actor-Network Theory and After* (pp. 113-135). Oxford, UK: Blackwell.

Dumit, J. (1997). A Digital Image of the Category of the Person: PET Scanning and Objective Self-Fashioning. In G. L. Downey and J. Dumit (Eds.), *Cyborgs and Citadels: Anthropological Interventions in Emerging Sciences* (pp. 83-102). Santa Fe, NM: School of Americal Research Press.

Dunning, J. (2003, April 27). Limon's Troupe Now Bears Her Signature. *New York Times,* p. 10 AR.

Ekins, R. (1997). *Male Femaling: A Grounded Theory Approach to Cross-Dressing and Sex Changing.* London: Routledge.

Elkins, J. (2003). *Visual Studies: A Skeptical Introduction.* New York: Routledge.

Ellis, C. (1995). Emotional and Ethical Quagmires of Returning to the Field. *Journal of Contemporary Ethnography, 24*(1), 68-98.

Ellis, C., & Bochner, A. P. (1996). *Composing Ethnography: Alternative Forms of Qualitative Writing.* Walnut Creek, CA: AltaMira Press.

Ellis, C., & Flaherty, M. (Eds.). (1992). *Investigating Subjectivity: Research on Lived Experience.* Newbury Park, CA: Sage.

Emmison, M., & Smith, P. (2000). *Researching the Visual: Images, Objects, Contexts and Interactions in Social and Cultural Inquiry.* London: Sage.

Epstein, S. (1996). *Impure Science: AIDS, Activism and the Politics of Knowledge.* Berkeley: University of California Press.

Epstein, S. (2004). Bodily Differences and Collective Identities: The Politics of Gender and Race in Biomedical Research in the United States. *Body and Society, 10*(2-3), 183-203.

Essed, P., & Goldberg, D. T. (2002). Cloning Cultures: The Social Injustices of Sameness. *Ethnic and Racial Studies, 25*(6), 1066-1082.

Estes, C. L. (1979). *The Aging Enterprise.* San Francisco: Jossey-Bass.

Evans, H., & Evans, M. (1996). *Picture Researcher's Handbook: An International Guide to Picture Resources and How to Use Them* (6th ed.). London: Routledge.

Evans, J., & Hall, S. (Eds.). (1999). *Visual Culture: The Reader.* London: Sage.

Ezzy, D. (2002). *Qualitative Analysis: Practice and Innovation.* London: Routledge.

Fairclough, N. (1999). Linguistic and Intertextual Analysis Within Discourse Analysis. In A. Jaworski & N. Coupland (Eds.), *The Discourse Reader* (pp. 183-212). London: Routledge.

Fairclough, N., & Wodak, R. (1997). Critical Discourse Analysis. In T. A. Van Dijk (Ed.), *Discourse as Social Interaction: Discourse Studies* (Vol. 2, pp. S.258-284). London: Sage.

Farberman, H. A. (1975). A Criminogenic Market Structure: The Automobile Industry. *Sociological Quarterly, 16,* 438-457.

Farnell, B., & Graham, L. R. (1998). Discourse-Centered Methods. In H. R. Bernard (Ed.), *Handbook of Methods in Cultural Anthropology* (pp. 411-458). Walnut Creek, CA: AltaMira Press.

Federation of Feminist Women's Health Centers. (1981/1995). *A New View of a Woman's Body.* New York: Simon & Schuster. Retrieved from http://www .fwhc.org/index.htm.

Fenstermaker, S., & West, C. (Eds.). (2002). *Doing Gender, Doing Difference: Inequality, Power, and Institutional Change.* New York: Routledge.

Ferguson, R., Gever, M., Minh-ha, T. T., & West, C. (Eds.). (1990). *Out There: Marginalization and Contemporary Culture.* Cambridge, MA: MIT Press.

Fine, G. A. (1993). The Sad Demise, Mysterious Disappearance and Glorious Triumph of Symbolic Interactionism. *Annual Review of Sociology, 19,* 61-87.

Fine, M. (1994). Working the Hyphens: Reinventing Self and Other in Qualitative Research. In N. Denzin & Y. Lincoln (Eds.), *Handbook of Qualitative Research* (pp. 70-82). Thousand Oaks, CA: Sage.

Fine, M., Mun Wong, L., Powell, L. C., & Weis, L. (Eds.). (1996). *Off White: Readings on Race, Power, and Society.* New York: Routledge.

Fine, M., Weis, L., Weseen, S., & Mun Wong, L. (2000). For Whom? Qualitative Research, Representations, and Social Responsibilities. In N. Denzin & Y. Lincoln (Eds.), *Handbook of Qualitative Research* (2nd ed., pp. 107-132). Thousand Oaks, CA: Sage.

Fishman, J. R. (2003). *Sex, Science, and Pharmaceutical Innovation: A Genealogy of Male and Female Sexual Dysfunction.* Doctoral dissertation in Sociology, University of California, San Francisco.

Flick, U. (1998). *An Introduction to Qualitative Research.* London: Sage.

Fontana, A. (2002). Postmodern Trends in Interviewing. In J. Gubrium & J. A. Holstein (Eds.), *Handbook of Interview Research: Context and Method.* Thousand Oaks, CA: Sage.

Fontana, A., & Preston, F. (1990). Postmodern Neon Architecture: From Signs to Icons. *Studies in Symbolic Interaction, 11,* 3-24.

Forsythe, D. E. (2001). *Studying Those Who Study Us: An Anthropologist in the World of Artificial Intelligence.* Stanford, CA: Stanford University Press.

Fosket, J. R. (2002). *Breast Cancer Risk and the Politics of Prevention: Analysis of a Clinical Trial.* Doctoral dissertation in Sociology, University of California, San Francisco.

Foucault, M. (1965). *Madness and Civilization.* New York: Random House.

Foucault, M. (1972). *The Archeology of Knowledge and the Discourse on Language.* New York: Harper.

Foucault, M. (1973). *The Order of Things: An Archeology of the Human Sciences.* New York: Vintage/Random House.

Foucault, M. (1975). *The Birth of the Clinic: An Archeology of Medical Perception.* New York: Vintage/Random House.

Foucault, M. (1978). *The History of Sexuality, Volume 1: An Introduction.* New York: Vintage.

Foucault, M. (1979). *Discipline and Punish: The Birth of the Prison.* New York: Vintage.

Foucault, M. (1980). *Power/Knowledge: Selected Interviews and Other Writings 1972-1977.* (C. Gordon, Ed.). New York: Pantheon.

Foucault, M. (1988). Technologies of the Self. In L. Martin, H. Gutman & P. Hutton (Eds.), *Technologies of the Self: A Seminar With Michel Foucault* (pp. 16-49). Amherst: University of Massachusetts Press.

Foucault, M. (1991). Questions of Method. In G. Burchell, C. Gordon, & P. Miller (Eds.), *The Foucault Effect: Studies in Governmentality* (pp. 73-86). Chicago: University of Chicago Press.

Foucault, M. (1995). *Dits et Ecrits, 1954-1988.* Paris: Gallimard.

Frank, A. W. (1995). *The Wounded Storyteller: Body, Illness, and Ethics.* Chicago: University of Chicago Press.

Fraser, N. (1997). *Justice Interruptus: Critical Reflections on the "Postsocialist" Condition.* New York: Routledge.

Fraser, N. (1989). *Unruly Practices: Power, Discourse, and Gender in Contemporary Social Theory.* Minneapolis: University of Minnesota Press.

Freidson, E. (1970). *Profession of Medicine: A Study of the Sociology of Applied Knowledge.* New York: Harper & Row.

Freidson, E. (1975). *Doctoring Together: A Study of Professional Social Control.* Chicago: University of Chicago Press.

Friedman, S. S. (1998). *Mappings: Feminism and the Cultural Geographies of Encounter.* Princeton, NJ: Princeton University Press.

Friese, C. (2003, October). Reporting Cloning: Journalists' Perceptions About the Relationships Between Science, the Media and the Public. Paper presented at the Annual Meeting of the Society for Social Studies of Science, Atlanta, Georgia.

Friese, C. (n.d.). Public Cultures of Sex Selection: An Analysis of the Controversy in Major American Newspapers, 1990-2002. Unpublished paper.

Fujimura, J. H. (1988). The Molecular Biological Bandwagon in Cancer Research: Where Social Worlds Meet. *Social Problems, 35,* 261-283.

Fujimura, J. H. (1991). On Methods, Ontologies and Representation in the Sociology of Science: Where Do We Stand? In D. Maines (Ed.), *Social Organization and Social Process: Essays in Honor of Anselm Strauss* (pp. 207-248). Hawthorne, NY: Aldine de Gruyter.

Fujimura, J. (1992). Crafting Science: Standardized Packages, Boundary Objects and "Translation." In A. Pickering (Ed.), *Science as Practice and Culture* (pp. 168-214). Chicago: University of Chicago Press.

Fujimura, J. H. (1996). *Crafting Science: A Socio-History of the Quest for the Genetics of Cancer.* Cambridge, MA: Harvard University Press.

Furneaux, W. S. (Ed.) (circa 1904). *Philips' Anatomical Model of the Female Human Body: An Illustrated Representation With Full and Descriptive Letterpress.* London: George Philip & Son.

Furneaux, W. S. (Ed.) (190?) *Philips' Popular Manikin or Model of the [Male] Human Body: An Illustrated Representation With Full and Descriptive Letterpress.* London: George Philip & Son.

Fyfe, G., & Law, J. (1988). Introduction: On the Invisibility of the Visual. In G. Fyfe & J. Law (Eds.), *Picturing Power: Visual Depiction and Social Relations* (pp. 1-14). New York: Routledge.

Gamson, J. (2000). Sexualities, Queer Theory and Qualitative Research. In N. Denzin & Y. Lincoln (Eds.), *Handbook of Qualitative Research* (2nd ed., pp. 347-365). Thousand Oaks, CA: Sage.

Ganchoff, C. (2004). Regenerating Movements: Embryonic Stem Cells and the Politics of Potentiality. *Sociology of Health and Illness, 26*(6), 757-774.

Gandhi, L. (1998). *Postcolonial Theory: A Critical Introduction.* New York: Columbia University Press.

Garrety, K. (1997). Social Worlds, Actor-Networks and Controversy: The Case of Cholesterol, Dietary Fat and Heart Disease. *Social Studies of Science, 27*(5), 727-773.

Garrety, K. (1998). Science, Policy, and Controversy in the Cholesterol Arena. *Symbolic Interaction, 21*(4), 401-424.

Geertz, C. (1973). Thick Description: Toward an Interpretive Theory of Culture. In *The Interpretation of Cultures: Selected Essays.* New York: Basic Books.

Gelder, K., & Thornton, S. (1997). *The Subcultures Reader.* London: Routledge.

Gerth, H., & Mills, C. W. (1964). *Character and Social Structure.* New York: Harcourt, Brace, & World.

Gieryn, T. F. (1999). *Cultural Boundaries of Science: Credibility on the Line.* Chicago: University of Chicago Press.

Gifford-Gonzales, D. (1993). You Can Hide But You Can't Run: Representations of Women's Work in Illustrations of Paleolithic Life. *Visual Anthropology Review, 9*(1), 22-41.

Gilman, S. L. (1985). *Difference and Pathology: Stereotypes of Sexuality, Race, and Madness.* Ithaca, NY: Cornell University Press.

Gilman, S. L. (1996). *Seeing the Insane.* Lincoln: University of Nebraska Press.

Ginsberg, F. (1999). Shooting Back: From the Ethnographic Film to the Ethnography of Media. In T. Miller & R. Stam (Eds.), *A Companion to Film Theory* (pp. 295-322). London: Blackwell.

Ginsberg, F., Abu-Lughod, L., & Larkin, B. (Eds.). (2002). *Media Worlds: Anthropology on New Terrain.* Berkeley: University of California Press.

Glaser, B. G. (1969). The Constant Comparative Method of Qualitative Analysis. In G. J. McCall & J. L. Simmons (Eds.), *Issues in Participant Observation* (pp. 216-228). Reading, MA: Addison-Wesley.

Glaser, B. G. (1978). *Theoretical Sensitivity: Advances in the Methodology of Grounded Theory.* Mill Valley, CA: Sociology Press.

Glaser, B. G. (1992). *Emergence Versus Forcing: Basics of Grounded Theory Analysis.* Mill Valley, CA: Sociology Press.

Glaser, B. G. (Ed.). (1993). *Examples of Grounded Theory: A Reader.* Mill Valley, CA: Sociology Press.

Glaser, B. G. (2002). Constructivist Grounded Theory? *FQS Forum: Qualitative Social Research, 3*(3). Retrieved from http:/www.qualitative-research.net/fqs.

Glaser, B. G., with Holton, J. (2004). Remodeling Grounded Theory. *Forum for Qualitative Social Research, 5*(2). Retrieved from www.qualitative-research .net/fqs-texte/2-04.

Glaser, B. G., & Strauss, A. L. (1964). Awareness Contexts and Social Interaction. *American Sociological Review, 29,* 669-679.

Glaser, B. G., & Strauss, A. L. (1965). *Awareness of Dying.* Chicago: Aldine.

Glaser, B. G., & Strauss, A. L. (1967). *The Discovery of Grounded Theory: Strategies for Qualitative Research.* Chicago: Aldine.

Glaser, B. G., & Strauss, A. L. (1968). *Time for Dying.* Chicago: Aldine.

Goffman, E. (1959). *Asylums: Essays on the Social Situation of Mental Patients and Other Inmates.* New York: Anchor/Doubleday.

Goffman, E. (1963a). *Behavior in Public Places: Notes on the Sociology of Gatherings.* New York: Free Press.

Goffman, E. (1963b). *Stigma: Notes on the Management of Spoiled Identity.* Englewood Cliffs, NJ: Prentice Hall.

Goffman, E. (1964). The Neglected Situation. *American Anthropologist, 66,* 133-136.

Goffman, E. (1974). *Frame Analysis: An Essay on the Organization of Experience.* Cambridge, MA: Harvard University Press.

Goffman, E. (1976). *Gender Advertisements.* New York: Harper & Row.

Goldberg, D. T. (2000). Heterogeneity and Hybridity: Colonial Legacy, Post Colonial Heresy. In H. Schwarz & S. Ray (Eds.), *Companion to Postcolonial Studies* (pp. 72-86). Malden, MA: Blackwell.

Gottdeiner, M., Collins, C., & Dickens, D. (1999). *Las Vegas: The Social Production of an All-American City.* Malden, MA: Blackwell.

Gottschalk, S. (1995). Videology: Video-Games as Postmodern Sites/Sights of Ideological Reproduction. *Symbolic Interaction, 18*(1), 1-18.

Gottweis, H. (1998). *Governing Molecules: The Discursive Politics of Genetic Engineering in Europe and the United States.* Cambridge, MA: MIT Press.

Graham, L. (1992). Archival Research in Intertextual Analysis: Four Represen-
tations of the Life of Dr. Lillian Moller Gilbreth. In C. Ellis & M. Flaherty
(Eds.), *Investigating Subjectivity: Research on Lived Experience* (pp. 31-52).
Newbury Park, CA: Sage.

Graham, L. (1998). *Managing on Her Own: Dr. Lillian Gilbreth and Women's
Work in the Interwar Era.* Norcross, GA: Engineering & Management Press.

Gramsci, A. (1971). *Selections From the Prison Notebooks* (Q. Hoare & G. N. Smith,
Trans.). New York: International Publishers.

Granoveter, M. (1983). The Strength of Weak Ties: A Network Theory Revisited.
In R. Collins (Ed.), *Social Theory* (pp. 201-233). San Francisco: Jossey-Bass.

Gray, H. (1995). *Watching Race: Television and the Struggle for "Blackness."*
Minneapolis: University of Minnesota Press.

Greenhalgh, S. (2001). *Under the Medical Gaze: Facts and Fictions of Chronic Pain.*
Berkeley: University of California Press.

Gross, P. R., & Levitt, N. (1994). *Higher Superstition: The Academic Left and Its
Quarrels With Science.* Baltimore: Johns Hopkins University Press.

Gubrium, J. F., & Holstein, J. A. (1997). *The New Language of Qualitative
Method.* New York: Oxford University Press.

Gubrium, J., & Holstein, J. A. (Eds.). (2002). *Handbook of Interview Research:
Context and Method.* New York: Oxford University Press.

Gunaratnam, Y. (2003). *Researching "Race" and Ethnicity.* Thousand Oaks, CA:
Sage.

Gupta, A., & Ferguson, J. (1997). *Culture, Power, Place: Explorations in Critical
Anthropology.* Durham, NC: Duke University Press.

Hacking, I. (1983). *Representing and Intervening: Introductory Topics in the
Philosophy of Natural Science.* Cambridge, UK: Cambridge University Press.

Hall, P. M. (1987). Interactionism and the Study of Social Organization.
Sociological Quarterly, 28(1), 1-22.

Hall, P. M. (1991). In Search of the Meso Domain: Commentary on the
Contributions of Pestello and Voydanoff. *Symbolic Interaction, 14*(2), 129-134.

Hall, P. M. (1997). Meta-Power, Social Organization, and the Shaping of Social
Action. *Symbolic Interaction, 20*(4), 397-418.

Hall, P. M., & McGinty, P. J. W. (2002). Social Organization Across Space and
Time: The Policy Process, Mesodomain Analysis, and Breadth of Perspective.
In S. C. Chew & D. Knottnerus (Eds.), *Structure, Culture and History:
Recent Issues in Social Theory* (pp. 303-322). Lanham, MD: Rowman &
Littlefield.

Hall, S. (1990). Cultural Identity and Diaspora. In J. Rutherford (Ed.), *Identity,
Community, Culture, Difference.* London: Lawrence & Wishart.

Hall, S. (1996). The West and the Rest: Discourse and Power. In S. Hall, D. Held,
D. Hubert, & K. Thompson (Eds.), *Modernity: An Introduction to Modern
Societies* (pp. 184-227). Oxford, UK: Blackwell.

Hall, S. (1997). *Representation: Cultural Representations and Signifying Practices.*
London: Blackwell.

Hammonds, E. M. (1994). Black (W)holes and the Geometry of Black Female Sexuality. *Differences: A Journal of Feminist Cultural Studies, 6*(2-3), 126-145.

Hammonds, E. M. (1997a). New Technologies of Race. In J. Terry & M. Calvert (Eds.), *Processed Lives: Gender and Technology in Everyday Life.* New York: Routledge.

Hammonds, E. M. (1997b). When the Margin Is the Center: African-American Feminism(s) and "Difference." In J. W. Scott, C. Kaplan, & D. Keates (Eds.), *Transitions, Environments, Translations: Feminisms in International Politics.* New York: Routledge.

Haraway, D. (1989). *Primate Visions: Gender, Race, and Nature in the World of Modern Science.* New York: Routledge.

Haraway, D. (1991a). *Simians, Cyborgs, and Women: The Reinvention of Nature.* New York: Routledge.

Haraway, D. (1991b). Situated Knowledges: The Science Question in Feminism and the Privilege of Partial Perspectives. In *Simians, Cyborgs, and Women: The Reinvention of Nature* (pp. 183-202). New York: Routledge.

Haraway, D. J. (1997). Modest_Witness@Second_Millenium. In *Modest_Witness@Second_Millenium.FemaleMan©_Meets_OncoMouse™: Feminism and Technoscience* (pp. 23-39). New York: Routledge.

Haraway, D. J. (1999). The Virtual Speculum in the New World Order. In A. E. Clarke & V. L. Olesen (Eds.), *Revisioning Women, Health, and Healing: Feminist, Cultural, and Technoscience Perspectives* (pp. 49-96). New York: Routledge.

Haraway, D. J. (2003). *The Companion Species Manifesto: Dogs, People, and Significant Otherness.* Chicago: Prickly Paradigm Press.

Harding, S. (1991). *Whose Science? Whose Knowledge? Thinking from Women's Lives.* Ithaca, NY: Cornell University Press.

Harding, S. (1998). *Is Science Multicultural? Postcolonialisms, Feminisms, and Epistemologies.* Bloomington: Indiana University Press.

Harper, D. (1994). On the Authority of the Image: Visual Methods at the Crossroads. In N. Denzin & Y. Lincoln (Eds.), *Handbook of Qualitative Research* (1st ed., pp. 403-412). Thousand Oaks, CA: Sage.

Harper, D. (2000). Reimagining Visual Methods: Galileo to Neuromancer. In N. Denzin & Y. Lincoln (Eds.), *Handbook of Qualitative Research* (2nd ed., pp. 717-732). Thousand Oaks, CA: Sage.

Harris, S. R. (2001). What Can Interactionism Contribute to the Study of Inequality? The Case of Marriage and Beyond. *Symbolic Interaction, 24*(4), 455-480.

Harrison, B. (1996). Every Picture "Tells a Story": Uses of the Visual in Sociological Research. In E. S. Lyon & J. Busfield (Eds.), *Methodological Imaginations* (pp. 75-94). London: Macmillan.

Harrison, B. (2002). Seeing Health and Illness Worlds: Using Visual Methodologies in a Sociology of Health and Illness: A Methodological Review. *Sociology of Health and Illness, 24*(6), 856-872.

Harrison, B., & Aranda, K. (1999). Photography, Power and Resistance: The Case of Health and Medicine. In J. Hearn & S. Roseneil (Eds.), *Consuming Cultures: Power and Resistance.* London: Macmillan.

Hayles, N. K. (1999). *How We Became Posthuman: Virtual Bodies in Cybernetics, Literature, and Informatics.* Chicago: University of Chicago Press.

Heath, D., Koch, E., Ley, B., & Montoya, M. (1999). Nodes and Queries: Linking Locations in Networked Fields of Inquiry. *American Behavioral Scientist, 43*(3), 452-463.

Hekman, S. J. (1999). *The Future of Differences: Truth and Method in Feminist Theory.* Malden, MA: Polity/Blackwell.

Hochschild, A. (1979). Emotion Work, Feeling Rules and Social Structure. *American Journal of Sociology, 85,* 551-575.

Hodder, I. (2000). The Interpretation of Documents and Material Culture. In N. Denzin & Y. Lincoln (Eds.), *Handbook of Qualitative Research* (2nd ed., pp. 703-715). Thousand Oaks, CA: Sage.

Hogle, L. (1996). Transforming Body Parts Into Therapeutic Tools: A Report from Germany. *Medical Anthropology Quarterly, 10*(4), 675-682.

Hogle, L. (1999). *Recovering the Nation's Body: Cultural Memory, Medicine, and the Politics of Redemption.* New Brunswick, NJ: Rutgers University Press.

Hollis, M., & Lukes, S. (Eds.). (1982). *Rationality and Relativism.* Cambridge, MA: MIT Press.

hooks, b. (1990). *Yearning: Race, Gender, and Cultural Politics.* Boston: South End Press.

hooks, b. (1992). *Black Looks: Race and Representation.* Boston: South End Press.

Hornstein, G., & Star, S. L. (1990). Universality Biases: How Theories About Human Nature Succeed. *Philosophy of the Social Sciences, 20,* 421-436.

Huber, J. (1973). Symbolic Interaction as a Pragmatic Perspective: The Bias of Emergent Theory. *American Sociological Review, 38,* 274-284.

Hughes, E. C. (1971). *The Sociological Eye.* Chicago: Aldine Atherton.

Irigaray, L. (1985). *Speculum of the Other Woman* (G. Gill, Trans.). Ithaca, NY: Cornell University Press.

Jackson, R. A., Gibson, K., Wu, Y. W., & Croughan, M. S. (2004). Adverse Perinatal Outcomes in Singletons Following In-Vitro Fertilization: A Meta-Analysis. *Obstetrics and Gynecology, 104*(2), 411-412.

Jasanoff, S. (1990). *The Fifth Branch: Science Advisers as Policymakers.* Cambridge, MA: Harvard University Press.

Jaworski, A., & Coupland, N. (1999a). Introduction: Perspectives on Discourse Analysis. In A. Jaworski & N. Coupland (Eds.), *The Discourse Reader* (pp. 1-44). London: Routledge.

Jaworski, A., & Coupland, N. (Eds.). (1999b). *The Discourse Reader.* London: Routledge.

Jay, M. (1993). *Downcast Eyes: The Denigration of Vision in Twentieth-Century French Thought.* Berkeley: University of California Press.

Jenkins, K. (Ed.). (1997). *The Postmodern History Reader.* London: Routledge.

Jenks, C. (1995). The Centrality of the Eye in Western Culture: An Introduction. In *Visual Culture: An Introduction* (pp. 1-16). London and New York: Routledge.

Joffe, C., & Weitz, T. A. (2003). Normalizing the Exceptional: Incorporating the "Abortion Pill" Into Mainstream Medicine. *Social Science & Medicine, 56,* 2353-2366.

Johnson, J. M. (1975). *Doing Field Research*. New York: Free Press.

Jones, A. (Ed.). (2003). *The Feminism and Visual Culture Reader*. New York: Routledge.

Jones, C., & Porter, R. (Eds.). (1994). *Reassessing Foucault: Power, Medicine and the Body*. London: Routledge.

Jones, J. H. (1981/1993). *Bad Blood: The Tuskegee Syphilis Experiment* (new and expanded ed.). New York: Free Press.

Jones, S. (Ed.). (1999). *Doing Internet Research: Critical Issues and Methods for Examining the Net*. Thousand Oaks, CA: Sage.

Jordanova, L. (1989). *Sexual Visions: Images of Gender in Science and Medicine Between the 18th and 20th Centuries*. Madison: University of Wisconsin Press.

Josselson, R., Lieblich, A., & McAdams, D. P. (Eds.). (2003). *Up Close and Personal: The Teaching and Learning of Narrative Research*. Washington, DC: American Psychological Association.

Kaiser, S. B. (1990). *The Social Psychology of Clothing: Symbolic Appearances in Context*. New York: Macmillan.

Karlberg, K. (2000). The Work of Genetic Care Providers: Managing Uncertainty and Ambiguity. *Research in the Sociology of Health Care, 17*, 81-97.

Katovich, M. A., & Reese, W. A. (1993). Postmodern Thought in Symbolic Interaction: Reconstructing Social Inquiry in Light of Late-Modern Concerns. *Sociological Quarterly, 34*(3), 391-411.

Kearney, M. H. (1998). Ready to Wear: Discovering Grounded Formal Theory. *Research in Nursing and Health, 21*, 179-186.

Kearney, M. H., Murphy, S., Irwin, K., & Rosenbaum, M. (1995). Salvaging Self: A Grounded Theory of Pregnancy on Crack Cocaine. *Nursing Research, 44*(4), 208-213.

Keating, P., & Cambrosio, A. (2000). Biomedical Platforms. *Configurations, 8*(3), 337-388.

Kendall, G., & Wickham, G. (1999). *Using Foucault's Methods*. London: Sage.

Kendall, G., & Wickham, G. (2004). The Foucaultian Framework. In C. Seale, G. Gobo, J. F. Gubrium, & D. Silverman (Eds.), *Qualitative Research Practice* (pp. 141-150). London: Sage.

Kevles, B. H. (1997). *Naked to the Bone: Medical Imaging in the 20th Century*. New Brunswick, NJ: Rutgers University Press.

Kinchelow, J., & McLaren, P. (2000). Rethinking Critical Theory and Qualitative Research. In N. Denzin & Y. Lincoln (Eds.), *Handbook of Qualitative Research* (2nd ed., pp. 279-314). Thousand Oaks, CA: Sage.

King, K. (1994). *Theory in Its Feminist Travels: Conversations in U.S. Women's Movements*. Bloomington: Indiana University Press.

King, K. (2002). Globalization, TV Technologies, and the Re-production of Sexual Identities: Researching and Teaching Layers of Locals and Globals in Highlander and Xena. In M. M. Lay, J. Monk, & D. S. Rosenfelt (Eds.), *Encompassing Gender: Integrating International Studies and Women's Studies*. New York: Feminist Press.

Kitzinger, C. (2004). Feminist Approaches. In C. Seale, G. Gobo, J. F. Gubrium, & D. Silverman (Eds.), *Qualitative Research Practice* (pp. 125-140). London: Sage.

Kleinman, S., & Copp, M. (1993). *Emotions and Fieldwork.* Newbury Park, CA: Sage.

Kolko, B., Nakamura, L., & Rodman, G. (2000). *Race in Cyberspace.* New York and London: Routledge.

Konecki, K. (2000). *Studies in Qualitative Methodology: Grounded Theory* (in Polish). Warszawa, Poland: PWN.

Kress, G., & van Leeuwen, T. (1999). Representation and Interaction: Designing the Position of the Viewer. In A. Jaworski & N. Coupland (Eds.), *The Discourse Reader* (pp. 377-404). London: Routledge.

Kurtz, L. R. (1984). *Evaluating Chicago Sociology: A Guide to the Literature, With an Annotated Bibliography.* Chicago: University of Chicago Press.

Kvale, S. (1996). *InterViews: An Introduction to Qualitative Research Interviewing.* Thousand Oaks, CA: Sage.

Ladson-Billings, G. (2000). Racialized Discourses and Ethnic Epistemologies. In N. Denzin & Y. Lincoln (Eds.), *Handbook of Qualitative Research* (2nd ed., pp. 257-278). Thousand Oaks, CA: Sage.

Lal, J. (1996). Situating Locations: The Politics of Self, Identity, and Other in Living and Writing the Text. In D. Wolf (Ed.), *Feminist Dilemmas in Fieldwork* (pp. 185-214). Boulder, CO: Westview Press.

Landstrom, C. (2000). The Ontological Politics of Staying True to Complexity. *Social Studies of Science, 30*(3), 475-480.

Lather, P. (1991). *Getting Smart: Feminist Research and Pedagogy With/In the Postmodern.* New York: Routledge.

Lather, P. (1993). Fertile Obsession: Validity After Poststructuralism. *Sociological Quarterly, 34*(4), 673-693.

Lather, P. (1994). Staying Dumb? Feminist Research and Pedagogy With/In the Postmodern. In H. W. Simons & M. Billig (Eds.), *After Postmodernism: Reconstructing Ideology Critique* (pp. 101-123). London: Sage.

Lather, P. (1995). The Validity of Angels: Interpretive and Textual Strategies in Researching the Lives of Women With HIV/AIDS. *Qualitative Inquiry, 1*(1), 41-68.

Lather, P. (1996). Troubling Clarity: The Politics of Accessible Language. *Harvard Educational Review, 66*(3), 525-545.

Lather, P. (1999). Naked Methodology: Research Lives of Women With HIV/AIDS. In A. Clarke & V. Olesen (Eds.), *Revisioning Women, Health and Healing: Feminist, Cultural and Technoscience Perspectives* (pp. 136-154). New York: Routledge.

Lather, P. (2000). Drawing the Line at Angels. In E. St. Pierre & W. Pillow (Eds.), *Working the Ruins: Feminist Poststructural Theory and Methods in Education* (pp. 284-311). New York: Routledge.

Lather, P. (2001a). Postbook: Working the Ruins of Feminist Ethnography. *Signs, 27*(1), 199-227.

Lather, P. (2001b). Postmodernism, Post-Structuralism, and Post(Critical) Ethnography: On Ruins, Aporias, and Angels. In P. Atkinson, A. Coffey, S. Delamont, J. Lofland, & L. Lofland (Eds.), *Handbook of Ethnography* (pp. 477-492). London: Sage.

Lather, P. (n.d.). *Getting Lost: Feminist Efforts Toward a Double(d) Science.* Unpublished manuscript.

Lather, P., & Smithies, C. (1997). *Troubling the Angels: Women Living With HIV/AIDS.* Boulder, CO: Westview.

Latour, B. (1986). Visualization and Cognition: Thinking With Eyes and Hands. In H. Kuklick & E. Long (Eds.), *Knowledge and Society: Studies in the Sociology of Culture Past and Present* (pp. 1-40). Greenwich, CT: JAI Press.

Latour, B. (1987). *Science in Action: How to Follow Scientists and Engineers Through Society.* Cambridge, MA: Harvard University Press.

Latour, B. (1988a). *The Pasteurization of France* (A. Sheridan & J. Law, Trans.). Cambridge, MA: Harvard University Press.

Latour, B. (1988b). Visualization and Social Reproduction: Opening One Eye While Closing the Other . . . A Note on Some Religious Paintings. In G. Fyfe & J. Law (Eds.), *Picturing Power: Visual Depictions and Social Relations* (pp. 15-38). New York: Routledge.

Latour, B. (1990). Drawing Things Together. In M. Lynch & S. Woolgar (Eds.), *Representation in Scientific Practice* (pp. 19-68). Cambridge, MA: MIT Press.

Latour, B. (1991). Materials of Power: Technology Is Society Made Durable. In J. Law (Ed.), *A Sociology of Monsters: Essays on Power, Technology and Domination* (pp. 103-131). New York: Routledge.

Latour, B. (1999). *Pandora's Hope: Essays on the Reality of Science Studies.* Cambridge, MA: Harvard University Press.

Law, J. (1999). After ANT: Complexity, Naming and Topology. In J. Law & J. Hassard (Eds.), *Actor Network Theory and After.* Oxford, UK: Blackwell.

Law, J. (2002). *Aircraft Stories: Decentering the Object in Technoscience.* Durham, NC: Duke University Press.

Law, J., & Hassard, J. (Eds.). (1999). *Actor Network Theory and After.* Oxford, UK: Blackwell.

Lay, M. M., Gurak, L. J., Gravon, C., & Myntii, C. (Eds.). (2000). *Body Talk: Rhetoric, Technology, Reproduction.* Madison: University of Wisconsin Press.

Lewin, E., & Leap, W. (Eds.). (1996). *Out in the Field: Reflections of Lesbian and Gay Anthropologists.* Urbana: University of Illinois Press.

Lieblich, A., Tuval-Mashiach, M. R., & Zilber, T. (1998). *Narrative Research.* Thousand Oaks, CA: Sage.

Lincoln, Y., & Denzin, N. (Eds.). (2003). *Turning Points in Qualitative Research: Tying Knots in a Handkerchief.* Walnut Creek, CA: AltaMira Press.

Lindee, S. M. (1997). *Suffering Made Real: American Science and the Survivors at Hiroshima.* Chicago: University of Chicago Press.

Lindesmith, A. R. (1981). Symbolic Interactionism and Causality. *Symbolic Interaction*, 4(1), 87-96.

Lister, M. (Ed.). (1995). *The Photographic Image in Digital Culture*. London: Routledge.

Litt, J. S. (2000). *Medicalized Motherhood: Perspective From the Lives of African-American and Jewish Women*. New Brunswick, NJ: Rutgers University Press.

Locke, K. (1996). Rewriting the Discovery of Grounded Theory After 25 Years? *Journal of Management Inquiry*, 5(1), 239-245.

Locke, K. (2001). *Grounded Theory in Management Research*. Thousand Oaks, CA: Sage.

Lofland, L. (1998). *The Public Realm: Exploring the City's Quintessential Social Territory*. Hawthorne, NY: Aldine de Gruyter.

Lyman, P., & Wakeford, N. (Guest Eds.). (1999). Special Issue on "Analyzing Virtual Societies: New Directions in Methodology." *American Behavioral Scientist 43*(3).

Lynch, M. (1991). Science in the Age of Mechanical Reproduction: Moral and Epistemic Relations Between Diagrams and Photographs. *Biology and Philosophy*, 6(2), 205-226.

Lynch, M. (1994). Representation Is Overrated: Some Critical Remarks About the Use of the Concept of Representation in Science Studies. *Configurations*, 2(1), 137-150.

Lynch, M., & Woolgar, S. (1988). Introduction: Sociological Orientations to Representational Practice in Science (special issue). *Human Studies*, 11(2-3), 99-361.

Lyotard, J. F. (1984). *Driftworks*. New York: Columbia University/Semiotext(e).

MacCannell, D. (1976). *The Tourist: A New Theory of the Leisure Class*. New York: Schocken.

Maines, D. R. (1978). Structural Parameters and Negotiated Orders: Comment on Benson, and Day and Day. *Sociological Quarterly, 19*, 491-496.

Maines, D. R. (1988). Myth, Text, and Interactionist Complicity in the Neglect of Blumer's Macrosociology. *Symbolic Interaction*, 11(1), 43-57.

Maines, D. R. (1995). In Search of Mesostructure: Studies in the Negotiated Order. In N. J. Herman & L. J. Reynolds (Eds.), *Symbolic Interaction: An Introduction to Social Psychology* (pp. 277-286). New York: General Hall.

Maines, D. R. (1996). On Postmodernism, Pragmatism and Plasterers: Some Interactionist Thoughts and Queries. *Symbolic Interaction*, 19(4), 323-340.

Maines, D. R. (2001). *The Faultline of Consciousness: A View of Interactionism in Sociology*. New York: Aldine de Gruyter.

Maines, D. R., & Charlton, J. C. (1985). The Negotiated Order Approach to the Analysis of Social Organization. *Studies in Symbolic Interaction* (Supp.), *1*, 271-308.

Mamo, L. (1999). Death and Dying: Confluence of Emotion and Awareness. *Sociology of Health and Illness, 21*(1), 13-26.

Mamo, L. (2002). *Sexuality, Reproduction, and Biomedical Negotiations: An Analysis of Achieving Pregnancy in the Absence of Heterosexuality*. Doctoral dissertation in Sociology, University of California, San Francisco.

Mamo, L., & Fishman, J. R. (2001). Potency in All the Right Places: Viagra as a Technology of the Gendered Body. *Body and Society, 7,* 13-35.

Manning, P. K. (1995). The challenges of postmodernism. In J. Van Maanen (Ed.), *Representation in ethnography* (pp. 245-272). Thousand Oaks, CA: Sage.

Manning, P. K. (2000). Semiotics, Semantics and Ethnography. In P. Atkinson, A. Coffey, S. Delamont, J. Lofland, & L. Lofland (Eds.), *Handbook of Ethnography* (pp. 145-159). London: Sage.

Manning, P. K., & Cullum-Swan, B. (1994). Narrative, Content and Semiotic Analysis. In N. Denzin & Y. Lincoln (Eds.), *Handbook of Qualitative Research* (1st ed., pp. 463-478). Thousand Oaks, CA: Sage.

Marcus, G. E. (1995). Ethnography in/of the World System: The Emergence of Multi-Sited Ethnography. *Annual Review of Anthropology, 24,* 95-117.

Marcus, G. E. (1998). *Ethnography Through Thick and Thin.* Princeton, NJ: Princeton University Press.

Marcus, G. E., & Fischer, M. M. J. (1986). The Crisis of Representation in the Human Sciences. In *Anthropology as Cultural Critique* (pp. 7-16). Chicago: University of Chicago Press.

Massumi, B. (2002). *Parables for the Virtual: Movement, Affect, Sensation.* Durham, NC: Duke University Press.

Mattingly, C., & Garro, L. C. (Eds.). (2000). *Narrative and the Cultural Construction of Illness and Healing.* Berkeley: University of California Press.

Mbembe, A. (2001). *On the Postcolony.* Berkeley: University of California Press.

McCarthy, D. (1984). Towards a Sociology of the Physical World: George Herbert Mead on Physical Objects. *Studies in Symbolic Interaction, 5,* 105-121.

McCarthy, D. (1996). *Knowledge as Culture: The New Sociology of Knowledge.* New York: Routledge.

McHugh, P. (1968). *Defining the Situation.* Indianapolis, IN: Bobbs-Merrill.

Mead, G. H. (1927/1964). The Objective Reality of Perspectives. In A. J. Reck (Ed.), *Selected Writings of George Herbert Mead* (pp. 306-319). Chicago: University of Chicago Press.

Mead, G. H. (1934/1962). *Mind, Self and Society.* (C. W. Morris, Ed.). Chicago: University of Chicago Press.

Mead, G. H. (1938/1972). *The Philosophy of the Act.* Chicago: University of Chicago Press.

Melia, K. M. (1996). Rediscovering Glaser. *Qualitative Health Research, 6*(3), 368-378.

Melia, K. M. (1997). Producing "Plausible Stories": Interviewing Student Nurses. In G. Miller & R. Dingwall (Eds.), *Context and Method in Qualitative Research* (pp. 26-36). London: Sage.

Meltzer, B. N., Petras, J. W., & Reynolds, L. T. (1975). *Symbolic Interactionism: Genesis, Varieties and Criticism.* Boston: Routledge & Kegan Paul.

Merriam, S. & Assoc. (2002). *Qualitative Research in Practice: Examples for Discussion and Analysis.* San Francisco: Jossey-Bass.

Messias, D. K., & DeJoseph, J. (n.d.). Feminist Narrative Interpretations: An Approach to Women's Stories. Unpublished paper.

Michael, M. (2004). On Making Data Social: Heterogeneity in Sociological Practice. *Qualitative Research, 4*(1), 5-23.

Miller, D. (1998). Why Some Things Matter. In his *Material Cultures: Why Some Things Matter* (pp. 3-21). London: University College of London Press.

Miller, G. (1997). Introduction: Context and Method in Qualitative Research. In G. Miller & R. Dingwall (Eds.), *Context and Method in Qualitative Research* (pp. 1-11). London: Sage.

Miller, S. (1996). Questioning, Resisting, Acquiescing, Balancing: New Mothers' Career Reentry Strategies. *Health Care for Women International, 17,* 109-131.

Mills, C. W. (1940). Situated Actions and Vocabularies of Motive. *American Sociological Review, 6,* 904-913.

Mills, C. W. (1959). *The Power Elite.* New York: Oxford University Press.

Mills, K., & Mills, P. (2000). *C. Wright Mills: Letters and Autobiographical Writings.* Berkeley: University of California Press.

Minh-Ha, Trinh T. (1989). *Woman, Native, Other: Writing Postcoloniality and Feminism.* Bloomington: Indiana University Press.

Mirzoeff, N. (1998). What Is Visual Culture? In his *The Visual Culture Reader* (pp. 1-11). New York: Routledge.

Mishler, E. (1995). Models of Narrative Analysis: A Topology. *Journal of Narrative and Life History, 5*(2), 87-123.

Mishler, E. (2000). *Storylines: Craftartists' Narratives of Identity.* Cambridge, MA: Harvard University Press.

Mitchell, E. (2003, August 17). Everyone's a Film Geek Now. *New York Times,* pp. AR 1, 15.

Mitchell, W. J. T. (1992). *The Reconfigured Eye: Visual Truth in the Post-Photographic Era.* Cambridge, MA: MIT Press.

Mitchell, W. J. T. (1994). *Picture Theory: Essays on Verbal and Visual Representation.* Chicago: University of Chicago Press.

Mitman, G. (1996). When Nature IS the Zoo: Vision and Power in the Art and Science of Natural History. *Osiris* (2nd Series), *11,* 117-143.

Mitman, G., Clarke, A., & Maienschein, J. (1993). Introduction to Special Issue on Biology at the University of Chicago, c. 1891-1950. *Perspectives on Science, 1*(3), 359-366.

Moore, L. J. (1996). *Producing Safer Sex: Knowledge, Latex Technologies, and Sex Workers in the Age of AIDS.* Doctoral dissertation in Sociology, University of California, San Francisco.

Moore, L. J. (1997). "It's Like You Use Pots and Pans to Cook. It's the Tool": The Technologies of Safer Sexualities. *Science, Technology and Human Values, 22*(4), 434-471.

Moore, L. J. (2002). Extracting Men From Semen: Masculinity in Scientific Representations of Sperm. *Social Text, 73,* 1-46.

Moore, L. J. (2003). "Billy the Sad Sperm With No Tail": Representations of Sperm in Children's Books. *Sexualities, 6*(3-4), 279-304.

Moore, L. J. (n.d.). *Sperm Tales: Social, Cultural and Scientific Representations of Human Semen*. Unpublished manuscript.

Moore, L. J., & Clarke, A. E. (1995). Genital Conventions and Transgressions: Graphic Representations in Anatomy Texts, c. 1900-1991. *Feminist Studies, 22*(1), 255-301.

Moore, L. J., & Clarke, A. E. (2001). The Traffic in Cyberanatomies: Sex/Gender/Sexuality in Local and Global Formations. *Body and Society, 7*(1), 57-96.

Moore, L. J., & Schmidt, M. (1999). On the Construction of Male Differences: Marketing Variations in Technosemen. *Men and Masculinities, 1*(4), 339-359.

Morrione, T. J. (1985). Situated Interaction. *Studies in Symbolic Interaction,* Supplement 1, 161-192.

Morrione, T. J. (1998). Persistence and Change: Fundamental Elements in Herbert Blumer's Metatheoretical Perspective. In L. Tomasi (Ed.), *The Tradition of the Chicago School of Sociology* (pp. 191-216). Aldershot, UK: Ashgate.

Morris, M., & Patton, P. (1979). *Michel Foucault: Power, Truth, Strategy*. Sydney, Australia: Feral Publications.

Mulvey, L. (1975/1989). Visual Pleasure and Narrative Cinema. In L. Mulvey (Ed.), *Visual and Other Pleasures*. London: Macmillan.

Mundy, J. (Ed.). (2001). *Surrealism: Desire Unbound*. Princeton, NJ: Princeton University Press.

Naples, N. A. (2003). *Feminism and Method: Ethnography, Discourse Analysis and Activist Research*. New York: Routledge.

Naples, N. A., with Clark, E. (1995). Feminist Participatory Research and Empowerment: Going Public as Survivors of Childhood Abuse. In H. Gottfried (Ed.), *Feminism and Social Change: Bridging Theory and Practice* (pp. 160-183). Champaign-Urbana: University of Illinois Press.

Naples, N. A., with Sachs, C. (2000). Standpoint Epistemology and the Uses of Self-Reflection in Feminist Ethnography: Lessons for Rural Sociology. *Rural Sociology, 65*(2), 194-214.

Ndaba-Mbata, R., & Seloilwe, E. S. (2000). Home-based Care of the Terminally Ill in Botswana: Knowledge and Perceptions. *International Nursing Review, 2000*(47), 4.

Nelkin, D. (1995). Scientific Controversies. In S. Jasanoff et al. (Eds.), *Handbook of Science & Technology Studies* (pp. 444-456). Thousand Oaks, CA: Sage.

Nicholson, L. (1999). *The Play of Reason: From the Modern to the Postmodern*. Ithaca, NY: Cornell University Press.

Okley, J. (1994). Thinking Through Fieldwork. In A. Bryman & R. G. Burgess (Eds.), *Analyzing Qualitative Data* (pp. 18-34). London: Routledge.

Olesen, V. L. (1994). Feminisms and Models of Qualitative Research. In N. Denzin & Y. Lincoln (Eds.), *Handbook of Qualitative Research* (1st ed., pp. 158-174). Thousand Oaks, CA: Sage.

Olesen, V. L. (2000). Feminisms and Qualitative Research at and Into the Millennium. In N. Denzin & Y. Lincoln (Eds.), *Handbook of Qualitative Research* (2nd ed., pp. 215-256). Thousand Oaks, CA: Sage.

Olesen, V. L., & Bone, D. (1998). Emotions in Rationalizing Organizations: Conceptual Notes for Professional Nursing in the USA. In G. Bendelow & S. J. Williams (Eds.), *Emotions in Social Life: Critical Themes and Contemporary Issues*. London: Routledge.

Omi, M., & Winant, H. (1994). *Racial Formation in the United States: From the 1960s to the 1990s*. New York: Routledge.

Orona, C. (1990). Temporality and Identity Loss Due to Alzheimer's Disease. *Social Science and Medicine, 30*(11), 1247-1256.

Oudshoorn, N. (2003). *The Male Pill: A Biography of a Technology in the Making*. Durham, NC: Duke University Press.

Oudshoorn, N., & Pinch, T. (Eds.). (2003). *How Users Matter: The Co-Construction of Users*. Cambridge, MA: MIT Press.

Papademas, D. (Ed.). (2002). *Visual Sociology: Teaching With Film/Video, Photography, and Visual Media*. Washington, DC: American Sociological Association Resource Materials for Teaching.

Park, R. E. (1925). *The City: Suggestions for the Investigation of Human Behavior in the Urban Environment*. Chicago: University of Chicago Press.

Park, R. E. (1952). *Human Communities*. Glencoe, IL: Free Press.

Park, R. E., & Burgess, E. W. (1921/1970). *Introduction to the Science of Sociology*. Chicago: University of Chicago Press.

Patton, C. (2000). Introduction: Helping Ourselves: Research After (the) Enlightenment. *Health, 4*(3), 267-287.

Peretz, H. (1995). Negotiating Clothing Identities on the Sales Floor. *Symbolic Interaction, 18*(1), 19-37.

Persaud, R. (1999). Race, Sex, and Referral for Cardiac Catheterization. *New England Journal of Medicine, 341*(26), 2021-2022.

Pfohl, S. J. (1985). *Images of Deviance and Social Control: A Sociological History*. New York: McGraw-Hill.

Phelan, M. P., & Hunt, S. A. (1998). Prison Gang Members' Tattoos as Identity Work: The Visual Communication of Moral Careers. *Symbolic Interaction, 21*(3), 277-298.

Phelan, P. (1996). *Unmarked: The Politics of Performance*. New York: Routledge.

Phillips, N., & Hardy, C. (2002). *Discourse Analysis: Investigating Processes of Social Construction*. Thousand Oaks, CA: Sage.

Pinch, T., & Bijker, W. (1987). The Social Construction of Facts and Artifacts: Or How the Sociology of Science and the Sociology of Technology Might Benefit Each Other. In W. Bijker, T. Pinch, & T. Hughes (Eds.), *The Social Construction of Technical Systems: New Directions in the Sociology and History of Technology* (pp. 17-50). Cambridge, MA: MIT Press.

Pink, S. (2001). *Doing Visual Ethnography*. London: Sage.

Plummer, K. (1995). *Telling Sexual Stories*. New York: Routledge.

Plummer, K. (2001a). The Call of Life Stories in Ethnographic Research. In P. Atkinson, A. Coffey, S. Delamont, J. Lofland, & L. Lofland (Eds.), *Handbook of Ethnography* (pp. 395-406). London: Sage.

Plummer, K. (2001b). *Documents of Life 2.* London: Sage.

Poland, B. (1995). Transcription Quality as an Aspect of Rigor in Qualitative Research. *Qualitative Inquiry, 1*(3), 290-310.

Poland, B. (1998). Reading Between the Lines: Interpreting Silences in Qualitative Research. *Qualitative Inquiry, 4*(2), 293-312.

Pollock, G. (1988). *Vision and Difference: Femininity, Feminism, and Histories of Art.* London: Routledge.

Poovey, M. (1998). *A History of the Modern Fact: Problems of Knowledge in the Sciences of Wealth and Society.* Chicago: University of Chicago Press.

Porter, T. M. (1995). *Trust in Numbers: The Pursuit of Objectivity in Science and Public Life.* Princeton, NJ: Princeton University Press.

Potter, E. (2001). *Gender and Boyle's Law of Gases.* Bloomington: Indiana University Press.

Prendergast, C., & Knotterus, J. D. (1993). The New Studies in Social Organization: Overcoming the Astructural Bias. In L. Reynolds (Ed.), *Interactionism: Exposition and Critique* (pp. 158-185). Dix Hills, NY: General Hall.

Press, A. L., & Cole, E. R. (1999). *Speaking of Abortion: Television and Authority in the Lives of Women.* Chicago: University of Chicago Press.

Price, M. (1994). *The Photograph: A Strange, Confined Space.* Stanford, CA: Stanford University Press.

Prior, L. (1988). The Architecture of the Hospital: A Study of Spatial Organization and Medical Knowledge. *British Journal of Sociology, 39*(1), 86-113.

Prior, L. (1997). Following in Foucault's Footsteps: Text and Context in Qualitative Research. In D. Silverman (Ed.), *Qualitative Research: Theory, Method, Practice* (pp. 63-79). London: Sage.

Prior, L. (2003). *Using Documents in Social Research.* London: Sage.

Prior, L. (2004). Documents. In C. Seale, G. Gobo, J. Gubrium, & D. Silverman (Eds.), *Qualitative Research Practice* (pp. 375-390). London: Sage.

Prosser, J. (Ed.). (1998). *Image-Based Research: A Sourcebook for Qualitative Researchers.* London: Falmer Press.

Pryce, A. (1996). Visual Imagery and Iconography of the Social World: Some Consideration of History, Art and Problems for Sociological Research. In E. S. Lyon & J. Busfield (Eds.), *Methodological Imaginations.* London: Macmillan.

Rabeharisoa, V., & Callon, M. (1998). The Participation of Patients in the Process of Production of Knowledge: The Case of the French Muscular Dystrophy Association. *Sciences Sociales et Sante, 16*(3), 41-65.

Rabinow, P. (1992). Artificiality and Enlightenment: From Sociobiology to Biosociality. In J. Crary & S. Kwinter (Eds.), *Incorporations* (pp. 234-252). New York: Zone.

Radnofsky, M. (1996). Qualitative Models: Visually Representing Complex Data in an Image/Text Balance. *Qualitative Inquiry, 2*(4), 385-410.

Rapp, R. (1999a). One New Reproductive Technology, Multiple Sites: How Feminist Methodology Bleeds in Everyday Life. In A. Clarke & V. Olesen (Eds.), *Revisioning Women, Health and Healing: Feminist, Cultural and Technoscience Perspectives.* New York: Routledge.

Rapp, R. (1999b). *Testing Women/Testing the Fetus: The Social Impact of Amniocentesis in America.* New York: Routledge.

Redfield, R. (Ed.). (1942). *Levels of Integration in Biological and Social Systems.* Lancaster, PA: Jacques Cattell Press.

Ree, J. (2001). Passions of a Prussian. *Lingua Franca,* July/August, 53-56.

Reed, J. (1984). *The Birth Control Movement and American Society: From Private Vice to Public Virtue* (2nd ed.). Princeton, NJ: Princeton University Press.

Rennie, D. L. (1998). Grounded Theory Methodology: The Pressing Need for a Coherent Logic of Justification. *Theory & Psychology, 8*(1), 1010-1119.

Reverby, S. M. (2000). *Tuskegee's Truths: Rethinking the Tuskegee Syphilis Study.* Chapel Hill: University of North Carolina Press.

Reynolds, L., & Herman-Kinney, N. (Eds.). (2003). *Handbook of Symbolic Interactionism.* Walnut Creek, CA: AltaMira Press.

Richardson, L. (1992). The Consequences of Poetic Representation: Writing the Other, Writing the Self. In C. Ellis & M. Flaherty (Eds.), *Investigating Subjectivity: Research on Lived Experience.* Newbury Park, CA: Sage.

Richardson, L. (2000). Writing: A Method of Inquiry. In N. Denzin & Y. Lincoln (Eds.), *Handbook of Qualitative Research* (2nd ed., pp. 923-948). Thousand Oaks, CA: Sage.

Riessman, C. K. (1993). *Narrative Analysis.* Newbury Park, CA: Sage.

Riessman, C. K. (Ed.). (1994). *Qualitative Studies in Social Work Research.* Thousand Oaks, CA: Sage.

Riessman, C. K. (2002). Analysis of Personal Narratives. In J. Gubrium & J. A. Holstein (Eds.), *Interview Research: Context and Method* (pp. 695-710). Thousand Oaks, CA: Sage.

Roberts, K. B., & Tomlinson, J. D. W. (1992). *The Fabric of the Body: European Traditions of Anatomical Illustration.* Oxford, UK: Clarendon Press.

Ronai, C. R. (1995). Multiple Reflections on Child Sex Abuse: An Argument for a Layered Account. *Journal of Contemporary Ethnography, 23*(4), 395-426.

Ronai, C. R. (1997). On Loving and Hating My Mentally Retarded Mother. *Mental Retardation, 35*(6), 417-432.

Rorty, R. (1979). *Philosophy and the Mirror of Nature.* Princeton, NJ: Princeton University Press.

Rorty, R. (1982). *Consequences of Pragmatism: Essays, 1972-1980.* Minneapolis: University of Minnesota Press.

Rosaldo, R. (1989). *Culture and Truth: The Remaking of Social Analysis.* Boston: Beacon.

Rose, G. (2001). *Visual Methodologies.* London: Sage.

Rose, N. (2001). The Politics of Life Itself. *Theory, Culture and Society, 18*(6), 1-30.

Rose, N., & Miller, P. (1992). Political Power Beyond the State: Problematics of Government. *British Journal of Sociology, 43*(2), 173-205.

Rosenberg, C. E. (1979). Toward an Ecology of Knowledge: On Discipline, Contexts and History. In A. Oleson & J. Voss (Eds.), *The Organization of Knowledge in Modern America.* Baltimore: Johns Hopkins University Press.

Rothfels, N. (2002). *Savages and Beasts: The Birth of the Modern Zoo.* Baltimore: Johns Hopkins University Press.

Rubington, E., & Weinberg, M. S. (Eds.). (1968). *Deviance—The Interactionist Perspective: Text and Readings in the Sociology of Deviance.* New York: Macmillan.

Said, E. (1978). *Orientalism.* New York: Random House.

Samik-Ibrahim, R. M. (2000). Grounded Theory Methodology as the Research Strategy for a Developing Country (FQS Online Text, retrieved from http://www.qualitative-research.net/fqs/fqs-eng.htm).

Sava, I., & Nuutinen, K. (2003). At the Meeting Place of Word and Picture: Between Art and Inquiry. *Qualitative Inquiry, 9*(4), 515-534.

Sawicki, J. (1991). *Disciplining Foucault: Feminism, Power and the Body.* New York: Routledge.

Schatzki, T. R., Knorr Cetina, K., & von Savigny, E. (Eds.). (2001). *The Practice Turn in Contemporary Theory.* London: Routledge.

Schatzman, L., & Strauss, A. (1973). *Field Research.* Englewood Cliffs, NJ: Prentice Hall.

Schoenberg, N. E., & Drew, E. M. (2002). Articulating Silences: Experiential and Biomedical Constructions of Hypertension Symptomatology. *Medical Anthropology Quarterly, 16*(4), 458-475.

Schreiber, R. S., & Stern, P. N. (Eds.). (2001). *Using Grounded Theory in Nursing.* New York: Springer.

Schuerich, J., & McKenzie, K. B. (2005). Foucault's Methodologies: Archeology and Genealogy. In N. Denzin & Y. Lincoln (Eds.), *Handbook of Qualitative Research* (3rd ed.). Thousand Oaks, CA: Sage.

Schwalbe, M., Goodwin, D. H., Schrock, S., Thompson, S., & Wolkomir, M. (2000). Generic Processes in the Reproduction of Inequality: An Interactionist Analysis. *Social Forces, 79,* 419-452.

Scott, J. (1989). History in Crisis? The Others' Side of the Story. *American Historical Review, 94,* 680-692.

Scott, J. W. (1992). Experience. In J. Butler & J. W. Scott (Eds.), *Feminists Theorize the Political.* New York: Routledge.

Scott, P., Richards, E., & Martin, B. (1990). Captives of Controversy: The Myth of the Neutral Social Researcher in Contemporary Scientific Controversies. *Science, Technology and Human Values, 15*(4), 474-494.

Scott, W. R., Meyer, J., et al. (1994). *Institutional Environments and Organizations: Structural Complexity and Individualism.* Thousand Oaks, CA: Sage.

Seboni, N. (1997). Young People's Health Needs in Botswana: A Challenge for Nursing. *International Nursing Review, 44*(4), 110-114.

Seboni, N. (2003). Commentary Regarding the Sub-Saharan African Region. *Journal of Nursing Scholarship, 35*(4), 313-315.

Sekula, A. (1982). On the Invention of Photographic Meaning. In V. Burgin (Ed.), *Thinking Photography.* London: Macmillan.

Seloilwe, E. S. (1998a). Family Caregiving of the Mentally Ill in Botswana: Experiences and Perceptions. *Mosenodi, 6*(1), 17-25.

Seloilwe, E. S. (1998b). Social Support Systems and the Care of the Mentally Ill in Botswana. *Mosenodi, 6*(2), 25-32.

Shaibu, S. (2002). Access to Health Care: Perspectives of Family Caregivers of the Elderly. *Mosenodi, 10*(2), 44-52.

Shaibu, S., & Wallhagen, M. I. (2003). Family Caregiving of the Elderly in Botswana: Boundaries of Culturally Acceptable Options and Resources. *Journal of Cross-Cultural Gerontology, 17*(2), 139-154.

Shapin, S. (1989). The Invisible Technician. *American Scientist, 77*(6), 554-563.

Shapin, S., & Schafer, S. (1985). *Leviathan and the Air-Pump: Hobbes, Boyle and the Experimental Life.* Princeton, NJ: Princeton University Press.

Shibutani, T. (1955). Reference Groups as Perspectives. *American Journal of Sociology, 60,* 562-569.

Shibutani, T. (1962). Reference Groups and Social Control. In A. Rose (Ed.), *Human Behavior and Social Processes* (pp. 128-145). Boston: Houghton Mifflin.

Shibutani, T. (1986). *Social Processes: An Introduction to Sociology.* Berkeley: University of California Press.

Shim, J. K. (2000). Biopower and Racial, Class, and Gender Formation in Biomedical Knowledge Production. In J. J. Kronenfield (Ed.), *Research in the Sociology of Health Care* (Vol. 17, pp. 173-195). Stamford, CT: JAI Press.

Shim, J. K. (2002a). *The Embodiment and Governance of "Difference": What Epidemiological Experts and Street Intellectuals Say About Race, Class, Gender, and Cardiovascular Risk.* Doctoral dissertation in Sociology, University of California, San Francisco.

Shim, J. K. (2002b). Understanding the Routinised Inclusion of Race, Socio-economic Status and Sex in Epidemiology: The Utility of Concepts From Technoscience Studies. *Sociology of Health and Illness, 24,* 129-150.

Shostak, S. (2003a). Locating Gene-Environment Interaction: At the Intersections of Genetics and Public Health. *Social Science and Medicine, 56,* 2327-2342.

Shostak, S. (2003b). *Locating Gene-Environment Interaction: Disciplinary Emergence in the Environmental Health Sciences, 1995-2000.* Doctoral dissertation in Sociology, University of California, San Francisco.

Silverman, K. (1996). *The Threshold of the Visible World.* New York: Routledge.

Simmel, G. (1903/1964). The Metropolis and Mental Life. In K. H. Wolff (Ed.), *The Sociology of Georg Simmel* (pp. 409-424). Glencoe, IL: Free Press.

Simmel, G. (1904/1971). Fashion. In D. L. Levine (Ed.), *Georg Simmel: On Individuality and Social Forms* (pp. 283-297). Chicago: University of Chicago Press.

Simmel, G. (1908/1970). Sociology of the Senses: Visual Interaction. In R. E. Park & R. G. Burgess (Eds.), *Introduction to the Science of Sociology* (Student abridged ed., pp. 146-151). Chicago: University of Chicago Press.

Simmel, G. (1908/1993). The Stranger. In C. Lemert (Ed.), *Social Theory: The Multicultural and Classic Readings* (pp. 200-203). Boulder, CO: Westview Press.

Simmel, G. (1955/1964). *Conflict and the Web of Group Affiliations* (K. H. Wolff and R. Bendix, Trans.). With a Foreword by Everett C. Hughes. New York: Free Press.

Simon, J. (1996). Discipline and Punish: The Birth of a Middle-Range Research Strategy. *Contemporary Sociology—A Journal of Reviews,* 316-319.

Sinding, C. (2004). The Power of Norms: Georges Canguilhem, Michel Foucault, and the History of Medicine. In F. Huisman & J. H. Warner (Eds.), *Locating Medical History: The Stories and Their Meanings* (pp. 262-284). Baltimore: Johns Hopkins University Press.

Smith, A. D. (1993). *Fires in the Mirror.* New York: Doubleday.

Smith, D. E. (1987). *The Everyday World as Problematic: A Feminist Sociology.* Boston: Northeastern University Press.

Smith, D. E. (1990). *The Conceptual Politics of Power.* Boston: Northeastern University Press.

Smith, S. M. (1999). Photographing the "American Negro": Nation, Race and Photography at the Paris Exhibition of 1990. In S. M. Smith (Ed.), *American Archives: Gender, Race, and Class in Visual Culture.* Princeton, NJ: Princeton University Press.

Snow, D. A. (2001). Extending and Broadening Blumer's Conceptualization of Symbolic Interaction. *Symbolic Interaction* 24(3), 367-377.

Snow, D. A., & Anderson, L. (1995). The Problem of Identity Construction Among the Homeless. In N. J. Herman & L. J. Reynolds (Eds.), *Symbolic Interaction: An Introduction to Social Psychology.* New York: General Hall.

Solomon-Godeau, A. (1996). The Other Side of Venus: The Visual Economy of Feminine Display. In V. DeGrazia & E. Furlough (Eds.), *The Sex of Things: Gender and Consumption in Historical Perspective* (pp. 113-150). Berkeley: University of California Press.

Soulliere, D., Britt, D. W., & Maines, D. R. (2001). Conceptual Modeling as a Toolbox for Grounded Theorists. *Sociological Quarterly,* 42(2), 253-269.

Spivak, G. (1993). *Outside in the Teaching Machine.* New York: Routledge.

Spivak, G. (1994). Responsibility. *Boundary 2: An International Journal of Literature and Culture,* 21(3), 19-64.

Spradley, J. R. (1979). *The Ethnographic Interview.* New York: Holt, Rinehart & Winston.

Stafford, B. M. (1991). *Body Criticism: Imaging the Unseen in Enlightenment Art and Medicine.* Cambridge, MA: MIT Press.

Stafford, B. M. (1996). *Good Looking: Essays on the Virtue of Images.* Chicago: University of Chicago Press.

Stanfield, J. H. (1994). Ethnic Modeling in Qualitative Research. In N. Denzin & Y. Lincoln (Eds.), *Handbook of Qualitative Research* (pp. 175-188). Thousand Oaks, CA: Sage.

Star, S. L. (1983). Simplification in Scientific Work: An Example From Neuroscience Research. *Social Studies of Science, 13,* 208-226.

Star, S. L. (1986). Triangulating Clinical and Basic Research: British Localizationists, 1870-1906. *History of Science, 24,* 29-48.

Star, S. L. (1989). *Regions of the Mind: Brain Research and the Quest for Scientific Certainty.* Stanford, CA: Stanford University Press.

Star, S. L. (1991a). Power, Technologies and the Phenomenology of Conventions: On Being Allergic to Onions. In J. Law (Ed.), *A Sociology of Monsters: Essays on Power, Technology and Domination* (pp. 25-56). New York: Routledge.

Star, S. L. (1991b). The Sociology of the Invisible: The Primacy of Work in the Writings of Anselm Strauss. In D. R. Maines (Ed.), *Social Organization and Social Processes: Essays in Honor of Anselm Strauss* (pp. 265-283). Hawthorne, NY: Aldine de Gruyter.

Star, S. L. (1992). The Trojan Door: Organizations, Work, and the "Open Black Box." *Systems/Practices, 5,* 395-410.

Star, S. L. (1995). The Politics of Formal Representations: Wizards, Gurus and Organizational Complexity. In S. L. Star (Ed.), *Ecologies of Knowledge: Work and Politics in Science and Technology* (pp. 88-118). Albany: State University of New York Press.

Star, S. L. (1999). The Ethnography of Infrastructure. *American Behavioral Scientist, 43,* 377-391.

Star, S. L., & Griesemer, J. (1989). Institutional Ecology, "Translations" and Boundary Objects: Amateurs and Professionals in Berkeley's Museum of Vertebrate Zoology, 1907-1939. *Social Studies of Science, 19,* 387-420.

Star, S. L., & Strauss, A. L. (1998). Layers of Silence, Arenas of Voice: The Ecology of Visible and Invisible Work. *Computer Supported Cooperative Work: The Journal of Collaborative Computing, 8,* 9-30.

Starrin, B., Dahlgren, L., Larsson, G., & Styrborn, S. (1997). *Along the Path of Discovery: Qualitative Methods and Grounded Theory.* Lund, Sweden: Studentlitteratur.

Stepan, N. (1986). Race and Gender: The Role of Analogy in Science. *Isis, 77,* 261-277.

Stern, P. N. (1994). Eroding Grounded Theory. In J. Morse (Ed.), *Critical Issues in Qualitative Research Methods* (pp. 212-223). Thousand Oaks, CA: Sage.

Strauss, A. L. (Ed.). (1956). *George Herbert Mead on Social Psychology.* Chicago: University of Chicago Press.

Strauss, A. L. (1959/1997). *Mirrors and Masks: The Search for Identity.* Glencoe, IL: Free Press (1st ed.); New Brunswick, NJ: Transaction Press (2nd ed.).

Strauss, A. L. (1970). Patterns of Dying. In O. Brim, H. Freeman, S. Levine, & N. Scotch (Eds.), *The Dying Patient* (pp. 129-155). New York: Basic Books.

Strauss, A. L. (1976). *Images of the American City.* New Brunswick, NJ: Transaction Books.

Strauss, A. L. (1978). A Social Worlds Perspective. *Studies in Symbolic Interaction, 1,* 119-128.

Strauss, A. L. (1979). *Negotiations: Varieties, Contexts, Processes and Social Order.* San Francisco: Jossey-Bass.

Strauss, A. L. (1982a). Interorganizational Negotiation. *Urban Life, 11*(3), 350-367.

Strauss, A. L. (1982b). Social Worlds and Legitimation Processes. In N. Denzin (Ed.), *Studies in Symbolic Interaction* (Vol. 4, pp. 171-190). Greenwich, CT: JAI Press.

Strauss, A. L. (1984). Social Worlds and Their Segmentation Processes. *Studies in Symbolic Interaction, 5,* 123-139.

Strauss, A. L. (1987). *Qualitative Analysis for Social Scientists*. Cambridge, UK: Cambridge University Press.

Strauss, A. L. (1988). The Articulation of Project Work: An Organizational Process. *Sociological Quarterly, 29,* 163-178.

Strauss, A. L. (1991a). Blumer on Industrialization and Social Change. Book Review of *Industrialization as an Agent of Social Change: A Critical Analysis* by Herbert Blumer. *Contemporary Sociology—A Journal of Reviews, 20,* 171-172.

Strauss, A. L. (1991b). *Creating Sociological Awareness: Collective Images and Symbolic Representation*. New Brunswick, NJ: Transaction Publications.

Strauss, A. L. (1991c). Mead's Multiple Conceptions of Time and Evolution: Their Contexts and Their Consequences for Theory. *International Sociology, 6,* 411-426.

Strauss, A. L. (1991d). Social Worlds and Spatial Processes: An Analytic Perspective. In W. R. Ellis (Ed.), *A Person-Environment Theory Series. The Center for Environmental Design Research Working Paper Series*. Berkeley: Department of Architecture, University of California. Available at www.ucsf.edu/anselmstrauss/.

Strauss, A. L. (1992). *Miroirs et Masques: Une Introduction a l'Interactionisme* (Maryse Falandry, Trans.). Paris: Editions Metailie.

Strauss, A. L. (1993). *Continual Permutations of Action*. New York: Aldine de Gruyter.

Strauss, A. L. (1995). Notes on the Nature and Development of General Theories. *Qualitative Inquiry, 1*(1), 7-18.

Strauss, A. L. (1996a). Everett Hughes: Sociology's Mission. *Symbolic Interaction, 19*(4), 271-285.

Strauss, A. L. (1996b). Fred Davis: An Appreciative Analysis. *Studies in Symbolic Interaction, 20,* 23-36.

Strauss, A. L. (1996c). A Partial Line of Descent: Blumer and I. *Studies in Symbolic Interaction, 20,* 3-22.

Strauss, A. L., & Corbin, J. (1990). *The Basics of Qualitative Analysis: Grounded Theory Procedures and Techniques* (1st ed.). Newbury Park, CA: Sage.

Strauss, A. L., & Corbin, J. (1994). Grounded Theory Methodology: An Overview. In N. Denzin & Y. Lincoln (Eds.), *Handbook of Qualitative Research* (pp. 273-285). Thousand Oaks, CA: Sage.

Strauss, A. L., & Corbin, J. (Eds.). (1997). *Grounded Theory in Practice*. Thousand Oaks, CA: Sage.

Strauss, A. L., & Corbin, J. (1998). *The Basics of Qualitative Analysis: Grounded Theory Procedures and Techniques* (2nd ed.). Thousand Oaks, CA: Sage.

Strauss, A. L., & Corbin, J. (2005). *The Basics of Qualitative Analysis: Grounded Theory Procedures and Techniques* (3rd ed.). Thousand Oaks, CA: Sage.

Strauss, A., Fagerhaugh, S., Suczek, B., & Wiener, C. (Eds.). (1985/1997). *Social Organization of Medical Work*. Chicago: University of Chicago Press (1st ed.); New Brunswick, NJ: Transaction Press (2nd ed.).

Strauss, A. L., & Glaser, B. G. (1970). *Anguish*. San Francisco: Sociology Press.

Strauss, A. L., Schatzman, L., Bucher, R., Ehrlich, D., & Sabshin, M. (1964). *Psychiatric Ideologies and Institutions*. Glencoe, IL: Free Press.

Strubing, J. (1998). Bridging the Gap: On the Collaboration Between Symbolic Interactionism and Distributed Artificial Intelligence in the Field of Multi-Agent Systems Research. *Symbolic Interaction, 21*(4), 441-464.

Sturken, M., & Cartwright, L. (2001). *Practices of Looking: An Introduction to Visual Culture.* Oxford, UK: Oxford University Press.

Suchman, L. (1987). *Plans and Situated Actions: The Problem of Human-Machine Communication.* New York: Cambridge University Press.

Swan-Jones, L. (1999). *Art Information and the Internet: How to Find It, How to Use It.* London: Fitzroy Dearborn.

Tagg, J. (1987). Evidence, Truth and Order: A Means of Surveillance. In his *The Burden of Representation* (pp. 60-102). London: Macmillan.

Talbot, M. (1999, July 11). The Little White Bombshell. *New York Times Magazine,* pp. 38-43.

Teslow, T. L. (1998). Reifying Race: Science and Art in "Races of Mankind" at the Field Museum of Natural History. In S. Macdonald (Ed.), *The Politics of Display: Museums, Science, Culture* (pp. 53-76). London: Routledge.

Thomas, W. I. (1923/1978). The Definition of the Situation. In R. Farrell & V. Swigert (Eds.), *Social Deviance* (pp. 54-57). Philadelphia: Lippincott.

Thomas, W. I., & Thomas, D. S. (1928/1970). Situations Defined as Real Are Real in Their Consequences. In G. P. Stone & H. A. Farberman (Eds.), *Social Psychology Through Symbolic Interaction* (pp. 154-155). Waltham, MA: Xerox College Publishing.

Timmermans, S. (1994). Dying of Awareness: The Theory of Awareness Contexts Revisited. *Sociology of Health and Illness, 16*(3), 322-339.

Timmermans, S. (1999). *Sudden Death and the Myth of CPR.* Philadelphia: Temple University Press.

Timmermans, S. (2002). Cause of Death vs. Gift of Life: Maintaining Jurisdiction in Death Investigation. *Sociology of Health and Illness, 24*(5), 550-574.

Timmermans, S. (in press). *Suspicious Death.* Chicago: University of Chicago Press.

Timmermans, S., & Berg, M. (2003). *The Gold Standard: The Challenge of Evidence-Based Medicine and Standardization in Health Care.* Philadelphia: Temple University Press.

Traweek, S. (1999). Warning Signs: Acting on Images. In A. Clarke & V. Olesen (Eds.), *Revisioning Women, Health and Healing: Feminist, Cultural and Technoscience Perspectives* (pp. 187-201). New York: Routledge.

Traweek, S. (2000). Faultlines. In R. Reid & S. Traweek (Eds.), *Doing Science and Culture* (pp. 21-48). New York: Routledge.

Treichler, P., Cartwright, L., & Penley, C. (1998). Introduction: Paradoxes of Visibility. In *The Visible Woman: Imaging Technologies, Gender, and Science* (pp. 1-20). New York: New York University Press.

Trepagnier, B. (2001). Deconstructing Categories: The Exposure of Silent Racism. *Symbolic Interaction, 24*(2), 141-163.

Tsing, A. L. (1993). *In the Realm of the Diamond Queen: Marginalities in Out of the Way Places.* Princeton, NJ: Princeton University Press.

Tuchman, G. (1994). Historical Social Sciences: Methodologies, Methods, and Meanings. In N. Denzin & Y. Lincoln (Eds.), *Handbook of Qualitative Research* (pp. 306-323). Thousand Oaks, CA: Sage.

Turnbull, D. (2000). *Masons, Trixters, and Cartographers: Comparative Studies in the Sociology of Scientific and Indigenous Knowledge*. Amsterdam: Harwood Academic.

Turner, B. A. (1983). The Use of Grounded Theory for the Qualitative Analysis of Organizational Behavior. *Journal of Management Studies, 20*(3), 333-347.

Twine, F. W., & Warren, J. W. (2000). *Racing Research, Researching Race: Methodological Dilemmas in Critical Race Studies*. New York: New York University Press.

Usher, R. (1997). Telling a Story About Research and Research as Story-Telling: Postmodern Approaches to Social Research. In G. McKenzie, J. Powell, & R. Usher (Eds.), *Understanding Social Research: Perspectives on Methodology & Practice* (pp. 27-41). London: Falmer Press.

Van den Hoonaard, W. C. (1997). *Working With Sensitizing Concepts: Analytical Field Research*. London: Sage.

Van Dijk, T. A. (Ed.). (1997a). *Discourse as Social Interaction, Vol. II*. London: Sage.

Van Dijk, T. A. (Ed.). (1997b). *Discourse as Structure and Process, Vol. I*. London: Sage.

Van Dijk, T. A. (1999). Discourse and the Denial of Racism. In A. Jaworski & N. Coupland (Eds.), *The Discourse Reader* (pp. 541-558). London: Routledge.

Van Leeuwen, T., & Jewitt, C. (2001). *Handbook of Visual Analysis*. London: Sage.

Van Maanen, J. (1995). An End to Innocence: The Ethnography of Ethnography. In J. Van Maanen (Ed.), *Representation in Ethnography* (pp. 1-35). Thousand Oaks, CA: Sage.

Veyne, P. (1971/1997). Foucault Revolutionizes History. In A. I. Davidson (Ed.), *Foucault and His Interlocutors* (pp. 146-182). Chicago: University of Chicago Press.

Visweswaran, K. (1994). *Fictions of Feminist Ethnography*. Minneapolis: University of Minnesota Press.

Wacquant, L. (2002). Scrutinizing the Street: Poverty, Morality, and the Pitfalls of Urban Ethnography. *American Journal of Sociology, 107*, 1468-1532.

Waldby, C. (1997). The Body and the Digital Archive: The Visible Human Project and the Computerization of Medicine. *Health, 1*(2), 227-243.

Watkins, E. S. (1998). *On the Pill: A Social History of Oral Contraceptives, 1950-1970*. Baltimore: Johns Hopkins University Press.

Weber, M. (1946). *From Max Weber* (H. Gerth & C. W. Mills, Trans.). New York: Oxford University Press.

Wiener, C. L. (1981). *The Politics of Alcoholism: A Social Worlds Analysis*. New Brunswick, NJ: Transaction Press.

Wiener, C. L. (1991). Arenas and Careers: The Complex Interweaving of Personal and Organizational Destiny. In D. R. Maines (Ed.), *Social Organization and Social Process: Essays in Honor of Anselm Strauss*. New York: Aldine de Gruyter.

Wiener, C. L. (2000a). *The Elusive Quest: Accountability in Hospitals*. New York: Aldine de Gruyter.

Wiener, C. L. (2000b). Applying the Straussian Framework of Action, Negotiation, and Social Arenas to a Study of Accountability in Hospitals. *Sociological Perspectives 43*(4), S59-S71.

Williams, L. (1989). *Hard Core: Power, Pleasure and the Frenzy of the Visible*. Berkeley: University of California Press.

Williams, R. (1980). Advertising: The Magic System. In his *Problems in Materialism and Culture* (pp. 170-195). London: Verso.

Wilson, H. S., & Hutchinson, S. A. (1996). Methodologic Mistakes in Grounded Theory. *Nursing Research, 45*(2), 122-124.

Winn, S. (2003, August 21). Every Picture Tells a Thousand Stories. *San Francisco Chronicle,* pp. E1-2.

Wirth, L. (1928). *The Ghetto*. Chicago: University of Chicago Press.

Wolf, D. L. (Ed.). (1996). *Feminist Dilemmas in Fieldwork*. Boulder, CO: Westview.

Wolf, E. R. (1982/1997). *Europe and the People Without History*. Berkeley: University of California Press.

Woolgar, S. (1991). Configuring the User: The Case of Usability Trials. In J. Law (Ed.), *A Sociology of Monsters: Essays on Power, Technology and Domination* (pp. 57-102). New York: Routledge.

Wuest, J. (1995). Feminist Grounded Theory: An Exploration of the Congruency and Tensions Between Two Traditions in Knowledge Discovery. *Qualitative Health Research, 5*(1), 125-137.

Zavella, P. (1996). Feminist Insider Dilemmas: Constructing Ethnic Identity With Chicana Informants. In D. Wolf (Ed.), *Feminist Dilemmas in Fieldwork* (pp. 138-159). Boulder, CO: Westview Press.

Zeruhavel, E. (2002). The Elephant in the Room: Notes on the Social Organization of Denial. In K. A. Cerulo (Ed.), *Culture in Mind: Toward a Sociology of Culture and Cognition* (pp. 21-27). New York: Routledge.

Zetka, J. R., Jr. (2003). *Surgeons and the Scope*. Ithaca, NY: ILR Press/Cornell University Press.

Zorbaugh, H. (1929). *The Gold Coast and the Slum*. Chicago: University of Chicago Press.

Index

About the Author

Adele E. Clarke is Professor of Sociology and Adjunct Professor of History of Health Sciences at the University of California, San Francisco. Trained by Anselm Strauss, she has been using and teaching grounded theory since 1980, especially the analysis of discourses. Her own research focuses on social, cultural, and historical studies of science, technology, and medicine. She is particularly interested in (bio)medicalization and common medical technologies pertinent to women's health such as contraception and the Pap smear.

She is the author of *Disciplining Reproduction: Modernity, American Life Scientists and the "Problem of Sex"* (1998). She also coedited *The Right Tools for the Job: At Work in Twentieth Century Life Sciences* (1992), *Women's Health: Complexities and Diversities* (1997), and *Revisioning Women, Health and Healing: Cultural, Feminist and Technoscience Perspectives* (1999). Her recent collaborative work on biomedicalization in the United States appeared in the *American Sociological Review* in 2003 and will include a coedited volume titled *Biomedicalization Studies: Technoscience and Transformation of Health and Illness*.

Clarke's current project takes up the history of biomedicalization and globalization by focusing on how medicines have traveled since the early 20th century, with special focus on Thailand and Puerto Rico. Visit her Web sites at www.sagepub.com/clarke and www.situationalanalysis.com.